Organic
Places to Stay
UK & IRELAND 3rd edition

Linda Moss

green books

This edition first published in the UK in 2009
by Green Books Ltd, Foxhole, Dartington, Totnes, Devon TQ9 6EB

Maps: ©MAPS IN MINUTES™ / Collins Bartholomew (2009)

PHOTO CREDITS
Front cover
Top left to right: Boath House Hotel and Spa, Inverness-shire
Clare Island Retreat Centre, County Mayo
The Traddock, Yorkshire
Main front cover picture: The Man of Aran Cottage, Aran Islands

Title page (p.1)
Croan Cottages, County Kilkenny

Back cover
Top to bottom: Penpont Self-Catering, Powys
Honeysuckle House, Argyll
Penpont Self-Catering, Powys
Ruddyglow Park, Sutherland
Strattons Hotel, Norfolk

ISBN 978 1 900322 44 7

Text printed on 75% recycled paper
by Latimer Trend, Plympton, Devon, UK

CONTENTS

FOREWORD

One couldn't conceive of a guide to 'Organic Places To Stay' being anything other than a brown rice and sandals sixties good-life guide a couple of decades back, but Linda Moss's book is anything but retro. If you're looking for organic, local and home-made food in a wide variety of accommodation, then this is the guide for you.

The word 'organic' may have become somewhat tainted over the years, mainly from over-use, but here it offers itself up on an earthy plate in locations of consummate beauty, where you may find anything from a tipi with a free organic hamper thrown in to a delicious organic breakfast in a boutique hotel.

If a working sheep farm or an organic smallholding with coppiced wood yurts is all too much for you, there are some city locations where the comforts are as homespun as in the sticks, but you can enjoy them under the bright lights of places like Edinburgh or Brighton. Alternatively you can pamper yourself in a fabulous spa at a Bio-Hotel in County Wicklow or enjoy contemporary 5-star bed and breakfast accommodation in the colourful market town of Llandeilo in West Wales.

This is really a small revolution for all of us who, when we leave home, don't just want home comforts, we want the good things too – the honey and free-range eggs, flowers from the garden and freshly baked bread, the fruit bowl that doesn't spell dismal supermarket fruit, the bedroom in the eaves where we really DO wake up and smell the coffee.

You may choose a biodynamic farm in Ireland's Blue Stack Mountains, a croft on the Isle of Iona, a 16th-century Welsh longhouse or hook up your caravan in a wild-flower meadow in Devon. That's what excites me about this guide – wherever I need to travel in the British Isles or Ireland, I no longer need to fear the horrors of nylon sheets and deep-fried greasy spoon breakfasts. I can plan a working trip or a break around an enchanting and well-priced place to stay.

I don't find many of the lovely things on offer in this guide even in some of the better and far more expensive hotels. If I book somewhere from between these covers I will be staying in the homes of a growing band of people who see an organic way of life, in its most catholic sense, as more important than lifestyle and excess. The simple luxuries are coming back to stay.

Tamasin Day-Lewis
Food Writer and Chef

INTRODUCTION

Over the last few years there has been a significant increase in the profile of all things organic, green and environmental. This includes an interest in the availability of locally produced food and drink products while on holiday, and much has been written about places to stay where there is an emphasis on food and regional cuisine. Farmers' markets, farm shops, and food and drink festivals – the largest being the Organic Food Festival in Bristol – have become opportunities for days out for both locals and tourists to see for themselves the variety of local food that is now on offer.

Reflecting their own passion for organic and locally sourced food, several hosts in Organic Places to Stay have written books on these subjects. Others have been nominated Organic Food Heroes by the Soil Association for their inspiring stories about being organic farmers. Five of the winners of the Taste of the West Awards 2008 feature in the book (one having received the gold award in the bed and breakfast category for promoting local food and drink on their menus), and two of the most recent Organic Food Awards were awarded to organic farmers with self-catering accommodation. The Organic Trophy, the highest accolade at the Organic Food Awards, was awarded to a couple who offer several accommodation options on their organic farm.

I'm certain there are more who have won awards or featured in articles in magazines and newspapers, and know there are many who quietly get on with things – be it farming in a traditional way, growing their own vegetables without using chemicals, baking their own bread and cakes like their grandparents did, or just serving their guests naturally good food. Around half the people in the book are involved in producing organic food, the rest are people who simply have an interest in organic food and try to source their produce carefully to create regional specialities and, in many instances, innovative cuisine.

I have spent many years putting these places together in order to make it easier for people to source an 'organic' place to stay. The majority of places that cater for guests endeavour to offer at least 50% organic food, often supplementing this with home-grown or local produce, and many of them offer a much higher percentage – up to 100%. Information about the availability of organic food is given for those who choose self-catering options on organic farms. If you see a place in the book where you would like to stay, the next step is to contact the owner of the accommodation who will be pleased to answer any queries regarding the organic food they offer or to discuss any special requirements that you may have.

Linda Moss

HOW TO USE THIS BOOK

There are four categories of accommodation in this book. The first lines of the entries are colour-coded for ease of recognition. Green denotes places that cater for guests, which have been divided into 'B&B' and 'Hotel'. Brown denotes places that are self-catering, which have been divided into 'S-C' and 'Camping'. The colours are also used on the maps to identify the type of accommodation.

66 TORPOINT *(B&B)*   BUTTERVILLA

231 LYONSHALL *(Hotel)*   PENRHOS MANOR HOUSE

351 HOWDEN *(S-C)*   THE STRAW BALE CABIN

489 ULLAPOOL *(Camping)*   LECKMELM FARM

Please note that the maps do not pinpoint the exact location of a particular place to stay. For directions, contact the accommodation owner.

There are a number of organic certification bodies in the UK. Where a place to stay is on a certified organic farm, or has a different organic certification (for example has its own organic restaurant or organic kitchen garden, or provides an organic breakfast), the name of the certifying body appears to the right of the photo.

A number of the organic farms in this book are members of the World Wide Opportunities on Organic Farms (WWOOF) network. The aims of WWOOF are:

• to enable people to learn first-hand about organic growing techniques
• to enable town-dwellers to experience living and helping on a farm
• to help farmers make organic production a viable alternative
• to improve communications within the organic movement

You can find out more at www.wwoof.org.uk.

The term 'CL' after the name of a caravan site means Certified Location. These are privately owned sites, which only allow five units on at any one time.

My advice to anyone with any particular dietary and other requirements is to ask the owner's when you first contact them regarding availability, as they will all try to be as flexible as possible in order to make their guests feel very welcome.

This third edition of *Organic Places to Stay* includes the following symbols:

○   Meals containing organic produce available on site

⑤   Meals containing organic produce available within 5 miles

●   Organic produce available on site

⑤   Organic produce available within 5 miles

👪   Accommodation which accepts children. Please note that some places displaying this symbol will only accept children under the age of one, others will only accept children over a certain age, and most people have opted not to display the child symbol if they only accept children over twelve.

🐕   Accommodation which accepts dogs. Bear in mind that there will be exceptions regarding the number of dogs, the size and behaviour of the dog etc, and most farmers will not accept dogs in the lambing season.

🚊   Accommodation within one mile of a train station. If this is a main line station, you will be able to complete your journey by taxi or bus.

🚌   Accommodation within one mile of a bus stop. Please bear in mind that a number of accommodations are very rural and buses only run infrequently.

Some of the hosts will pick you up from the train station or bus stop if you arrange this beforehand – ask when you book – and if you are arriving after dark, and walking the last part of your journey, don't forget your torch!

We will be grateful for any feedback on the places where you stay, and there is a form on page 336 for this purpose.

MAPS

Pavillion Cottage, Wigtownshire

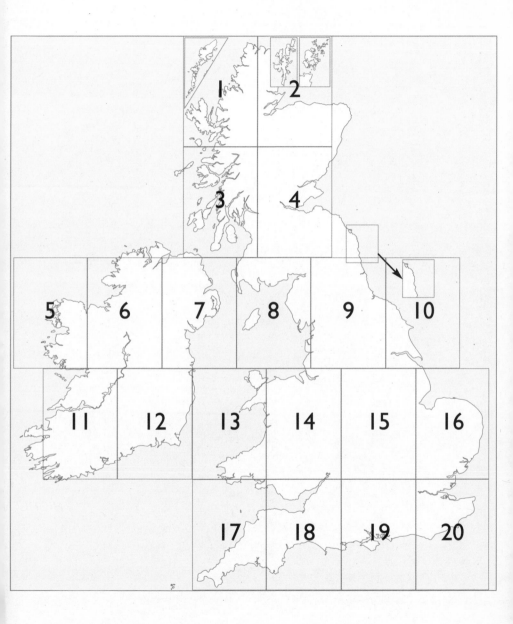

MAP I

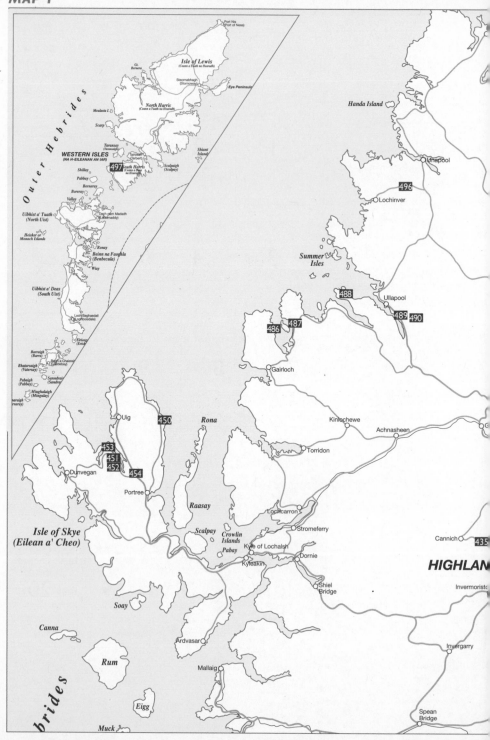

MAP 2

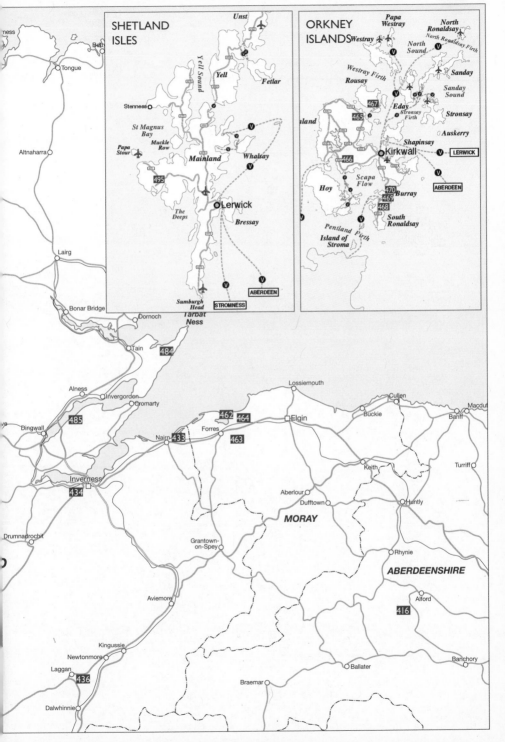

SHETLAND ISLES

Unst
Belt
Yell Sound
Yell
Fetlar
Stenness
St Magnus Bay
Muckle Row
Papa Stour
Mainland
Whalsay
495
The Deeps
Bressay
Lerwick
Sumburgh Head
Tarbat Ness
ABERDEEN
STROMNESS

ORKNEY ISLANDS

Papa Westray
North Ronaldsay
Westray
North Ronaldsay Firth
North Sound
Sanday
Westray Firth
Rousay
Sanday Sound
467
Eday
Stronsay
465
Stronsay Firth
Auskerry
island
Shapinsay
466
Kirkwall
LERWICK
Hoy
Scapa Flow
ABERDEEN
470
Burray
467
468
South Ronaldsay
Pentland Firth
Island of Stroma

ness
Tongue
Altnaharra
Lairg
Bonar Bridge
Dornoch
Tain
484
Alness
Invergordon
Cromarty
Lossiemouth
Cullen
Macduf
485
462
464
Buckie
Banff
Dingwall
Forres
Elgin
Nairn
433
463
Keith
Turriff
Inverness
434
Aberlour
Dufftown
Huntly
Drumnadrochit
MORAY
Grantown-on-Spey
Rhynie
ABERDEENSHIRE
Aviemore
Alford
416
Kingussie
Newtonmore
Ballater
Banchory
Laggan
436
Braemar
Dalwhinnie

MAP 3

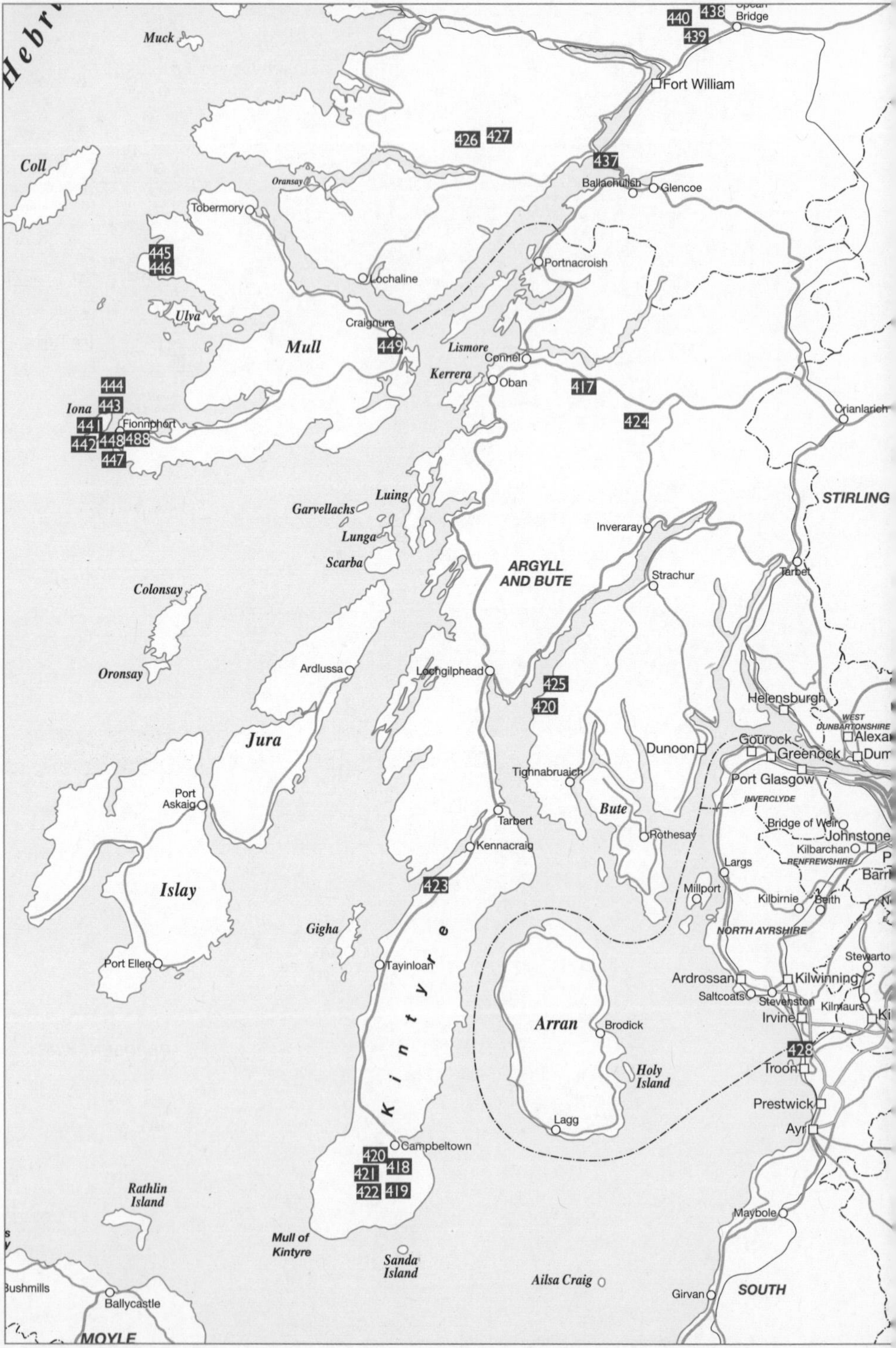

Hebr...

Muck

440 438 Spean Bridge
439

□Fort William

Coll

426 427

Oransay 437

Balachulish □Glencoe

Tobermory

445
446

Lochaline

Portnacroish

Ulva

Craignure

Mull

449 Lismore

Connel

Kerrera 417

Oban

424

Orianlarich

STIRLING

444
Iona 443
441 Fionnphort
442 448 488
447

Luing

Garvellachs

Lunga

Inveraray

Scarba

*ARGYLL
AND BUTE*

Strachur

Tarbet

Colonsay

Oronsay

Ardlussa

Lochgilphead

425
420

Helensburgh

*WEST
DUNBARTONSHIRE*
□Alexa

Jura

Dunoon□

Gourock□
□Greenock □Dum

Port Glasgow

Tighnabruaich

INVERCLYDE

Port
Askaig

Bute

Bridge of Weir

Johnstone

Tarbert

Rothesay

Kilbarchan □

RENFREWSHIRE

Kennacraig

Largs

P

Islay

423

Millport

Kilbirnie

Barr

Beith

N

NORTH AYRSHIRE

Gigha

Stewarto

Port Ellen

Tayinloan

Ardrossan□

□Kilwinning

Saltcoats□

Stevenston□ Kilmaurs

Arran Brodick

Irvine□

□Kil

*Holy
Island*

428
Troon□

Lagg

Prestwick□

Ayr□

420
421 418
422 419

Campbeltown

*Rathlin
Island*

Maybole

*Mull of
Kintyre*

*Sanda
Island*

Ailsa Craig

Girvan□ *SOUTH*

Bushmills

Ballycastle

MOYLE

MAP 4

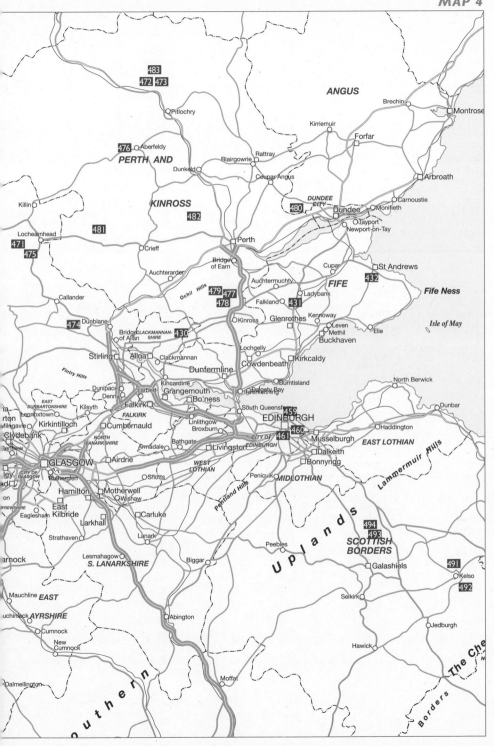

MAP 5

Inishkea
North

Inishkea
South

Duvillaun More

397

MAYO

E

Achill
Island

Clare
Island
394

Castlebar

Westport

Caher
Island

Inishturk

396

Clarer

Inishbofin

Ballinrobe

Inishark

Clifden

385

Galway

Gorumna

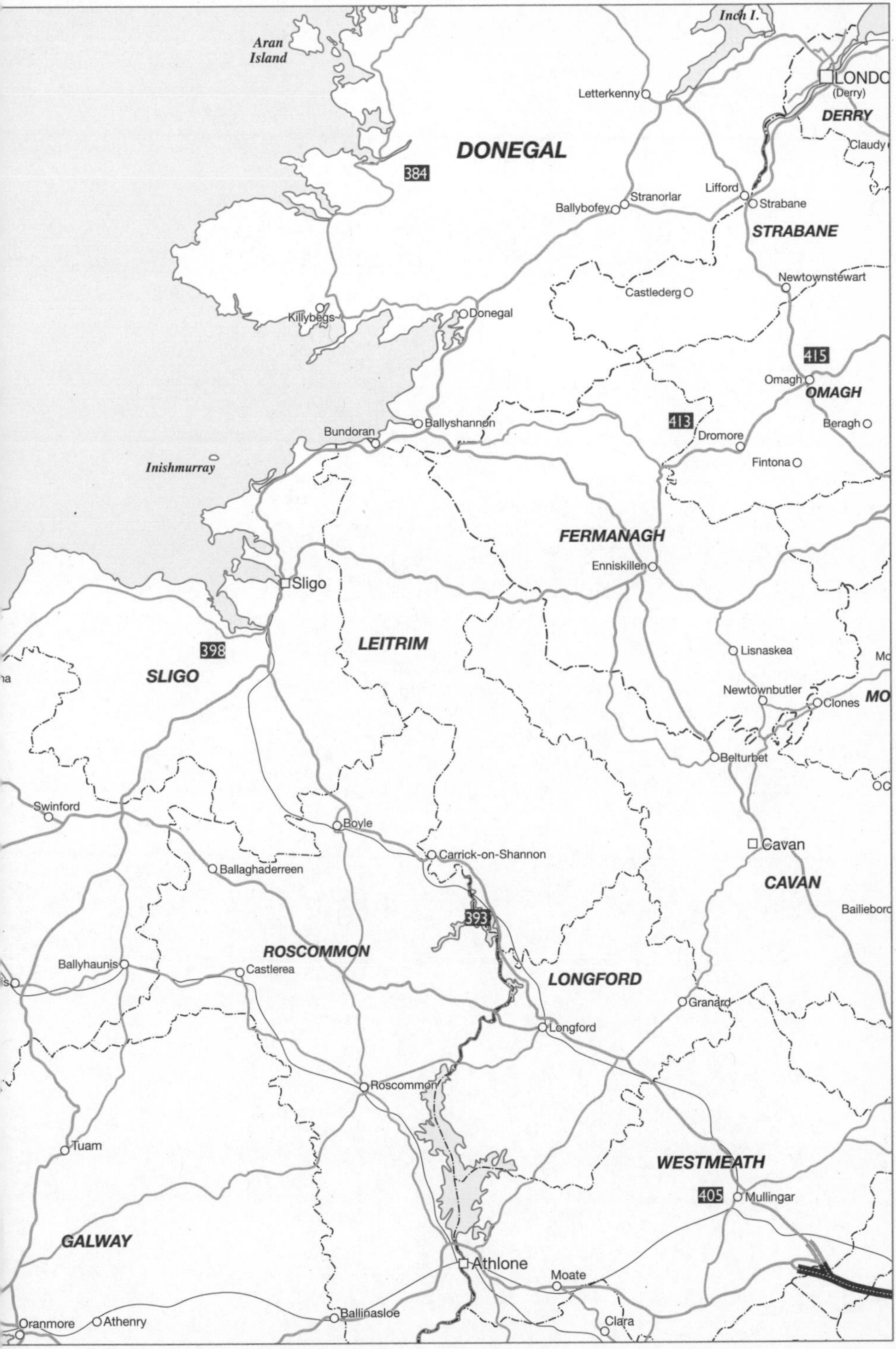

MAP 6

Inch I.

*Aran
Island*

Letterkenny ○

□ LONDO
(Derry)

DERRY

Claudy ○

DONEGAL

384

Lifford

Stranorlar ○ Strabane

Ballybofey ○

Ballybofey ○

STRABANE

Castlederg ○

Newtownstewart ○

Killybegs ○ Donegal

415

Omagh ○

OMAGH

Beragh ○

Bundoran ○ Ballyshannon

413

Dromore ○

Fintona ○

Inishmurray

FERMANAGH

Enniskillen ○

□ Sligo

LEITRIM

Lisnaskea ○

Mo

398

Newtownbutler ○

Clones ○ **MO**

SLIGO

Belturbet ○

na

CC

Swinford ○

Boyle

□ Cavan

Ballaghaderreen ○

Carrick-on-Shannon ○

CAVAN

Bailiebor ○

393

Ballyhaunis ○

ROSCOMMON

Castlerea ○

LONGFORD

Granard ○

s ○

Longford ○

Tuam ○

Roscommon ○

WESTMEATH

405 ○ Mullingar

GALWAY

□ Athlone

Moate ○

Oranmore ○ Athenry ○

Ballinasloe ○

Clara ○

MAP 7

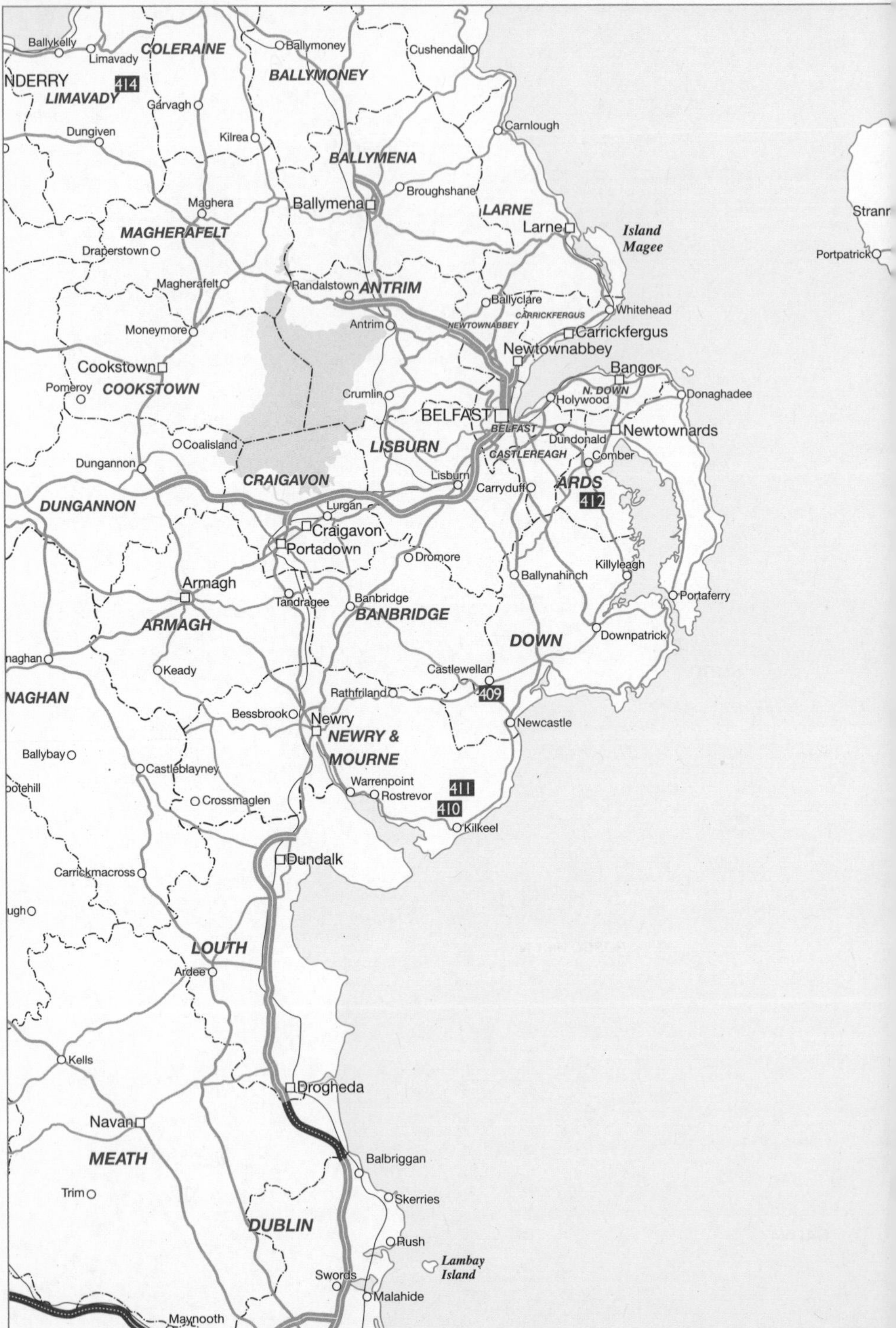

Ballykelly
Limavady
COLERAINE
Ballymoney
Cushendall

NDERRY
LIMAVADY 414
Garvagh
BALLYMONEY

Dungiven
Kilrea
Carnlough

BALLYMENA

Maghera
Ballymena
Broughshane
LARNE
Larne
Island
Magee

MAGHERAFELT
Draperstown
Magherafelt
Randalstown ANTRIM

Moneymore
Antrim
Ballyclare
CARRICKFERGUS
NEWTOWNABBEY
Whitehead
Carrickfergus
Newtownabbey

Cookstown
Pomeroy COOKSTOWN
Crumlin
BELFAST
N. DOWN
Holywood
Bangor
Donaghadee

Dungannon
Coalisland
LISBURN
BELFAST
CASTLEREAGH
Dundonald
Comber
Newtownards

DUNGANNON
CRAIGAVON
Lisburn
Carryduff
ARDS 412

Lurgan
Craigavon
Portadown
Dromore
Killyleagh

Armagh
Tandragee
Banbridge
BANBRIDGE
Ballynahinch
Portaferry

ARMAGH
DOWN
Downpatrick

naghan
Keady
Castlewellan

NAGHAN
Rathfriland
409

Ballybay
Bessbrook
Newry
NEWRY &
MOURNE
Newcastle

Castleblayney
Warrenpoint
411

ootehill
Crossmaglen
Rostrevor
410
Kilkeel

Carrickmacross

ugh

Dundalk

LOUTH
Ardee

Kells

Drogheda

Navan

MEATH
Balbriggan

Trim
Skerries

DUBLIN
Rush
Lambay
Island

Swords

Maynooth
Malahide

Stranr

Portpatrick

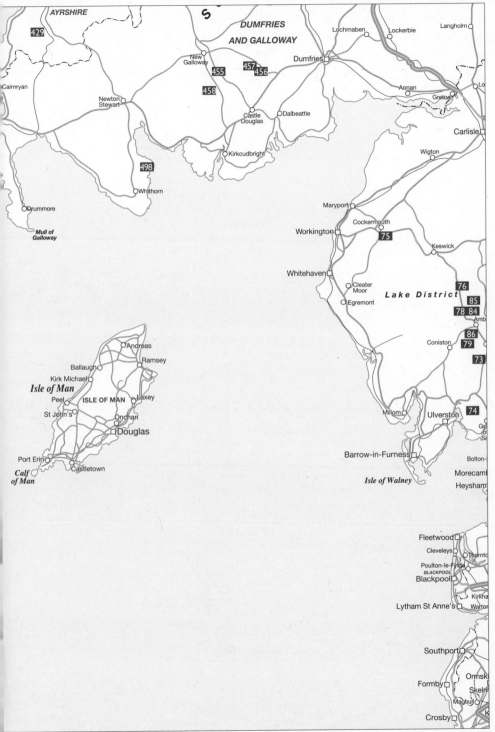

MAP 8

NORTHUMBERLAND

Ashington
Newbiggin-by-the-Sea
Morpeth
Bedlington
Blyth
Cramlington
Seaton Delaval
Ponteland
Dudley
Whitley Bay
Darras Hall
North Shields
Tynemouth
Longbenton
Gosforth
South Shields
Corbridge
Ryton
Blaydon
NEWCASTLE UPON TYNE
Hexham
Prudhoe
Whitburn
Brampton
Whickham
Gateshead
Jarrow
TYNE & WEAR
Burnopfield
Birtley
SUNDERLAND
Stanley
Washington
Consett
Houghton le Spring
Leadgate
Seaham
Castleside
Chester-le-Street
Great Lumley
Hetton-le-Hole
Murton
Lanchester
Alston
Easington
Durham
Haswell
Peterlee
Brandon
Thornley
Crook
Willington
Wingate
DURHAM
Penrith
Spennymoor
Cornforth
Trimdon
Hartlepool
Bishop Auckland
Ferryhill
Sedgefield
HARTLEPOOL
Shildon
Billingham
Newton Aycliffe
STOCKTON-ON-TEES
Redcar
Appleby-in-Westmorland
Stockton-on-Tees
Middlesbrough
Brotton
New Marske
Skelton
Brough
DARLINGTON
Egglescliffe
Eston
REDCAR & CLEVELAND
Darlington
MIDDLESBROUGH
Guisborough
Hurworth-on-Tees
Yarm
Stokesley
CUMBRIA
Scotch Corner
NORTH YORKSHIRE M
Windermere
Richmond
NATIONAL PARK
Catterick
North Yo
Kendal
Sedbergh
Northallerton
Hawes
Leyburn
Thirsk
Kirkby Lonsdale
Sowerby
NORTH YORKSHIRE
Carnforth
-e-Sands
YORKSHIRE DALES
Ripon
Easingwold
NATIONAL PARK
Lancaster
Settle
Forest of Bowland
Knaresborough
YORK
York
Harrogate
Skipton
Ilkley
Wetherby
Garstang
Barnoldswick
Earby
Silsden
Otley
Tadcaster
LANCASTRE
Clitheroe
Bramhope
Barrowford
Colne
Guiseley
Yeadon
Preston
Keighley
Bingley
Shipley
Sherburn in Elmet
Selby
Padiham
Nelson
Haworth
Wilsden
Pudsey
LEEDS
Garforth
Freckleton
Brierfield
Burnley
BRADFORD
Queensbury
WEST YORKSHIRE
Morley
Castleford
Longton
Blackburn
Accrington
Oswaldtwistle
Halifax
Batley
Knottingley
Leyland
Rawtenstall
Todmorden
Brighouse
Elland
Mirfield
Dewsbury
Normanton
Pontefract
Eccleston
Darwen
BLACKBURN WITH DARWEN
Whitworth
Ossett
Wakefield
Walton
Burscough Bridge
Chorley
Ramsbottom
Rochdale
Littleborough
Huddersfield
Horbury
Hemsworth
Askern
Standish
Horwich
Bury
Milnrow
Kirkburton
Royston
South Kirby
Hatfield
Wigan
Bolton
Heywood
Shaw
Meltham
Holmfirth
Oudwell
Adwick Le Street
Atherton
Radcliffe
Middleton
Oldham
Barnsley
Thurnscoe
Doncaster
Rainford
Walkden
Mossley
Penistone
Wombwell
Maxborough
Bessacarr
St Helens
Leigh
Swinton
Salford
GREATER MANCHESTER
Stocksbridge
Swinton
New
MANCHESTER
Rawmarsh
Conisborough

83 82 270 272 274 271 273 278 77 281 283 282 81 202 203 359 349 87 80 357 353 358 355 35 255 363 256 362 364 366 367 252 254 253 350 352 5

MAP 10

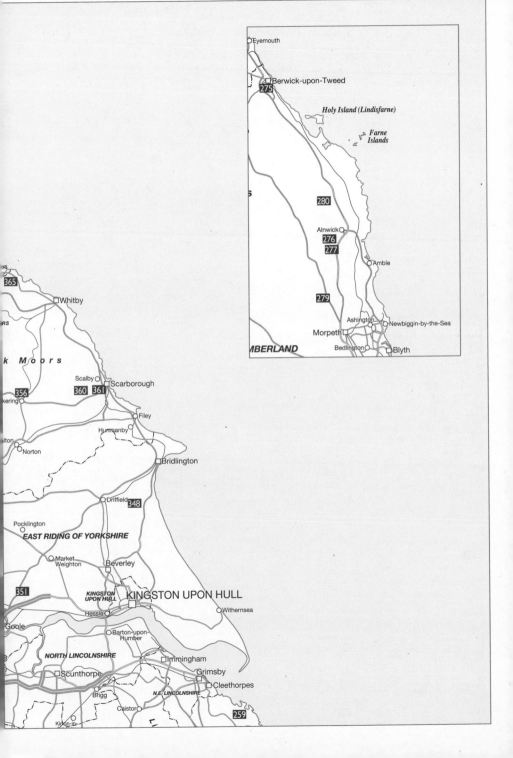

Eyemouth

Berwick-upon-Tweed
275

Holy Island (Lindisfarne)

Farne
Islands

280

Alnwick
276
277

Amble

279

Ashington   Newbiggin-by-the-Sea

Morpeth

Bedlington   Blyth

MBERLAND

365

Whitby

RS

k M o o r s

356
kering

Scalby   Scarborough
360 361

Filey

Hunmanby

ilton
Norton

Bridlington

Driffield 348

Pocklington

EAST RIDING OF YORKSHIRE

Market
Weighton   Beverley

351

*KINGSTON
UPON HULL* KINGSTON UPON HULL

Hessle

Withernsea

Goole

Barton-upon-
Humber

NORTH LINCOLNSHIRE

Immingham

Scunthorpe

Grimsby

Cleethorpes

Brigg

N.E. LINCOLNSHIRE

Caistor

259

Kirton-in-

MAP II

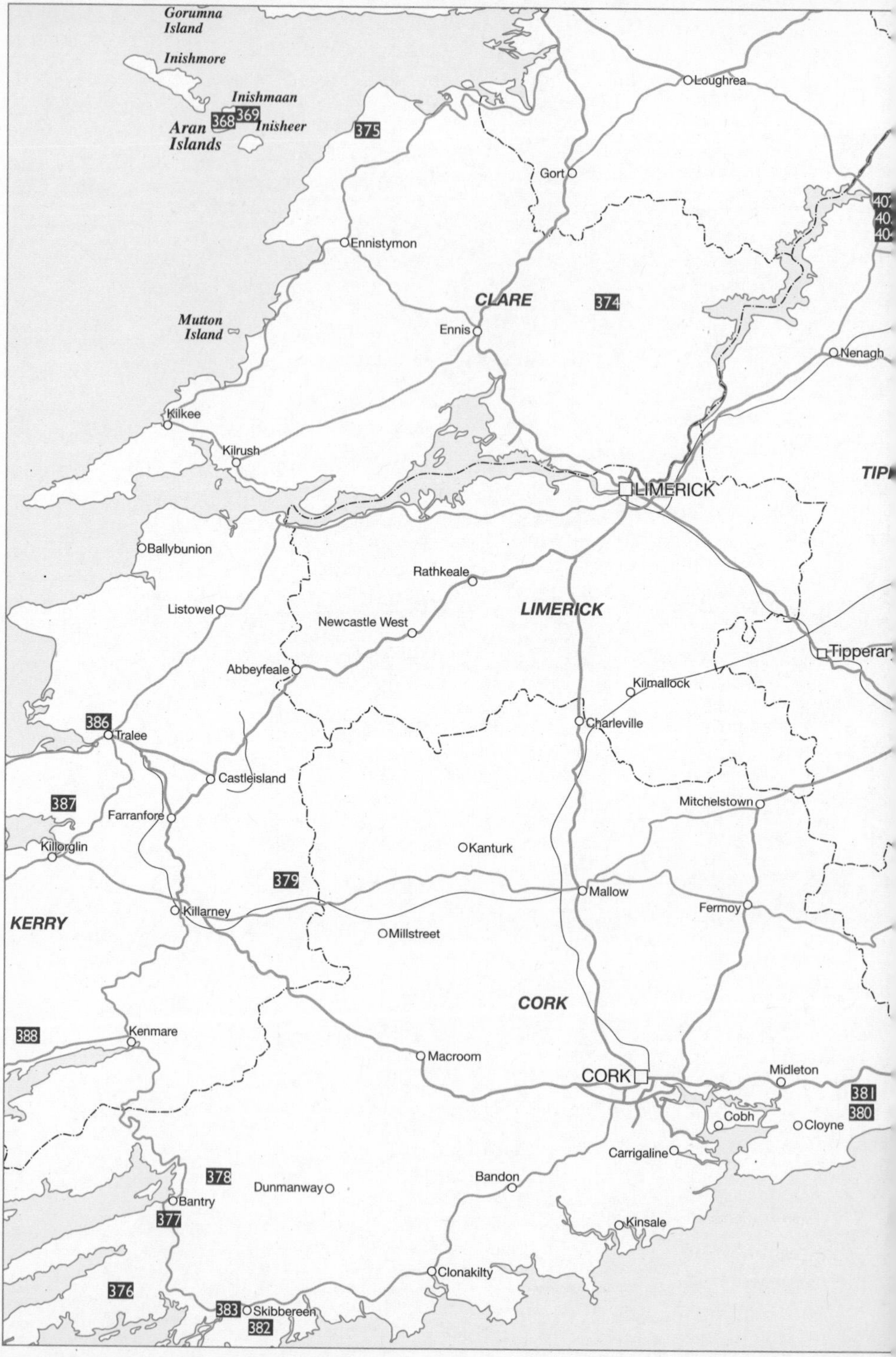

Gorumna
Island

Inishmore

Inishmaan

Aran
Islands
| 368 | 369 | Inisheer

| 375 |

Loughrea

Gort

Ennistymon

CLARE

| 374 |

Nenagh

Mutton
Island

Ennis

40.
40.
40-

Kilkee

Kilrush

LIMERICK

TIP

Ballybunion

Rathkeale

LIMERICK

Listowel

Newcastle West

Tipperar

Abbeyfeale

Kilmallock

| 386 | Tralee

Charleville

Castleisland

| 387 |

Farranfore

Mitchelstown

Killorglin

Kanturk

| 379 |

Mallow

Fermoy

KERRY

Killarney

Millstreet

CORK

| 388 |

Kenmare

Macroom

Midleton

CORK

| 381 |
| 380 |

Cobh

Cloyne

Carrigaline

| 378 |

Dunmanway

Bandon

Bantry

| 377 |

Kinsale

| 376 |

Clonakilty

| 383 | Skibbereen
| 382 |

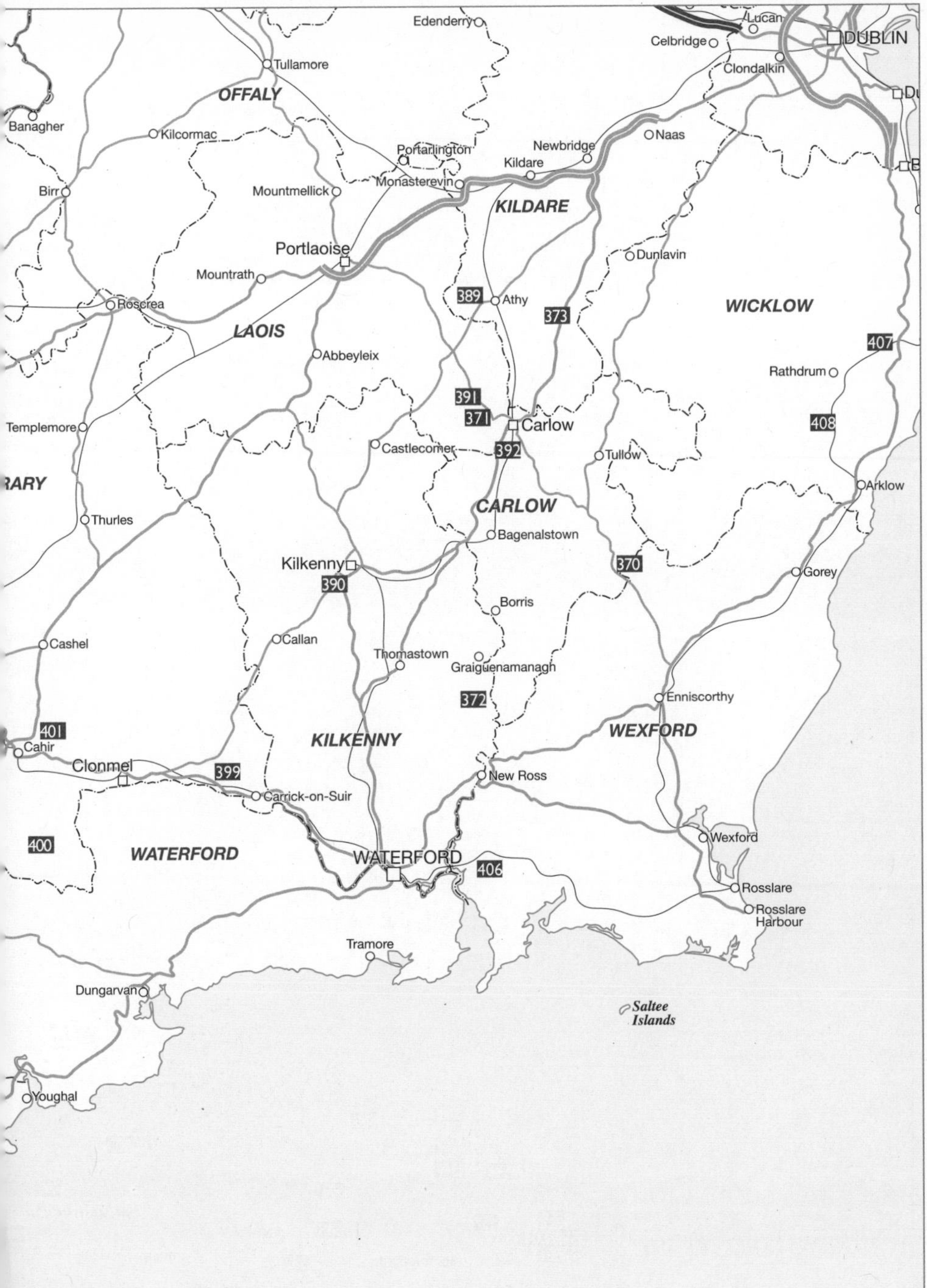

MAP 12

Lucan
Edenderry
Celbridge
DUBLIN
Tullamore
Clondalkin
OFFALY
D
Banagher
Kilcormac
Portarlington
Newbridge
Naas
Kildare
B
Birr
Mountmellick
Monasterevin
KILDARE
Portlaoise
Mountrath
Dunlavin
WICKLOW
Roscrea
389 Athy
373
LAOIS
Rathdrum
Abbeyleix
407
391
Templemore
371 Carlow
408
Castlecomer
392
Tullow
Arklow
CARLOW
RARY
Thurles
Bagenalstown
Kilkenny
370 Gorey
390
Borris
Cashel
Callan
Thomastown
Graiguenamanagh
Enniscorthy
372
KILKENNY
WEXFORD
401
Cahir
Clonmel
399
New Ross
Carrick-on-Suir
WATERFORD
Wexford
400
WATERFORD
WATERFORD
406
Rosslare
Rosslare
Harbour
Tramore
Dungarvan
Saltee
Islands
Youghal

MAP 13

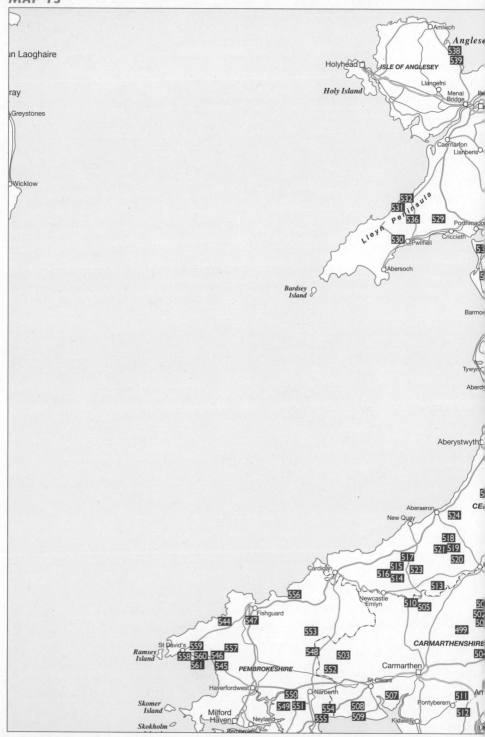

un Laoghaire

ray

Greystones

Wicklow

Amlwch

Anglese

538
539

Holyhead *ISLE OF ANGLESEY*

Holy Island

Llangefni

Menai
Bridge

Be

Caernarfon
Llanberis

Lleyn Peninsula

532
531
536 529 Porthmado
530 Pwllheli Criccieth
Abersoch

5

5

Bardsey
Island

Barmo

Tywyn

Aberd

Aberystwyth

5

Aberaeron *CE*
New Quay 524

518
521 519
520
517
515 523
Cardigan 516 514
513

556 Newcastle 510 505 50
Emlyn 50
50

Fishguard 499

544 547 *CARMARTHENSHIRE*
553
St David's 559 548 503 50
Ramsey 557
Island 558 560 546 552 Carmarthen
561 545 *PEMBROKESHIRE* St Clears
Haverfordwest 507 511 An
550 Narberth Pontyberem 512
Skomer 549 551 508
Island 554 509
Milford 555 Kidwelly
Skokholm Haven Neyland
Pembroke

MAP 14

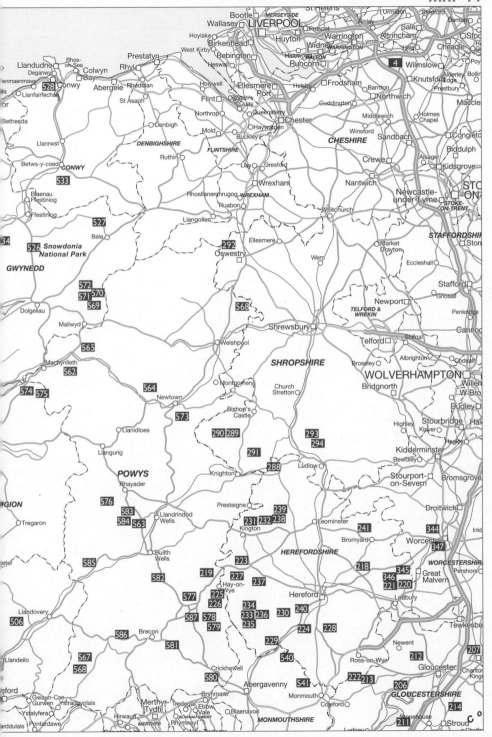

MAP 15

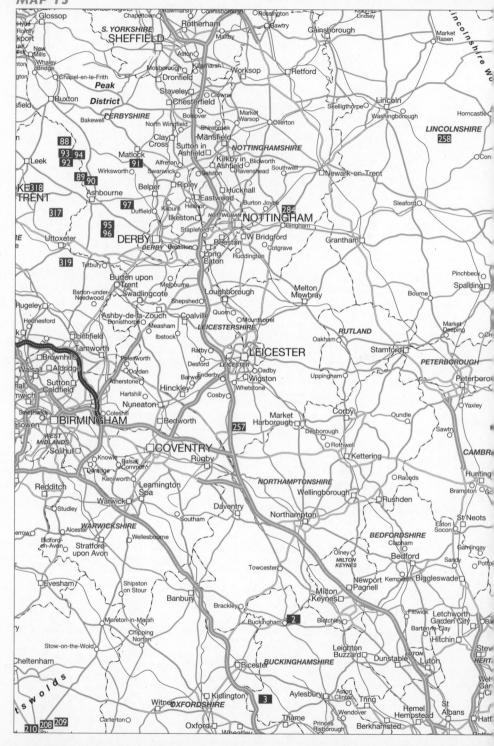

MAP 16

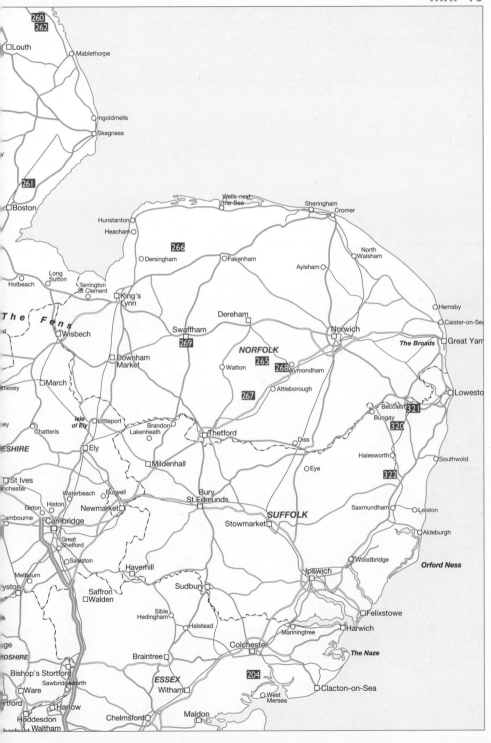

MAP 17

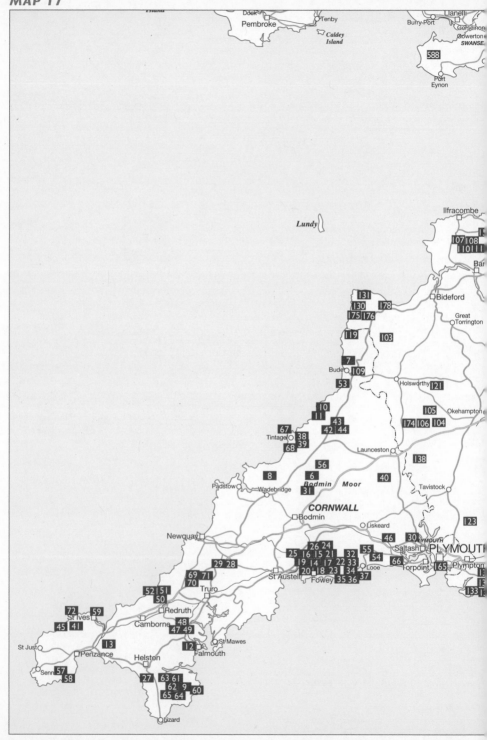

MAP 18

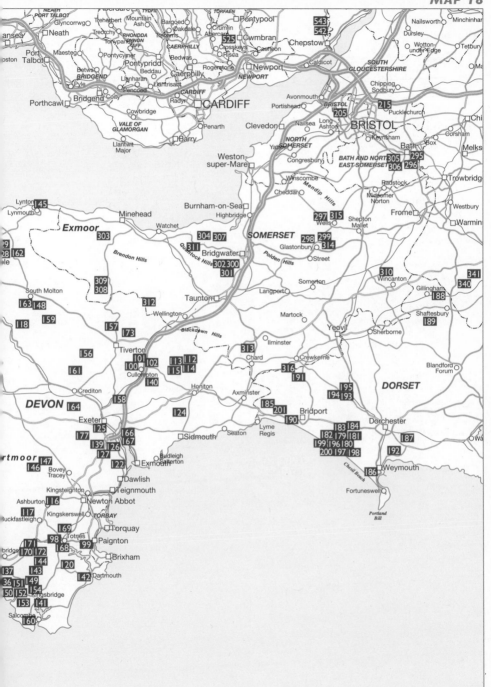

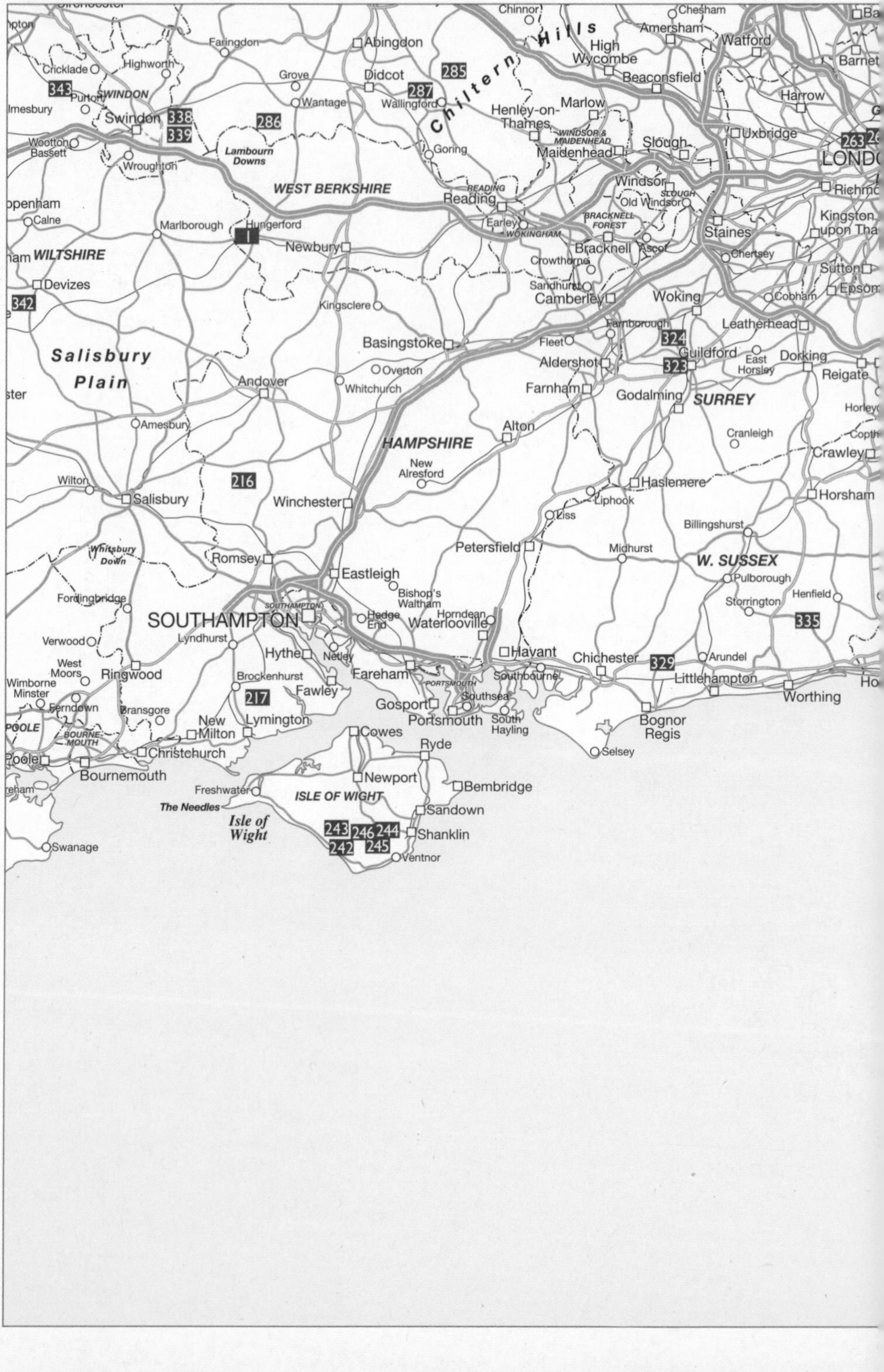

MAP 19

Chinnor
Chesham
Amersham
Watford
Ba
High Wycombe
Beaconsfield
Barnet
Faringdon
Abingdon
Chiltern Hills
Harrow
Grove
Didcot
285
Marlow
Henley-on-Thames
Uxbridge
LOND
Highworth
Wantage
287
Wallingford
WINDSOR & MAIDENHEAD
Slough
263
Cricklade
Purton
SWINDON
Swindon
338
339
286
Goring
Maidenhead
Imesbury
Wootton Bassett
Wroughton
Lambourn Downs
WEST BERKSHIRE
READING
Reading
Windsor
Old Windsor
SLOUGH
Richm
openham
Calne
Marlborough
Hungerford
Newbury
Earley
WOKINGHAM
BRACKNELL FOREST
Staines
Kingston upon Tha
am WILTSHIRE
Crowthorne
Bracknell
Ascot
Chertsey
Sutton
Epsom
Devizes
Kingsclere
Sandhurst
Camberley
Woking
Cobham
342
Farnborough
Leatherhead
Basingstoke
Fleet
324
Guildford
East Horsley
Dorking
Salisbury Plain
Andover
Overton
Whitchurch
Aldershot
323
Reigate
Farnham
Godalming
SURREY
Horley
Amesbury
Alton
Cranleigh
Copth
Crawley
HAMPSHIRE
New Alresford
Wilton
216
Winchester
Haslemere
Horsham
Salisbury
Liphook
Liss
Billingshurst
Petersfield
Midhurst
W. SUSSEX
Whitsbury Down
Romsey
Eastleigh
Pulborough
Fordingbridge
Bishop's Waltham
Storrington
Henfield
Verwood
SOUTHAMPTON
Hedge End
Horndean
Waterlooville
335
Lyndhurst
West Moors
Ringwood
Hythe
Netley
Havant
Chichester
329
Arundel
Littlehampton
Wimborne Minster
Ferndown
Bransgore
Brockenhurst
Fareham
PORTSMOUTH
Southbourne
Worthing
POOLE
BOURNE-MOUTH
New Milton
217
Fawley
Lymington
Gosport
Southsea
Portsmouth
South Hayling
Bognor Regis
Ho
oole
Christchurch
Cowes
Ryde
Selsey
reham
Bournemouth
Freshwater
Newport
Bembridge
Swanage
The Needles
Isle of Wight
ISLE OF WIGHT
Sandown
243
246
244
Shanklin
242
245
Ventnor

MAP 20

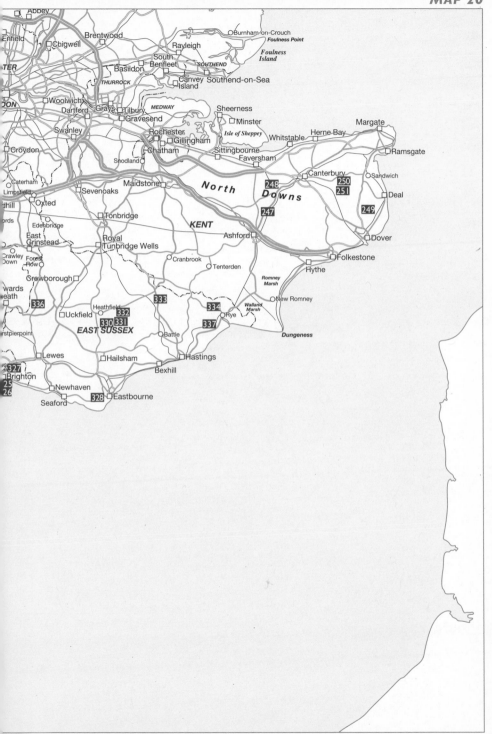

ENGLAND

Orchard Keeper's Cottage, Devon

HUNGERFORD *(B&B)*

WILTON HOUSE   1

33 High Street
Hungerford RG17 0NF
Tel: 01488 684228   MAP 19

Town House Bed and Breakfast
Double, from £76 pn

80% organic (local farm and home-grown)

Wilton House offers the very highest standard of accommodation and comfort in an historic, classic English town house with a documented history that predates 1470. An early 18th-century façade conceals its medieval origins. It has been described by Pevsner as the most ambitious house in Hungerford. The two guest rooms and the dining room are in the elegant 18th-century part of the house, which has wood panelling, open fireplaces and many other period features. The delicious wholesome English breakfast is made with local farm and home-grown organic produce. It is just four minutes walk to Hungerford railway station. The River Kennet and the Kennet and Avon Canal both run through the historic market town. welfares@hotmail.com   www.wiltonhouse-hungerford.co.uk

BEACHAMPTON *(B&B)*

FULLERS FARM HOUSE   2

Manor Farm
Beachampton MK19 6DT
Tel: 01908 562412   MAP 15

Bed and Breakfast,
Double, £60 pn

Breakfast includes our own home-grown organic produce

Organic Farmers & Growers

Manor Farm is the last remaining working farm in the village of Beachampton. Our charming period farmhouse is situated on the edge of the picturesque village. We offer very comfortable and stylish bed and breakfast accommodation in the old dairy, giving you independence from the main house. Breakfast is served in the farmhouse in the elegant and cosy breakfast room, where we provide guests with our home-grown and home-cured bacon, home-made sausage from our old native breed pigs, along with locally produced preserves. Enjoy the peace and beauty of the unspoilt countryside around us or explore the historic towns of Stony Stratford and Buckingham, both only five minutes drive away. info@fullersatmanorfarm.co.uk www.fullersatmanorfarm.co.uk

WORMINGHALL (B&B)

LOWERBROOK FARM 3

Ickford Road
Worminghall HP18 9LA
Tel: 01844 339641   MAP 15

Bed and Breakfast, double £80 pn, single £65 pn. Dinner 3 course £30, Supper £15

Honest food using produce in season, home-grown, local and organic whenever possible

500 year old farmhouse set in lovely well kept grounds on a 15-acre farm in the village of Worminghall, five miles from Thame and ten from Oxford on the Bucks / Oxon border. We have one large oak beamed guest suite (sitting / breakfast room, *en suite* bathroom) with its own private entrance off an outside patio area, excellent for breakfast when the sun shines. We serve quality food made with the freshest of ingredients using produce in season, home-grown, local and organic whenever possible. Meals are available by prior arrangement. Mary has been a chef for fifteen years; her background is in New Zealand cuisine. Her cookery is essentially based on good food cooked well, partly invented or inspired.
james_cox@talktalk.net   www.lowerbrookfarm.typepad.com

ASHLEY (B&B)

SUGAR BROOK FARM 4

Mobberley Road
Ashley WA14 3QB
Tel: 0161 928 0879   MAP 14

Farmhouse Bed and Breakfast
Double, £50 pn

100% organic breakfast on request

Soil Association

Sugar Brook Farm is a working organic farm set within the picturesque location of the Cheshire countryside. Environmental issues are given highest priority and the farm has recently joined the Countryside Stewardship Scheme to encourage wildlife further. If time allows, you can explore the farm's nature walks and discover its hidden gems – a Grade A site of biological interest at Arden Wood, a Grade B site at Erlam's Pasture in the old tile yard, the brook by the Birkin, and Sugar Brook itself. The proximity of Manchester airport (five minutes away) and Tatton Park does not encroach upon the peaceful setting, rather they add to the convenience of its location.
mail@sugarbrookfarm.co.uk   www.sugarbrookfarm.co.uk

LOWTON (S-C)

JOHNSONS ORCHARD 5

Johnsons Farm
Lowton WA3 1LQ
Tel: 01942 671020   MAP 9

Cottage: sleeps 5+cot, £400-£600 pw
Bed and Breakfast, £25-£35 pppn

Fruit and vegetables in season from the farm
and gardens gratis

Organic Farmers & Growers

Situated in a quiet corner of an organic dairy farm, the cottage has been refurbished to a high standard. It is the ideal location for a family holiday with a difference. Visitors can experience the joys of bringing in the cows for milking (with help from Jess the wonder dog), feeding the calves, and harvesting fresh fruit and vegetables in season – all totally organic since 2000. There is a secure garden for children and many local child-friendly attractions. Short stays on request. To the south of Lowton is Highfield Moss, part of which has been designated a SSSI. The 53-acre site was designated in 1986 for its biological interest (mainly mire communities, of which it is the best example in Greater Manchester). johnsons.farm@tinyworld.co.uk   www.johnsonsorchardcottage.co.uk

BLISLAND (Camping)

SOUTH PENQUITE FARM 6

Blisland
Bodmin PL30 4LH
Tel: 01208 850491   MAP 17

Yurts: sleep 2-6, £220-£360 pw
VW camper van hire, £70-£100 pd

Our own mutton burgers and sausages
available from the farmhouse

Soil Association

200 acre working organic sheep farm, with a flock of two hundred ewes and a herd of twenty cows, on Bodmin Moor between the villages of Blisland and St Breward. The small campsite (May-Oct, £3-£6 pppn) is intended to have a low impact on the surroundings with modern solar / rainwater showers. The four yurts are well spaced in their own field on the campsite, with stunning views across the moors. Short breaks June and Sept. Local village shop and pub will provide all your daily needs. The farm is rich in archaeological remains and wildlife. A demonstration farm for the SA and West Country Rivers Trust, the farm walk takes in diverse wildlife habitats, 1500m of beautiful river bank and a Bronze Age hut settlement. thefarm@bodminmoor.co.uk   www.southpenquite.co.uk

BUDE (S-C)

BEACHMODERN NO. 28   7

Downs View Road
Bude EX23 8RG
Tel: 01288 275006   MAP 17

Self-Catering: sleeps up to 20
£1300-£5000 pw

Private chef offering in-house organic meals at No. 28 or organic dining locally

Beachmodern No. 28 is one of the largest, most stylish and contemporary self-catering destinations in Cornwall. It has large living rooms, open fires, high ceilings, eight bedrooms, three bathrooms, and sleeps up to twenty. Hire Beachmodern's private chef to prepare modern organic cuisine using fresh, local and organic ingredients sourced from the very best Cornish suppliers. Outside there's a safe enclosed rear garden and a barbecue area. No. 28 is perfectly located close to Crooklets Beach and overlooking Bude's links golf course on the stunning North Cornwall coast. Bude's beautiful sandy beaches are great for swimming, surfing, kayaking, fishing and rock pooling – all just 400 metres from No. 28's front door. stay@beachmodern.com   www.beachmodern.com/no28.asp

○ ⑤

CHAPEL AMBLE (B&B)

DAVID'S HOUSE   8

Chapel Amble
Wadebridge PL27 6EU
Tel: 01208 814514   MAP 17

Bed and Breakfast
£40-£50 pppn

100% organic breakfast, locally sourced or home-made

Chemical-free, organic bed and breakfast. A spacious guest house with warm, friendly hospitality situated close to the dramatic north coast of Cornwall. The stunning beaches of Daymer Bay and Polzeath are both within five minutes drive. We provide delicious organic breakfasts. All the food served is locally produced and organic. Special diets can be catered for. All bedding, furniture and cleaning products are organic / environmentally friendly. Drinking and bathing water is filtered. Chapel Amble is in a conservation area, and is surrounded by National Trust land and organic farmland. Explore the quaint fishing villages of Port Isaac and Port Quin, and the bustling market town of Wadebridge. info@davidshouse.co.uk   www.davidshouse.co.uk

○ ⑤ ⑤ ♣

COVERACK *(B&B)*

GARDEN COTTAGE 9

Coverack
Helston TR12 6SD
Tel: 01326 281010   MAP 17

Bed and Breakfast
£32 pppn
High quality food, mainly organic

The cottage is in a tranquil location, and is within walking distance of the unspoilt fishing village of Coverack. Guests can relax in the large sunny gardens. No herbicides or pesticides are used so the bird population is visible and thriving. High quality organic breakfasts are tailored to individual preferences and served in a garden room where you can watch the birds feeding. We do not provide other meals but we are near two places which do, both organic farms and lovely to visit. Roskillys has beautiful ponds to walk around and you can eat delicious freshly prepared food in the Croust House courtyard (organic farm products include fudge and ice-cream). Rosuick Organic Farm also has a café serving home-made food. deryl.dart@hotmail.co.uk www.coverack.org.uk

CRACKINGTON HAVEN *(S-C)*

WOODA FARM COTTAGE 10

Wooda Farm
Crackington Haven EX23 0LF
Tel: 01840 230129 / 230140   MAP 17

Cottage: sleeps 4, £285-£595 pw
Short Breaks, from £150

Organic lamb, eggs, home-grown apples and vegetables in season, home baking

Soil Association

Spectacular walks, stunning surf and total seclusion on this 20-acre organic farm. Explore our pastures bordered by Cornish banks and hedgerows. Discover our old orchard, bluebell woods, wildflower meadows and stream. Walk the two miles to the magnificent beach at Crackington Haven. Simple and comfortable accommodation in Wooda Farm Cottage, a self-contained annexe of the 16th-century farmhouse. Organic lamb and eggs produced on the farm, seasonal fruit and vegetables, and organic home-baking to order. Organic dairy products (milk, ice cream, etc) are available from a nearby farm. Natural spring water comes from a well. A beautiful art studio is also available with the cottage. max@woodafarm.co.uk www.woodafarm.co.uk/cottage.html

CRACKINGTON HAVEN (B&B)

WOODA FARMHOUSE   11

Wooda Farm
Crackington Haven EX23 0LF
Tel: 01840 230140 / 230129   MAP 17

Stay and Work at Wooda, from £145 pp 2
nights all inc. From £350 pppw all inc

Organic lamb, eggs, vegetables, fruit from farm

Soil Association

Find comfort, space and freedom in an inspirational setting. Wooda is a working organic farm set in a secluded south-facing valley two miles from the sea. A place for creative people to come and work away from their usual routine. The 16th-century farmhouse is available to those who are also using our award-winning barn space or stunning stable studio for creative work, retreats, celebrations. Groups of up to 12 are then invited to join us as house guests with all their meals included. We naturally turn to our own organic produce first and you're guaranteed some exciting cooking. Our setting provides the focus, our delicious organic food is the fuel. Bring your creative ideas to Wooda and let them take flight.
max@woodafarm.co.uk   www.woodafarm.co.uk

○

FALMOUTH (Hotel)

HAWTHORNE DENE HOTEL 12

12 Pennance Road
Falmouth TR11 4EA
Tel: 01326 311427   MAP 17

Small Edwardian Hotel, £40-£65 pppn
Evening Meal (as priced on menus daily)

The finest locally produced meat, fish and
vegetables (around 55%-85% organic)

Soil Association

Family-owned and run, the Hawthorne Dene is a small Edwardian hotel of character and distinction. Steeped in tradition, the hotel has fine rooms furnished to a very high standard. Most have fantastic sea views overlooking Falmouth's magnificent bay and a panorama that stretches from the Roseland to the Lizard. We are committed to green tourism and sustainable practices. We serve only the finest locally sourced produce, organic or free-range where possible. All our food is prepared fresh here on the premises by our award-winning kitchen team. Special diets catered for. We are members of the Soil Association and the CoaST Project, and involved with Organic South West and Recycle Cornwall.
enquiries@hawthornedenehotel.co.uk   www.hawthornedenehotel.com

GERMOE (B&B)

GROVE COTTAGE B&B 13

Trescowe
Germoe TR20 9RW
Tel: 01736 763624 MAP 17

Bed and Breakfast
£30-£49 pppn

We support local farmers and growers and all foods are organic wherever possible

Nestled in the higgledy piggledy hamlet of Trescowe, Grove Cottage was once the home of the village cartwright. All three rooms have a private bathroom – the Hayloft, with original A-frame beams, Cartwright's, with a comfy bedstead, and Ivy's, which overlooks the gardens. Next morning, you'll enjoy food that has never journeyed inside a supermarket lorry. You'll find milk fresh from cows which graze Cornish clifftops, eggs laid that morning from a nearby farm, succulent gammons and bacon for breakfast, all meat sausages, handmade bread from 'Promises and Piecrust' using organic flours (rye, white, granary and wholemeal), Cornish marmalade on Cornish toast – a great way to start the day.
enquiry@cornishcottagewithrooms.co.uk   www.cornishcottagewithrooms.co.uk

GOLANT (S-C)

CHURCH MEADOW 14

Penquite Farm
Golant PL23 1LB
Tel: 01726 833319 MAP 17

Split Level House: sleeps 6
£300-£820 pw

Home-made Cornish cream tea to welcome you on arrival

Organic Farmers & Growers

Church Meadow is a spacious split level-house that has been tastefully furnished and decorated to a very high standard. There are wonderful views from the upstairs sitting room of the Fowey River Valley and surrounding open countryside. Patio doors open onto a paved balcony leading to the fenced garden which has a large secluded lawn. Church Meadow is a five minute stroll from the peaceful riverside village of Golant, where you'll find a traditional local pub and a children's play area. Penquite is a 150-acre organic farm with forty suckler cows and their calves. Bring your boots and enjoy the circular walk over the farm with its abundant wildlife. Help feed our friendly farm animals and collect the free-range eggs.
ruth@penquitefarm.co.uk   www.penquitefarm.co.uk

GOLANT *(S-C)*

COACHES REST 15

Penquite Farm
Golant PL23 1LB
Tel: 01726 833319 MAP 17

Barn Conversion: sleeps 4
£200-£770 pw

Home-made Cornish cream tea to welcome
you on arrival

Organic Farmers & Growers

Coaches Rest is a very spacious sympathetically restored barn conversion. Tastefully furnished to a superior 5-star quality, it retains all the traditional old beams. Designed with a wet room (level entry shower with handrails) for wheelchair users, it is also ideal for people with restricted walking ability. There is a paved patio area with garden furniture and gas barbecue, and steps that lead up to a large fenced lawn with extensive views of the river with boats resting on their moorings. Penquite is a 150-acre organic farm with forty suckler cows and their calves. Nestling beside the farm is a beautiful 13th-century church in this peaceful riverside village with wonderful views of the river and open countryside. ruth@penquitefarm.co.uk   www.penquitefarm.co.uk

GOLANT *(B&B)*

GILLYFLOWER COTTAGE 16

South Torfrey Farm
Golant PL23 1LA
Tel: 01726 833126 MAP 17

Cottage: sleeps 4+
£460-£790 pw

Farm gate sales of eggs, chicken, beef,
(turkeys, geese at xmas)

Soil Association

A stylish new property, Gillyflower is contemporary and bright, fabulously furnished, a real treat to return to after a day on the beach. It is situated in the heart of a working organic farm that nestles above the Fowey estuary. The cottage adjoins the back of the original stone farmhouse, away from the courtyard with a private aspect looking out over a grass meadow. Designed on two levels, the open-planned kitchen and living area is entered from the decked patio. The two comfortable bedrooms, both with *en suite* wet rooms, are downstairs. We hope you enjoy the cottage gardens, which are a delight throughout the year – drawing you outside to barbeque on your private patio on sunny afternoons and warm summer evenings. stf7@onetel.com   www.southtorfreyfarm.com

GOLANT *(S-C)* HONEYPIN 17

South Torfrey Farm
Golant PL23 1LA
Tel: 01726 833126   MAP 17

Cottage: sleeps 4
£310-£740 pw

Farm gate sales of eggs, chicken, beef,
(turkeys, geese at xmas)

Soil Association

Honeypin has been created from the original stone and slate wagon house. The accommodation is all on a single level and is wheelchair accessible. It has a gated garden, connected by a level path to the indoor swimming pool and games room. Mobile shower chair and pool hoist available if needed. Gated swings, slide and sand pit area for our younger visitors. The peaceful village of Golant is within easy walking distance. A footpath connects the farm to the picturesque port of Fowey. Within easy reach are stunning coastline, coastal walks, small beaches great for families and safe for little swimmers. A vegetable garden is being planned and visitors will be able to pick and purchase fresh organic vegetables in season. stf7@onetel.com   www.southtorfreyfarm.com

GOLANT *(S-C)* LINDEN COTTAGE 18

South Torfrey Farm
Golant PL23 1LA
Tel: 01726 833126   MAP 17

Cottage: sleeps 2-4
£290-£700 pw

Farm gate sales of eggs, chicken, beef,
(turkeys, geese at xmas)

Soil Association

Linden Cottage is one of two adjoining barns, with inverted accommodation to take advantage of the rural views, in the heart of a working organic farm. The use of reclaimed timber and lime paints complement the many original features. Gated garden, gated swings, slide and sand pit area for our younger visitors. Inside games room. Indoor swimming pool and sauna for fun, relaxation or complete fitness – in total privacy. Located above the village of Golant, a path connects South Torfrey Farm to Fowey. Stunning coastline, coastal walks, small beaches great for families and safe for little swimmers. A vegetable garden is being planned and visitors will be able to pick and purchase fresh organic vegetables in season. stf7@onetel.com   www.southtorfreyfarm.com

GOLANT *(S-C)*

MULBERRY LODGE   19

South Torfrey Farm
Golant PL23 1LA
Tel: 01726 833126   MAP 17

Converted Barn: sleeps 6
£380-£990 pw

Farm gate sales of eggs, chicken, beef,
(turkeys, geese at xmas)

Soil Association

Mulberry Lodge is a very spacious, beautifully renovated detached barn, with a sloping path of granite setts winding through the patio garden to a wide front door. The use of reclaimed timber and lime paints complement the many original features. Gated swings, slide and sand pit area for our younger visitors. Inside games room. Indoor swimming pool and sauna for fun, relaxation or complete fitness – in total privacy. Located above the village of Golant, a footpath connects South Torfrey Farm to Fowey. Stunning coastline, coastal walks, small beaches great for families and safe for little swimmers. A vegetable garden is being planned and visitors will be able to pick and purchase fresh organic vegetables in season. stf7@onetel.com   www.southtorfreyfarm.com

GOLANT *(S-C)*

OLD GRANARY   20

Penquite Farm
Golant PL23 1LB
Tel: 01726 833319   MAP 17

Converted Barn: sleeps 8-10
£400-£1385 pw

Home-made Cornish cream tea to welcome you on arrival

Organic Farmers & Growers

The Old Granary has been beautifully restored to a superior 5-star quality with traditional beams and lovely oak flooring. All the rooms have wonderful views over the Fowey Valley and the surrounding countryside, and from upstairs you can see the river with sailing and pleasure boats going up and down the estuary to visit other creeks and inlets. There is a large fenced garden, a gas barbecue and ample parking. Penquite is a 150-acre organic farm with forty suckler cows and their calves. Come and help feed our friendly farm animals and collect the free-range eggs – children just love it. Bring your boots and enjoy the circular walk over the farm with breathtaking views of the river, wildlife and open countryside.
ruth@penquitefarm.co.uk   www.penquitefarm.co.uk

GOLANT (S-C)

ROWAN COTTAGE 21

South Torfrey Farm
Golant PL23 1LA
Tel: +44 (01726 833126   MAP 17

Cottage: sleeps 2-4
£290-£700 pw

Farm gate sales of eggs, chicken, beef,
(turkeys, geese at xmas)

Soil Association

Rowan Cottage is entered at ground floor level through its own walled and gated garden. Two steps lead up to the front door which opens to a slate-floored hallway. The use of reclaimed timber and lime paints complements the many original features. Gated swings, slide and sand pit area for our younger visitors. Inside games room. Indoor swimming pool and sauna for fun, relaxation or complete fitness – in total privacy. Located above the village of Golant, a footpath connects South Torfrey Farm to Fowey. Stunning coastline, coastal walks, small beaches great for families and safe for little swimmers. A vegetable garden is being planned and visitors will be able to pick and purchase fresh organic vegetables in season. stf7@onetel.com   www.southtorfreyfarm.com

GORRAN (S-C)

DOVECOTE 22

Treveague Farm
Gorran PL26 6NY
Tel: 01726 842295   MAP 17

Converted Barn: sleeps 4
£300-£600 pw

Our organic beef, lamb and pork is cooked in our café (open summer holidays)

Soil Association

This converted barn can be found nestled amongst a hamlet of attractively-converted farm buildings, at the bottom of a long private drive. Treveague is a family-run organic farm on the renowned Roseland peninsula, and has breathtaking sea views in two directions. It is a 200-acre working farm breeding sheep, cattle, and pigs. All our guests are encouraged to take part in caring for the animals. We have live webcams which can be viewed from the cottages. See the badgers up close in the wildlife hide, where we also have cameras in nest boxes and an infra red camera for watching at night. With a natural spring-fed pond we attract a wide variety of birds. There are three beaches within walking distance from the farm. treveague@btconnect.com   www.treveaguefarm.co.uk/dovecote.html

GORRAN (S-C)

FOXES DEN 23

Treveague Farm
Gorran PL26 6NY
Tel: 01726 842295   MAP 17

Barn Cottage: sleeps 6
£350-£800 pw

Our organic beef, lamb and pork is cooked in our café (open summer holidays)

Soil Association

Foxes Den is one of three barns built to the highest standard and finished in 2007. The barns are in a secluded walled garden with far reaching views across the countryside and to the sea. Treveague is a family-run organic farm on the renowned Roseland peninsula. It is a 200-acre working farm breeding sheep, cattle, and pigs. A welcome pack will be provided at the beginning of your stay, which includes produce from our farm or from local farm producers. Local amenities include village grocery shops, post office, fish and chip shop, two local pubs, restaurants and beach cafés. There are three beaches within walking distance from the cottage. Heligan Gardens and the Eden Project are a short drive from the farm. treveague@btconnect.com   www.treveaguefarm.co.uk/foxesden.html

GORRAN (B&B)

PENVERGATE 24

Penvergate Farm
Gorran PL26 6LX
Tel: 01726 842768   MAP 17

Bed and Breakfast
£25-£30 pppn

90% organic, includes own organic produce

Soil Association

A 15th-century house and organic farm situated just five minutes walk from the local beach. Although modernised, it retains much of its character with thick cob walls and beamed ceilings. The house is set in extensive grounds with an organic fruit orchard, small streams, garden and children's play area. All the rooms overlook the orchard and streams. At Penvergate Farm we raise organic rare breed Large Black Pigs, traditional Herefords, and most rare breeds of chickens and ducks (all free-range), giving the most wonderful eggs for your breakfast or even to take home. We also use our own sausage and bacon in the full English breakfast. Cornish cream teas are served in our idyllic country garden. penvergate@hotmail.com   www.penvergateorganicfarm.co.uk

GORRAN *(Camping)*

TREVEAGUE FARM CAMPSITE 25

Gorran
St Austell PL26 6NY
Tel: 01726 842295   MAP 17

Camping and Touring
£6-£18 pn

Our organic beef, lamb and pork is cooked in our café (open summer holidays)

Soil Association

Treveague Farm truly is traditional camping as it should be, with room to roam and space to relax with extensive sea views in every direction. We offer water and electric hook-ups for forty pitches and generous tent space situated around a safe area for children to play. Our heated shower and loo block is designed to the highest standard. Open daily is our campsite shop offering a range of essentials and organic farm produce. We can order fresh bread and cakes from the local baker, hot out of the oven just in time for breakfast. Amble down the coastal footpaths and explore a selection of beautiful Cornish beaches, or stay on the farm and experience daily farm life.

treveague@btconnect.com   www.treveaguefarm.co.uk/camp.html

GORRAN HIGH LANES *(B&B)*

MOUNT PLEASANT FARM   26

Gorran High Lanes
St Austell PL26 6LR
Tel: 01726 843918   MAP 17

Bed and Breakfast
£24-£30 pppn

80%-90% organic breakfasts

An organic smallholding set in a peaceful rural location with fine views over traditional stone-walled fields to the sea beyond. We are environmentally friendly and have been awarded the Green Tourism Gold Award. We are developing half an acre of organic vegetable plots and are now growing our own organic food. Delicious organic breakfasts served with eggs from our own hens. Substantial and wholesome home-made vegetarian / vegan suppers may be available with prior notice. Provenance local and organic. You are welcome to wander in the garden and meet the ducks and hens. Spectacular cliffs and the beautiful south Cornish coastline, with some of the finest sandy beaches in Cornwall, just a mile away.

jill@mpfarm.aquiss.com   www.vegetarian-cornwall.co.uk

GUNWALLOE *(B&B)*

GLENDOWER 27

Gunwalloe
Helston TR12 7QG
Tel: 01326 561282 MAP 17

Bed and Breakfast
£37.50 pppn

We try to serve food that is organic, locally sourced, or grown here in the garden

A stylish B&B in an elevated setting surrounded by farmland, just minutes from the coast, beaches and the village pub. Breakfast is served in the conservatory, which overlooks the cottage garden. We source our ingredients locally and almost everything is organic, from Cornwall, or grown at Glendower. Our garden has an abundance of fruit trees, and vegetables are grown in the raised beds and greenhouse. The menu changes seasonally. A typical breakfast would include kippers from Tregida Smokehouse near Bude, a full English breakfast (including home produce in season), home-made fruit compote with yogurt from Gwavas Jersey Farm, local honey and organic almonds. Organic bread is made nearby at Gear Farm.
ian.mandy.turner@virgin.net www.glendower-gunwalloe.co.uk

LADOCK *(S-C)*

ARRALLAS FARM COTTAGE 28

Arrallas Farm
Ladock TR2 4NP
Tel: 01872 510032 MAP 17

Cottage: sleeps 6-8, £330-£1100 pw
Short Breaks (out of season)

Fresh unpasteurised milk available by arrangement

Soil Association

The cottage is the west wing of a partly Georgian Grade II listed farmhouse on a 300-acre Duchy of Cornwall organic dairy farm. We have 180 cows and a viewing area from which to watch the milking. We sell our milk through OMSCO, and our milk regularly gets used to produce Yeo Valley cheese and sometimes to make organic Cornish brie. We are happy to show our guests around the farm. Visitors might enjoy helping give the young calves their milk or collecting the eggs from our friendly chickens. Below the farm is a large area of mixed woodland, a great place for wildlife enthusiasts. Lots of walks in the area. The farm is twenty minutes from the sea. An organic vegetable box can be ordered.
aliceebush@aol.com www.arrallasfarmholidays.co.uk

LADOCK *(S-C)*

ARRALLAS FARM STABLES 29

Arrallas Farm
Ladock TR2 4NP
Tel: 01872 510032   MAP 17

Cottage: sleeps 6, £325-£1050 pw
Short Breaks (out of season)

Fresh unpasteurised milk available by
arrangement

Soil Association

A stylish single storey property with high ceilings and a slate floor on a 300-acre Duchy of Cornwall organic dairy farm. We have 180 cows and a viewing area from which to watch the milking. We sell our milk through OMSCO, and our milk regularly gets used to produce Yeo Valley cheese and sometimes to make organic Cornish brie. We are happy to show our guests around the farm. Visitors might enjoy helping give the young calves their milk or collecting the eggs from our friendly chickens. Below the farm is a large area of mixed woodland, a great place for wildlife enthusiasts. Lots of walks in the area. The farm is only twenty minutes drive from the sea. An organic vegetable box can be ordered.
aliceebush@aol.com   www.arrallasfarmholidays.co.uk

LANDRAKE *(B&B)*

LANTALLACK FARM 30

Landrake
Saltash PL12 5AE
Tel: 01752 851281   MAP 17

Farmhouse Bed and Breakfast
£47.50-£50 pppn

Organic milk, yogurt, meat, eggs, fruit,
vegetables

Lovely Georgian farm with breathtaking views. ETC 5 diamond Gold Award. Delicious breakfast of fresh fruit salad, organic yogurt, Lantallack orchard apple juice, local organic sausages, Cornish smoked bacon, free-range eggs, home-made bread, or smoked haddock en-cocotte straight from the Aga. All produce, including milk, meat, bread, eggs (from our own free-range hens) and vegetables, sourced organically. We are not officially registered organic but pesticides or fertilizers have not been used on the land for 20 years. We produce our own lamb and pork. Other locally reared meat comes from our butcher. Outdoor solar-heated swimming pool (May-Sept). Residential and non-residential art courses throughout the year.
nickywalker44@tiscali.co.uk   www.lantallack.co.uk

LANIVET *(B&B)*

STEPHEN GELLY FARM   31

Lanivet
Bodmin PL30 5AX
Tel: 01208 831213   MAP 17

Bed and Breakfast, £20-£25 pppn.
Evening meal, £12-£15 pp

Nearly everything in the wholefood
breakfast is home-grown or home-made

Soil Association

We offer one double *en suite* and one family room in our comfortable Victorian farmhouse. Your wholefood breakfast of cereals, milk, eggs, yogurt, fruit, bread, butter, jams, honey, etc is served in the south-facing conservatory. Stephen Gelly Farm is a pleasant rural retreat, situated in a quiet lane south of Bodmin. It's a 120-acre traditional grassland farm with small fields and wildlife friendly hedgerows. We organically farm a herd of Devon suckler cows, a small flock of sheep, free-range chickens and laying hens. Our home-produced organic meats are sold directly from our farm. We have a large kitchen garden and keep a house cow, geese, bees and horses. Water comes from a spring on the farm.
stephengelly.farm@btinternet.com   www.stephengellyfarm.co.uk/html/accommodation.htm

LANSALLOS *(B&B)*

LESQUITE B&B   32

Lansallos
Looe PL13 2QE
Tel: 01503 220315   MAP 17

Farmhouse Bed and Breakfast
Double £30-£32 pppn, Single £45 pn

Includes organic farm produce, home-made
preserves

Soil Association

An attractive farmhouse, of 17th-century origin, on a working organic farm in a peaceful wooded valley between Polperro and Fowey, which can be reached by picturesque ferry crossing. Lesquite nestles at the end of our farm drive in the midst of beautiful countryside. We offer bed and breakfast for up to six persons in the renovated farmhouse. Full Cornish breakfast of fresh fruit or yogurt, cereals or muesli, and traditional cooked fare including our own hens' eggs, toast and home-made preserves. The breakfast room has french doors onto a patio overlooking the garden. Our newly built garden apartments, which are all on ground level and independent from the farmhouse, can also be taken on a bed and breakfast basis.
stay@lesquite.co.uk   www.lesquite.co.uk

LANSALLOS (S-C)

LESQUITE GARDEN APTS 33

Lansallos
Looe PL13 2QE
Tel: 01503 220315 MAP 17

Self-Catering or B&B Apartments: sleep 2
S/C £65 pn, B&B £38-£40 pppn, (weekly rates)

Organic farm produce may be available to buy and is included in the breakfast

Soil Association

Three newly built garden apartments, all on ground level with wheelchair users in mind, situated on a working organic farm in a peaceful wooded valley between Polperro and Fowey. The apartments can be used as a self-catering option as they each have kitchen facilities; alternatively they can be taken on a bed and breakfast basis. Wake up to the sound of birds singing. Contemplate the absolute tranquillity that our setting bestows on you. Take a walk and feed the waterfowl on our pond. Our stream is a tributary of the Fowey River, and our pond is home to mallard and moorhen. You may even be lucky enough to see the turquoise flash of a very shy kingfisher. Woodland walks and the Cornwall Coast Path are nearby. stay@lesquite.co.uk www.lesquite.co.uk

LANSALLOS (S-C)

MEADOW BANK 34

West Kellow Farm
Lansallos PL13 2QL
Tel: 01503 272089 MAP 17

Cottage: sleeps 4, £275-£650 pw
Breakfast (on request)

Organic produce used whenever possible

Organic Farmers & Growers

An attractive stone cottage on a 160-acre organic beef farm in an Area of Outstanding Natural Beauty. Recently converted, it retains much of its original charm, with exposed wooden beams and galleried accommodation. Breakfast for guests of the cottage can be provided in the farmhouse for an additional cost (details on request). The hearty cooked Cornish breakfast is prepared on the farmhouse Aga. Home-made bread and preserves. Organic produce used whenever possible. The farm buildings are set in a peaceful location in a large garden with two ponds and panoramic countryside views. You can explore the garden, the wildlife ponds and surrounding farm (children must be accompanied). westkellow@aol.com www.westkellow.co.uk

LANSALLOS *(S-C)*

LITTLE COTTAGE 35

Lesquite
Lansallos PL13 2QE
Tel: 01503 220315 MAP 17

Cottage: sleeps 2
£200-£450 pw

Organic farm produce may be available

Soil Association

Little Cottage is a tastefully and sympathetically converted wagon house and stable, adjacent to Lesquite farmhouse. The accommodation, which is all on ground level, includes a sitting room with french doors opening onto its own patio looking out onto lawns, the woods and the pond. Wake up to the sound of birds singing. Contemplate the absolute tranquillity that our setting bestows on you. Take a walk and feed the waterfowl on our pond. Our stream, which feeds the pond, is a tributary of the Fowey River, and our pond is home to mallard and moorhen. You may even be lucky enough to see the turquoise flash of a very shy kingfisher. Woodland walks and the Cornwall Coast Path are nearby.
tolputt@lesquite-polperro.fsnet.co.uk   www.lesquite-polperro.fsnet.co.uk/selfcater.html

LANSALLOS *(S-C)*

VALLEY VIEW 36

West Kellow Farm
Lansallos PL13 2QL
Tel: 01503 272089 MAP 17

Cottage: sleeps 2, £250-£400 pw
Breakfast (on request)

Organic produce used whenever possible

Organic Farmers & Growers

A delightful stone cottage on a 160-acre organic beef farm in an Area of Outstanding Natural Beauty. The farm overlooks the beautiful and tranquil Cornish countryside only one mile from Polperro. Breakfast for guests of the cottage can be provided in the farmhouse for an additional cost (details on request). The hearty cooked Cornish breakfast is prepared on the farmhouse Aga. Home-made bread and preserves. Organic produce is used whenever possible. The farm buildings are set in a peaceful location in a large garden with two ponds and panoramic countryside views. You are welcome to explore the garden, the wildlife ponds and the surrounding farm (all children must be accompanied).
westkellow@aol.com   www.westkellow.co.uk

LANSALLOS *(B&B)*

WEST KELLOW FARM 37

Lansallos
Looe PL13 2QL
Tel: 01503 272089 MAP 17

Bed and Breakfast
£28-£32 pppn

Organic produce used whenever possible

Organic Farmers & Growers

A Victorian farmhouse on a 160-acre organic beef farm in an Area of Outstanding Natural Beauty. It is set in a peaceful location in a large garden with two ponds and panoramic views of unspoilt countryside. On arrival, sample a cream tea in the conservatory. Enjoy a hearty cooked Cornish breakfast prepared on the farmhouse Aga. Home-made bread and preserves. Organic produce is used whenever possible. Explore the garden and surrounding farm. The more adventurous may walk down the valley to the unspoilt fishing village of Polperro about a mile away, where you can also join the famous coastal path. Then take a horse drawn bus down the quaint narrow streets to the picturesque fishing harbour. westkellow@aol.com   www.westkellow.co.uk

LESNEWTH *(S-C)*

HELSETT BUNGALOW 38

Helsett Farm
Lesnewth PL35 0HP
Tel: 01840 261207 MAP 17

Bungalow: sleeps 6
Contact for prices

Milk, ice cream, yogurts, smoothies, clotted cream, beef, veal, pork, bread

Soil Association

Helsett Bungalow is a modern three bedroom bungalow overlooking Helsett Farm. Visitors can feel part of the working organic dairy farm. A family-run business, Helsett is home to a pedigree herd of organic Ayrshire cows. Milk is processed in an on-farm factory into delicious award-winning dairy products. The bungalow comfortably sleeps six, and has a bathroom, large sitting room and a kitchen with a Rayburn. Enjoy the spectacular view over the whole farm, with the cattle grazing in the fields, from the garden and sitting room. There are wonderful walks through woods to the picturesque fishing village of Boscastle, where you'll find tea gardens, restaurants, a baker's and a fruit shop on the high street. helsett.icecream@btconnect.com   www.helsettfarm.com/stay_with_us.htm

LESNEWTH *(S-C)*

OSTLERS 39

Helsett Farm
Lesnewth PL35 0HP
Tel: 01840 261207 MAP 17

Converted Barn: sleeps 4-10
Contact for prices

Organic dairy produce, organic beef and pork

Soil Association

Ostlers is a converted barn which sleeps up to ten people, tastefully furnished in a farmhouse style. Helsett Farm is a 265-acre organic dairy farm, which is home to a pedigree herd of a hundred Ayrshire cows and their calves. The organic milk from the cows is processed in the on farm factory to produce a variety of organic dairy products – milk, ice cream, yogurt, smoothies, mascarpone, clotted cream, soured cream and frozen yogurts. Organic beef and pork are also available. With stunning views across the farm, visitors are welcome to roam through the fields and woods, watch the cows being milked, feed the young stock, and generally enjoy living on this working organic farm in North Cornwall.
helsett.icecream@btconnect.com   www.helsettfarm.com/stay_with_us.htm

LEZANT *(S-C)*

EAST PENREST BARN 40

East Penrest Farm
Lezant PL15 9NR
Tel: 01579 370186 MAP 17

Converted Barn: sleeps 10, £400-£1400 pw
Home cooked meals (by arrangement)

Where possible our own organic produce is used

Soil Association

East Penrest is a 120-acre organic beef and sheep farm in the lovely Inny Valley, on the fringes of the Tamar Valley Area of Outstanding Natural Beauty. Free-range children are especially welcome. Home cooked meals by prior arrangement, with lots of fresh vegetables and potatoes or rice. Where possible I use our own organic produce, otherwise it is sourced locally from non-intensive environmentally friendly systems. Enjoy a plate of fresh warm scones with clotted cream and home-made strawberry jam at teatime (£10 for eighteen scones). Main course and pudding for supper (£10 pp, minimum of six persons). Or a candlelit three-course-dinner in the farmhouse (£20 pp, four to six persons).
jrider@lineone.net   www.organicfarmholiday.co.uk

MORVAH *(B&B)*

KEIGWIN FARMHOUSE   41

Morvah
St Ives TR19 7TS
Tel: 01736 786425   MAP 17

Bed and Breakfast
£30 pppn

80%-95% organic (local or home-grown /
home-made)

The house is about 300 years old, set in two acres of gardens and a field overlooking the Atlantic near the small village of Morvah. I provide an organic breakfast with fruit, yogurt, cereal, toasts, croissants and home-made marmalade, with a cooked breakfast if required. We are Wholesome Food Association producers. A large potager provides us with plenty of ·vegetables, herbs and salads – all grown without the use of chemicals. We get eggs from our own naturally reared ducks, and also from nearby hens. Enjoy home-made scones or a cake and a pot of tea on your arrival. A sandy / rocky beach and the South West Coast Path are just a few minutes' walk away. We are six miles from St Ives, on the B3306.
gilly@yewtreegallery.com   www.yewtreegallery.com/gardens.htm

OTTERHAM *(S-C)*

NUTMEG COTTAGE   42

Old Newham Farm
Otterham PL32 9SR
Tel: 01840 230470   MAP 17

Cottage: sleeps 4
£300-£650 pw

Local shop (less than 2 miles) sells fresh and local produce

Soil Association

Nutmeg Cottage is one of three old stone and slate cottages formed around the centre of a 30-acre organic beef and sheep farm dating back to medieval times. It has two bedrooms (a double and a twin), an open log fire, and WiFi internet. The cottages have been restored and converted, with great care taken to retain as much character as possible. Old Newham Farm is deep in the country, yet is only a few miles from North Cornwall's most spectacular coastal scenery. The land is grazed in the traditional manner by cattle and sheep, and we also keep horses and other smaller livestock. There's plenty of room to get away from it all here and find the real peace of Cornwall's unspoiled countryside.
orghol@old-newham.co.uk   www.old-newham.co.uk

OTTERHAM *(S-C)*

SKYBER COTTAGE · 43

Old Newham Farm
Otterham PL32 9SR
Tel: 01840 230470 · MAP 17

Cottage: sleeps 2
£250-£350 pw

Local shop (less than 2 miles) sells fresh and local produce

Soil Association

One of three cottages formed from the old stone and slate buildings around the centre of a 30-acre organic beef and sheep farm. The cottages have been restored and converted, with great care being taken to retain as much character as possible. Old Newham Farm is deep in the country with no passing traffic, yet is only a few miles from the West Country's most spectacular coastal scenery. Dating back to medieval times, the farm is found at the end of a quiet country lane. The land is grazed in the traditional manner by cattle and sheep, and we also keep horses and other smaller livestock. There's plenty of room to get away from it all here and find the real peace of North Cornwall's unspoiled countryside.
cottages@old-newham.co.uk   www.old-newham.co.uk

OTTERHAM *(S-C)*

THE STABLES · 44

Old Newham Farm
Otterham PL32 9SR
Tel: 01840 230470 · MAP 17

Cottage: sleeps 4
£300-£650 pw

Local shop (less than 2 miles) sells fresh and local produce

Soil Association

One of three old stone and slate cottages formed around the centre of a 30-acre organic beef and sheep farm dating back to medieval times. It has two bedrooms (a double four-poster bed with *en suite* bathroom and a twin with shower room) and WiFi internet. The cottages have been restored and converted, with great care taken to retain as much character as possible. The land is grazed in the traditional manner by cattle and sheep, and we also keep horses and other smaller livestock. Deep in the country with no passing traffic, there's plenty of room to get away from it all and find the real peace of the unspoiled countryside. The farm is only a few miles from North Cornwall's most spectacular coastal scenery.
orghols@old-newham.co.uk   www.old-newham.co.uk

PENDEEN (S-C)

POLMINA   45

Bosigran Farm
Pendeen TR20 8YX
Tel: 01326 555555   MAP 17

Converted Barn: (REF 1222) sleeps 2+cot
£282-£588 pw

Rare-breed lamb (subject to availability)

Soil Association

Found at the end of a bumpy track, this charming barn conversion overlooks the wild Penwith moorland and the Atlantic Ocean. Part of a working organic National Trust farm (beef, sheep, poultry), it has been thoughtfully restored under the watchful eye of the Trust. On the first floor and reached by exterior granite steps, this delightful, compact, open-plan apartment is unique. Antique pine furniture, stripped floorboards, and whitewashed walls enhance the attractive décor. Set within its own grounds, Polmina offers total seclusion. It is perfect for couples seeking peace and tranquillity close to the sea, and ideally located for coastal walking. Short breaks are available from October to March.
www.classic.co.uk/holiday-cottage/desc-1222.html

PILLATON (B&B)

SMEATON FARM   46

Pillaton
Saltash PL12 6RZ
Tel: 01579 351833   MAP 17

Farmhouse Bed and Breakfast, from £30 pppn
Evening Meal, from £15 (pre-book)

Home-produced organic food is always used whenever available

Soil Association

Smeaton is a 450-acre working organic farm situated within the Duchy of Cornwall. A choice of breakfasts includes full English, continental, or fresh local fish, taken in our cosy breakfast room. Guests can enjoy the beautiful gardens here at the farm whilst enjoying a true Cornish cream tea. If you require an organic evening meal (complimentary glass of wine included), this can be pre-booked. Home-produced organic food is always used whenever available, including beef, pork, lamb, free-range eggs and seasonal vegetables. The Aberdeen Angus beef cattle, Dorset Horn sheep, and Saddleback and Tamworth pigs can always be seen around the farm. Farm fresh organic meats are available for sale.
info@smeatonfarm.co.uk   www.smeatonfarm.co.uk

PONSANOOTH *(S-C)*

MILLERS   47

Kennall Vale Mills
Ponsanooth TR3 7HL
Tel: 01209 861168   MAP 17

Cottage: sleeps 4, £300-£550 pw
Short breaks, 2 person discounts available

Organic welcome tray plus fruit from the
forest garden when available

A granite stone cottage in a secluded woodland valley setting next to the River Kennall. There are riverside seating areas and gardens around an attractive mill leat. The cottage also has its own private courtyard. You will receive a friendly welcome and some home-made Cornish biscuits. We have a private nature reserve with a wildlife conservation lake and bluebell woodland and we are part of the Agroforestry Research Trust garden network. Guests may like a tour of our forest garden, where we grow some unusual fruit and vegetables. There are peaceful country walks from the door and at the same time we are within easy travelling distance of both north and south coast beaches and many popular Cornish attractions. natasha@austin-uk.co.uk   www.kennallvale.co.uk

PONSANOOTH *(S-C)*

OFFICE   48

Kennall Vale Mills
Ponsanooth TR3 7HL
Tel: 01209 861168   MAP 17

Cottage: sleeps 2
£250-£450 pw

Organic welcome tray plus fruit from the
forest garden when available

A granite stone cottage in a secluded woodland valley setting next to the River Kennall. It has its own private riverside seating area and small garden (the cottage is not recommended for young children). You will receive a friendly welcome and home-made Cornish biscuits. We have a private nature reserve, with a wildlife conservation lake and bluebell woodland. We are part of the Agroforestry Research Trust garden network. Guests may like a tour of our forest garden, where we grow some unusual fruit and vegetables. There are peaceful country walks from the door and at the same time we are within easy travelling distance of both north and south coast beaches as well as many Cornish gardens and other attractions. natasha@austin-uk.co.uk   www.kennallvale.co.uk

PONSANOOTH (S-C)

STABLES 49

Kennall Vale Mills
Ponsanooth TR3 7HL
Tel: 01209 861168   MAP 17

Cottage: sleeps 4+1, £300-£630 pw
Short breaks, 2 person discounts available

Organic welcome tray plus fruit from the
forest garden when available

A granite stone cottage in a secluded woodland valley setting. It is set back from the river and has its own private garden with steps leading down to a mill leat (the cottage is not recommended for under fours). You will receive a friendly welcome and some home-made Cornish biscuits. We have a private nature reserve with a wildlife conservation lake and bluebell woodland and we are part of the Agroforestry Research Trust garden network. Guests may like a tour of our forest garden, where we grow some unusual fruit and vegetables. There are peaceful country walks from the door and at the same time we are within easy travelling distance of both north and south coast beaches and many popular Cornish attractions.
natasha@austin-uk.co.uk   www.kennallvale.co.uk

PORTREATH (S-C)

BYRE COTT 50

Higher Laity Farm
Portreath TR16 4HY
Tel: 01209 842317   MAP 17

Cottage: sleeps 4, £230-£740 pw
Short Breaks, £200-£255

Organic farm produce (beef, lamb, pork,
eggs, cauliflower in season), local organic veg

Soil Association

This ground floor, level access cottage (previously the former milking parlour for the farm's pedigree Holstein herd) is full of character and offers a truly delightful holiday retreat. Our working farm is just a mile from the old mining port of Portreath. We have an organic suckler herd of South Devon cattle, all naturally reared on our 60 acres of grassland. Organic pigs, sheep and chickens can also be seen on the farm. We are ideally placed for walkers, with the recently upgraded Mineral Tramways Coast to Coast Path and the nearby beach at Portreath on the South West Coast Path. Higher Laity Farm is also close to the spectacular north coast, with its breathtaking scenery and abundant bird and wildlife.
info@higherlaityfarm.co.uk   www.higherlaityfarm.co.uk/cottages/byre_cott.asp

PORTREATH *(S-C)*

THE LOFT 51

Higher Laity Farm
Portreath TR16 4HY
Tel: 01209 842317   MAP 17

Loft: sleeps 4, £220-£710 pw
Short Breaks, £185-£240

Organic farm produce (beef, lamb, pork,
eggs, cauliflower in season), local organic veg

Soil Association

Approached by granite steps, the accommodation (with exposed wooden beams) is on the first floor. Views over superb open countryside can be enjoyed from this delightful cottage. Our working farm is just a mile from the old mining port of Portreath. We have an organic suckler herd of South Devon cattle, naturally reared on our 60 acres of grassland. Organic pigs, sheep and chickens can also be seen on the farm. Ideally placed for walkers, with the recently upgraded Mineral Tramways Coast to Coast Path and the nearby beach at Portreath on the South West Coast Path. Higher Laity Farm is also close to the spectacular north coast, with its breathtaking scenery and abundant bird and wildlife.

info@higherlaityfarm.co.uk   www.higherlaityfarm.co.uk/cottages/loft.asp

PORTREATH *(S-C)*

TROTTERS 52

Higher Laity Farm
Portreath TR16 4HY
Tel: 01209 842317   MAP 17

Converted Barn: sleeps 4-6,
£250-£780 pw / Short Breaks, £215-£270

Organic farm produce (beef, lamb, pork,
eggs, cauliflower in season), local organic veg

Soil Association

Formerly the farm's pig farrowing house, this stylish and superbly-equipped ground floor barn has been converted to provide a charming, spacious holiday home. Our working farm is situated just a mile from the old mining port of Portreath. We have an organic suckler herd of South Devon cattle, all naturally reared on our 60 acres of grassland. Organic pigs, sheep and chickens can also be seen on the farm. We are ideally placed for walkers, with the recently upgraded Mineral Tramways Coast to Coast Path and the nearby beach at Portreath on the South West Coast Path. Higher Laity Farm is also close to the spectacular north coast, with its breathtaking scenery and abundant bird and wildlife.

info@higherlaityfarm.co.uk   www.higherlaityfarm.co.uk/cottages/trotters.asp

POUNDSTOCK *(B&B)*

BANGORS ORGANIC 53

Poundstock
Bude EX23 0DP
Tel: 01288 361297 MAP 17

Bed and Breakfast, £47.50-£75 pppn
Bed and Breakfast Dinner, £71.25-£95 pppn

All food at breakfast and in the restaurant is 100% certified organic

Soil Association

An elegant restored Victorian house from which Gill and Neil Faiers run the UK's first certified 'Bed and Organic Breakfast'. The main house has fabulous views towards the sea, and offers two spacious *en suite* double bedrooms, both with roll top baths and separate showers. The adjoining coach house comprises two newly-created luxury suites, each with a bedroom, bathroom and private sitting room. We offer a three-course-dinner on most evenings in our totally organic restaurant, where we serve seasonal home-grown organic food. The emphasis is on freshly picked, carefully prepared, simple and delicious dishes. All the fresh ingredients we use are grown in our own organic gardens and greenhouse.
info@bangorsorganic.co.uk www.bangorsorganic.co.uk

SEATON *(Camping)*

KEVERAL FARM 54

Seaton
Looe PL13 1PA
Mobile: 07772 155967 MAP 17

Camping, from £3 per adult pn
Yurts, from £18 pn

Organic produce sometimes available in season

Soil Association

Keveral Farm is a community of sixteen adults and ten children. We have been organic for over thirty years. Our Orchard Camping is quiet, sheltered and car free. Tents are well spaced for privacy, and there are camp-fires. We also have yurts available for hire. Our Visitors' Barn, with kitchen facilities and indoor space, can be used for an extra charge. The farm is very safe and secure. It is only fifteen minutes walk through the woods to the beach and the seaside village of Seaton with its café, shop and pub. The coast path, the Monkey Sanctuary and some great beaches are nearby, and Bodmin Moor and the Eden Project are within an hour's drive. The farm is four miles east of the small coastal town of Looe.
oak@keveral.org www.keveral.org

SEATON *(Camping)*

TRERIEVE FARM CAMPING 55

Seaton
Looe PL11 3DJ
Tel: 01503 250376   MAP 17

Caravan and Camping Site
£8 per pitch pn for caravans or tents

You certainly will be able to sample the
freshest of local produce

Soil Association

Trerieve is a 150-acre working organic farm on the south-east coast with fantastic views over the sea. We aim to provide quiet relaxing holidays where you can enjoy nature and the stunning scenery. The caravan and camping field has views across Whitsand Bay to Rame Head. It is sheltered from westerly winds by a hedge and enjoys good views of the countryside. There are five electric hook-up points including one on the hard standing for wet weather use. Mains water tap and chemical disposal points are sited in the field. Across the lane (which is very quiet with less than ten vehicles per day) and adjacent to the house is the WC block. You can enjoy the variety of wildlife and plants on circular walks around the farm.
info@trerieve.co.uk   www.trerieve.co.uk

ST BREWARD *(Camping)*

CORNISH YURT HOLIDAYS 56

Greyhayes
St Breward PL30 4LP
Tel: 01208 850670   MAP 17

Yurts: sleep 2-6, £295-£475 pw
Short Breaks (available out of season)

Organic sausages, beefburgers, minced beef,
bacon, eggs usually available

One 16ft and one 20ft yurt on a 40 acre smallholding on the edge of Bodmin Moor. The yurts, professionally built on the farm from locally coppiced wood, stand on wooden decks each with a wood-burning stove to one side (wood supplied), and carpets and rugs on the floor. They are totally secluded in two separate fields surrounded by gnarly oaks, granite stones, moorland and pasture. The coast is twelve miles away, the cycle path along the River Camel is less than two miles away, and the moor is underfoot. Depending on the time of year fresh produce from the farm, which is run on organic lines, or local producers is available (sausages, burgers, minced beef, bacon, eggs), as is locally produced charcoal.
nfo@yurtworks.co.uk   www.yurtworks.co.uk/holidays/index.htm

ST BURYAN *(S-C)*

BOSKENNA COTTAGE   57

Boskenna Home Farm
St Buryan TR19 6DQ
Tel: 01736 810705   MAP 17

Cottage: sleeps 2
£390-£660 pw

Organic eggs, (organic beef may be available)

Organic Farmers & Growers

Boskenna Cottage is an idyllic self-catering cottage designed especially for two. The cottage has been built with traditional local materials including granite and slate. Inside the light and airy classic open-beamed accommodation you'll appreciate the fine craftsmanship in the spacious modern surroundings. With contemporary furnishings and appliances it has under-floor heating throughout. In a peaceful setting with a private garden the cottage is just footsteps from a tranquil cove on the South West Coast Path. Enjoy the culinary delights of the region's high quality locally produced food and drink and experience the real beauty of Cornwall and everything this spectacular region has to offer.
stay@luxury-cornwall.co.uk   www.luxury-cornwall.co.uk/cottage.asp

ST BURYAN *(B&B)*

BOSKENNA HOME FARM   58

St Buryan
Penzance TR19 6DQ
Tel: 01736 810705   MAP 17

Bed and Breakfast Suites
Double, £37 pppn

Breakfasts with home-made and local produce used wherever possible

Organic Farmers & Growers

Set in a small hamlet, Boskenna is a working organic beef farm with a herd of pedigree south Devon cows. You are very welcome to take a farm tour and meet the animals. It is a wonderful rural location only six miles from Penzance on the south coast of the Land's End peninsula. Our two superior bed and breakfast suites provide spacious *en suite* accommodation with king-size beds, and both are accessed directly from the farmhouse cobbled courtyard. Delicious breakfasts, a veritable feast with home-made and local produce used wherever possible, are served in the adjacent farmhouse dining room from 8am to 9am. St Loys Cove, a peaceful rocky bay, is a few minutes walk from Boskenna through an enchanting wooded valley.
stay@luxury-cornwall.co.uk   www.luxury-cornwall.co.uk

ST IVES *(B&B)*

ORGANIC PANDA   59

1 Pednolver Terrace
St Ives TR26 2EL
Tel: 01736 793890   MAP 17

Bed and Breakfast, £40-£70 pppn
Packed Lunch (order night before)

Organic breakfast and complimentary cakes
or biscuits

The Organic Panda is situated in the vibrant community of St Ives. Our B&B has stunning views overlooking the harbour and the sea. With its use of natural materials and eco-friendly products the Organic Panda offers beautiful, spacious, contemporary accommodation. Enjoy breakfast at our ten seater rustic table. All our food is fresh, organic, and locally sourced where possible. Choose your breakfast (meat, fish, vegetarian, vegan) from an extensive menu. Dietary requirements are welcomed and catered for, including gluten-free, sugar-free, dairy free, but never taste free. We bake all our own bread (wholemeal, gluten-free, yeast-free), as well as specialist cakes and biscuits. Green Tourism Business Scheme Gold Award. info@organicpanda.co.uk   www.organicpanda.co.uk

ST KEVERNE *(S-C)*

THE WING   60

Tregellast Barton Farm
St Keverne TR12 6NX
Tel: 01326 280479   MAP 17

Converted Barn: sleeps 6
£200-£595 pw

Our own organic milk, cream, ice cream, etc

Soil Association

The Wing has been converted from an old barn which forms the south-facing wing of the farmhouse. It has its own entrance and a small lawn outside. Tregellast Barton has always been home to Channel Island cows. The farm has grown to 200 acres and has around a hundred milking Jersey cows. Both the land and the herd are certified organic. Farm produce includes organic milk, organic cream, organic ice cream, organic clotted cream fudge, apple juice, cider, pasties, mustards, chutneys, jams and marmalade. Enjoy delicious home-made food and locally made organic beers at our licensed tearoom / restaurant. There is a mile of easy walking in a charming valley of ponds, meadows and woods. silke@roskillys.co.uk   www.roskillys.co.uk/cottages

ST MARTIN *(Camping)*

CORNISH YURTS   61

Tregeague Farm
St Martin TR12 6EB
Tel: 01326 231211   MAP 17

Yurts: sleeps 6
£240-£450 pw

Organic farm shops and restaurant nearby

Organic Farmers & Growers

Two 18-foot yurts on an organic beef and dairy farm in an Area of Outstanding Natural Beauty on the Lizard Peninsula. The farm has been in the Williams family for five generations. The yurts are set in a one-acre field, sheltered by hedges and trees (you're more than welcome to explore the farm). There is a Wood-burning stove in your yurt, and we also allow campfires. Each yurt comes with its own barbecue, and depending on the season we can supply organic barbecue packs. Rosuick Organic Farm shop is about ten minutes walk away, and Gear Organic Farm shop is a five minute drive away. Within a five mile radius you'll find many beaches, the scenic Helford river, and the beautiful countryside that's all around us. mail@cornishyurts.co.uk   www.cornishyurts.co.uk

ST MARTIN *(S-C)*

ELMTREE FARM HOUSE   62

Rosuick Organic Farm
St Martin TR12 6DZ
Tel: 01326 231302   MAP 17

Cottage: sleeps 6
£200-£600 pw

Farm shop and café sell home and local produce

Soil Association

Rosuick Organic Farm is situated in its own picturesque valley in an Area of Outstanding Natural Beauty. The farm has been in the Oates family since the 1700s, ours being the 6th generation to farm here. The cottages are all in their own private grounds, but with access to the tennis court and farm trail. Elmtree is a traditional cob and stone cottage with its own half-acre of garden. It has a sunny aspect, looking out across the fields. We sell as much of our own home produce as possible at our farm shop, located on the edge of the farm. Spring water supply. Wonderful walking, both on the farm and the Goonhilly Downs. We have nine Bactrian camels, to be used for camel treks. Visitor centre and café.
oates@rosuick.co.uk   www.rosuick.co.uk

ST MARTIN *(Camping)*

GEAR ORGANIC CAMPING 63

St Martin
Helston TR12 6DE
Tel: 01326 221364   MAP 17

Simply Camping (open May-Sept)
£7.50-£8.50 per adult pn

Farm shop sells organic produce and home-made food

Biodynamic Agricultural Association

The camping field is one and a half acres of level mown grass overlooking the Helford River. Our organic farm shop sells organic and local produce – fresh fruit and vegetables, apple juice, milk, ice cream, etc. Organic and local produce is also used in the home-made takeaway food, including hot pizzas, bread and cakes. Real Cornish pasties made on-site daily. The farm slopes down to the beautiful Helford River off Falmouth Bay. Boats for hire at Helford and St Anthony to explore Frenchman's Creek and along the river. Beaches and small fishing ports within six miles. Wet weather activities in the area – Ships and Castles swimming pool in Falmouth, Paradise Park in Hayle, Flambards in Helston.
pathosking@btinternet.com

ST MARTIN *(S-C)*

ROSUICK COTTAGE 64

Rosuick Organic Farm
St Martin TR12 6DZ
Tel: 01326 231302   MAP 17

Cottage: sleeps 6
£250-£650 pw

Farm shop and café sell home and local produce

Soil Association

Rosuick Organic Farm is situated in its own picturesque valley in an Area of Outstanding Natural Beauty. The farm has been in the Oates family since the 1700s, ours being the 6th generation to farm here. The cottages are all in their own private grounds, but with access to the tennis court and farm trail. Rosuick Cottage has just been refurbished. It is a very grand house with its own amazing two-acre garden. It has a sunny aspect, looking out across its own garden and the fields beyond. We sell as much of our own home produce as possible at our farm shop, located on the edge of the farm. Spring water supply. Wonderful walks on the farm and the Goonhilly Downs. We now have nine Bactrian camels.
oates@rosuick.co.uk   www.rosuick.co.uk

ST MARTIN *(S-C)*

ROSUICK FARM HOUSE 65

Rosuick Organic Farm
St Martin TR12 6DZ
Tel: 01326 231302   MAP 17

Cottage: sleeps 10
£450-£975 pw

Farm shop and café sell home and local produce

Soil Association

Rosuick Organic Farm is situated in its own picturesque valley in an Area of Outstanding Natural Beauty. Rosuick Farm House is a beautiful traditional stone farmhouse, with a history reaching back to the Domesday. The main property of the valley, it has 15th-century doors and many character features, and nestles in its country surroundings. Access from the farmhouse to the tennis court and farm trail. We sell as much of our own home produce as possible at our farm shop, which is located on the edge of the farm. Spring water supply. Wonderful walking on the farm and the Goonhilly Downs. We have nine Bactrian camels, which are to be used for camel treks. Visitor centre and café.
oates@rosuick.co.uk   www.rosuick.co.uk

TORPOINT *(B&B)*

BUTTERVILLA 66

Polbathic
Torpoint PL11 3EY
Tel: 01503 230315   MAP 17

Bed and Breakfast, £47.50-£57.50 pppn
Evening Meal, £30 pp

Local seasonal produce, organic wherever possible

Soil Association

Fifteen organic acres of exceptionally beautiful countryside two miles from the Cornish coast. Comfortable large double *en suite* rooms with modern conveniences and eco-friendly solar-heated power showers. Local seasonal produce for breakfasts and evening meals, home-grown organic or sourced from organic suppliers whenever possible. We grow a range of fresh fruit and vegetables in our extensive kitchen garden. We care for our land in a sustainable, natural, eco-friendly way and have an abundance of wildlife to help you feel close to nature. Buttervilla has no farm animals so guests can roam freely in the delightful grounds. The environment is clean, pure and influenced by sweet Atlantic breezes.
info@buttervilla.com   www.buttervilla.com

TREKNOW *(B&B)*

MICHAEL HOUSE   67

Trelake Lane
Treknow PL34 0EW
Tel: 01840 770592   MAP 17

Vegetarian Guest House, B&B £25-£34 pppn
Evening Meal, 3 course £18.50

60%-80% of the food we offer is organic or home grown

A vegetarian and vegan guest house offering delicious food and a peaceful atmosphere, Michael House is one mile from Tintagel in the pretty hamlet of Treknow. It looks down towards the sea over rolling fields and the valley leading to Trebarwith Strand, whose stunning beach is five minutes drive away (fifteen minutes on foot). As well as delicious and extensive breakfasts we offer three-course evening meals to guests by arrangement. These are on a set menu basis and draw inspiration from traditional and world cuisine. Colour and flavour are paramount. We aim to use the best local, fairly-traded, home-produced and / or organic produce that we can obtain. We are licensed. Open all year. Children and pets welcome.
info@michael-house.co.uk   www.michael-house.co.uk

TREVALGA *(B&B)*

REDDIVALLEN   68

Reddivallen Farm
Trevalga PL35 0EE
Tel: 01840 250854   MAP 17

Bed and Breakfast, £34-£42 pppn
Dinner, £15 (by arrangement)

Our organic beef can be tasted by our guests when it is on the menu for dinner

Soil Association

Secluded 17th-century farmhouse and converted barn on a 339-acre working organic farm. Reddivallen is close to Boscastle and just a few minutes away from the breathtaking coastline. Relax in this peaceful location overlooking lake and valley. Spacious accommodation, two storied gabled porch, slate hallway, granite mullion windows. Superb home cooking. Dinner by arrangement using our home-produced organic beef, lamb and other produce. The grounds are landscaped with grass and shrubs. We have developed a lake where we have introduced mirrored carp for anyone who is keen to fish, or you can just stroll around the lake taking in the wildlife and surrounding valley. We welcome walkers and cyclists.
liz@redboscastle.com   www.redboscastle.com

ZELAH *(S-C)*

CALLESTOCK COURTYARD 69

Little Callestock Farm
Zelah TR4 9HB
Tel: 01872 540445   MAP 17

Apartments: sleep 2
£295-£520 pw

Organic milk, scones, jam, clotted cream, eggs

Organic Farmers & Growers

Set in a rural location, these charming barns have been lovingly-restored to an excellent standard (4-star). The properties have four-posters (some of which are kingsize), whirlpool baths, wood-burning stoves, exposed stonework, wooden floors and beautiful pine beams. Little Callestock is an organic dairy farm with a herd of pretty Jersey cows. Organic produce includes milk, home-made scones, jam, clotted cream, eggs. A welcome tray with an organic clotted cream tea is provided on arrival. Ramble through the farm and surrounding tranquil countryside. Use our bikes and explore picturesque unspoilt country lanes. Visit Truro and superb sandy beaches. Come and find out why our guests keep returning. GTBS Silver Award. liznick@littlecallestockfarm.co.uk   www.callestockcourtyard.com/courtyard.html

ZELAH *(S-C)*

ORCHARD COTTAGE 70

Little Callestock Farm
Zelah TR4 9HB
Tel: 01872 540445   MAP 17

Converted Barn: sleeps 4
£320-£625 pw

Organic milk, scones, jam, clotted cream, eggs

Organic Farmers & Growers

A detached barn conversion set in its own private garden. Renovated to a high standard (3-star property) it offers year round family holidays and breaks. Large garden with patio and garden furniture. Barbecue available. Little Callestock is an organic dairy farm with a herd of pretty Jersey cows. Our organic produce includes milk, home-made scones, jam, clotted cream, butter, eggs. A welcome tray with an organic clotted cream tea is provided on arrival. Ramble through the farm and surrounding tranquil countryside. Use our bikes and explore picturesque unspoilt country lanes. Visit the cathedral city of Truro, the Eden Project, and superb sandy beaches. Come and find out why our guests keep returning. GTBS Silver Award. liznick@littlecallestockfarm.co.uk   www.callestockcourtyard.com/orchard.html

ZELAH (S-C)

WHEAL BUSY 71

Little Callestock Farm
Zelah TR4 9HB
Tel: 01872 540445   MAP 17

Converted Barn: sleeps 3
£340-£660 pw

Organic milk, scones, jam, clotted cream, eggs

Organic Farmers & Growers

A detached barn conversion (5-star property), Wheal Busy is on the edge of the courtyard. The living area has a beautiful oak floor and a wood-burning stove. The gallery bedroom is accessed via a stunning claret spiral staircase. Little Callestock is an organic dairy farm with a herd of pretty Jersey cows. Organic produce includes milk, home-made scones, jam, clotted cream, butter, eggs. A welcome tray with an organic clotted cream tea is provided on arrival. Ramble through the farm and surrounding tranquil countryside. Use our bikes and explore picturesque unspoilt country lanes. Visit the cathedral city of Truro, the Eden Project, and superb sandy beaches. Come and see why our guests keep returning. GTBS Silver Award.
liznick@littlecallestockfarm.co.uk   www.callestockcourtyard.com/whealbusy.html

ZENNOR (B&B)

BOSWEDNACK MANOR 72

Zennor
St Ives TR26 3DD
Tel: 01736 794183   MAP 17

Vegetarian Bed and Breakfast
Open April-Sept, £21-£28 pppn

Exclusively organic food if requested in advance

Spacious granite farmhouse set in 3 acres of eco-friendly meadows, vegetable, fruit and flower gardens. We are one mile west of Zennor and surrounded by an ancient, unspoiled landscape of moorland, stone-walled fields and magnificent coastal cliffs and coves. Fine views from all the guest rooms. Solar-powered panels provide much of the hot water. Our delicious breakfast is vegetarian and around 50% of the fare is organic (100% organic on request). Home-made, home-grown blackcurrant jam is usually available. We also offer guided wildlife walks. If you prefer to explore on your own there are free walk sheets of circular routes from Boswednack, with notes on local archaeology, wild flowers and birds.
boswednack@ravenfield.co.uk   www.boswednackmanor.co.uk

BOWNESS *(B&B)*

APHRODITES HOTEL   73

Longtail Hill
Bowness LA23 3JD
Tel: 015394 45052   MAP 8

Boutique Hotel, B&B from £35 pppn
Breakfast, Snacks, Evening Meal

We serve organic, local, seasonal and fair
trade foods whenever it is possible

Aphrodites is a boutique hotel offering guest accommodation in both classical and themed suites. Often described as 'the hip hotel' in the Lake District, it is not just a bed and breakfast but a hotel serving food that is all organic, with a strong emphasis on Slow Food. Most of the organic food is locally sourced and is fairly-traded where possible. The restaurant is exclusively for the use of our guests (a Soil Association licence is to be applied for). When the weather is fine you can enjoy the outside gallery eating and drinking area, which overlooks a unique dancing fountain. Set in two acres of beautiful gardens, Aphrodites Hotel is just a few minutes walk from Lake Windermere and the bustling village of Bowness.
enquiries@21thelakes.co.uk   www.aphroditeslodge.co.uk

CARTMEL *(B&B)*

HOWBARROW ORGANIC   74

Cartmel
Grange-over-Sands LA11 7SS
Tel: 015395 36330   MAP 8

Bed and Organic Breakfast, £57.50 room pn
Dinner, 4 course £19.50 (by arrangement)

100% organic food (licensed with the Soil
Association)

Soil Association

Howbarrow is an organic smallholding with panoramic views of the Lake District and the Cumbrian coast. The 16th-century family farmhouse has slate floors and oak beams. We provide a full organic breakfast and evening meals by arrangement. 100% of the food provided is organic, much of which is produced on the farm. Farm produce includes meat, vegetables, herbs and soft fruit. The land is in an environmentally sensitive area, and is managed under a scheme to enhance the wildlife and landscape features. Forty four varieties of birdlife have been recorded, as well as deer, badgers and bats. Part of the Soil Association's Open Farm Network, Howbarrow also has a farm shop, a display area and a farm walk.
enquiries@howbarroworganic.co.uk   www.howbarroworganic.co.uk

COCKERMOUTH *(S-C)*

LOW STANGER FARM   75

Stanger
Cockermouth CA13 9TS
Tel: 01900 823558   MAP 8

Cottage: sleeps 4+, £245-£410 pw
Short Breaks, 1 night £100/2 nights from £130

Seasonal fruit and vegetables available from
the farm

In Conversion

Low Stanger Farm is situated within the small settlement of Stanger, two miles south of Cockermouth in the beautiful Lorton Valley. Stable Cottage is a spacious two bedroom barn conversion adjoining the farmhouse on our small lakeland farm and organic market garden. The living accommodation is on the first floor to take advantage of the view across open fields. There are footpaths and a bridleway running from the farmyard. Visitors can also explore the farm itself including a long stretch of the river Cocker (fishing available). You can buy organic fruit and vegetables from the farm in season and usually eggs as well. Hot water is supplied by an advanced solar water heating system with electrical back-up for cloudy days. enquiries@lowstanger.co.uk   www.lowstanger.co.uk

EASEDALE *(Hotel)*

LANCRIGG HOTEL   76

Easedale
Grasmere LA22 9QN
Tel: 015394 35317   MAP 8

Bed and Breakfast, £50-£95 pppn.
Organic vegetarian Restaurant

Delicious organic vegetarian food, organic
wines and beers

Biodynamic Agricultural Association

The hotel is set in the picturesque valley of Easedale in the heart of the Lake District, half a mile from the village of Grasmere. It provides comfortable and relaxing accommodation and makes a wonderful escape from a busy world. There are some lovely walks from the door. The house has many connections with past and present writers, poets, artists and musicians. The Green Valley Organic Restaurant at Lancrigg is open daily for breakfast, lunch, tea, evening meals. The food is freshly-prepared, and the imaginative menu has been designed by experienced chefs and a qualified nutritionist. Special diets are well catered for. Most of the dishes have a vegan alternative. Booking is advisable for evening meals. info@lancrigg.co.uk   www.lancrigg.co.uk

GILSLAND (B&B)

WILLOWFORD FARM 77

Gilsland
Brampton CA8 7AA
Tel: 016977 47962   MAP 9

Bed and Breakfast, £35-£40 pppn
Evening Meal, £18-£20 pp

Organic and local food provided where possible

In Conversion

A 100-acre farm, currently converting to the organic standards of the Soil Association (due to be fully converted 01/04/09). Guest accommodation is in a Grade II listed farmhouse and a beautifully converted stone byre. Being food producers ourselves, we are passionate about what goes on your plate. We use local and organic ingredients wherever possible, including from our own farm and garden, and place great importance on knowing where our food comes from. Hearty breakfasts include home-made bread, and delicious freshly-made organic evening meals, and packed lunches are also available. Our farm is on the Hadrian's Wall National Trail and contains impressive sections of the wall and other Roman remains. stay@willowford.co.uk   www.willowford.co.uk

GRASMERE (Hotel)

MOSS GROVE HOTEL 78

Grasmere
Ambleside LA22 9SW
Tel: 015394 35251   MAP 8

Small Hotel, £65-£120 pppn
Mediterranean buffet style breakfast

Buffet breakfast in the country kitchen (70%-95% organic)

Centrally located in the village of Grasmere, within the Lake District National Park. The hotel features beautiful bathroom suites with spa baths, showers and underfloor heating, mostly superking-size beds (handmade from reclaimed timbers or natural leather), highspeed internet access and flat screen TVs in all rooms, an extensive Mediterranean buffet breakfast serving only organic, local and fair trade food. The organic ethos includes recycling wherever possible, redecoration with organic clay paints, oak hardwood flooring, furnishings predominantly free from man-made fibres and chemicals, cotton and wool used for all soft furnishings, natural duck down duvets and pillows, filtered water throughout. enquiries@mossgrove.com   www.mossgrove.com

HAWKSHEAD *(B&B)*

YEWFIELD   79

Hawkshead Hill
Hawkshead LA22 0PR
Tel: 015394 36765   MAP 8

Vegetarian Bed and Breakfast, £35-£60 pppn

We have a vegetarian restaurant in
Ambleside

Breakfast is between 70% and 90% organic

A peaceful 5-star retreat in the heart of the English Lake District. We offer a continental vegetarian buffet including fresh fruits, muesli, cereals, home-baked bread, yogurt, preserves, coffee and teas, and a full cooked vegetarian breakfast using locally sourced organic produce and ingredients where possible. There are over 30 acres of land around the house, including native woodland, rough fell pasture, a small tarn and a stream. The grazed pasture is managed carefully, giving priority to ecological considerations. Newly-developed ornamental areas closer to the house include orchards, vegetable gardens, a herb patio, and a mixed border. A nature trail through the land and gardens guides you round the grounds.
derek.yewfield@btinternet.com   www.yewfield.co.uk

KENDAL *(B&B)*

ARDRIG VEGETARIAN B&B   80

144 Windermere Road
Kendal LA9 5EZ
Tel: 01539 736879   MAP 9

Bed and Breakfast
From £28 pppn

Most of the food we serve is organic

Ardrig Vegetarian is a quiet, friendly bed and breakfast in Kendal run by vegetarians. Breakfast is fresh, tasty, healthy and filling. It is all vegetarian and mostly organic, fair trade and non-GM. Vegan options are normally available, and we can cater for other dietary needs if you let us know when you book. Bedding and towels are washed with Ecover products and we aim for cleanliness without wastefulness. Soaps are environmentally and animal-friendly. Ecover products are also used for household cleaning. Kendal is a lively town with good restaurants, museums, an art gallery, theatre and cinemas, and is the home of the Quaker Tapestry. Kendal is three miles from the mainline railway station at Oxenholme.
enquiry@ardrigvegetarian.com   www.ardrigvegetarian.com

LITTLE SALKELD *(S-C)*

TOWN END FARM COTTAGE 81

Town End Farm
Little Salkeld CA10 1NN
Tel: 01768 881336   MAP 9

Cottage: sleeps 6, £260-£380 pw
Short breaks available pro rata

Organic milk, organic eggs (when available)

Organic Farmers & Growers

A cottage and barn attached to the main farmhouse have been converted into comfortable accommodation without sacrificing character. It's full of rustic oak beams, sandstone alcoves and many other charming features. There's a small walled garden to the front of the cottage, in which you might enjoy a barbecue whilst admiring the views across the countryside. Town End Farm is a working farm and the family has farmed here for many generations. Visitors to the cottage are invited to wander over the 200 acres of farmland running along the beautiful river Eden. Fly fishing is available for two rods, please ask for details. The farm welcomes well behaved children to help on the farm at the owner's discretion.

joyce@tumpline.com   www.tumpline.com/property/townend

LONGTOWN *(S-C)*

SHANK WOOD LOG CABIN 82

Whitecloserigg
Longtown CA6 5TY
Tel: 01228 791801   MAP 9

Log Cabin: sleeps 4
£70-£110 pn

Fresh caught fish for the barbeque, organic milk and organic eggs from 05/09

In Conversion

The cabin is situated amongst 140 acres of picturesque privately-owned ancient woodland in the middle of a two mile beat of the River Lyne. The split-level accommodation has been designed to work in conjunction with nature as much as possible. The house rod is provided with the cabin so please limit one rod to being in the water at any one time. There are eleven pools on the two mile beat, each having its own place where fish love to lie. Another opportunity to fish is just five minutes walk from the cabin into open farm land, where there is a stocked rainbow trout pond. Guests will be able to buy organic milk from us when we are fully converted to organic, and as we have chickens organic eggs will also be available.

info@fishinghideaway.co.uk   www.fishinghideaway.co.uk

ROWELTOWN (S-C)

LOW LUCKENS 83

Low Luckens Farm
Roweltown CA6 6LJ
Tel: 016977 48186 MAP 9

Self-Catering: sleeps 9+3, £12-£15 pppn
Full Centre: £100 pn, £395 pw

Organic produce can be purchased from the farm when available

Soil Association

The Organic Resource Centre is housed in a traditional farm building at Low Luckens Farm. It is situated in beautiful countryside close to the Scottish Borders and Hadrian's Wall. Part of the Soil Association's Open Farm Network, the farm produces organic beef, lamb and vegetables. The centre provides simple, clean and inexpensive self-catering accommodation for groups and families who enjoy the countryside, or want to become actively involved in farming or conservation. It is also an excellent base for walkers and cyclists. An extensive Countryside Stewardship agreement covers the farm's 220 acres, including riverside and woodland footpaths. Organic produce can be purchased from the farm when available. lowluckensorc@hotmail.com www.lowluckensfarm.co.uk

RYDAL (B&B)

COTE HOW ORGANIC 84

Rydal
Ambleside LA22 9LW
Tel: 015394 32765 MAP 8

Bed and Breakfast, from £54.50 pppn
Minimum two nights stay

Fully Soil Association licensed for 'Restaurant and Catering' and 'Processing'

Soil Association

Centrally located within the Lake District National Park, Cote How is a 16th-century country guest house and tearoom offering luxury accommodation and organic food. We are Soil Association licensed for our breakfast and tearoom to provide our visitors with the best organic, seasonal, local and wholesome food available. Packed lunches on request. Enjoy a home-made organic cream tea. We bake all our own scones, cakes and bread, and make our own preserves and chutneys using organic produce. Set in four acres and close to Rydal Water, Cote How is within easy reach of Ambleside and Grasmere. Green Tourism Business Scheme Gold Award. Winners of Cumbria Tourism Sustainable Tourism Award 2008. info@cotehow.co.uk www.cotehow.co.uk

RYDAL *(B&B)*

NAB COTTAGE  85

Rydal
Ambleside LA22 9SD
Tel: 015394 35311   MAP 8

B&B (Oct-July), £29-£32 pppn
Dinner, 3 course £20 (by arrangement)

We make our own bread, and use organic
produce wherever possible

Nab Cottage is between Grasmere and Ambleside in the heart of the Lake District, with beautiful views over the lake. It dates from the 16th-century and stands alone near the shores of Rydal Water, surrounded by mountains. Many original features remain – beams, flagged floors, spice cupboard, mullioned windows, open fire. Enjoy our home-made bread and a long breakfast. The atmosphere is easy going and guests can enjoy spending time inside. Outside, the views, and the walks, are stunning. Excellent low level routes and longer treks directly from the cottage. Packed lunches, dinner or lighter snacks by arrangement using fresh, organic and fair trade ingredients. Massage, Reiki, Shiatsu available. tim@nabcottage.com www.nabcottage.com

ULPHA *(S-C)*

HIGH WALLABARROW   86

High Wallabarrow Farm
Ulpha LA20 6EA
Tel: 01229 715011   MAP 8

Cottage: sleeps 4-5, £250-£480 pw
Camping Barn: sleeps 10, £8.50 pppn

Free-range eggs, lamb, beef, fruit and
vegetables may be available to buy

A beautiful sheltered corner of Dunnerdale amongst native oakwoods and flower-rich meadows in a sweeping bend of the River Duddon. Adjoining the farmhouse the accommodation overlooks the garden, beck, rocky crags and the farmyard. The woodlands, garden and vegetable beds are all managed without using chemicals. Visitors are free to roam over 450 acres of farm woodland and pastures. Free-range eggs, Hebridean lamb, Galloway beef and naturally grown fruit and vegetables may be available to buy. Home-produced charcoal is often available. The camping barn is situated in the farmyard, but is safely enclosed. The Newfield Inn, a delightful fifteen minute walk through the woods, serves real ales and food all day. info@wallabarrow.co.uk www.wallabarrow.co.uk

WINDERMERE (S-C)

HELM FARM 87

Matson Ground
Windermere LA23 2HF
Tel: 015394 45756 MAP 9

Apartments: sleep 2-5
£190-£700 pw

Cuts of organic beef and lamb can be
delivered to Helm Farm

Organic Farmers & Growers

Four self-catering holiday apartments in a converted barn near Windermere in the English Lake District. The buildings, some of which date back to 1691, and the adjacent farmland are part of a family-run farming estate. The apartments are close to Bowness-on-Windermere, but are very quiet and right on the edge of pleasant wooded countryside. Helm Farm is not a working farm, although the land has been farmed as part of Matson Ground Farm for many years. Matson Ground Farm, with eighty beef shorthorn cows and about a thousand ewes, has been registered as organic since 2002. We are members of Cumbria Organics. There are footpaths from the door connecting with a wide network of paths, including the Dales Way. info@matsonground.co.uk www.matsonground.co.uk/homehelm.html

ILAM (S-C)

BEECHENHILL COTTAGE 88

Beechenhill Farm
Ilam DE6 2BD
Tel: 01335 310274 MAP 15

Cottage: sleeps 2, £270-£410 pw
Short breaks, £190-£270

Seasonal range of locally produced ready-
meals and puddings

Soil Association

Romantic small cottage hideaway on an organic dairy farm. Ready meals are available to buy, made with produce from environmentally sensitive local farms. Tiny, warm and peaceful, the beautifully decorated stone cottage is in its own walled garden with not another house in sight. Relax by the real fire for cosy evenings. Virtually allergy-free, so no pets. The farmhouse garden has garden games, 'book in advance' Swedish style hot tub, sculptures, stunning views. The farm trail is a lovely way to spend an hour or so. Beechenhill Haybarn is an ideal venue for parties and events. The farm and tourism business have achieved the Peak District Environmental Quality Mark and a Green Tourism Business Scheme Silver Award. beechenhill@btinternet.com www.beechenhill.co.uk/cottage.htm

ILAM *(B&B)*

BEECHENHILL FARM 89

Ilam
Ashbourne DE6 2BD
Tel: 01335 310274   MAP 15

Farmhouse Bed and Breakfast
£36-£39 pppn

Local and organic produce where possible

Soil Association

Working organic dairy farm (Peak District Environmental Quality Mark and Silver Award Green Tourism Business Scheme) in a beautiful area of the Peak District National Park. The long, low, ivy-clad farmhouse, built from local limestone, has been added to since the 1500s. Wonderful views over the garden and fields with grazing cows. Farmhouse breakfasts are prepared with local and organic produce where possible. Fruit, cereals, home-made organic yogurt, our famous porridge, home-made bread toasted with home-made jam and honey from the farm, feature alongside a delicious traditional farmhouse breakfast. Farm walks, garden games, table tennis, Swedish style hot tub. Events and parties welcome at the Haybarn. beechenhill@btinternet.com   www.beechenhill.co.uk

ILAM *(S-C)*

COTTAGE BY THE POND 90

Beechenhill Farm
Ilam DE6 2BD
Tel: 01335 310274   MAP 15

Cottage: sleeps 6, £380-£710 pw
Short breaks, £200-£580

Seasonal range of locally produced ready-meals and puddings

Soil Association

Beautifully decorated cottage (converted from the old milking barn) on an organic dairy farm near Dovedale. It is virtually allergy-free, so no pets, and designed to be accessible to everybody, including those with wheelchairs. The large sitting room has a patio window which looks due south over a little courtyard, the walled pond and rolling farmland. Savour the distinctive foods of the area – a delicious range of locally made ready-meals and puddings is available to buy from the farmhouse. The seasonal range includes Dovedale Beef, Peak Feast vegetarian dishes, and Peak Puddings. The farm and tourism business have achieved the Peak District Environmental Quality Mark and a Green Tourism Business Scheme Silver Award. beechenhill@btinternet.com   www.beechenhill.co.uk/cottagebypond.htm

RIBER *(B&B)*

HEARTHSTONE FARM 91

Hearthstone Lane
Riber DE4 5JW
Tel: 01629 534304 MAP 15

Farmhouse B&B, double £75 pn
Discount for three nights or more

We use our own organic produce wherever possible

Organic Farmers & Growers

Hearthstone Farm is a traditional working family farm producing organic beef, pork and lamb, plus bacon, gammon and sausage made from organic pork. Organic home produce can be bought from our farm shop. Nestling at the edge of the Peak District, our 16th-century stone farmhouse is the perfect location for a relaxing break in some of Britain's most breathtaking countryside. Situated on the edge of the village, the farm offers a comfortable environment from which to explore the surrounding area. We pride ourselves on the quality of our breakfasts, using our own organic produce wherever possible. Guests are welcome to go out onto the farm, and we are delighted to answer any questions about our farming methods.
enquiries@hearthstonefarm.co.uk   www.hearthstonefarm.co.uk

STANSHOPE *(S-C)*

ANCESTRAL BARN 92

Church Farm
Stanshope DE6 2AD
Tel: 01335 310243 MAP 15

5-star Ancestral Barn: sleeps 6
£550-£960 pw

Home-produced meat, free-range eggs, our own honey, bread

Organic Farmers & Growers

Award-winning 5-star 200 year old Grade II listed barn on a working organic farm. We are situated on top of Halldale, which meanders down to Dovedale in the breathtaking scenery of the Peak District National Park. Come and see our lambs being born in the spring, our wild flower meadows in the summer, or enjoy cosy open fires in the winter to snooze by. locally produced foods can be delivered to your barn door. Just ask at Church Farm door for our organic beef and lamb. Proud holders of the Peak District Environmental Quality Mark for our accommodation and organic farming practices (use of locally grown or locally produced products, use of environmentally friendly products, conservation of landscape).
sue@fowler89.fsnet.co.uk   www.dovedalecottages.co.uk/ancestralbarn/index.html

STANSHOPE *(S-C)*

CHURCH FARM COTTAGE 93

Church Farm
Stanshope DE6 2AD
Tel: 01335 310243   MAP 15

Grade II Listed Cottage: sleeps 4
£450-£750 pw

Home-produced meat, free-range eggs, our own honey, bread

Organic Farmers & Growers

lovingly-restored Grade II listed 16th-century country cottage in a tranquil setting on a working organic farm. It is situated on top of Halldale, which meanders down to Dovedale in the breathtaking countryside of the Peak District National Park. Come and see our lambs being born in the spring, our wild flower meadows in the summer, or cosy open fires to snooze by in the winter. Locally produced foods can be delivered to the cottage door. Just ask at Church Farm door for our organic beef and lamb. We are proud holders of the Peak District Environmental Quality Mark for supporting environment practices such as conservation of landscape, use of locally grown / produced products, use of environmentally friendly products. sue@fowler89.fsnet.co.uk   www.dovedalecottages.co.uk/farmcottage/index.html

STANSHOPE *(S-C)*

DALE BOTTOM COTTAGE 94

Church Farm
Stanshope DE6 2AD
Tel: 01335 310243   MAP 15

Cottage: sleeps 2-6
£650-£1160 pw

Home-produced meat, free-range eggs, our own honey, bread

Organic Farmers & Growers

Dale Bottom Cottage is situated in a charming hamlet in Dovedale in the Peak District National Park. It is in a little enclave on its own, with the cottage's front and the delightful garden soaking up the sun. Its stone walls are smothered in clematis and there's a medley of colour from roses and sweet peas which clamber up the wall beside the front door. From whichever direction you approach you can't ignore the display of English cottage garden flowers at their best. locally produced foods can be delivered to your door. Just ask at the farm door for our organic beef and lamb. Also ask for our free-range eggs or a jar of our delicate flavoured honey.
sue@fowler89.fsnet.co.uk   www.dovedalecottages.co.uk/dalebottom/index.html

SUTTON ON THE HILL *(S-C)*

THE CHOP HOUSE 95

Windlehill Farm
Sutton on the Hill DE6 5JH
Tel: 01283 732377   MAP 15

Converted Barn: sleeps 6, £300-£520 pw
Short Breaks (out of season)

Organic produce available locally

Organic Farmers & Growers

The Chop House has been carefully converted from the farm corn shed. It features original beams and has pleasant views of the farmyard, duck pond and surrounding countryside. There has been a farm on this site since at least the 16th-century. Set in tranquil countryside, the 10-acre working organic smallholding specialises in traditional and rare breeds of livestock. We keep pure-breed Poll Dorset Sheep and Kerry Cattle, which are milked on the family organic farm next door, as well as pedigree beagles. We have a fully accessible meeting room which caters for up to fifteen people. Spinning and weaving and other courses run by local specialists are available. Please contact us for more information.
windlehill@btinternet.com   www.windlehill.btinternet.co.uk

SUTTON ON THE HILL *(S-C)*

THE HAYLOFT 96

Windlehill Farm
Sutton on the Hill DE6 5JH
Tel: 01283 732377   MAP 15

Apartment: sleeps 2, £180-£280 pw
Short breaks out of season

Organic produce available locally

Organic Farmers & Growers

The Hayloft is a first floor apartment over the old stable. It features original beams and pleasant views of the farmyard, duck pond and surrounding countryside. There has been a farm on this site since at least the 16th-century. Set in tranquil countryside, this 10-acre working organic smallholding specialises in traditional and rare breeds of livestock. We keep pure breed Poll Dorset Sheep and Kerry Cattle, which are milked on the family organic farm next door, as well as pedigree beagles. We have a fully accessible meeting room which caters for groups of up to fifteen people. Spinning and weaving and other courses run by local specialists are also available. Please contact us for more information.
windlehill@btinternet.com   www.windlehill.btinternet.co.uk

WESTON UNDERWOOD *(B&B)*

PARK VIEW FARM 97

Bullhurst Lane
Weston Underwood DE6 4PA
Tel: 01335 360352   MAP 15

Farmhouse Bed and Breakfast
£80-£85 two persons in double *en suite* room
Organic and locally produced where possible
Organic Farmers & Growers

Enjoy country house hospitality in our elegant farmhouse, set in large gardens overlooking the National Trust's magnificent Kedleston Park. Park View is a working sheep farm, managed organically. Sheep graze peacefully in the fields beyond the farmhouse, which dates back to 1860. Beautiful four-poster *en suite* rooms, crisp white sheets, flowers and books. The delightful dining room and drawing room overlook the south-facing vine covered terrace. Delicious breakfasts are cooked on the Aga. Eggs are collected each morning from the hens who wander from their house to the garden and clover-filled fields beyond. Fresh fruits from the farm are made into delicious compote for breakfast and Mike bakes the bread.
enquiries@parkviewfarm.co.uk   www.parkviewfarm.co.uk

BERRY POMEROY *(B&B)*

NORWEGIAN WOOD 98

Berry Pomeroy
Totnes TQ9 6LE
Tel: 01803 867462   MAP 18

Bed and Breakfast
£35-£45 pppn
95% organic, locally sourced where possible

Beautifully converted Devon long barn, full of colour and atmosphere, in a stunning location overlooking the edge of Dartmoor. Relaxing, restful, refreshing. Start the day with a healthy organic traditional English meat, vegan, lacto-vegetarian, wheat-free, raw food or other customised breakfast to suit your dietary needs. Organic beverages in double and twin rooms with filtered water. Our food is certified organic and locally sourced where possible (average 95% organic). We adhere to the Soil Association's open book certification for small businesses. We are a non-smoking, ecologically sensitive, environmentally friendly household. Children welcome. In-house nutritional naturopathy / iridology / tutorials / PGCE, MIfL.
heather@norwegianwood.eclipse.co.uk   www.organicbedandbreakfast.info

BLAGDON BARTON (B&B)

WEST BLAGDON 99

Blagdon Barton
Paignton TQ4 7PU
Tel: 01803 665599 MAP 18

Vegetarian Bed and Breakfast, from £25 pppn
Evening Meal (by arrangement)

We can offer 100% organic if required

A smallholding run on organic lines on the edge of Torbay – the 'English Riviera'. It is contained in a small medieval hamlet, yet is secluded and surrounded by views of fields and hills. We have a small menagerie of animals including goats and ducks, and children are welcome to feed and pet them. We have two double rooms with views of the garden – one *en suite* and the other with a private, but separate, bathroom. Food is vegetarian and we can offer 100% organic if required. Some of the food will be home-grown. In addition to bed and breakfast we also offer an evening meal by arrangement. We run art retreat weekends for those who would enjoy a restful and creative diversion from the rigours of modern living. ronigail@aol.com

BRADNINCH (S-C)

POORMAN'S COT 100

Highdown Farm
Bradninch EX5 4LJ
Tel: 01392 881028 MAP 18

Cottage: sleeps 4
£250-£530 pw

Delivery service from Riverford Organic Farm

Soil Association

A family-run organic dairy farm peacefully situated with stunning views of the Culm Valley and surrounding hills. The farm is in Countryside Stewardship as well as in a Grey Partridge Regeneration Area, which has helped encourage a diverse and thriving habitat for the bird population. Guests are welcome to wander through the farm's fields and lanes, where an abundance of wildlife is waiting to be discovered. Organic produce can be delivered for your stay from Riverford Farm. There are some excellent farm shops nearby selling locally produced and organic produce. The coast, including the world famous Jurassic coast, Dartmoor and Exmoor are within easy reach. Green Tourism Business Scheme Bronze Award. svallis@highdownfarm.co.uk www.highdownfarm.co.uk/poormans.htm

DEVON

BRADNINCH *(S-C)*

THE CIDER BARN

101

Highdown Farm
Bradninch EX5 4LJ
Tel: 01392 881028 MAP 18

Converted Barn: sleeps 2
£225-£415 pw

Delivery service from Riverford Organic Farm

Soil Association

A family-run organic dairy farm peacefully situated with stunning views of the Culm Valley and surrounding hills. The farm is in Countryside Stewardship as well as in a Grey Partridge Regeneration Area, which has helped encourage a diverse and thriving habitat for the bird population. Guests are welcome to wander through the farm's fields and lanes, where an abundance of wildlife is waiting to be discovered. Organic produce can be delivered for your stay from Riverford Farm. There are some excellent farm shops nearby selling locally produced and organic produce. The coast, including the world famous Jurassic coast, Dartmoor and Exmoor are within easy reach. Green Tourism Business Scheme Bronze award. svallis@highdownfarm.co.uk   www.highdownfarm.co.uk/ciderbarn.htm

BRADNINCH *(S-C)*

THE OLD FARMHOUSE 102

Highdown Farm
Bradninch EX5 4LJ
Tel: 01392 881028 MAP 18

House: sleeps 7
£375-£830 pw

Delivery service from Riverford Organic Farm

Soil Association

A family-run organic dairy farm peacefully situated with stunning views of the Culm Valley and surrounding hills. The farm is in Countryside Stewardship as well as in a Grey Partridge Regeneration Area, which has helped encourage a diverse and thriving habitat for the bird population. Guests are welcome to wander through the farm's fields and lanes, where an abundance of wildlife is waiting to be discovered. Organic produce can be delivered for your stay from Riverford Farm. There are some excellent farm shops nearby selling locally produced and organic produce. The coast, including the world famous Jurassic coast, Dartmoor and Exmoor are within easy reach. Green Tourism Business Scheme Bronze award. svallis@highdownfarm.co.uk   www.highdownfarm.co.uk/farmhouse.htm

BRADWORTHY *(S-C)*

BREXWORTHY FARM 103

Bradworthy
Holsworthy EX22 7TR
Tel: 01409 241488   MAP 17

Cottages: sleep 2-3, £180-£650 pw
Bed and Breakfast, £25-£40 pppn

Home produce (sausages, bacon, pork, lamb,
free-range eggs, fruit, vegetables)

In Conversion

Set in a pretty lawned courtyard, the cottages have been carefully renovated from farm buildings and feature original beams and exposed stonework. Our smallholding is in its second year of organic conversion. Fresh produce, including sausages, bacon and pork from our Gloucester Old Spot pigs, lamb from our flock of Devon and Cornwall sheep, eggs from our free-range hens, as well as fruit and vegetables (when in season) available to buy, all of which is grown on our holding. Breathtaking country and coastal walks can be found nearby and there are stunning beaches within easy distance of the farm, many of them owned by the National Trust. Bradworthy, two miles away, has a large village square, pub, tearooms, etc.
lesley@brexworthyfarm.net   www.brexworthyfarm.net

BRATTON CLOVELLY *(S-C)*

BULL'S COTTAGE 104

Ellacott Barton
Bratton Clovelly EX20 4LB
Tel: 01837 871480   MAP 17

Cottage: sleeps 4
£250 pw

Organic meat and local produce available to purchase

Soil Association

Set within a working organic farm, Bull's Cottage nestles in the courtyard next to Eversfield Lodge. With wonderful views overlooking Dartmoor, it is perfect for a small family or four adults. The accommodation is appointed to a high standard and is well equipped. Patio doors open out onto the delightful natural garden, where guests can wander and enjoy the plants, flowers and wild birds that visit our large pond. An ideal place for photographers and artists. The 850-acre estate is situated in the beautiful rolling scenery of the Devon hills, and the hedgerows, meadows and garden are a haven for wildlife. Guests will enjoy the peace, tranquillity and stunning views, with many tourist attractions within easy reach.
info@eversfieldlodge.co.uk   www.eversfieldlodge.co.uk/accommodation/bulls%20cottage.aspx

BRATTON CLOVELLY *(S-C)*

EVERSFIELD COACH HOUSE 105

Ellacott Barton
Bratton Clovelly EX20 4JF
Tel: 01837 871480   MAP 17

Cottage: sleeps 8
From £250 pw

Organic breakfast pack includes our own bacon and sausages

Soil Association

Luxury self-catered accommodation on an 850-acre organic estate. The Coach House is set in an attractive courtyard of old stone buildings next to the manor house. Outside, guests can enjoy soaking up the sun in their own sheltered private courtyard. At the rear of the house there is easy access onto a public footpath, which winds across lovely farmland to the village pub. Eversfield breeds and rears Aberdeen Angus cattle, Large Black pigs and Romney sheep in a truly organic and traditional way. Organic produce (meat, poultry, eggs, vegetables, fruit, salad) is available for guests to purchase from the farm, subject to availability. An organic breakfast can be provided in Eversfield Lodge with prior notice.
info@eversfieldlodge.co.uk   www.eversfieldlodge.co.uk

BRATTON CLOVELLY *(B&B)*

EVERSFIELD LODGE 106

Ellacott Barton
Bratton Clovelly EX20 4LB
Tel: 01837 871480   MAP 17

Country House Bed and Breakfast
From £65 per room pn

Organic where possible, home-made, local and regional

Soil Association

In a peaceful and tranquil setting on the edge of Dartmoor, Eversfield Lodge forms part of an 850-acre organic working farm producing award-winning meat. We offer luxury *en suite* accommodation for up to sixteen people, and provide a full English organic breakfast served in the elegant dining room with glorious views towards Dartmoor. Organic orange juice, locally made organic apple juice, award-winning Eversfield organic bacon and sausages, eggs from our own chickens, local organic marmalade, jams and honey, a selection of toast, croissants and pastries, fresh fruit and yogurts, West Country milk and butter. Complimentary hot and cold drinks and home-made cakes. Dinner option is available for house parties.
info@eversfieldlodge.co.uk   www.eversfieldlodge.co.uk

BRAUNTON *(S-C)*

CAEN BYRE 107

Little Comfort Farm
Braunton EX33 2NJ
Tel: 01271 812414   MAP 17

Cottage: sleeps 4-5, £405-£869 pw
Short Breaks from £219, Meals from £5.95

Organic sausages, bacon, pork, lamb, beef,
eggs, jam, apple juice

Soil Association

Working organic family farm in an exceptionally secluded, peaceful valley through which the little River Caen flows. Caen Byre is a spacious two bedroom detached cottage with a large entrance porch. Converted from a traditional stone farm building it is set in its own lovely garden. Enjoy a home-made Devonshire cream tea on arrival, prepared with organic and local produce. We supply our own organic sausages, bacon, pork, lamb, beef and eggs, as well as home-made meals using our own meat. Feed the animals and collect the eggs. Explore the Devon Wildlife Trust private nature trail. Coarse fishing on our tranquil well stocked lake. Fifteen minutes from secluded coves, miles of golden sand, super surfing.
info@littlecomfortfarm.co.uk   www.littlecomfortfarm.co.uk

BRAUNTON *(S-C)*

CAEN END 108

Little Comfort Farm
Braunton EX33 2NJ
Tel: 01271 812414   MAP 17

Cottage: sleeps 6, £463-£993 pw
Short Breaks from £219, Meals from £5.95

Organic sausages, bacon, pork, lamb, beef,
eggs, jam, apple juice

Soil Association

Working organic family farm in a secluded, peaceful valley through which the little River Caen flows. Caen End is a completely self-contained three bedroom single storey wing of the farmhouse, with level access and its own terrace and lawn running down to the river. Enjoy a home-made Devonshire cream tea on arrival, prepared with organic and local produce. We supply our own organic sausages, bacon, pork, lamb, beef and eggs, as well as home-made meals using our own meat. Feed the animals and collect the eggs. Explore the Devon Wildlife Trust private nature trail. Coarse fishing on our tranquil well stocked lake. The farm is fifteen minutes from secluded coves, miles of golden sand, and super surfing.
info@littlecomfortfarm.co.uk   www.littlecomfortfarm.co.uk

DEVON

BRAUNTON *(S-C)*

GRANARY 109

Little Comfort Farm
Braunton EX33 2NJ
Tel: 01271 812414 MAP 17

Cottage: sleeps 4, £314-£828 pw
Short Breaks from £219, Meals from £5.95

Organic sausages, bacon, pork, lamb, beef,
eggs, jam, apple juice

Soil Association

Working organic family farm in a secluded valley through which the little River Caen flows. The Granary is a spacious two bedroom single storey cottage with level access from the parking area. Converted from a traditional stone farm building it is set in its own lovely garden. Enjoy a home-made Devonshire cream tea on arrival, prepared with organic and local produce. We supply our own organic sausages, bacon, pork, lamb, beef and eggs, as well as home-made meals using our own meat. Feed the animals. Collect the eggs. Explore the Devon Wildlife Trust private nature trail. Coarse fishing on our well stocked lake. Fifteen minutes from secluded coves, miles of golden sand, and super surfing.
info@littlecomfortfarm.co.uk   www.littlecomfortfarm.co.uk

BRAUNTON *S-C)*

MILL HOUSE 110

Little Comfort Farm
Braunton EX33 2NJ
Tel: 01271 812414 MAP 17

Cottage: sleeps 10, £463-£1635 pw
Short Breaks from £219, Meals from £5.95

Organic sausages, bacon, pork, lamb, beef,
eggs, jam, apple juice

Soil Association

Working organic family farm in an exceptionally secluded, peaceful valley through which the little River Caen flows. The Mill House is a spacious five bedroom cottage on two levels. Converted from a traditional stone farm building it is set in its own lovely garden. Enjoy a home-made Devonshire cream tea on arrival, prepared with organic and local produce. We supply our own organic sausages, bacon, pork, lamb, beef and eggs, as well as home-made meals using our own meat. Feed the animals and collect the eggs. Explore the Devon Wildlife Trust private nature trail. Coarse fishing on our tranquil well stocked lake. The farm is fifteen minutes from secluded coves, miles of golden sand, and super surfing.
info@littlecomfortfarm.co.uk   www.littlecomfortfarm.co.uk

BRAUNTON *(S-C)*

WOODLARK   111

Little Comfort Farm
Braunton EX33 2NJ
Tel: 01271 812414   MAP 17

Cottage: sleeps 4, £314-£752 pw
Short Breaks from £219, Meals from £5.95

Organic sausages, bacon, pork, lamb, beef,
eggs, jam, apple juice

Soil Association

Working organic family farm in an exceptionally secluded, peaceful valley through which the
little River Caen flows. Woodlark is a two bedroom 'upside down' cottage, with lovely views
from its first floor living room over the gardens. Outside is a lawned area with terrace. Enjoy
a home-made Devonshire cream tea on arrival, prepared with organic and local produce. We
supply our own organic sausages, bacon, pork, lamb, beef and eggs, as well as home-made
meals using our own meat. Feed the animals and collect the eggs. Explore the Devon Wildlife
Trust private nature trail. Coarse fishing on our tranquil well stocked lake. The farm is fifteen
minutes from secluded coves, miles of golden sand, and super surfing.
info@littlecomfortfarm.co.uk   www.littlecomfortfarm.co.uk

BROADHEMBURY *(S-C)*

CLEW PARK   112

Upcott Farm
Broadhembury EX14 3LP
Tel: 01404 841444   MAP 18

Converted Barn: sleeps 6
£450-£1250 pw

Superb organic stall in Honiton market
twice weekly, box deliveries available

Organic Farmers & Growers

Clew Park is one of four high quality cottages at Hembury Court. It is situated on a 240-
acre organic farm at the edge of the Blackdown Hills in East Devon, a mile from the thatch
village of Broadhembury. The four cottages, all with quality finishes of granite, oak and
terracotta are complemented by superb additional facilities. These include a large hot tub,
fitness suite, games lawn, barbecue veranda and two large oak cruck structures providing a
communal sitting room and games room. When all four cottages are hired together, sleeping
a maximum of seventeen, an additional kitchen is available and the games room, which also
has oak tables and chairs, makes a stunning setting for celebrations.
persey@upcottfarm.fsnet.co.uk   www.hembury-court-barns.co.uk

BROADHEMBURY *(S-C)*   POCKETS   113

Upcott Farm
Broadhembury EX14 3LP
Tel: 01404 841444   MAP 18

Converted Barn: sleeps 2
£260-£560 pw

Superb organic stall in Honiton market
twice weekly, box deliveries available

Organic Farmers & Growers

Pockets is one of four high quality cottages found at Hembury Court. It is situated on a 240-acre organic farm at the edge of the Blackdown Hills in East Devon, a mile from the thatch village of Broadhembury. The four cottages, all with quality finishes of granite, oak and terracotta are complemented by superb additional facilities. These include a large hot tub, fitness suite, games lawn, barbecue veranda and two large oak cruck structures providing a communal sitting room and games room. When all four cottages are hired together, sleeping a maximum of seventeen, an additional kitchen is available and the games room, which also has oak tables and chairs, makes a stunning setting for celebrations.
persey@upcottfarm.fsnet.co.uk   www.hembury-court-barns.co.uk

BROADHEMBURY *(S-C)*   POPPY'S   114

Upcott Farm
Broadhembury EX14 3LP
Tel: 01404 841444   MAP 18

Converted Barn: sleeps 4
£335-£950 pw

Superb organic stall in Honiton market
twice weekly, box deliveries available

Organic Farmers & Growers

Poppy's is one of four high quality cottages found at Hembury Court. It is situated on a 240-acre organic farm at the edge of the Blackdown Hills in East Devon, a mile from the thatch village of Broadhembury. The four cottages, all with quality finishes of granite, oak and terracotta are complemented by superb additional facilities. These include a large hot tub, fitness suite, games lawn, barbecue veranda and two large oak cruck structures providing a communal sitting room and games room. When all four cottages are hired together, sleeping a maximum of seventeen, an additional kitchen is available and the games room, which also has oak tables and chairs, makes a stunning setting for celebrations.
persey@upcottfarm.fsnet.co.uk   www.hembury-court-barns.co.uk

BROADHEMBURY *(S-C)*

SMART'S HOUSE 115

Upcott Farm
Broadhembury EX14 3LP
Tel: 01404 841444   MAP 18

Converted Barn: sleeps 5
£380-£1050 pw

Superb organic stall in Honiton market
twice weekly, box deliveries available

Organic Farmers & Growers

One of four high quality cottages found at Hembury Court. It is situated on a 240-acre organic farm at the edge of the Blackdown Hills in East Devon, a mile from the thatch village of Broadhembury. The four cottages, all with quality finishes of granite, oak and terracotta are complemented by superb additional facilities. These include a large hot tub, fitness suite, games lawn, barbecue veranda and two large oak cruck structures providing a communal sitting room and games room. When all four cottages are hired together, sleeping a maximum of seventeen, an additional kitchen is available and the games room, which also has oak tables and chairs, makes a stunning setting for celebrations.
persey@upcottfarm.fsnet.co.uk   www.hembury-court-barns.co.uk

BROADPARK *(B&B)*

CUDDYFORD 116

Rew Road
Broadpark TQ13 7EN
Tel: 01364 653325   MAP 18

Vegetarian Bed and Breakfast
£25-£30 pppn

Evening Meal (optional), from £15

Cuddyford is a family-run vegetarian guest house in a rural setting amongst peaceful rolling landscape within Dartmoor National Park. Wholesome cooking is prepared using home-grown fruit and vegetables (no chemicals), free-range eggs, honey from our own hives and home-baked bread. You can also sample some of our home-pressed apple juice. There are river and woodland walks nearby, where you'll find a wide range of lichen, ferns, primroses and sage, as well as a variety of birds such as the redstart, flycatcher and wood wren. We are ideally situated for exploring the heather-covered moors and the Dart Valley, with easy access to the South Devon coast, as the A38 is only a mile away. There is ample off road parking.
a.vevers@csl.gov.uk   www.ashburton.org/directory/cuddyford/index.htm

BUCKFASTLEIGH *(S-C)*

MOORVIEW 117

Bowden Farm
Buckfastleigh TQ11 0JG
Tel: 01364 643955   MAP 18

Caravan: sleeps 6
£150-£360 pw

Home-reared beef, lamb, free-range eggs

Soil Association

Bowden Farm is set in some of Devon's most striking countryside. It has panoramic views from Widecombe on the foothills of Dartmoor, right around to Dawlish, Teignmouth, Torquay, Brixham et al on the South Devon coastline. Moorview is a luxury caravan set in its own individual plot. It is fully equipped, double glazed, with heaters in every room. The veranda and lounge area enjoy spectacular views over the surrounding countryside. Situated on a working organic farm, visitors are welcome to take a guided tour of the farm to meet the animals. These include cattle, sheep, chickens and miniature Shetland ponies. There are fantastic walks adjoining the farm and also within Dartmoor National Park.
cowsnsheepnponies@bowdenfarm.org.uk   www.holidaydevon.org.uk

BURRINGTON *(S-C)*

BRIDLEWAY COTTAGES  118

Golland Farm
Burrington EX37 9JP
Tel: 01769 520550   MAP 18

Cottages: sleep 4-6+2
£250-£955 pw

Welcome pack to help you settle in includes wine, milk, butter, eggs, loaf of bread

Soil Association

Three cottages converted from traditional farm buildings on a small mixed organic farm in the rolling hills of the Taw Valley. As an organic and environmentally aware farm, we encourage our guests not to shop at supermarkets while they are staying on the farm. Devon produces some of the best food and drink in the country, grown and made by people who are passionate about providing quality food. We can provide free-range eggs to guests at most times of the year, and local shops include a butcher's, baker's, greengrocer's, and general organic store. A tributary of the River Taw runs through the farm and walkers can enjoy acres of farmland including water meadows filled with glorious wild flowers and fantastic wildlife.
gollandfarm@btconnect.com   www.gollandfarm.co.uk

BURRINGTON *(B&B)*

BURRINGTON BARTON 119

Burrington
Umberleigh EX37 9JQ
Tel: 01769 520216   MAP 17

Farmhouse Bed and Breakfast
From £30 pppn

The full English breakfast is made with local produce

Soil Association

Burrington Barton is a 175-acre mixed working organic farm. Relax in the peaceful surroundings of the ancient farmhouse and awake to the crow of the cockerel and the sound of bird song. Enjoy a full English breakfast made with local produce. Alongside sheep, cattle and cereals the land hosts an abundance of wildlife such as badgers, foxes, squirrels, roe and red deer. The woodlands and the water meadows are also a tranquil home to a variety of plant and bird life. On the edge of the small village of Burrington this is a good base for exploring Dartmoor, Exmoor and the beautiful North Devon coast. We are also near to Eggesford Forest, woodland walks, the Tarka Trail and Tarka Line, and local pannier markets. bartonfarm@yahoo.com   www.burrington-barton.co.uk

CAPTON *(S-C)*

HONEYSUCKLE BUNGALOW 120

Dittisham Farm
Capton TQ6 0JE
Tel: 07768 625333   MAP 18

Bungalow: sleeps 2-5, £239-£459 pw
Reduced tariff for parties of two people

Organic Berkshire rare breed pork, Red Ruby beef, sausages, organic eggs, honey

Soil Association

A two bedroom bungalow on a 21-acre organic farm in the unspoilt hamlet of Capton, between Dartmouth and Dittisham (both three miles). Here live prize-winning rare breed organic Berkshire pigs, Red Ruby cattle, poultry, bees and Poppy the labrador. The accommodation has been refurbished in a farm and country style. The layout has been designed to appeal to couples of any age, a family with up to three children (travel cot available) or up to four adults. south-facing sun trap area with sun loungers, barbecue and picnic table. You can walk to Dittisham for a pub lunch or take the undulating walk around our land, from the top of which are spectacular views to Dartmoor and Torbay, and to Portland Bill on a really clear day. sue@self-cater.co.uk   www.self-cater.co.uk/DittishamFarmHolidayLet

CHILLA *(S-C)*

ORCHARD COTTAGE 121

West Lake Farm
Chilla EX21 5XF
Tel: 01409 221991   MAP 17

Cottage: sleeps 2
£200-£400 pw

Award-winning organic apple juices and
ciders, free-range eggs

Soil Association

A 13-acre organic farm dating from 1482, off the beaten track in the heart of Ruby Country. Old varieties of apple and some rare Devon varieties are grown, and award-winning apple juices are pressed. Rare breed chickens range the orchard providing breakfast eggs. The cottage has been tastefully reconstructed using green oak beams and rafters with open-plan design. Oak staircase to the spacious mezzanine floor with a large patio window and balcony with 180-degree views over the picturesque landscape. Special farmers' market food ferry arranged for your visit. Ponds, willow coppice and wildflower conservation areas have been established, gaining us a Devon Wildlife Trust Gold Award for environmentally friendly farming. info@orchardkeeperscottage.co.uk   www.orchardkeeperscottage.co.uk

DAWLISH *(S-C)*

DUCKALLER FARM 122

Port Road
Dawlish EX7 0NX
Tel: 01626 863132   MAP 18

Holiday Home: sleeps 6
£185-£440 pw

Organic pork, sausages and bacon plus a
limited range of seasonal vegetables

Soil Association

Situated in its own garden and bordering open fields, the accommodation is a well equipped six berth holiday home with main facilities throughout. It is comprised of a double bedroom, a twin bedroom and a small double bed in the lounge area. A large and private decking area, with views across open countryside, complements an ideal place to relax and unwind. Duckaller Farm is a small organic farm of around 90 acres, primarily growing organic vegetables for local distribution. The farm walk follows a combination of arable margins designed to enhance the habitat for farmland birds. Approached by a private road, Duckaller Farm is well located for exploring the surrounding area and nearby beaches. holidays@duckallerfarm.co.uk   www.duckallerfarm.co.uk

DOUSLAND *(B&B)*

LAMMERGEIER 123

Yennadon
Dousland PL20 6NA
Tel: 01822 855837　　　　MAP 17

Bed and Breakfast, from £25 pppn
Evening Meal (by arrangement)

We offer a high percentage of organic
produce to our visitors

Lammergeier is a detached individual residence with beautiful views and pleasant gardens. Enjoy good quality home-cooked food at our family-run traditional bed and breakfast. We offer a high percentage of organic produce to our visitors, almost all sourced locally, as well as our own free-range eggs. The generous wholesome breakfast is served in our lovely Victorian conservatory overlooking the garden. Packed lunches and evening meals are available by special arrangement. Situated in one of Dartmoor's picturesque and peaceful locations, there is direct access from Lammergeier to open moorland. Burrator Reservoir, a local beauty spot within walking distance, is surrounded by some of Devon's finest tors. yvonne.parkinson@virgin.net　freespace.virgin.net/yvonne.parkinson

EAST HILL *(S-C)*

THE HAY HOUSE 124

Blacklake Farm
Ottery St Mary EX11 1QA
Tel: 01404 812122　　　　MAP 18

Holiday House: sleeps 6
£350-£895 pw

Home-bred, grass-fed Red Ruby Devon beef
and Dorset Down lamb

Soil Association

Blacklake Farm is set on the upper slopes of East Hill. The Hay House has been converted using the original structure and natural materials such as lime plaster and natural oak. Being the only holiday house on the farm the Hay House offers peace and privacy, with only the ebb and flow of traditional farm life to punctuate the day. The farmland is varied – a mix of permanent old pasture, deciduous woodland and old apple orchards. We are a Soil Association Organic Demonstration Farm and welcome opportunities to talk to people about our organic farming experience. The coast is three miles from the farm. Catherine is a qualified aromatherapist and offers guests treatments from her practice room in the farmhouse. catherine@blacklakefarm.com　www.blacklakefarm.com

EXETER *(B&B)*

RAFFLES 125

11 Blackall Road
Exeter EX4 4HD
Tel: 01392 270200   MAP 18

Bed and Breakfast
£36-£37 pppn
We offer around 75% organic produce

Centrally located in historic Exeter, Raffles offers excellent bed and breakfast accommodation. The Victorian town house is furnished with antiques and has been sympathetically restored. A full range of breakfast menus is served in the comfortable and spacious dining room. Where possible, much of the fare is organically produced. Guests have use of the well stocked garden. Exeter is one of the few cities to have free guided tours. These tours allow you to experience the detail and history of this beautiful city. The National Parks of Dartmoor and Exmoor are within easy reach. Exeter also provides easy access to unspoiled coastal regions such as Sidmouth, Exmouth, Beer and Seaton.
raffleshtl@btinternet.com   www.raffles-exeter.co.uk

EXMINSTER *(B&B)*

LOWER POTTLES 126

Days-Pottles Lane
Exminster EX6 8BB
Tel: 01392 833961   MAP 18

Bed and Breakfast
£30-£35 pppn

Locally sourced produce, own organic free-range eggs, fresh organic fruit salad

In Conversion

A tastefully renovated old barn providing beautifully appointed accommodation and organic breakfasts. It is situated within the village of Exminster on a 25-acre smallholding undergoing organic conversion. The double rooms are both *en suite* with organic towels and tea / coffee tray. Mouth-watering organic breakfasts are served in the exclusive guest sitting / dining room or outside on the patio. Breakfasts include eggs from our organic free-range hens, fresh fruit salad or compote and a full 'Devon' – all from locally sourced organic produce. Explore the nearby historic city of Exeter, the rugged landscape of Dartmoor, National Trust properties, Powderham Castle, local beaches and the breathtaking coastal area.
sj.nott@btconnect.com   www.lowerpottles.co.uk

EXMINSTER (S-C)

LOWER TOWSINGTON   127

Days-Pottles Lane
Exminster EX6 8BB
Tel: 01392 833961   MAP 18

Thatched Cottage, Ref HGGM: sleeps 5
£498-£1066 pw (late availability offers)

Organic welcome pack with home-made
cake, organic free-range eggs

In Conversion

Beautifully renovated 300 year old detached thatched cottage situated on the owner's 25-acre smallholding (in organic conversion). Newly painted with natural paints, the accommodation includes a spacious beamed sitting room with a wood-burning stove, a spacious dining room, and a large farmhouse-style kitchen with a slate floor. Relax in the fabulous surroundings and enjoy a barbecue in the garden. The cottage is just half a mile from the village of Exminster with local pubs and shops. There is also a golf course in the village. Beaches and coastal walks are within a fifteen minute drive. For nature lovers there is an abundance of wildlife. Local attractions include Haldon Forestry Centre with walks and cycle trails.
sj.nott@btconnect.com   www.chooseacottage.co.uk

GOODLEIGH (S-C)

THE HAVEN AT BAMPFIELD   128

Bampfield Farm
Goodleigh EX32 7NR
Tel: 01271 346566   MAP 18

Cottage: sleeps 4-6, £290-£780 pw
Short Breaks (minimum stay 2 nights)

Try our delicious home-produced beef

Organic Farmers & Growers

A perfect location for a special break. The Haven is a charming 17th-century cottage on an organic dairy farm with stunning views of the sea. Peace, tranquillity, fresh air. The farm nestles in rolling hills and overlooks the River Yeo. A favourite with young families and walkers. Enjoy a Devon cream tea on arrival. Collect the eggs and cook them for your breakfast. Watch the farmer working hand in hand with the land and wildlife. Identify an abundance of wildlife and plants on the farm's nature trail. The lanes around the farm are scented with wild flowers. With their traditional high Devon hedges they have remained the same for centuries. Come and discover this unspoilt corner of North Devon.
lynda@bampfieldfarm.co.uk   www.bampfieldfarm.co.uk/haven.htm

GOODLEIGH *(S-C)*

THE OLD GRANARY 129

Bampfield Farm
Goodleigh EX32 7NR
Tel: 01271 346566   MAP 18

Cottage: sleeps 2-8, £310-£930 pw
Short Breaks (minimum stay 2 nights)

Succulent Bampfield beef for you to eat

Organic Farmers & Growers

The Old Granary is a delightful cottage on an organic dairy farm with stunning views of the sea. Peace, tranquillity, fresh air. The farm nestles in rolling hills and overlooks the River Yeo. A favourite with young families and walkers. Enjoy a Devon cream tea on arrival. Watch the cows come home for milking, and the farmer working the land and caring for the wildlife. If you try our organic beef you will definitely want to take some home. Identify an abundance of wildlife and plants on the farm's nature trail. The lanes around the farm are scented with wild flowers. With their traditional high Devon hedges they have remained the same for centuries. Come and discover this unspoilt corner of North Devon.
lynda@bampfieldfarm.co.uk   www.bampfieldfarm.co.uk/granary.htm

HARTLAND *(S-C)*

LITTLE BARTON 130

Hartland
Bude EX39 6DY
Tel: 01237 441259   MAP 17

Farmhouse: sleeps 10, £700-£1500 pw
Cottage: sleeps 6, £300-£800 pw

Organic produce, local meat and vegetables:
Organic SE Asian catering available

A large Victorian farmhouse with panoramic sea views, set in an Area of Outstanding Natural Beauty four miles north of Bude. It is less than a mile from the coastal path, Atlantic beaches and wild beautiful countryside. A variety of locally sourced food is available in the village and there's a farmers' market on the first Sunday of each month. Online orders for organic food and organic SE Asian catering can be arranged. We have our own water supply. A wide range of wildlife lives on the land surrounding the house. The long access track passes through culm grassland, full of seasonal wildflowers. Hartland is a thriving community with many craftspeople. The area is wonderful for swimming, surfing, walking, etc. A cottage (sleeping six) is also available.
enquiries@littlebartonhartland.co.uk   www.littlebartonhartland.co.uk

HARTLAND (S-C)

LONG FURLONG 131

East Long Furlong
Hartland EX39 6AT
Tel: 01237 441337   MAP 17

Coastal Cottages: sleep 2-9
£575-£2750 pw

Evening meals available, prepared with organic
ingredients and delivered to your door

An award-winning complex of twelve self-catering cottages, with a special organic catering service delivered to your door. Home-made organic evening meals are prepared and cooked to order, including local venison and hot chocolate pudding. I am passionate about the food we eat and cook for our guests, and have been sourcing organic produce for over twenty years. We offer a local and organic food hamper at a small extra cost, and have a comprehensive list of local suppliers of organic food in each cottage. We can also organise an organic vegetable box to be delivered directly to your cottage. Indoor swimming pool, outdoor swim spa, etc. On the Hartland Peninsula close to the South West Coast Path.
info@longfurlongcottages.co.uk   www.longfurlongcottages.co.uk

HOLBETON (S-C)

CORNER COTTAGE 132

Carswell Farm
Holbeton PL8 1HH
Tel: 01752 830020   MAP 17

Cottage: sleeps 8, £520-£1800 pw
Short breaks in winter, £215-£480

Organic meat, local organic fruit and veg:
organic breakfast hamper (to order)

Soil Association

We are organic dairy farmers on the South Devon coast. Carswell Farm is deep in unspoilt countryside in the heart of the South Hams, and overlooks the sea. Our farm cottages are situated along secluded farm lanes a few minutes walk from the coast and Wadham beach. We put local fresh organic milk in the cottage ready for your arrival. Try our award-winning organic lamb and beef (Carswell is the birthplace of The Well Hung Meat Company). Organic Devon breakfast hamper to order. Because we are organic you will see an exceptional quantity and variety of wildlife, including some resident barn owls. Beautiful coves and beaches are nearby, with acres of sand at low tide and some dramatic coastal walks.
enquiries@carswellcottages.com   www.carswellcottages.com/cornercottage

HOLBETON (S-C)

LAMBSIDE HOUSE 133

Carswell Farm
Holbeton PL8 1HH
Tel: 01752 830020 MAP 17

Georgian House: sleeps 11+3, £650-£2295 pw
Short breaks in winter, £130-£600

Organic meat, local organic fruit and veg:
organic breakfast hamper (to order)

Soil Association

We are organic dairy farmers on the South Devon coast. Carswell Farm is deep in unspoilt countryside in the heart of the South Hams, and overlooks the sea. Our farm cottages are situated along secluded farm lanes a few minutes walk from the coast and Wadham beach. We put local fresh organic milk in the house ready for your arrival. Try our award-winning organic lamb and beef (Carswell is the birthplace of The Well Hung Meat Company). Organic Devon breakfast hamper to order. Because we are organic you will see an exceptional quantity and variety of wildlife, including some resident barn owls. Beautiful coves and beaches are nearby, with acres of sand at low tide and some dramatic coastal walks. enquiries@carswellcottages.com   www.carswellcottages.com/lambsidehouse

HOLBETON (S-C)

SHEPHERD'S COTTAGE 134

Carswell Farm
Holbeton PL8 1HH
Tel: 01752 830020 MAP 17

Cottage: sleeps 6, £295-£995 pw
Short breaks in winter, £150-£260

Organic meat, local organic fruit and veg:
organic breakfast hamper (to order)

Soil Association

We are organic dairy farmers on the South Devon coast. Carswell Farm is deep in unspoilt countryside in the heart of the South Hams, and overlooks the sea. Our farm cottages are situated along secluded farm lanes a few minutes walk from the coast and Wadham beach. We put local fresh organic milk in the cottage ready for your arrival. Try our award-winning organic lamb and beef (Carswell is the birthplace of The Well Hung Meat Company). Organic Devon breakfast hamper to order. Because we are organic you will see an exceptional quantity and variety of wildlife, including some resident barn owls. Beautiful coves and beaches are nearby, with acres of sand at low tide and some dramatic coastal walks. enquiries@carswellcottages.com   www.carswellcottages.com/shepherdscottage

HOLBETON *(S-C)*

SPRING COTTAGE 135

Carswell Farm
Holbeton PL8 1HH
Tel: 01752 830020　　　　　　MAP 17

Cottage: sleeps 6, £250-£945 pw
Short breaks in winter, £135-£250

Organic meat, local organic fruit and veg:
organic breakfast hamper (to order)

Soil Association

We are organic dairy farmers on the South Devon coast. Carswell Farm is deep in unspoilt countryside in the heart of the South Hams, and overlooks the sea. Our farm cottages are situated along secluded farm lanes a few minutes walk from the coast and Wadham beach. We put local fresh organic milk in the cottage ready for your arrival. Try our award-winning organic lamb and beef (Carswell is the birthplace of The Well Hung Meat Company). Organic Devon breakfast hamper to order. Because we are organic you will see an exceptional quantity and variety of wildlife, including some resident barn owls. Beautiful coves and beaches are nearby, with acres of sand at low tide and some dramatic coastal walks.
enquiries@carswellcottages.com　www.carswellcottages.com/springcottage

HOLBETON *(S-C)*

THE LODGE, CARSWELL 136

Carswell Farm
Holbeton PL8 1HH
Tel: 01752 830020　　　　　　MAP 18

Eco-Lodge: sleeps 4, £275-£795 pw
Short breaks in winter, £140-£230

Organic meat, local organic fruit and veg:
organic breakfast hamper (to order)

Soil Association

We are organic dairy farmers on the South Devon coast. Carswell Farm is deep in unspoilt countryside in the heart of the South Hams, and overlooks the sea. Our farm cottages are situated along secluded farm lanes a few minutes walk from the coast and Wadham beach. We put local fresh organic milk in the lodge ready for your arrival. Try our award-winning organic lamb and beef (Carswell is the birthplace of The Well Hung Meat Company). Organic Devon breakfast hamper to order. Because we are organic you will see an exceptional quantity and variety of wildlife, including some resident barn owls. Beautiful coves and beaches are nearby, with acres of sand at low tide and some dramatic coastal walks.
enquiries@carswellcottages.com　www.carswellcottages.com/thelodge

HOLBETON (S-C)

THE MEWS 137

Carswell Farm
Holbeton PL8 1HH
Tel: 01752 830020 MAP 18

Converted Barn: sleeps 2+1, £235-£570 pw
Short breaks in winter, £130-£200

Organic meat, local organic fruit and veg:
organic breakfast hamper (to order)

Soil Association

We are organic dairy farmers on the South Devon coast. Carswell Farm is deep in unspoilt countryside in the heart of the South Hams, and overlooks the sea. Our farm cottages are situated along secluded farm lanes a few minutes walk from the coast and Wadham beach. We put local fresh organic milk in The Mews ready for your arrival. Try our award-winning organic lamb and beef (Carswell is the birthplace of The Well Hung Meat Company). Organic Devon breakfast hamper to order. Because we are organic you will see an exceptional quantity and variety of wildlife, including some resident barn owls. Beautiful coves and beaches are nearby, with acres of sand at low tide and some dramatic coastal walks.
enquiries@carswellcottages.com   www.carswellcottages.com/themews

KELLY (S-C)

DEVON YURT 138

Borough Farm
Kelly PL16 0HJ
Tel: 01822 870366 MAP 17

Yurts: sleep 4-6
From £95 yurt pn, £475 pw

Free-range eggs, salad, potatoes, seasonal
fruit and vegetables, jams, cordials

Soil Association

Escape to the country on this organic family smallholding bordering the Tamar Valley, an Area of Outstanding Natural Beauty. We stock the farm with rare breed animals and have created gardens and wildlife areas. The two yurts are each in their own private space. You can experience the wildlife and see buzzards, pipistrelle bats and swallows, and listen to numerous songbirds. The eco-bath tent is a regular highlight. Eco-loos. Enjoy the sunrise over Dartmoor, which provides a dramatic back-drop to the yurts, and the sunset over Cornwall. Choose to pick your own salads, dig potatoes, feed a lamb or ride a pony. For a truly pampered stay you can pre-book cotton bedlinen and order an organic breakfast to be delivered to your door.
contactus@devonyurt.co.uk   www.devonyurt.co.uk

KENN (S-C)

HUXLEY'S HOME 139

Bickham Farm
Kenn EX6 7XL
Tel: 01392 833833   MAP 18

Farmhouse: sleeps 5
£237-£561 pw

When available, pre-order a box of organic vegetables, fruit, bacon, sausages, lamb

Soil Association

Approached by a quiet country lane, this charming farmhouse enjoys peace and seclusion with far-reaching views over open countryside. The property is decorated and furnished to a high standard and retains much of its original charm and character. With some lovely walks adjoining the land and Dartmoor National Park within a short driving distance, walkers and nature lovers will be in their element. The farmhouse is situated on a 120-acre organic farm with sheep, pigs, Huxley the pet pig, turkeys, chickens, cattle. In the evenings enjoy a guided tour around the farm. You will have the opportunity to pre-order a box of organic veg, fruit, bacon, sausages, lamb to await your arrival (when available).
roddy@rodandbens.com   www.rodandbens.com

KENTISBEARE (S-C)

THE HAY LOFT 140

Maddocks Farm
Kentisbeare EX15 2BU
Tel: 01647 433593   MAP 18

Cottage: sleeps 12, from £738 pw
Short Breaks (minimum stay 3 nights)

Seasonal produce (vegetables, salads, strawberries) when available

Soil Association

Spacious converted barn, attached to other uninhabited barns, across a courtyard from our part 17th-century listed farmhouse. A welcome pack includes organic, local and fair trade items plus a home-made organic chocolate banana loaf and six of our own organic eggs. Guests have their own large lawned garden with a patio. We have a 5-acre organic smallholding and specialise in salads, supplying various local shops and a pub with unusual spicy and herb salads. We also run a vegetable box scheme (June-December). You are welcome to walk around the farm and enjoy the lovely views across miles of countryside. Kentisbeare is an attractive village in the middle of the rolling farmland of the Lower Culm Valley.
help@helpfulholidays.com   www.helpfulholidays.com/microresults.asp?search_value=g40

KINGSBRIDGE *(S-C)*

GARDEN ROOMS 141

Lower Coombe Royal
Kingsbridge TQ7 4AD
Tel: 01548 852880   MAP 18

Self-Catering Retreat: sleeps 2+
£450-£1100 pw

Where we can, we use and supply organic
products and produce

Lower Coombe Royal is set in its own private valley in the heart of the South Hams. The one bedroom five star self-catering accommodation opens straight out onto the gardens and its own Italianate terrace. It has been as organically prepared as possible, with the bed made from sustainable wood, a mattress made of entirely organic fibres, organic towels, linens and aromatherapy toiletries. A welcome hamper of local and organic produce is supplied, with home-grown vegetables and fruit when in season. We have 8 acres of historic gardens and a growing vegetable patch tended by a qualified organic gardener. Plans for the future include a freshwater swimming pond, chickens to provide eggs, bees to make our own honey. susi@lowercoomberoyal.co.uk   www.lowercoomberoyal.co.uk

KINGSWEAR *(B&B)*

FIR MOUNT HOUSE 142

Higher Contour Road
Kingswear TQ6 0DE
Tel: 01803 752943   MAP 18

Bed and Breakfast, £40-£45 pppn
Evening Meal, £30 pp

Mainly local and organic food used in all our
cooking

Victorian period home in the lovely village of Kingswear, with wonderful views of the River Dart and the surrounding South Hams countryside. Start the day with one of our fabulous breakfasts – organic breads, jams and marmalades, home-made granola, fresh fruits and yogurt with freshly-squeezed juices, eggs from our own hens, scrummy bacon and sausages from our friends' organically reared rare-breed pigs. We offer an evening meal of the very finest locally sourced organic meat, fish and vegetables, followed by truly luscious puddings. We also run the Manna from Devon Cookery School, providing relaxed courses concentrating on the great seasonal local food that is on our doorstep. enquiries@mannafromdevon.com   www.mannafromdevon.com

LODDISWELL (S-C)

CRANNACOMBE FARM 143

Hazelwood
Loddiswell TQ7 4DX
Tel: 01647 433593   MAP 18

Farmhouse: sleeps 9, from £378 pw
Cider House: sleeps 8, from £370 pw

Our own apple-based products, organic food shop three miles away

Soil Association

17th-century farmhouse on a working family farm (80 acres, including apple orchards and sheep). Set in a beautiful unspoilt valley in a designated Area of Outstanding Natural Beauty. Producers of farm pressed organic apple juices and skilfully blended organic cider from old varieties of apples. Hand selected organic apples are used to make the delicious apple juice and apple with grape fruit. The 3 acres of organic orchards are certified by the Soil Association. Half a mile of the River Avon runs through the farm, where you can picnic, paddle and swim. Wildlife abounds around the farm, and there are lovely walks. Kingsbridge is just five miles away, and there are many sandy beaches nearby.
help@helpfulholidays.com   www.helpfulholidays.com/property.asp?ref=1200a

LODDISWELL (B&B)

HAZELWOOD HOUSE 144

Loddiswell
Kingsbridge TQ7 4EB
Tel: 01548 821232   MAP 18

Bed and Breakfast, £37.50-£80 pppn
Lunch from £10, Dinner £18-£30

Delicious food using local produce (around 80% organic)

Hazelwood House, set in lush South Devon countryside, reflects this beautiful setting in the food it serves. Every attempt is made to use the fresh, locally grown, organic produce for which Devon is so well known. Hazelwood House has its own water supply. The accommodation is gracious and comfortable, with fifteen bedrooms (seven of them *en suite*). Situated in 67 acres of woodland, meadows and orchards in a wild, unspoilt river valley, it is the perfect place to relax, reflect, and refuel. At Hazelwood we put the earth first. The resulting unspoiled natural beauty of the valley provides a haven for a wide range of wildlife, with otters, badgers, deer and foxes among its residents. Camping is available, £15 per night.
info@hazelwoodhouse.com   www.hazelwoodhouse.com

LYNTON *(B&B)*

NORTH WALK HOUSE   145

Lynton
Lynmouth EX35 6HJ
Tel: 01598 753372   MAP 18

Bed and Breakfast, from £37 pppn
Evening Meal, 4 course from £25.95 pp

We pride ourselves on using only the
freshest local organic produce

A beautiful Victorian house overlooking the sea – wooden floor boards, oriental rugs, Egyptian cotton linen, open fireplaces, breathtaking views. We specialise in local organic produce. Breakfasts include fresh fruit salad, organic local yogurt, milk and eggs from West Hill Farm, free-range bacon from Hindon Organic Farm, free-range award-winning sausages from Hidden Valley Farm (all local small producers in Exmoor), muesli, organic bread, organic coffee or tea. The smoked haddock and kippers are also local. Evening meals (book in advance) are personally prepared on the Aga, using organic and local food, including free-range duck and chicken as well as freshly picked seasonal vegetables. We are members of Slow Food UK. walk@northwalkhouse.co.uk   www.northwalkhouse.co.uk

MANATON *(B&B)*

EASDON COTTAGE   146

Long Lane
Manaton TQ13 9XB
Tel: 01647 221389   MAP 18

Vegetarian Bed and Breakfast, double £65 pn
Evening Meal (by arrangement)

At least 95% organic food all year round

Beautiful location, peaceful surroundings, comfort, relaxation, and a warm welcome are all to be found at Easdon Cottage – a classic stone house on the edge of Dartmoor with historic roots back beyond the seventeenth-century. Bed and breakfast accommodation is a cosy *en suite* double / twin room. A vegetarian or vegan breakfast is prepared using organically produced food wherever possible, including home-grown in season. Packed lunches are from £5 per person. Evening meal by prior arrangement. At different times of the year the countryside is rich with native species of wildlife and wild flowers. Artists and photographers find much to inspire them. Good walking, riding and bicycling country. easdondown@btopenworld.com

MANATON (S-C)

THE BARN AT EASDON 147

Long Lane
Manaton TQ13 9XB
Tel: 01647 221389   MAP 18

Barn: sleeps 2-3, £220-£380 pw
Winter Breaks, £145 (minimum 3 nights)

Organic food available locally, home-grown
in season

Nestling into the hill and on the edge of the bridlepath leading on to Easdon Tor, the Barn, with its thick granite walls, provides a comfortable hideaway in the landscape. The setting, on the east side of Dartmoor, is remote and tranquil. A short flight of steps leads up through a stable door into the main open-plan accommodation, with views over the surrounding countryside and moorland. An area of garden is available to sit and enjoy the views, or for meals outside. You can buy organic food locally, and home-grown vegetables may be available in season for purchase from the owner's nearby garden. Spring water. Good walking and wildlife watching with excellent views in the surrounding area.
easdondown@btopenworld.com

MESHAW (B&B)

FERN TOR 148

Meshaw
South Molton EX36 4NA
Tel: 01769 550339   MAP 18

Vegetarian Guest House, B&B £23-£33 pppn
Evening Meal, £12-£18 pp

Vegetarian / vegan meals, home-grown
organic produce when available

Fern Tor's 5 acres of culm grassland along the Little Silver River has been awarded a Countryside Stewardship grant and is rich with wild flowers, particularly in spring. The remaining land is used for our many rescued animals and for growing organic fruit and vegetables. Jane is a Cordon Vert trained cook and provides gourmet vegetarian or vegan meals using fair trade and organic produce when available (special diets on request). Dining is at separate tables and, when the nights are long, by candlelight. Fern Tor was Voted Best Vegan Accommodation 2007 and selected by The Guardian as one of the UK's Ten Best Vegetarian B&B's in 2008. Many local walks. Ideally located for exploring North and Mid-Devon and Exmoor.
veg@ferntor.co.uk   www.ferntor.co.uk

MODBURY *(B&B)*

CUCKOO FARM 149

Torr Down
Nr Modbury PL21 0SD
Tel: 01548 550700   MAP 18

Bed and Breakfast
£30 pppn

Organic milk, beverages, sugar, bread, butter, free-range eggs, bacon, sausages

We designed our strawbale house to resemble a Devon farmhouse. It has been a joy to build and we very much look forward to sharing it with our guests. From the windows you will be able to see far-reaching rural views across beautiful farmland and woodland. We have plenty of space for you to stretch your legs, have a picnic and relax and enjoy true peace and quiet. We support our local free-range and organic farming friends whenever possible. Beverages and sugar are organic and fair trade. Heat, electricity and hot water are provided by renewables. Fantastic South Devon beaches, the South West Coast Path, Dartmoor and delightful market towns are all within easy reach. We look forward to meeting you soon. woodham3@fsmail.net   www.cuckoofarmholidays.co.uk

MOTHECOMBE *(S-C)*

EFFORD HOUSE 150

Flete Estate
Haye Farm PL8 1JZ
Tel: 01752 830234   MAP 18

Country House: sleeps 12, £814-£2255 pw
Short Breaks, £150 pn (min 3 nights)

Home-produced organic beef and lamb delivered to the cottage

Soil Association

A beautifully proportioned detached country house set in its own grounds bordered by mature woodlands. It is one of several properties on our 1000-acre organic farm, part of the Flete Estate. We are in an Area of Outstanding Natural Beauty by the River Erme estuary, a designated SSSI on the South Devon coast with six miles of drives for walking and bird watching and access to beaches and coastal paths. The estate offers beef and lamb produced on the home farm to our cottage guests. Riverford organic farm shop and café is three miles away, and it's fifteen miles to their farm and field kitchen. Nearby Modbury, the UK's first plastic bag-free town, is a great supporter of organic and local produce traders. cottages@flete.co.uk   www.flete.co.uk

MOTHECOMBE (S-C)

FLETE MILL COTTAGE 151

Flete Estate
Haye Farm PL8 1JZ
Tel: 01752 830234   MAP 18

Cottage: sleeps 5, £638-£1485 pw
Short Breaks, £150 pn (min 3 nights)

Home-produced organic beef and lamb
delivered to the cottage

Soil Association

Flete Mill Cottage, one mile along a four mile private drive, has been completely restored and exquisitely renovated. It is one of several properties on our 1000-acre organic farm, part of the Flete Estate. We are in an Area of Outstanding Natural Beauty by the River Erme estuary, a SSSI on the South Devon coast with six miles of drives for walking and bird watching and access to beaches and coastal paths. The estate offers beef and lamb produced on the home farm to our cottage guests. Riverford organic farm shop and café is three miles away, and it's fifteen miles to their farm and field kitchen. Nearby Modbury, the UK's first plastic bag-free town, is a great supporter of organic and local produce traders.
cottages@flete.co.uk   www.flete.co.uk

MOTHECOMBE (S-C)

NEPEANS COTTAGE 152

Flete Estate
Haye Farm PL8 1JZ
Tel: 01752 830234   MAP 18

Cottage: sleeps 8, £770-£1821 pw
Short Breaks, £150 pn (min 3 nights)

Home-produced organic beef and lamb
delivered to the cottage

Soil Association

This fairy tale cottage, with stunning views across the estuary, is hidden in a small clearing deep in the woods. It is one of several properties on our 1000-acre organic farm, part of the Flete Estate. We are in an Area of Outstanding Natural Beauty by the River Erme estuary, a SSSI on the South Devon coast with six miles of drives for walking and bird watching and access to beaches and coastal paths. The estate offers beef and lamb produced on the home farm to our cottage guests. Riverford organic farm shop and cafe is three miles away, and it's fifteen miles to their farm and field kitchen. Nearby Modbury, the UK's first plastic bag-free town, is a great supporter of organic and local produce traders.
cottages@flete.co.uk   www.flete.co.uk

MOTHECOMBE (S-C)

THE BOSUN'S COTTAGE   153

Flete Estate
Haye Farm PL8 1JZ
Tel: 01752 830234   MAP 18

Cottage: sleep 7, £638-£1705 pw
Short Breaks, £150 pn (min 3 nights)

Home-produced organic beef and lamb
delivered to the cottage

Soil Association

The Bosun's Cottage is surrounded by its own garden with tranquil views over the valley and woods beyond. It is one of several properties on our 1000-acre organic farm, part of the Flete Estate. We are in an Area of Outstanding Natural Beauty by the River Erme estuary, a SSSI on the South Devon coast with six miles of drives for walking and bird watching and access to beaches and coastal paths. The estate offers beef and lamb produced on the home farm to our cottage guests. Riverford organic farm shop and cafe is three miles away, and it's fifteen miles to their farm and field kitchen. Nearby Modbury, the UK's first plastic bag-free town, is a great supporter of organic and local produce traders.
cottages@flete.co.uk   www.flete.co.uk

MOTHECOMBE (S-C)

COASTGUARDS COTTAGES 154

Flete Estate
Haye Farm PL8 1JZ
Tel: 01752 830234   MAP 18

Cottages: sleep 6, £660-£1760 pw
Short Breaks, £150 pn (min 3 nights)

Home-produced organic beef and lamb
delivered to the cottage

Soil Association

These three cottages are perched above Coastguards Beach with spectacular ever changing views. The cottages share a children's games room, complete with table tennis. Our 1000 acre organic farm is in an Area of Outstanding Natural Beauty by the River Erme estuary, a designated SSSI on the South Devon coast with six miles of drives for walking and bird watching and access to beaches and coastal paths. The estate offers beef and lamb produced on the home farm to our cottage guests. Riverford organic farm shop and café is three miles away, and it's fifteen miles to their farm and field kitchen. Nearby Modbury, the UK's first plastic bag-free town, is a great supporter of organic and local produce traders.
cottages@flete.co.uk   www.flete.co.uk

MUDDIFORD *(B&B)*

BOWDEN FARM 155

Muddiford
Barnstaple EX31 4HR
Tel: 01271 850502   MAP 17

Bed and Breakfast, £35-£42.50 pppn
Packed lunches available on request

Organic and local produce offered wherever possible

Soil Association

Bowden is a beautiful 82-acre organic farm in a secluded valley with stunning views to the sea and Dartmoor. Enjoy walks directly from the house, see our rare breed cows, sheep, alpacas and chickens, meet the lambs and calves, and collect fresh eggs. The Grade II listed house was originally built in the 16th-century. On arrival you will be served with a Devon cream tea – home-made scones, local preserves and clotted cream and a choice of fine teas. Delicious breakfasts are served in the tranquil dining room – fresh fruit and organic yogurt, warm baked bread, smoked salmon with free-range scrambled eggs, traditional cooked breakfast, kippers or kedgeree. We aim to serve local organic produce whenever possible.
stay@bowdenfarm.com   www.bowdenfarm.com

○

NOMANSLAND *(S-C)*

MIDDLEWICK BARTON 156

Nomansland
Tiverton EX16 8NP
Tel: 01884 861693   MAP 18

Apartment: sleeps 2, £295-£369 pw
Short Breaks, from £145

Organic and natural food store and café (Griffin's Yard) in South Molton

Soil Association

A spacious one bedroom ground floor self-catering apartment in a character Georgian farmhouse on a working organic farm. All the rooms are furnished to a very high standard. Escape from the pressures of everyday life on our idyllic organic farm situated in the heart of rural Devon in beautiful unspoilt countryside. Explore over 200 acres of secluded farmland with hilltop views, wooded valleys, streams, and a wonderful variety of plant and wildlife. Take advantage of the excellent local facilities for walking, riding and cycling. Sample the best of local Devonian eating establishments. Discover this undiscovered part of Devon for yourself. We are open all year. Short breaks (three or four nights) available out of season.
middlewick.barton@tiscali.co.uk   www.middlewick-barton-devon.co.uk

5

OAKFORD (B&B)

HARTON FARM 157

Oakford
Bampton EX16 9HH
Tel: 01398 351209 MAP 18

Farmhouse Bed and Breakfast, £22-£24 pppn
Evening Meal, £12

Vegetables home-grown and pesticide free, meat home-produced without additives

Our stone-built 17th-century farmhouse faces south in one of the hidden valleys above the River Exe on the southern edge of Exmoor. Come and enjoy a unique rural experience on our friendly working farm, where we take pride in real food and genuine hospitality. We grow our own pork, beef and lamb, and the garden and greenhouse provide many different types of vegetables, fruit and herbs. By walking the farm trail, you can enjoy the changing seasons, as summer flowers follow primroses, bluebells and orchids. You can sit on a bench under the oaks and watch the sun go down in the company of red deer and owls. We have achieved the Gold Award from both the Green Tourism Business Scheme and Devon Wildlife Trust.
lindy@hartonfarm.co.uk   www.hartonfarm.co.uk

POLTIMORE (S-C)

MALLARD COTTAGE 158

Poltimore Farm
Nr Exeter EX4 0AA
Tel: 01647 433593 MAP 18

Cottage: sleeps 6
£243-£734 pw

We can organise an organic vegetable box to be delivered

Soil Association

Mallard Cottage is within the grounds of the owner's 60-acre organic farm. Old farm buildings are close by, but beyond are stunning views. The cottage has its own entrance via steps up to a little wooden balcony. Enclosed garden and games barn. It is totally peaceful – ducks in the yard, a Shetland pony, goats, some domestic animals and a half acre lake. Picturesque Poltimore is a mainly thatched and red-stone hamlet in farmland on the outskirts of Exeter. There's an organic farm shop in Thorverton. Darts Farm Village in Topsham (food hall, deli bar, restaurant) offers a wide range of local farm / organic / high quality produce. Otterton Mill (bakery, restaurant) uses locally sourced ingredients, organic if available.
help@helpfulholidays.com   www.helpfulholidays.com:80/microresults.asp?search_value=g619

ROMANSLEIGH *(B&B)*

CATSHEYS

159

Romansleigh
South Molton EX36 4JW
Tel: 01769 550580   MAP 18

Bed and Breakfast
£60-£65 pppn

Breakfasts include homegrown, organic and locally sourced produce

A contemporary rural retreat set in eleven tranquil acres of organic gardens and woodland, a natural habitat for deer, badgers, foxes and birds. Spacious, light and airy, eclectically furnished double *en suite* rooms, large comfortable beds, crisp linens, down duvets, and fresh flowers from the garden. All our food is prepared with fresh, organic (wherever possible) produce from the kitchen garden, plus quality local produce. We make our own marmalade, bread and cereals. Swim in the solar-heated pool, relax in the garden, walk in the woods, explore Exmoor and Dartmoor, surf the dramatic North Devon coast, and visit many gardens and historic houses. Regret no children, no pets, no smoking.
rosie@catsheys.co.uk   www.catsheys.co.uk

SALCOMBE *(B&B)*

THRESHOLD

160

20A Longfield Drive
Salcombe TQ8 8NT
Tel: 01548 842877   MAP 18

Bed and Breakfast
£27.50-£42.50 pppn

Home baked organic bread, milk, soya, spreads, yogurt, butter, free-range eggs

A warm welcome awaits you at our organic bed and breakfast. It is in a tranquil setting overlooking North Sands valley and farmland, just a short walk from Salcombe town centre and North Sands beach (down a footpath from our garden). Our luxury room has a kingsize waterbed and *en suite* / steam room with aromatherapy oils. Large choice of breakfast menu. Full English or vegetarian, including organic home-baked bread, organic milk, butter, yogurt, preserves. Sausages and bacon from local farms. All drinks are organic, also on beverage trays in bedrooms. Free WiFi internet access. Good café selling organic food and drinks at East Portlemouth beach. Two restaurants / cafés in Kingsbridge provide organic meals.
info@salcombebedandbreak.co.uk   www.salcombebedandbreak.co.uk

SANDFORD *(B&B)*

ASHRIDGE FARM   161

Sandford
Crediton EX17 4EN
Tel: 01363 774292   MAP 18

Farmhouse Bed and Breakfast
£27-£35 pppn

Home and local organic produce used in the breakfast

Soil Association

Set in the beautiful mid Devon countryside, Ashridge Farm is a 200-acre working organic farm with cattle, sheep, pigs, chickens and cereals. You will stay in a warm friendly barn conversion with home cooking. All rooms are on the ground floor with *en suite* facilities and underfloor heating (one room has a mobility M3A certificate). Farm holidays are great fun on Ashridge. Guests can help feed the chickens and collect the eggs for breakfast, and feed the lambs. There's a large lawn where children can play safely, and there are 200 acres to roam with wildlife in abundance. Ideal for a holiday or a short break. The north and south Devon coasts, Dartmoor and Exmoor are all within an hour's drive from the farm. jill@ashridgefarm.co.uk www.ashridgefarm.co.uk

○ ⑤ 🧑

SHIRWELL *(Camping)*

PARKHILL FARM   162

Shirwell
Barnstaple EX31 4JN
Tel: 01271 850323   MAP 18

Caravan: sleeps 6, £20-£25 pn
Camping, £8 per unit

Organic lamb is sometimes available from the farm

Soil Association

Parkhill Farm is a level field with outstanding views, but with shelter from hedges. We are a quiet site on an organic beef and sheep farm. We also have free-range chickens. Our holiday caravan is situated in a private and quiet garden area surrounded by trees. Enjoy our farm walks. There are spectacular views across the countryside, including Exmoor. This is a wonderful place to come on holiday, with a great mixture of beaches and countryside. There are more than enough places to visit and things to do to keep even the most active perfectly happy. Close to both Arlington Court and the Broomhill Sculpture Gardens. Barnstaple town centre is two and a half miles away. Coastal resorts nearby.
ray.toms@virgin.net

SOUTH MOLTON *(B&B)*

GREAT STONE FARM 163

Exeter Road
South Molton EX36 4HX
Tel: 01769 574461   MAP 18

Farmhouse Bed and Breakfast
£25-£35 pppn

Breakfast includes local and organic produce

Organic Farmers & Growers

Great Stone Farm is a working organic dairy farm situated in a quiet location just one and a half miles from the market town of South Molton. At Great Stone you can enjoy our 15th-century thatched farmhouse (Grade II listed) and large garden. Comfortable *en suite* bedrooms. A full English, continental or vegetarian breakfast is served, using local and organic produce. South Molton is in one of the last remaining rural areas of Britain. Visit a honey farm where you can watch the bees working behind glass. The local countryside and villages are interesting too, with lovely country pubs for eating out. If you enjoy walking or visits to the beach, Exmoor and the North Devon coast are only a short drive away.

bgreatstone@aol.com   www.greatstonefarm.co.uk

TEDBURN ST MARY *(B&B)*

GREAT CUMMINS FARM 164

Tedburn St Mary
Exeter EX6 6BJ
Tel: 01647 61278   MAP 18

Farmhouse Bed and Breakfast
Double £55 pn, Single £40 pn

Mainly organic (100% organic by prior arrangement)

Soil Association

An exceptionally comfortable four star bed and breakfast in a 16th-century farmhouse with wonderful rural views. The delicious breakfast, cooked to order, is either wholly organic (by prior arrangement) or mainly organic using farm produce. Great Cummins is a small family-run organic farm in the glorious rolling hills of mid Devon. It comprises about 40 acres of permanent pasture, some 12 acres of woodland – hardwoods like oak and ash, most of which we planted when we came here ten years ago, an acre of (mainly cider) apple trees and an acre of land for growing vegetables. We sell our organic produce (fruit, vegetables, eggs, meat) direct to our customers via a box scheme and direct orders.

davidgaraway@yahoo.co.uk   www.greatcumminsfarm.co.uk

THE HOE *(B&B)*

BERKELEY'S OF ST JAMES 165

4 St James Place East
The Hoe PL1 3AS
Tel: 01752 221654   MAP 17

Guest House
Double B&B, £60-£70 pn

Organic / free-range where possible (40%-60% organic)

Berkeley's of St James is an elegant Victorian guest house situated in a secluded square on Plymouth Hoe. Quiet, exclusive, and furnished to a very high standard, it is tucked away from the main thoroughfare in pleasant and relaxing surroundings. We offer a substantial traditional full English breakfast with a choice of menu. Fresh fruit and fish. Organic and free-range produce is used wherever possible (average 40%-60% organic food during the year). Vegetarians are welcome. We are within easy walking distance of the sea front, the historic Barbican, the theatre and the pavilions. Plymouth is an ideal base for touring Dartmoor, Devon and Cornwall, and is within travelling distance of the Eden Project.
enquiry@onthehoe.co.uk   www.onthehoe.co.uk

TOPSHAM *(Camping)*

HIGHFIELD FARM 166

Clyst Road
Topsham EX3 0BY
Tel: 01392 876388   MAP 18

Caravan and Camping Site
£7.50 pn per pitch

Organic produce in season from the farm gate

Soil Association

Enjoy a truly green break on this family-run organic farm situated in the beautiful Clyst Valley. The family have been farming these 118 acres for the past three generations. Always farmed in a traditional manner, wild flower-rich hay meadows and hedgerows abound. There is a circular nature trail on the farm that passes through fields of sheep or cattle down to the River Clyst (watch out for otters and other wildlife). You can buy organic free-range eggs and other organic produce in season from the farm gate. The camping area is level and has five electric hook-ups. The site has only cold water and no showers. Caravans, motorcaravans, tents welcome. The farm is ten minutes walk walk from the riverside town of Topsham.
ian@highfieldfarm.org   www.highfieldfarm.org/camping.php

TOPSHAM *(B&B)*

REKA DOM 167

43 The Strand
Topsham EX3 0AY
Tel: 01392 873385   MAP 18

Bed and Breakfast
£37.50-£45 pppn

Our food is organic / free-range and locally
sourced whenever possible

Family-run bed and breakfast in an unusual 17th-century riverside property, with a choice of
three very different suites. Facing south, all rooms enjoy views over the beautiful Exe estuary
towards Exmouth and the wooded Haldon hills. Our famously-extensive breakfast includes
home-made breads, jams and marmalades, and is served at your leisure in our ground floor
dining room. Please note that our food is organic / free-range and locally sourced whenever
possible. Massage, healing and beauty treatments are available. An excellent base for
exploring Devon, Topsham itself offers river walks, wildlife, quiet spaces, independent shops,
a Saturday market and a range of pubs and restaurants championing West Country produce.
beautifulhouse@hotmail.com   www.rekadom.co.uk

TOTNES *(B&B)*

DART VILLAS B&B 168

3 Dart Villas
Totnes Down Hill TQ9 5ET
Tel: 01803 865895   MAP 18

Vegetarian Bed and Breakfast
Double from £60 pn, Single from £35 pn

We like to provide good quality organic
food (at least 95% organic)

Dart Villas organic vegetarian bed and breakfast is situated up on the hill overlooking the
River Dart and the town. It has lovely views of the town and the surrounding countryside.
All our food and drinks are organic where possible, including locally made organic bread,
eggs, butter, yogurt and milk, fresh organic fruits and fruit spreads. We believe organic food
is healthier for you and the environment, and it tastes better too. We operate an
environmental policy as far as washing sheets and towels is concerned, and use all
biodegradable cleaning products. It is only a five minute walk to the interesting and unique
town of Totnes, with its individual shops, restaurants and cafés to suite all tastes.
mounivk@yahoo.co.uk   www.dartvillasbb.co.uk

TOTNES *(B&B)*

NUMBER 12 169

12 Cistern Street
Totnes TQ9 5SP
Tel: 01803 840359 MAP 18

Organic Vegetarian B&B
£40-£45 pppn

Organic vegetarian using locally sourced
foods or fair traded wherever possible

Number 12 offers an extensive organic vegetarian breakfast with comfortable contemporary accommodation. Our Georgian house is located in the heart of Totnes, just two minutes walk from the high street. All three guest rooms are *en suite*, and there's a range of organic tea and freshly ground coffee in each room. Some of our linen is organic or fair-traded. We use local organic farm suppliers Riverford, for over 80% of our menu. Committed to reducing our carbon footprint, we offer discounts for long stays using public transport. All are very welcome – for families we offer travel cot and high chairs. Totnes is the second oldest borough in England and has many historic buildings within walking distance of Number 12. bookings@bedandbreakfasttotnes.com   www.bedandbreakfasttotnes.com

UGBOROUGH *(S-C)*

BARN OWL COTTAGE 170

Fowlescombe Farm
Ugborough PL21 0HW
Tel: 01548 821000 MAP 18

Cottage: sleeps 6+cot
£480-£1200 pw

Our own award-winning beef and rare breed
lamb plus other local produce

Soil Association

One of two 5-star cottages in an architect designed barn conversion on this historic estate. Now a 470-acre organic wildlife-rich working farm, Fowlescombe lies in an idyllic spot in its own hidden valley. Enjoy roaming the estate seeing flower-rich pastures, bluebell woods, primrose lanes, and wildlife ponds. Watch out for badgers, foxes, deer, hare, owls and other wildlife. Meet rare breed and pedigree farm animals and enjoy aspects of farming, countryside management and organic produce. This is an ideal location for exploring the wonderful Devon countryside, South Hams coast and scenic Dartmoor. Book both cottages for parties of up to ten. The cottages have each attained the Green Tourism Business Scheme Gold Award. richard@fowlescombe.com   www.fowlescombe.co.uk/Lets/Barn%20Owl%20Cottage.htm

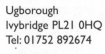

UGBOROUGH *(B&B)*

HILLHEAD FARM · 171

Ugborough
Ivybridge PL21 0HQ
Tel: 01752 892674   MAP 18

Farmhouse Bed and Breakfast
£28-£31 pppn, single supplement £5

Locally sourced, home-made, much of it
organic

Soil Association

Hillhead is a traditional working beef and sheep farm surrounded by tranquil fields yet only five minutes stroll from the village of Ugborough. There are lovely views over the peaceful South Hams countryside. We grow organic vegetables on a field scale as part of a co-operative of like-minded local farmers. Our produce goes to supply a thriving box scheme. Our own garden is organic and we grow vegetables, herbs and soft fruit. We also have a flock of about twenty hens which are truly free-range. Enjoy delicious farmhouse breakfasts in the sunny conservatory, using local produce and home-made organic bread and preserves. We have been awarded the South Hams Green Tourism Silver Award. Camping available, £6-£9 per night.
info@hillhead-farm.co.uk   www.hillhead-farm.co.uk

UGBOROUGH *(S-C)*

SWALLOW COTTAGE · 172

Fowlescombe Farm
Ugborough PL21 0HW
Tel: 01548 821000   MAP 18

Cottage: sleeps 4+cot
£400-£1000 pw

Our own award-winning beef and rare breed
lamb plus other local produce

Soil Association

One of two 5-star cottages in an architect-designed barn conversion on this historic estate. Protection of the environment and wildlife and farm animal conservation are priorities. Rare breed Manx Loaghtan and Hebridean sheep, pedigree Angus and Devon cattle graze ancient pastures. Rare breed Golden Guernsey goats help with scrub management. Rare breed chickens wander round the orchard and organic vegetable plot on pest control duty (eggs usually available). Organically managed woodland for amenity and wildlife provides fuel for all our wood burners. Meat and pies, pasties and ready-meals from our own, local and organic ingredients are often available. Green Tourism Business Scheme Gold Award.
richard@fowlescombe.com   www.fowlescombe.co.uk/Lets/Swallow%20Cottage.htm

UPLOWMAN *(S-C)*

MIDDLE COOMBE FARM 173

Uplowman
Tiverton EX16 7QQ
Tel: 01884 821176   MAP 18

House: sleeps 16, from £1000 pw / £800 w/end
Barn: holds 70 for events, £650 per w/end

Seasonal organic vegetables and organic beef, honey may be available

Soil Association

Beautiful Grade II listed 16th/17th-century cob and thatched farmhouse set in its own sheltered valley. It is surrounded by a gatehouse, barns (including a thatched cider barn), gardens, and 400 acres of organic farm and mixed woodland with an extensive footpath network. We are licensed for weddings. Mountain bikes for loan. solar-heated swimming pool. 5.5kw solar photovoltaic generator. The woodland is sustainably-managed. The farm produces organic beef, willow, comfrey plant feed, and seasonal vegetables. We have replanted our organic orchard with traditional apple varieties and undertaken extensive pasture management, hedge laying, planting schemes, with noticeable positive impact on flora and fauna.
info@coombefarmwoods.co.uk   www.coombefarmwoods.co.uk

VIRGINSTOW *(Hotel)*

PERCY'S COUNTRY HOTEL 174

Coombeshead Estate
Virginstow EX21 5EA
Tel: 01409 211236   MAP 17

Small Hotel (contact for prices)
Restaurant (breakfast, lunch, dinner)

Contemporary country cooking, delicious home-produced organic breakfast

Soil Association

Located in one of England's three designated areas of tranquillity, the tasteful and eco-friendly hotel offers superbly appointed rooms. The cuisine delivers exceptional country cooking. The award-winning dishes – food created on the estate with zero food miles, burst with colour and flavour and include organic pork and lamb reared on the estate together with organic vegetables, herbs and salads from the well-stocked vegetable garden. Stroll around the gardens, woodland and peaceful lakes to experience the outstanding beauty of the 130-acre organic estate. The 60,000 tree plantation, comprising mixed broadleaves and edible shrubs, goes a long way to making Percy's a carbon neutral hotel.
info@percys.co.uk   www.percys.co.uk

WELCOMBE *(B&B)*

CRANHAM HOUSE   175

Welcombe
Hartland EX39 6ET
Tel: 01288 331351   MAP 17

Bed and Breakfast, £35 pppn
Supper £10, Evening Meal (3 course) £18.50

Home-grown organic veg, herbs, eggs, bread, meat, apple juice, chutneys, preserves

Cranham House is an old stone farmhouse set in 18 acres of a spectacular wooded valley in North Devon. In an Area of Outstanding Natural Beauty the house is within a short walk of the beach at Welcombe Mouth. Our bed and breakfast accommodation offers two luxurious double *en suite* bedrooms. Our vegetables, salads and herbs are home-grown and organic, eggs are from our own hens and we serve rare breed meats from local organic smallholders (who are also friends) and local cheeses. Bread and apple juice are produced by us. Our self-catering annexe, sleeping 2-4 people, is a lovely oak-framed barn with a wood burner and a private garden (£300-£500 pw). Organic home-made meals available on request.
info@cranhamhouse.co.uk   www.cranhamhouse.co.uk

WELCOMBE *(S-C)*

WELCOMBE BARTON   176

Welcombe
Bideford EX39 6HF
Tel: 01288 331692   MAP 17

Farmhouse: sleeps 6
£595-£700 pw

Home-grown produce is available in season (honesty box for payments)

Welcombe Barton is a hidden gem just one mile from the Hartland heritage coastline. The Grade II listed medieval farmhouse is set in a stunning remote location in an Area of Outstanding Natural Beauty. Four simple bedrooms, one bathroom, a kitchen, a lounge with original slate flooring and woodburner. A 4-acre field with composting loos and thatched celtic roundhouse is part of the holiday. Local producers Holsworthy Organics deliver vegetable boxes once a week if you pre-order. Eggs are available from local organic Black Rock chickens. The Yarner Trust demonstrates sustainable living and natural food production. Come and see the demonstration organic kitchen garden and the stunning organic willow beds.
info@yarnertrust.org   www.yarnertrust.org

WESTCOTT *(B&B)*

HIGHER WESTCOTT FARM 177

Westcott
Moretonhampstead TQ13 8SU
Tel: 01647 441205   MAP 18

Boutique Guesthouse, B&B £40-£55 pppn
Afternoon Tea £5, Dinner (weekends) £15-£25

Our produce is carefully sourced and,
wherever possible, organic

Delicious locally sourced mostly organic food, sumptuous beds, contemporary bathrooms, stunning views. Westcott is a tiny hamlet in a breathtaking landscape of moors and woodlands in Dartmoor National Park. A perfect location for family or friends looking to relax or enjoy a celebration (exclusive hire, B&B from £460 pn for 8-10 persons). We prepare our own food and take time to source ingredients locally. Breakfasts feature home-made organic bread and our neighbour's organic free-range eggs. Hamper rucksacks can be tailor-made for your requirements, perfect for picnics or long walks. Three course dinner menu using seasonal Devonshire produce served at weekends. Wild food foraging, fishing and shooting arranged locally.
info@higherwestcottfarm.com   www.higherwestcottfarm.com

WOOLSERY *(S-C)*

THE OLD POUND HOUSE 178

Woolsery
Bideford EX39 5QA
Tel: 01237 431589   MAP 17

Converted Barn: sleeps 2-4, £235-£385 pw
Short Breaks, £40-£45 pn (minimum 2 nights)

Home-grown naturally produced vegetables
in season

The small converted barn is separated from our house by a drive and a large herb bed. A single dwelling beside a single track road, the barn backs onto a small field full of wild flowers in summer. We are surrounded by 13 acres of fields with a large wildlife pond. All our vegetables are organic (available to purchase in season) and are grown on our land. Herbs are free. The house and barn are situated about half a mile outside the rural village of Woolfardisworthy (Woolsery) between Bideford and Bude. The village has a pub and a general store and post office. An outside tennis court is available by the new village hall. Many sand and stone beaches nearby, and lovely walks both coastal and inland.
david.baker8@virgin.net

ABBOTSBURY *(S-C)*

BRIDE COTTAGE 179

Gorwell Farm
Abbotsbury DT3 4JX
Tel: 01305 871401   MAP 18

Cottage: sleeps 4
From £225 pw

Organic beef, lamb and pork available to buy,
plus ready-made meals

Soil Association

Oak beams and a hayloft roof add to the atmosphere of this cosy little cottage. Carefully converted, it retains many original features. Doors from the living room lead to a small, private garden. Gorwell is a family-run organic farm. We can help with meals as we have our own frozen beef, lamb and pork, and frozen ready-meals are also available for you to buy. The farm is ideally positioned in its own secret wooded valley. Birds, wildlife, wildflowers in abundance. Nesting boxes and feeding posts with cameras for wildlife tourists. There is easy access to a wonderful network of footpaths from the farm, including the South West Coast Path and the MacMillan Way. Gorwell is just two miles from Chesil Beach.
mary@gorwellfarm.co.uk   www.gorwellfarm.co.uk/bride.asp

ABBOTSBURY *(S-C)*

GORWELL FARM GRANARY 180

Gorwell Farm
Abbotsbury DT3 4JX
Tel: 01305 871401   MAP 18

Converted Barn: sleeps 8
From £300 pw

Organic beef, lamb and pork available to buy,
plus ready-made meals

Soil Association

A spacious barn with beautiful wooden ceilings and oak beams, two miles from Chesil Beach. With views of amazing sunsets down the valley, the south-west-facing garden is the perfect place to relax and enjoy a drink or an evening barbecue. Gorwell is a family-run organic farm. We can help with meals as we have our own frozen beef, lamb and pork, and frozen ready-meals are also available for you to buy. The farm nestles in its own secret wooded valley. Birds, wildlife and wildflowers in abundance. Nesting boxes and feeding posts with cameras for wildlife tourists. There is easy access to a wonderful network of footpaths from the farm, including the South West Coast Path and the MacMillan Way.
mary@gorwellfarm.co.uk   www.gorwellfarm.co.uk/granary.asp

ABBOTSBURY *(S-C)*

GREYMARE COTTAGE   181

Gorwell Farm
Abbotsbury DT3 4JX
Tel: 01305 871401   MAP 18

Cottage: sleeps 4 (+2 Bunkbeds)
From £250 pw

Organic beef, lamb and pork available to buy,
plus ready-made meals

Soil Association

An attractive stone-built Victorian semi-detached cottage. The conservatory overlooks the large garden, and the sitting room faces south with views overlooking the hills. Gorwell is a family-run organic farm. We can help with meals as we have our own frozen beef, lamb and pork, and frozen ready-meals are also available for you to buy. The farm is ideally positioned in its own secret wooded valley. Birds, wildlife and wildflowers in abundance. Nesting boxes and feeding posts with cameras for wildlife tourists. There is easy access to a wonderful network of footpaths from the farm, including the South West Coast Path and the MacMillan Way. Gorwell is just two miles from West Dorset's Chesil Beach.

mary@gorwellfarm.co.uk   www.gorwellfarm.co.uk/greymare.asp

ABBOTSBURY *(S-C)*

MEAD COTTAGE   182

Gorwell Farm
Abbotsbury DT3 4JX
Tel: 01305 871401   MAP 18

Cottage: sleeps 8
From £250 pw

Organic beef, lamb and pork available to buy,
plus ready-made meals

Soil Association

The cottage has recently been completely refurbished to a high standard. The dining room will seat ten for meals, and the living room is comfortable with a log burner in the fireplace and patio doors to the garden. Gorwell is a family-run organic farm. We can help with meals as we have our own frozen beef, lamb and pork, and frozen ready-meals are also available for you to buy. The farm nestles in its own secret wooded valley. Birds, wildlife and wildflowers in abundance. Nesting boxes and feeding posts with cameras for wildlife tourists. Easy access to a wonderful network of footpaths from the farm, including the South West Coast Path and the MacMillan Way. Gorwell is two miles from Chesil Beach.

mary@gorwellfarm.co.uk   www.gorwellfarm.co.uk/mead.asp

SrrsSSSS

ABBOTSBURY *(S-C)*

SPINDLE COTTAGE 183

Gorwell Farm
Abbotsbury DT3 4JX
Tel: 01305 871401 MAP 18

Cottage: sleeps 6
From £275 pw

Organic beef, lamb and pork available to buy, plus ready-made meals

Soil Association

The original features of this former barn have been retained wherever possible, and a fireplace has been added to keep you cosy in cooler weather. Patio doors lead onto the garden with plenty of space all on one level. Gorwell is a family-run organic farm. We can help with meals as we have our own frozen beef, lamb and pork, and frozen ready-meals are also available for you to buy. The farm nestles in its own secret wooded valley. Birds, wildlife, wildflowers in abundance. Nesting boxes and feeding posts with cameras for wildlife tourists. Easy access to a wonderful network of footpaths, including the South West Coast Path and the MacMillan Way. Gorwell Farm is just two miles from Chesil Beach.
mary@gorwellfarm.co.uk   www.gorwellfarm.co.uk/spindle.asp

ABBOTSBURY *(S-C)*

SUNDIAL COTTAGE 184

Gorwell Farm
Abbotsbury DT3 4JX
Tel: 01305 871401 MAP 18

Cottage: sleeps 5
From £250 pw

Organic beef, lamb and pork available to buy, plus ready-made meals

Soil Association

Sundial is a cosy Victorian semi-detached farm cottage with its own fenced garden. The sitting / dining room is south-facing and retains the original features of a cottage of its period. Gorwell is a family-run organic farm. We can help with meals as we have our own frozen beef, lamb and pork, and frozen ready-meals are also available for you to buy. The farm nestles in its own secret wooded valley. Birds, wildlife and wildflowers in abundance. Nesting boxes and feeding posts with cameras for wildlife tourists. There is access to a wonderful network of footpaths, including the South West Coast Path and the MacMillan Way, which both cross our farm. Gorwell is two miles from Chesil Beach in West Dorset.
mary@gorwellfarm.co.uk   www.gorwellfarm.co.uk/sundial.asp

CHARMOUTH *(B&B)*

MONKTON WYLD COURT   185

Charmouth
Bridport DT6 6DQ
Tel: 01297 560342   MAP 18

Bed and Breakfast, £22-£26 pppn
Breakfast, Lunch, Supper (by arrangement)

Home cooked organic vegetarian food, some
grown in our own garden

Holistic education centre set in beautiful countryside near Lyme Regis. We run courses on permaculture, yoga, arts, crafts, voice, movement and family weeks. We also welcome B&B visitors when possible. All our food is vegetarian and we are proud that we provide mainly organic food. We use small local businesses to purchase food, and our one acre walled kitchen garden provides some of our fruit, vegetables and salads. Our kitchen garden is not certified organic, but has been cultivated on organic principles since 1940. Located in a beautiful Dorset valley three miles from the sea, the 11-acre estate includes a small dairy and chicken farm, terraced lawns, woods and a stream. Camping from £5.50 per night.
bookings@monktonwyldcourt.org   www.monktonwyldcourt.org

CHICKERELL *(Camping)*

EAST FLEET FARM   186

Chickerell
Weymouth DT3 4DW
Tel: 01305 785768   MAP 18

Touring Park, £10-£19 pn
£3 extra for electric hook-up

Organic milk (shop), organic beef (bar
meals)

Soil Association

The touring park is situated at the heart of our 300-acre organic dairy farm. We are delighted to have been chosen to receive a Gold David Bellamy Award for five consecutive years, naming us one of the most environmentally friendly parks in the UK. We offer a unique location on the shores of the Fleet Lagoon, overlooking Chesil Beach and the sea. Relax and unwind in the truly peaceful Dorset countryside. The Old Barn fully licensed family bar opens at Easter for the summer. This converted 19th-century grain barn has stunning views over the Fleet. Bar meals served (our own organic beef is on the menu). Local beers on sale. Peak season can get busy, so best avoided for those looking for tranquillity.
enquiries@eastfleet.co.uk   www.eastfleet.co.uk

CROSSWAYS *(B&B)*

FROME VALLEY HOUSE   187

15 Frome Valley Road
Crossways DT2 8WP
Tel: 01305 851583   MAP 18

Bed and Breakfast
Double £30 pppn, Single £40 pppn

Organic breakfast (bacon, eggs, milk, home-made bread, tea, coffee, fruit, etc)

Frome Valley House has a warm and friendly atmosphere and is situated in the glorious and rolling countryside of Dorset. We serve a fresh organic breakfast every morning, tailored to your taste. Most of the food is locally sourced and has been selected from the best organic farms in the region. Breakfast includes cereal, juice, toast, bacon, egg, mushrooms, sausages, tomatoes, coffee, tea, with vegetarian being an option. All three guest rooms are large in size and all have double beds. Each room has tea and coffee making facilities and sofas where you can relax and unwind after a busy day exploring. You can walk into neighbouring fields and for miles along country paths and bridleways from the doorstep.
patwhiskey@aol.com   www.fromevalleyhouse.co.uk

GILLINGHAM *(B&B)*

ANSTYROSE COTTAGE   188

Wyke Road
Gillingham SP8 4NH
Tel: 01747 825379   MAP 18

Bed and Breakfast
From £25 pppn

Mainly organic (at least 95%) and local where possible

Charming 18th-century detached cottage with a working pottery in a beautiful cottage garden. Situated on the western outskirts of Gillingham, a small rural town in North Dorset. Keen gardener and professional potter offers very comfortable accommodation (one twin room and one single room) with full continental breakfast. Mostly organic and local where possible, breakfast includes cereal, juice, toast and marmalade or honey, ham, cheese, hard-boiled eggs. Eco-friendly accessories. The cottage is only a couple of minutes walk to fields and the same to a small pub with good food. It is ten minutes walk to the town centre and twenty minutes walk to the train station. Gillingham is on the North Dorset Cycleway.
kazworks@waitrose.com   www.kazworks.co.uk

HARTGROVE *(S-C)*

HARTGROVE FARM 189

Hartgrove
Shaftesbury SP7 0JY
Tel: 01747 811830   MAP 18

Cottages: sleep 2-5
£310-£895 pw

We have a small farm shop selling eggs, honey, real Dorset dairy ice cream

Hartgrove is a family farm set in the glorious Dorset countryside. The farm is run on organic lines, with cows and sheep grazing the gently undulating fields. The award-winning cottages are furnished and equipped to a high standard. Old beams, log fires, full central heating. Help feed our friendly farm animals (goats, sheep, pigs, geese, chickens), collect eggs, bottle feed a lamb or watch the milking. Tennis court. Games Barn. Free local swimming. The village nestles below the majestic Cranborne Chase. Stroll the valley paths or drink in the views from the top of the Downs. It is absolutely beautiful. Visit the local farmers' markets and buy fresh organic produce. Pretty thatched villages have excellent pubs serving food.
cottages@hartgrovefarm.co.uk   www.hartgrovefarm.co.uk

HIGHER EYPE *(Camping)*

DOWNHOUSE FARM 190

Higher Eype
Bridport DT6 6AH
Tel: 01308 421232   MAP 18

Campsite, £11-£13 pn per pitch
Café open mid March to mid October

You can purchase our organic meat, sausages, bacon, etc from the farm

Soil Association

Downhouse Farm is set on 500 acres of National Trust land. We produce top quality free-range pork, lamb and beef, which are all reared to organic standards. The campsite is a small relaxed site with a beautiful view and an easy stroll down to a quiet beach with safe bathing. At the farmhouse we run our Garden Café, which has a wonderful view of part of Lyme Bay and across to Portland. We serve good home-made, unpretentious and wholesome food made using our own organic meats, herbs and vegetables alongside other equally superb local produce. Our cakes and scones are baked on the premises daily. Many footpaths cross the farmland, offering stunning views along the coast and inland over the Dorset landscape.
nikki@downhouse-farm.co.uk   www.downhouse-farm.co.uk/camping.htm

MOSTERTON *(B&B)*

BOWES HOUSE 191

Mosterton
Beaminster DT8 3HN
Tel: 01308 868862   MAP 18

Bed and Breakfast
£30-£40 pppn

Breakfast is sourced locally and is organic
wherever possible

Family-run bed and breakfast set in three quarters of an acre of beautiful established garden with stunning views across the Dorset and Somerset countryside. The guest rooms are large and comfortable, with feather pillows and duvets and white cotton bed linen (some organic), and thick white towels. Soap and paper products are organic. Breakfast is sourced locally and is organic wherever possible, eggs are our own, organic (not certified) stewed fruit is from the garden, and we make our own organic yogurt and preserves. We try to be as environmentally friendly / organic as possible in all that we do, and have installed solar-heated hot water. Tea and refreshments on arrival include home-made organic cakes or biscuits.
info@boweshousebandb.com   www.boweshousebandb.com

OSMINGTON *(S-C)*

THE CARTSHED 192

Church Lane
Osmington DT3 6EW
Tel: 01305 833690   MAP 18

Cottage: sleeps 6+cot, £340-£780 pw
Camping (August only)

Organic beef, lamb, pork, eggs, vegetables,
milk, bread from Eweleaze Farmshop

Soil Association

The Cartshed is a delightful converted stone barn in an Area of Outstanding Natural Beauty. It is located on a very quiet no-through road in the pretty village of Osmington. Renovated to a very high standard its traditional features include a large open fireplace, beamed ceilings, and polished wood and flagstone floors. There are gardens to the front and rear, with a patio area and barbecue. Located a mile off the coast, the cottage is within easy reach of the beaches at Osmington Mills and Ringstead, as well as having the facility for private parking at Eweleaze Farm for access to our own private beach at Redcliff Point. Organic produce (beef, lamb, pork, eggs, vegetables, milk, bread) available from our farm shop.
peter@eweleaze.co.uk   www.eweleaze.co.uk/cottage.htm

TOLLER PORCORUM *(S-C)*

STABLE COTTAGE 193

Lower Road
Toller Porcorum DT2 0DH
Tel: 01300 321413   MAP 18

Cottage: sleeps 2-4, £180-£400 pw
Short Breaks (October-March)

Our own organic milk, local organic produce

Soil Association

A converted stable adjoining the farmhouse on a family-run organic dairy farm. Cosy and well equipped, the cottage has two bedrooms and its own private garden. It is situated in the village of Toller Porcorum in an area renowned for wildlife. Toller is a lovely village off the beaten track, surrounded by heavenly West Dorset countryside including the farm itself and Dorset Wildlife Trust's reserves at Kingcombe and Powerstock. There are many local walks to enjoy without the use of a car. Midway between Bridport and Dorchester, it is only twenty minutes drive (with stunning views) to the Heritage coast. Perfect for nature and beach lovers. If you want a great holiday with a very small ecological footprint, this is it.
janetchaffey@hotmail.co.uk

TOLLER PORCORUM *(S-C)*

SUNNYSIDE ORGANIC FARM 194

Lower Kingcombe
Toller Porcorum DT2 0EQ
Tel: 01300 321537   MAP 18

Cottage: sleeps 2-4, £450-£650 pw
Organic Supper, £8.50 per head

Organic home produce may be available to buy

Soil Association

Beautifully converted from an old cow byre, The Old Barn is on a working organic farm situated in an Area of Outstanding Natural Beauty. Home-produced organic beef and lamb (subject to availability) can be purchased during your stay. A night off? Supper on arrival? I will cook you an organic casserole with a bottle of wine between two for £8.50 per head. Sunnyside Organic Farm is set in the Kingcombe Valley, famous for its wild flower meadows, amid 600 acres of the Dorset Wildlife Trust. The Wessex Ridgeway and the Jubilee Trail cross the farm and there are many long and short walks for you to enjoy without the need of a car. There is fishing in the River Hooke and the holiday cottage is only six miles from the sea.
sunnyside.farm@tiscali.co.uk   www.sunnysideorganicfarm.co.uk

TOLLER PORCORUM *(B&B)*

THE KINGCOMBE CENTRE 195

Toller Porcorum
Dorchester DT2 OEQ
Tel: 01300 320684   MAP 18

Holidays, Courses (contact for more info)
B&B £34-£36 pppn, Evening Meal £20 pp

As much organic and organically grown as possible

Kingcombe is a study centre offering holidays, courses, bed and breakfast, and guided walks. Situated in converted farm buildings at the heart of Lower Kingcombe beside the River Hooke, the centre is on 4 acres of riverside pasture and is surrounded by the Kingcombe Meadows Nature Reserve. The food we cook for our guests is seasonal, organic if possible and local. The garden is chemical-free and we grow a substantial amount of our own fruit and vegetables. We have a small flock of sheep at Kingcombe, so produce our own lamb. Pork and beef is sourced from farms along the Lower Kingcombe Valley. The milk and cream come from a nearby organic dairy farm from cows grazing in this valley and the next.
office@kingcombecentre.org.uk   www.kingcombecentre.org.uk

WEST BEXINGTON *(S-C)*

GRANARY LODGE 196

Tamarisk Farm Cottages
Beach Road DT2 9DF
Tel: 01308 897784   MAP 18

Cottage: sleeps 7
£425-£980 pw

Our own organic produce (vegetables, fruit, beef, lamb, mutton) for sale

Soil Association

A disabled-friendly (M1) stone-built bungalow. Tamarisk Farm slopes down to Chesil beach in the tiny village of West Bexington. Our organic market garden has 6 acres of vegetables and fruit in season. Organic wheat and rye are grown and milled on the farm as organic wholemeal stoneground flour. Organic beef, lamb, mutton joints, sausages available in individual packs or freezer boxes to take home. Conservation is a major interest on the farm. In the Stewardship Scheme we repair forest marble walls, plant hedges and trees, have flower-rich meadows, North Devon cattle and sheep. The whole coastline is now of World Heritage status. The Dorset Wildlife Trust has designated extensive areas as SSSI and SNCI.
holidays@tamariskfarm.com   www.tamariskfarm.com/holidays/?p=granary

WEST BEXINGTON *(S-C)*

MIMOSA COTTAGE 197

Tamarisk Farm Cottages
Beach Road DT2 9DF
Tel: 01308 897784 MAP 18

Cottage: sleeps 4
£375-£860 pw

Our own organic produce (vegetables, fruit, beef, lamb, mutton) for sale

Soil Association

A large comfortable cottage (M3i disabled access), Tamarisk Farm slopes down to Chesil beach in the tiny village of Bexington. Our organic market garden has 6 acres of vegetables and fruit in season. Organic wheat and rye are grown and milled on the farm as organic wholemeal stoneground flour. Organic beef, lamb, mutton joints, sausages available in individual packs or freezer boxes to take home. Conservation is a major interest on the farm. In the Stewardship Scheme we repair forest marble walls, plant hedges and trees, have flower-rich meadows, sheep, North Devon cattle. The whole coastline is now of World Heritage status. The Dorset Wildlife Trust has designated extensive areas as SSSI and SNCI.
holidays@tamariskfarm.com   www.tamariskfarm.com/holidays/?p=mimosa

WEST BEXINGTON *(S-C)*

THE FOSSIL AND THE CROSS 198

Tamarisk Farm Cottages
Beach Road DT2 9DF
Tel: 01308 897784 MAP 18

Cottage: sleeps 4
£260-£600 pw

Our own organic produce (vegetables, fruit, beef, lamb, mutton) for sale

Soil Association

The Fossil and the Cross is 800 metres from the sea. The farm slopes down to Chesil beach in the tiny village of Bexington. Our organic market garden has 6 acres of vegetables and fruit in season. Organic wheat and rye are grown and milled on the farm as organic wholemeal stoneground flour. Organic beef, lamb, mutton joints, sausages are available in individual packs or freezer boxes to take home. Conservation is a major interest on the farm. In the Stewardship Scheme we have flower-rich meadows, repair forest marble walls, plant hedges and trees, keep sheep, cattle, horses. The whole coastline is now of World Heritage status. The Dorset Wildlife Trust has designated extensive areas as SSSI and SNCI.
holidays@tamariskfarm.com   www.tamariskfarm.com/holidays/?p=fossil

WEST BEXINGTON *(S-C)*

THE MOAT   199

Tamarisk Farm Cottages
Beach Road DT2 9DF
Tel: 01308 897784   MAP 18

Cottage: sleeps 5
£295-£680 pw

Our own organic produce (vegetables, fruit, beef, lamb, mutton) for sale

Soil Association

The Moat looks straight down the village road towards the sea. The farm slopes down to Chesil beach in the tiny village of West Bexington. Our organic market garden has 6 acres of vegetables and fruit in season. Organic wheat and rye are grown and milled on the farm as organic wholemeal stoneground flour. Organic beef, lamb, mutton joints, sausages available in individual packs or freezer boxes to take home. Conservation is a major interest. In the Stewardship Scheme we have flower-rich meadows, repair forest marble walls, plant hedges and trees, keep sheep and cattle. The whole coastline is now of World Heritage status. The Dorset Wildlife Trust has designated extensive areas as SSSI and SNCI.
holidays@tamariskfarm.com   www.tamariskfarm.com/holidays/?p=moat

WEST BEXINGTON *(S-C)*

WHISPERING PINES   200

Tamarisk Farm Cottages
Beach Road DT2 9DF
Tel: 01308 897784   MAP 18

Cottage: sleeps 5
£260-£600 pw

Our own organic produce (vegetables, fruit, beef, lamb, mutton) for sale

Soil Association

A cottage bungalow of local stone 800 metres from the sea. Tamarisk Farm slopes down to Chesil beach in the tiny village of West Bexington. Our organic market garden has 6 acres of vegetables and fruit in season. Organic wheat and rye are grown and milled on the farm as organic wholemeal stoneground flour. Organic beef, lamb, mutton joints, sausages available in individual packs or freezer boxes to take home. Conservation is a major interest on the farm. In the Stewardship Scheme we repair forest marble walls, plant hedges / trees, have flower-rich meadows, sheep, cattle, horses. The whole coastline is of World Heritage status. The Dorset Wildlife Trust has designated extensive areas as SSSI and SNCI.
holidays@tamariskfarm.com   www.tamariskfarm.com

WHITCHURCH CANONICORUM   BECKLANDS ORGANIC FARM 201

Whitchurch Canonicorum
Bridport DT6 6RG
Tel: 01297 560298   MAP 18

Bed and Organic Breakfast, £32.50-£37.50 pn
Packed lunches (by arrangement)

Fully organic English breakfast (certified by
the Soil Association)

Soil Association

Becklands thatched farmhouse lies in an Area of Outstanding Natural Beauty, two and a half miles from Charmouth beach. Our 100% organic breakfast includes the farm's eggs, beef sausages and home-made preserves. Organic linen and eco-friendly paints have been used throughout, while the bedhead and the dining table have been made from Beckland's ash. The 12-hectare farm has been managed organically since 1973. Visitors are welcome to collect eggs, help move cattle, etc. Our organic produce is sold in the small farm shop. Self-guided walks (map and guide at farm shop). One night bookings taken from Sept to June, £37.50 pppn. Minimum stay two nights July and August (try last minute for single nights). becklandsorganicfarm@btopenworld.com   www.becklandsorganicfarm.co.uk

TRIMDON GRANGE (B&B)   POLEMONIUM B&B   202

28 Sunnyside Terrace
Trimdon Grange TS29 6HF
Tel: 01429 881529   MAP 9

Bed and Breakfast, £28 pppn
Evening Meal, £10 pp

Our own and local fresh organic produce,
home-made bread and preserves

Organic environmentally friendly bed and breakfast, with one double four-poster room and two singles. Organic soaps and shampoos. Room refreshments include organic biscuits. Fresh organic milk on request. Our own and local fresh organic produce, home-made bread and preserves for breakfast. Packed lunches and evening meals on request. Polemonium Plantery is a specialist organic and peat-free nursery, supplying hardy perennials, shrubs and trees. Weekend courses on organic / wildlife gardening (£100 pp). Organic nappy-washing service, organic baby dressing gowns, cot / high chair provided, children's activity basket. Good access for cyclists, walkers, and also from public transport.
bandb@polemonium.co.uk   www.polemonium.co.uk/bnb.html

WEARHEAD *(B&B)*

LOW CORNRIGGS FARM 203

Cowshill
Wearhead DL13 1AQ
Tel: 01388 537600   MAP 9

Farmhouse Bed and Breakfast, £29-£39 pppn
Dinner, £17 (book in advance)

Organic when possible, naturally reared
Hereford beef, local Weardale lamb

Lovely old farmhouse, built over 200 years ago, with spectacular views over the top of Weardale in an AONB. We pride ourselves in good home-cooked food, organic when possible or wild / local. Home-produced beef, wild salmon, trout, game, some vegetables grown in our garden or from our neighbour's organic farm. Most of our meals are traditional – good clean honest food – and are served in the delightful dining room. AA Pie Award for evening meals. Breakfast is taken in the conservatory. Home-made bread and jams, local sausages, home-made muffins. Green Tourism Business Scheme Silver Award. Environmentally sensitive area. Stunning scenery, waterfalls, open moorland, old green roads, hills, birds, flowers.
cornriggsfarm@btconnect.com   www.britnett.net/lowcornriggsfarm

FINGRINGHOE *(B&B)*

HAMS FARM 204

Abberton Road
Fingringhoe CO5 7AL
Tel: 01206 735247   MAP 16

Bed and Breakfast, £30 pppn
Evening Meal, from £18 (by arrangement)

Our own produce and locally sourced produce

Not a farmhouse, but a spacious bungalow with outstanding countryside views over the Pyfleet and Colne Estuary set in quiet surroundings about fifty yards from the road. Picnic lunches and evening meals are available with prior notice. Emma is a qualified cook, and uses our own fresh farm produce as well as locally sourced produce in the home-made meals. Andrew works with 7 acres of apple orchard and 2 acres of vegetables, and also manages some acres of grass, woodland and ponds. The fruit and vegetables are sold by farm gate sales, and also to local shops. Emma manages the vegetable stall and retail outlets. Our aim is to sell fresh, naturally grown farm produce at the best price to the consumer.
info@hamsfarm.com   www.hamsfarm.com

BRISTOL *(B&B)*

FULL MOON BACKPACKER 205

1 North Street
Stokes Croft BS1 3PR
Tel: 0117 9245007   MAP 18

Bunk bed dormitory style and twin rooms
£16-£19 pppn

Organic and free-range food (restaurant
open 9am-9.30pm)

We are an eco-friendly independent backpacker hotel, suitable for like-minded travellers. We have an on-site pub / restaurant open to both guests and the public, providing quality fresh organic and local free-range food with beers, wines and spirits to match. Our linen and bedding is all organic, and where possible we do as much as we can to reduce our impact on the environment. Over 20% discount when paying for seven nights in advance. Getting here is easy. The city bus station is a one minute walk away. The bus station has regular links to and from Bristol international airport departing every hour. If you are arriving by train there is also a bus link taking you between the two every hour.
info@fullmoonbristol.co.uk   www.fullmoonbristol.co.uk

BULLO PILL *(B&B)*

GROVE FARM B&B 206

Bullo Pill
Newnham On Severn GL14 1EA
Tel: 01594 516304   MAP 14

Farmhouse Bed and Breakfast, £30-£35 pppn
Packed Lunch, £3.50 (on request)

Locally sourced organic food wherever
possible

Soil Association

A traditional farmhouse on an organic dairy and sheep farm. Grove Farm is quiet and secluded, with panoramic views over the Severn Vale towards the Cotswolds. The peace is broken only by the roaming guinea fowl. There are two double guest bedrooms. Guests have their own lounge with an open log fire in the oldest part of the farmhouse, full of exposed beams and a circular staircase. Garden and terrace for your use. Children are welcome. Wonderful walking on our doorstep, and your horse can come too. There is riding and walking access to the Royal Forest of Dean, with its many miles of waymarked trails. The Wye Valley and the Cotswolds are both nearby. There's an organic restaurant locally.
davidandpennyhill@btopenworld.com   www.grovefarm-uk.com

CHELTENHAM *(Hotel)*

CHELTENHAM LAWN 207

5 Pittville Lawn
Cheltenham GL52 2BE
Tel: 01242 526638 MAP 14

Vegetarian Hotel
£35-£50 pppn

Award-winning vegetarian breakfasts include locally sourced organic products

A unique experience awaits you at our beautiful Regency hotel in the heart of Cheltenham. Pittville Park is literally feet away from the hotel and it's only a few minutes to the Pittville Pump Rooms. Close to the town centre, with its superb selection of independent restaurants, this is the perfect place to explore the delights of Cheltenham and the Cotswolds. Our award-winning vegetarian breakfasts include local organic ingredients, freshly cooked to order. For those who are interested we offer art courses and creative workshops to run alongside your stay. These courses are available throughout the year and are also open to non-residents. Course fees and details are available on request.
anthea.millier@cheltenhamlawn.com   www.cheltenhamlawn.co.uk

CIRENCESTER *(Camping)*

FOUR YURT ECO-CAMP 208

Abbey Home Farm
Cirencester GL7 5HF
Tel: 01285 640441 MAP 15

Yurts: sleep 18 in total
Mon-Thu £475, Fri-Mon £559, Fri-Fri £975

Organic Farm Shop and Café (open Tuesday-Saturday)

Soil Association

On the edge of a wood with lovely views. Suitable for holidays, friends or family gatherings, outdoor residential workshops, retreats. All cooking utensils and mattresses provided. Outside fireplace, gas ring and woodburner in the larger yurt. The four yurts sleep eighteen maximum. Bookings taken for a full week (Fri-Fri), three day weekends (Fri-Mon), four day week (Mon-Fri). Use our large green oak meeting room simultaneously for workshops. In the award-winning farm shop you'll find organic food – fresh meat, eggs, milk, vegetables and soft fruit – all grown on the farm, plus general groceries and organic bed and table linen. Shop, eat and drink in the garden or the café and watch the vegetables grow.
info@theorganicfarmshop.co.uk   www.theorganicfarmshop.co.uk/produce.htm

CIRENCESTER *(Camping)*

HUT BY THE POND 209

Abbey Home Farm
Cirencester GL7 5HF
Tel: 01285 640441   MAP 15

Hut by the Pond: sleeps 2, from £45 pn
Yurt: from £40 pn, Camping: adult £4, child £1

Organic Farm Shop and Café (open Tuesday
to Saturday)

Soil Association

The hut by the pond (adults only) is surrounded by trees at the water's edge, and is perfect for romance or retreat all year round. The yurt (sleeps five, available Apr-Oct) is in a woodland glade, twenty minutes walk from the farm shop. All stays minimum two nights. The green field campsite is in a lovely spot next to the old oak wood. Quiet space, trees, walks and wildlife abound. Our farm shop and café is open Tuesday to Saturday. Lunches in the café change daily, closely following progress in the garden. We always have a good selection of fresh salads, a fresh soup of the day and a main dish of the day. The shop sells everything organic you can imagine, including lots of organic produce from the farm itself.
info@theorganicfarmshop.co.uk   www.theorganicfarmshop.co.uk/produce.htm

CIRENCESTER *(S-C)*

LOWER WIGGOLD 210

Abbey Home Farm
Cirencester GL7 5HF
Tel: 01285 640441   MAP 15

Cottage: sleeps 4+ £395-£600 (Fri-Fri)
Short Breaks (available in low season)

Organic Farm Shop and Café (open Tuesday-Saturday)

Soil Association

A two bedroom semi-detached cottage with woodburner in the depths of the farm, far from the hustle and the bustle. Furnished with unusual old and reclaimed furniture from our travels. Beautiful organic bed linen to hire on request. Environmentally friendly cleaning products. Guests have sole use of a small south-facing garden to the side of the cottage, and the whole farm to roam. Twenty minutes walk away down our quiet lane is our award-winning 100% organic farm shop and café where you'll find organic food – fresh meat, eggs, milk, vegetables and soft fruit – all grown on the farm, plus general groceries and organic bed and table linen. Shop, eat and drink in the garden or the café. Watch the vegetables grow.
info@theorganicfarmshop.co.uk   www.theorganicfarmshop.co.uk/produce.htm

FRAMPTON ON SEVERN *(B&B)*

THE TRUE HEART 211

Frampton on Severn
Gloucester GL2 7ED
Tel: 01452 740504 · MAP 14

Bed and Breakfast
£37.50-£42.50 pppn

All organic, locally sourced and home-made where possible

A village pub until the 1960s, The True Heart has been transformed (ecologically and with at least 75% of hot water solar-powered) into a homely bed and breakfast. Wonderful views of the Gloucester & Sharpness Canal, the River Severn (both within walking distance) and across to the Forest of Dean. Traditional breakfasts. All ingredients of the finest quality. Everything is local, home-made and organic where possible. Organic home-made jam for sale. Frampton on Severn is a Conservation Area within the glorious Severn Vale. It has reputedly the longest village green in England, where fairs and events are held throughout the year. Great walking and cycling country (wellies and cycles can be provided).
veronica@thetrueheart.co.uk   www.thetrueheart.co.uk

HIGHLEADON *(S-C)*

HIGHLEADON COTTAGES 212

New House Farm
Highleadon GL18 1HQ
Tel: 01452 790209 · MAP 14

Cottages: sleep 2-6, £190-£450 pw
Touring caravans £10 pn

Organic free-range eggs are available from the farm

Organic Farmers & Growers

Three self-catering cottages on a 330-acre working organic farm. Situated in the Leadon Vale on the northern edge of the Forest of Dean, the three well-equipped units have been converted from a stable and a cartshed. Organic free-range eggs are available to buy from the farm. The farm abounds with wildlife. You can try your hand at badger watching or bird spotting. Buzzards regularly breed on the farm. The route of the now redundant Gloucester to Hereford canal runs through New House Farm. In places this has been reclaimed into the fields, but a long length is still evident and today used as a farm track. The cottages are ideally located for exploring the Malverns and the beautiful Cotswolds villages.
cjojan@aol.com

LOWER LYDBROOK *(S-C)*

GREENWAY COTTAGE   213

Stowfield Road
Lower Lydbrook GL17 9NJ
Tel: 01594 860075   MAP 14

Cottage: sleeps 4, £450 pw
B&B and Short Breaks on application

Award-winning restaurant on the same
estate, all local food

The cottage is set in 3 acres of Lydbrook House estate just yards from the River Wye, with superb views from all the windows. The restaurant is in the converted Malt House extension on the estate. The food policy at the restaurant is to use only local produce. All the meats, fish, vegetables, dairy products, breads and puddings are from ingredients sourced in the south-west. Wherever possible they are also organic. Almost all the vegetables we use are grown naturally in our own walled Georgian kitchen garden. We serve organic wines and locally made beers, cider and fruit juice. Visitors can also buy some of the fresh ingredients we use in the kitchen, such as organic vegetables, olives, olive oil and flour.
gardencafe@btinternet.com   www.gardencafe.co.uk

PAINSWICK *(B&B)*

ST ANNES   214

Gloucester Street
Painswick GL6 6QN
Tel: 01452 812879   MAP 14

Bed and Breakfast
From £32.50 pppn

Organic, local free-range, home-made
organic breads and jams

A Grade II listed, early 18th-century town house in the centre of beautiful Painswick. We offer one twin and two kingsize double-bedded rooms, all with *en suite* or private bathroom. Relax by the open fire with a delicious Aga-cooked English breakfast, which includes organic porridge and other organic cereals, organic milk and butter, local free-range meats and eggs, organic fair trade teas and coffee, home-made organic breads, and local or home-made organic jams and marmalade. Painswick offers several excellent options for dinner, all within just a few minutes walk. The village is on the scenic Cotswold Way. Walkers, cyclists and children are all welcome in our comfortable English family home.
greg.iris@btinternet.com   www.st-annes-painswick.co.uk

PUCKLECHURCH *(B&B)*

FERN COTTAGE B&B   215

188 Shortwood Hill
Pucklechurch BS16 9PG
Tel: 01179 374966   MAP 18

B&B, double *en suite* £75-£78 pn
Award-winning breakfast

Organic / local / home-grown / home-made /
seasonal British food

Award-winning Fern Cottage is a smallholding in South Gloucestershire set in two acres of greenbelt / conservation area, fifteen minutes from the World Heritage City of Bath. Guests are free to wander around our cottage garden or wildlife field. Our beautiful guest bedrooms are in the stable block with panoramic countryside views towards Bath and Bristol. All rooms are doubles with *en suites*. We are passionate about good quality food and use only organic / local / home-grown / home-made / seasonal and British food. Our delicious West Country breakfast has now won us many top awards, and we have also won prestigious awards for our commitment to the environment and wildlife.
sueandpete@ferncottagebedandbreakfast.co.uk   www.ferncottagebedandbreakfast.co.uk

BROUGHTON *(Camping)*

THE ANCHORAGE   216

Salisbury Road
Broughton SO20 8BX
Tel: 01794 301234   MAP 19

Camping, £5 pppn
WWOOF Host

Farm shop (fruit, vegetables, salads, eggs etc)

Soil Association

A permaculture farm of 3.5 acres producing fruit, vegetables, salads, poultry and eggs. Organic farm produce and other organic products are for sale. We aim to provide an alternative to globalisation by supplying quality local food to the local community whilst minimising negative impact on the environment. The campsite is small and quiet – the perfect place to relax and observe the English countryside. The farm is situated below rolling chalk hills – a rich habitat for flora and fauna. Nature reserves (including a Site of Special Scientific Interest), chalk streams, bridleways, footpaths and historic churches are all within walking distance. Broughton is known as one of the best kept villages in Hampshire.
tidtidy@googlemail.com

LYMINGTON *(S-C)*

WARBORNE FARM 217

1 Warborne Farm Cottages
Lymington SO41 5QD
Tel: 01590 610785 MAP 19

Farm Cottage: sleeps 5
£500-£900 pw

Award-winning vegetables and meat are for sale in the organic farm shop

Soil Association

Situated in the New Forest within the New Forest National Park you will find this delightful two / three bedroom semi-detached cottage that will sleep up to five people. Being part of Warborne Organic Farm gives the cottage an extra dimension, with fresh organic vegetables and meat for sale in the farm shop. With horses stables, sheep and chickens around and vegetables growing in front of the house, this cottage makes and excellent base for a family holiday. Being situated in the New Forest and only three miles from the Solent, this is an ideal place for people who love walking, cycling or sailing. You can even bring your own horse – there is room and accommodation is possible, and there are many beautiful rides around.
holiday@organicfarmcottage.com   www.organicfarmcottage.com

CANON FROME *(S-C)*

CANON FROME COURT 218

Canon Frome
Ledbury HR8 2TD
Tel: 0870 765 0714 MAP 14

Apartment: sleeps 1-5
£29-£42 pn, £175-£254 pw

Small shop sells some organic, wholefood, fair trade items

Georgian manor house overlooking a lake on a working farm in rural Herefordshire. The 40-acre community farm is farmed co-operatively and naturally (though not certified organic). Stock includes cattle, sheep, goats, poultry, bees. We have a 2-acre walled kitchen garden growing vegetables and soft fruits, a large greenhouse, two polytunnels and a couple of orchards. Our arable land provides wheat for our flour, potatoes and further vegetables. The apartment, a recently converted space with a large kitchen / sitting room, is in the stable block. Whilst we provide a good deal of organic food for ourselves, unfortunately we only occasionally have enough surplus to sell from the shop to guests.
playroom@canonfromecourt.org.uk   www.canonfromecourt.org.uk

CLYRO *(S-C)*

TONY'S CABIN 219

Clyro Hill Farm
Clyro HR3 6JU
Tel: 01497 820520 MAP 14

Holiday Cabin: sleeps 6-8
£480-£830 pw (contact re festival prices)

Organic produce (eggs, beef, lamb, turkey, fruit, vegetables, herbs) as available

Organic Farmers & Growers

Clyro Hill Farm overlooks the Wye Valley and the Brecon Beacons National Park. We produce home bred organic poultry, lamb and beef. Chickens are our biggest seller and we specialise in Christmas turkeys. We sell direct from the farm and can deliver our organic food anywhere in the UK. We're at the Brecon Farmers Market on the second Saturday of every month. Tony's Cabin is a modern, fully insulated chalet-style cabin with French windows onto balcony area, set in private grounds on the south-east side of our farm. Organic eggs, and an organic beef / lamb joint (or turkey at Christmas and New Year) are included in the rental. Organic fruit and vegetables and herbs as available. Farm walks are encouraged.
info@clyrohillfarm.co.uk   www.clyrohillfarm.co.uk

COLWALL *(Camping)*

CAVES FOLLY ECO-CAMPSITE 220

Caves Folly Nurseries
Evendine Lane WR13 6DU
Tel: 01684 540631 MAP 14

Campsite, £7 pppn
Tent and breakfast, £15 pppn

On-site shop selling organic fruit and vegetables, free-range eggs, etc

Soil Association

Have a quiet night camping in our meadow at just £7 pppn. The onsite nursery shop sells fresh organic fruit and vegetables and other local produce. Our wildflower meadow has secluded little areas to allow you to spend a tranquil night with nature. Old codgers (or other) camping with tent and breakfast provided, £15 pp. We provide a two man tent, sleeping mats, pillows, a cooker to cook your own breakfast (food supplied by us). You provide the sleeping bags. Please note that our eco-campsite is only available to anyone who turns up either on foot or by bicycle. We are lucky to have an excellent public transport network in Colwall, with regular buses and trains. The eco-campsite is ten minutes walk from the train station.
pleck@cavesfolly.com   www.cavesfolly.co.uk

COLWALL (S-C)

THE PLECK   221

Caves Folly Nurseries
Evendine Lane WR13 6DU
Tel: 01684 540631   MAP 14

Bungalow: sleeps 6, £90 pn, £175-£350 pw
B&B self-catering style £35 pppn

Our on-site shop sells organic fruit and
vegetables, free-range eggs, etc

Soil Association

Situated in the village of Colwall and in the Malvern Hills Area of Outstanding Natural Beauty, The Pleck is an idyllic place to stay. The two bedroom bungalow has all modern facilities with its own private garden and patio / barbecue area. Wormery and recycling facilities on-site. Our organic nursery is always full of flora and fauna to delight everyone. We also have a farm shop selling local and organic produce. Local facilities include five pubs, a bakery, shop, post office, fishing and horse riding. We have a brilliant network of footpaths, and the Malvern hills on our doorstep. Visitors can walk up the lane and collect Malvern spring water. Come and share this little haven with us. Ideal for groups, families or individuals. Everyone is welcome. pleck@cavesfolly.com   www.cavesfolly.co.uk

COUGHTON (B&B)

THE HILL HOUSE   222

Howle Hill
Coughton HR9 5ST
Tel: 01989 562033   MAP 14

Bed and Breakfast, £30-£40 pppn
Evening Meal, £10-£20 pp

Mostly organic, local (named sources) and
seasonal

The Hill House is family-run, laid back and relaxed. We adhere to the principles of permaculture. The food we offer guests is mostly organic, local (named sources) and seasonal. The bedrooms are wonderful, the sauna and cinema are popular, the outdoor spa is favourite. We have achieved Gold status with Wildlife Action, and have a Green Business Award from Herefordshire Nature Trust. Set in four acres of woodland at five hundred feet the views are spectacular – south over the beautiful Wye Valley to Wales, and west towards the ancient Forest of Dean. Wildlife abounds. We have our own happy hens, and ducks and pigs are planned in the future. Phase one of the willow maze is established to be completed this year. thehillhouse2000@hotmail.com   www.thehowlinghillhouse.com

EARDISLEY *(B&B)*

UPPER HOUSE BARN 223

Eardisley
Hereford HR3 6PW
Tel: 01544 327833 MAP 14

Bed and Breakfast
£70-£75 per room pn

Organic breakfasts, made with locally produced products where possible

This historic Grade-2-listed barn conversion, with its wealth of exposed beams, lies in Eardisley on the famous Black and White Villages Trail. Breakfast is taken in the charming dining room, overlooking the garden and patio. Fresh produce is all sourced within four miles and is locally produced and organic wherever possible. We use produce from our gardens in season and garden to organic principles. Organic milk and yogurt are from September Organic Dairy, two miles to the north, and home-produced organic sausages, bacon and eggs are from Oakchurch Farm Shop, four miles to the south. All bathroom consumables are organic and we use organic cleaning products where possible.
jill@upperhousebarn.co.uk   www.upperhousebarn.co.uk

GARWAY HILL *(S-C)*

THE SUMMER HOUSE 224

Garway House
Garway Hill HR2 8RT
Tel: 01981 580314 MAP 14

Cottage: sleeps 4
£236-£582 pw

Organic and locally sourced welcome pack, home-grown vegetables, eggs, home baking

This detached cottage is a family-run rural retreat with its own private garden area. Set in three acres of stunning rolling countryside belonging to Garway House, it is a haven for walkers, families or couples. The cottage has recently been renovated using locally sourced materials and solvent-free organic paint. You'll find comfy beds, quality bed linen, vintage Welsh wool blankets and organic toiletries. All tea and coffee provided is organic and fair trade. Guests have shared use of our heated outdoor pool. We use organic methods in all our gardens. The grounds contain a natural wildlife pond, a stream, a natural spring, and grassland with over a hundred and twenty species of native British plants including orchids.
thesummerhouse@garwayhouse.co.uk   www.garwayhouse.co.uk

HAY-ON-WYE *(B&B)*

LOWER HOUSE   225

Cusop Dingle
Hay-on-Wye HR3 5RQ
Tel: 01497 820773   MAP 14

Bed and Breakfast, from £40 pppn
Occasional suppers

Organic eggs, milk, butter, yogurt, bread, and
most fruit and vegetables

Three double rooms in a romantic old house set in its own secluded 7-acre valley, just over the border into Wales and a mile from the famous book town of Hay-on-Wye. Magical garden with topiary and luxuriant planting, traditional vegetable garden, wilderness, meadows and wildlife pond. Featured in several national magazines, in the Brecon Beacons National Park, on the Offa's Dyke Path, near the Black Mountains and close to the River Wye. Breakfasts are largely organic, locally sourced and fair trade where possible. We use rare breed additive-free pork and have good home-made vegetarian options. We have solar panels, recycle as much as possible and use environmentally friendly cleaning products and toiletries.
nicky.daw@btinternet.com   www.lowerhousegardenhay.co.uk

HAY-ON-WYE *(B&B)*

TY MYNYDD   226

Llanigon
Hay-on-Wye HR3 5RJ
Tel: 01497 821593   MAP 14

Mountain Farmhouse Bed and Breakfast
Double, £35-£40 pppn

Breakfast is made with our own organic
produce when available

Organic Farmers & Growers

Ty Mynydd is a small, family-run working organic farm situated amidst the beautiful Black Mountains of Wales. From your room you can enjoy breathtaking panoramic views and stunning sunsets. The mountains offer a dramatic changeable aura to the vast space surrounding us here at Ty Mynydd (Welsh for 'Mountain House'). We serve a delicious organic breakfast using organic produce from our farm, and have a fresh mountain spring supplying our water. We run our home and farm on a chemical-free basis using only eco-friendly renewable and recycled products. We are currently undertaking an environment scheme, which helps us provide and maintain natural habitats for wildlife and vegetation.
nikibarber@tymynydd.co.uk   www.tymynydd.co.uk

HAY-ON-WYE *(B&B)*

WINDLE PARK FARM 227

Hardwicke
Hay-on-Wye HR3 5HA
Tel: 01497 831666 MAP 14

Farmhouse Bed and Breakfast, £20 pppn
Camping, £3 pppn

Organic food served and available for sale

Biodynamic Agricultural Association

This working organic farm rears rare breed stock, producing Hereford beef, Portland lamb and Tamworth pork, all reared outside. Bed and Breakfast is in the 17th-century cottage farmhouse, with one double bedroom and one single bedroom. Water colour or pastel painting days can be arranged. There are walks in ancient oak woodlands for nature lovers. On the nearby hills the scenery is magnificent. On the western end of the village you can visit the site on which the ruins of Clifford Castle (built in the 11th-century) stand. Although Windle Park Farm is in a delightfully secluded position, it's only ten minutes from the famous 'book' town of Hay-on-Wye. This is an ideal area for both walking and touring.

HOARWITHY *(B&B)*

ASPEN HOUSE 228

Hoarwithy
Hereford HR2 6QP
Tel: 01432 840353 MAP 14

Bed and Breakfast, £35 pppn
Dinner, £25

Cosy dining room, real food, and the absolute best of local produce

Aspen House is much more than just a Bed and Breakfast. We are advocates of real food, and everything here is about the celebration of food. We stand against factory food and everything processed and, as members of the Slow Food movement, we champion artisan producers everywhere. We are tireless in our efforts to ensure that everything we prepare contains the finest ingredients sourced directly from local producers, growers and independent shops. Taste is paramount, and we cook everything from scratch using the best of what is available in season. Why not make food your focus, bring along some friends and savour the Aspen House private dining experience for yourselves?
sallyandrob@aspenhouse.net   www.aspenhouse.net

KIMBOLTON *(B&B)*

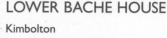

LOWER BACHE HOUSE 229

Kimbolton
Leominster HR6 0ER
Tel: 01568 750304   MAP 14

Country House, B&B from £39.50 pppn
Evening Meal, £19.50-£24.50

Home and locally grown organic produce,
outsourcing committed to fair trade principles

Nestling in a tiny tranquil valley, this award-winning 17th-century farmhouse is a haven for those seeking peace, quiet and beautiful countryside. We have three suites, each of which has its own bath or shower room and private sitting room. For our renowned cuisine we source from our own kitchen garden and, as far as possible, from local organic suppliers. Our wine list is totally organic. Lower Bache House is set in 14 acres of private nature reserve, lovingly nurtured to provide a diversity of habitats for wildlife, with traditional hay meadows, a stream, woodland, marshland, and gardens that complement the surrounding acres. Wildlife Action Gold Award and the Green Business Award from Herefordshire Nature Trust.
leslie.wiles@care4free.net   www.smoothhound.co.uk

○ ⑤

KINGSLAND *(S-C)*

THE BUZZARDS COTTAGES 230

Kingsland
Leominster HR6 9QE
Tel: 01568 708941   MAP 14

Cottages: sleep 2-6, £295-£495 pw
Camping, from £9 pn

Seasonal organic produce is available to buy

Biodynamic Agricultural Association

Our three self-contained cottages are spacious, comfortable, and attractively furnished with antique and modern furniture. The accommodation is equipped to a very high standard, and is located along a secluded country lane in the middle of 200 acres of farmland. Our award-winning, working organic and biodynamic smallholding produces fruit and vegetables. We have rare breed pigs, old breed sheep, hens and a goose. This practical and replicable lifestyle conserves, recycles and enriches. Seasonal organic produce is available to buy. There is an abundance of wildlife on our 16 acres of woodland, pasture land, orchards and ponds. Bed and Breakfast is occasionally available, from £35 per person per night.
holiday@thebuzzards.co.uk   www.thebuzzards.co.uk

LYONSHALL *(Hotel)*

PENRHOS MANOR HOUSE 231

Lyonshall
Kington HR5 3LH
Tel: 01544 230720   MAP 14

Weddings, Conferences, Retreats
Seminars, Meetings

Fundamental to the philosophy of Penrhos is
the use of fresh organic produce

Soil Association

A creative and inspiring setting for weddings, retreats, courses, team building events, business / corporate meetings. The group of medieval and Elizabethan timber frame buildings makes a large square around a courtyard with a pond in the centre. Surrounded by 5 acres of homestead it makes a unique venue for a company or individuals requiring space and total privacy away from day to day pressures, helping to build a team spirit which will enable the business to flourish. Penrhos is the perfect setting for a green wedding. Your wedding becomes a house party for your family and friends with preparations the day before, the ceremony, the banquet, a party in the evening and breakfast the next morning.
info@penrhos.com   hotel.penrhos.com

LYONSHALL *(S-C)*

SKYLARK AND BARN OWL 232

Penrhos Court
Lyonshall HR5 3LH
Tel: 01544 230720   MAP 14

Apartments: sleep 2-3
£250-£350 pw

Welcome organic food box on arrival,
organic shop

Soil Association

Skylark and Barn Owl are two self-catering apartments in part of an 18th-century thrashing barn at Penrhos Court. The apartments have been sympathetically converted and maintain many of the original features. They are on three levels, with the kitchen and dining room on the ground floor, lounge and bathroom on the second, and a balcony bedroom on the third. The old manor farm is in a peaceful setting with beautiful views. There is an organic shop on-site selling organic foods, superfoods, herbs and wines. Organic produce is also available locally. This is an excellent base from which to enjoy the untamed countryside of the borderlands. The area is delightful all year around, each season quite distinct.
info@penrhos.com   www.penrhos.co.uk

MICHAELCHURCH ESCLEY *(S-C)* HOLT FARM BARN 233

Rhydunnog Farm
Michaelchurch Escley HR2 0PS
Tel: 01747 828170   MAP 14

Converted Barn: sleeps 6-8, £581-£975 pw
Short Breaks (contact for prices)

Organic potatoes and vegetables grown on
the farm

Soil Association

Holt Farm lies in attractive, rolling hill country on the borders of Herefordshire and Monmouthshire. The farm has been in the family for generations, and is now farmed organically. The Grade II listed barn has been transformed into superb holiday accommodation, its original features contrasted with 21st-century luxury and comfort. An imaginative full height living and dining area is set between the two large glassed-in barn doors, with dining for up to twenty three guests for special occasions. The barn has retained a wealth of original features – oak beams, glazed high trusses, spiral staircases, stone paved floor, a woodburner. For outdoor dining the barn also has a large paved patio with a lovely outlook. enq@hideaways.co.uk   www.hideaways.co.uk

MICHAELCHURCH ESCLEY *(S-C)* HOLT FARM HOUSE 234

Rhydunnog Farm
Michaelchurch Escley HR2 0PS
Tel: 01747 828170   MAP 14

House: sleeps 6-7, £535-£897 pw
Short Breaks (contact for prices)

Organic potatoes and vegetables grown on
the farm

Soil Association

Dating from the 17th-century, this Grade II listed building has recently been completely restored, retaining many of its original features. Full of an atmosphere of age and history, Holt Farm House has flagstone floors, a bread oven, and a stone spiral stair. There is an enclosed garden around the house with an orchard beyond. Holt Farm lies in attractive, rolling hill country on the borders of Herefordshire and Monmouthshire, at the end of a long private track. It is a wonderful, peaceful location, and has immediate access to superb walks and rides. The organic farm is situated at 900 feet, and a footpath rises behind to a hill with direct access to Offa's Dyke and the Black Mountains, affording extensive views. enq@hideaways.co.uk   www.hideaways.co.uk

MICHAELCHURCH ESCLEY (S-C)   HOLT FARM STABLE   235

Rhydunnog Farm
Michaelchurch Escley HR2 0PS
Tel: 01747 828170   MAP 14

Cottage: sleeps 2-4, £331-£548 pw
Short Breaks (contact for prices)

Organic potatoes and vegetables grown on
the farm

Soil Association

Holt Farm Stable is a recent conversion, resulting in a very bright and cosy hideaway to very high specifications. Attached to Holt Farm House, with which it can be jointly booked, Holt Farm Stable has its entrance from the courtyard with its own patio, garden and barbecue. Holt Farm, which is organically run, lies in attractive rolling hill country on the borders of Herefordshire and Monmouthshire. At the end of a long private track, it is a wonderful, peaceful location, and has immediate access to superb walks and rides. Situated at nine hundred feet, a footpath rises behind to a hill with direct access to Offa's Dyke and the Black Mountains, affording extensive views.

enq@hideaways.co.uk   www.hideaways.co.uk

MICHAELCHURCH ESCLEY (S-C)   THE WAIN HOUSE   236

Rhydunnog Farm
Michaelchurch Escley HR2 0PS
Tel: 01747 828170   MAP 14

Cottage: sleeps 4, £413-£693 pw
Short Breaks (contact for prices)

Organic potatoes and vegetables grown on
the farm

Soil Association

Opposite and across from Holt Farm Stable, The Wain House has been expertly converted from the old cart shed. All the accommodation is on the ground floor and offers level access for disabled visitors. As well as having access to the communal courtyard shared with the other cottages, it has its own attractively landscaped garden area at the rear. Holt Farm lies in rolling hill country on the borders of Herefordshire and Monmouthshire, at the end of a long private track. It is a wonderful, peaceful location, and has immediate access to superb walks and rides. The organic farm is situated at 900 feet, and a footpath rises behind to a hill with direct access to Offa's Dyke and the Black Mountains.

enq@hideaways.co.uk   www.hideaways.co.uk

MONNINGTON-ON-WYE *(B&B)* DAIRY HOUSE FARM 237

Monnington-on-Wye
Hereford HR4 7NL
Tel: 01981 500143 MAP 14

Farmhouse Bed and Breakfast, £35 pppn
Evening Meal (by arrangement)

Breakfast includes organic and local produce

Soil Association

A secluded farmhouse located between Hereford and Hay-on-Wye. It is beautifully furnished with oak floors and beams. The spacious rooms have lovely open views across our working organic farm to the surrounding hills. Delicious Aga-cooked breakfasts with home-made preserves and organic / local produce. Packed lunches. Evening meals by prior arrangement. There are wonderful walks from the doorstep. Dairy House Farm is close to the river and adjacent to the Wye Valley Walk. Children, dogs and horses are welcome. The Three Rivers Ride crosses Herefordshire for sixty miles. The route passes nearby through beautiful countryside, and riders get the opportunity to cross the River Wye.
clare@dairyhousefarm.org www.dairyhousefarm.org

PEMBRIDGE *(B&B)* LEEN FARM 238

The Leen
Pembridge HR6 9HN
Tel: 01544 388305 MAP 14

Farmhouse Bed and Breakfast
£30 pppn

Organic home produce includes milk and seasonal vegetables

Organic Farmers & Growers

A 500-acre family farm, mentioned in the Domesday Book. Leen Farm is home to the oldest herd of Hereford cattle in the world, a wildlife haven with butterflies, trout pools and award-winning nature reserves, including a marshland Site of Special Scientific Interest. Farms do not come this old without very careful management over a long period, backed by a great knowledge of the countryside and its flora and fauna. The farm is an ideal base for naturalists, historians, painters and photographers, and there is wonderful walking around the beautiful black and white villages of the Welsh Marches. Organic home produce includes milk and seasonal vegetables. There are two good organic restaurants nearby.
tony@leenfarmorganics.co.uk www.leenfarmorganics.co.uk

PEMBRIDGE *(Camping)*

THE LEEN CARAVAN SITE 239

Leen Farm
Pembridge HR6 9HN
Tel: 01544 388305   MAP 14

Certified Location Caravan Site
£10 per caravan pn

Seasonal vegetables available to purchase

Organic Farmers & Growers

Exclusive five pitch 'Certified Location' situated beside the River Arrow. We have a one-acre, level, well drained, lawned site with well spaced pitches, all with electric hook-ups and water taps. The site is in the middle of our 500-acre organic farm, home to the oldest herd of Hereford cattle in the world, a wildlife haven with butterflies, trout pools and award-winning nature reserves, including a marshland Site of Special Scientific Interest. Miles of tracks for quiet enjoyment of the countryside. Leen Farm is only a mile from the medieval village of Pembridge with its pubs and shop. There are two good organic restaurants nearby. Wonderful walking around the beautiful black and white villages of the Welsh Marches.
tony@leenfarmorganics.co.uk   www.leenfarmorganics.co.uk

WINNAL *(S-C)*

THE OLD DAIRY 240

Winnal Common Farm
Winnal HR2 9BS
Tel: 01432 277283   MAP 14

Cottage: sleeps 5, £227-£382 pw
Short Breaks, 3 nights £127

Soil Association

A holiday cottage in the heart of the Herefordshire countryside. The Old Dairy is a tastefully converted milking parlour and dairy. It is situated in a beautiful rural location on a working organic farm and livery yard. We began the farm's organic conversion In 1999, and became fully organic in 2001. We keep a small herd of organic single sucklers, mostly Aberdeen Angus. Alongside this we run a livery yard and a small stud. Children will love playing football with our dogs, Ted and Pickles, and seeing the mares and foals, as well as the cows and calves. The nearby village of Allensmore has a shop and a pub. We are five miles from the ancient cathedral city of Hereford. Dogs welcome. Horses by arrangement.
info@winnal.co.uk   www.winnal.co.uk

WINSLOW *(S-C)*

WICTON FARM COTTAGE 241

Wicton Farm
Winslow HR7 4LR
Tel: 01747 828170   MAP 14

Cottage: sleeps 6-10
£810-£1361 pw

Organic farm produce is available to buy

Soil Association

Very spacious Victorian farm cottage deep in the Herefordshire countryside, a mile and a half from the nearest road. The wisteria clad cottage is situated on an organic dairy farm. We also produce organically reared pork, lamb, eggs, and vegetables for home consumption, emphasising the quality of good. Children can watch the cows being milked, help collect the farm eggs, or take part in one of the cookery workshops organised at the farm. There are lots of walks on the farm using the foot and bridlepaths, or the disused railway line which runs the length of the farm. The large half-acre garden has an above-the-ground swimming pool for the summer months. A games room in an old oast house has a pool table, darts, etc. enq@hideaways.co.uk   www.hideaways.co.uk/property.cfm/H185

CHALE *(B&B)*

BUTTERFLY PARAGLIDING 242

Sunacre, The Terrace
Chale PO38 2HL
Tel: 01983 731611   MAP 19

Bed and Breakfast, from £25 pppn
Camping, from £5 pppn

95% of the food and drink provided is organic

For a thrilling organic experience, Butterfly Paragliding run tandem flights, fun days and courses (from £65) all year round. Set up in 1994 as a centre of excellence on the Isle of Wight to provide paragliding tuition for all levels of pilot, from beginner to competition level. As a registered BHPA school we offer a relaxed and comprehensive service, and with our contacts overseas we are the original paragliding holiday company. Stay in our beautiful Edwardian house, with its unrivalled sea views, set in an acre of grounds in an Area of Outstanding Natural Beauty. 95% of the food and drink provided is organic. Any other food that you require can be bought from our organic shop. Green Island Tourism Gold Award. butterfly@paraglide.uk.com   www.paraglide.uk.com/organic_bed_and_breakfast.htm

CHALE *(B&B)*

GOTTEN MANOR 243

Gotten Lane
Chale PO38 2HQ
Tel: 01983 551368   MAP 19

Bed and Breakfast, £35-£48 pppn
(based on two people sharing a room)

Home-made, organic and local produce

The Old House offers unique accommodation. Dating back to the early 14th-century it is one of the few, and probably oldest, first floor houses on the Isle of Wight. The two huge guest rooms are both traditionally decorated, with lime washed walls and wooden floors. The cast iron baths within the rooms and Persian rugs create an old-fashioned opulence. A hearty breakfast, including home-made jams and marmalades, is made from organic and local produce and served in the old creamery. A private walled garden is reserved for guests. We also have three self-catering cottages. They are traditionally decorated with lime washed walls and every effort has been made to make them as ecologically acceptable as possible. organic@gottenmanor.co.uk   www.gottenmanor.co.uk

GODSHILL *(S-C)*

GODSHILL PARK COTTAGE 244

Shanklin Road
Godshill PO38 3JF
Tel: 01983 840781   MAP 19

Cottage: sleeps 4
£220-£875 pw

Produce from our own farm is available to buy

Soil Association

This detached two-bedroom cottage will appeal to those wanting peace and tranquillity in a luxurious environment. French windows open into the garden, where there is seating for al fresco dining. Breakfast can be taken in the Great Hall of the farmhouse by arrangement if wished. The cottage is on a working organic farm a quarter of a mile from the public road. We have a lake stocked with roach and carp for the exclusive use of our guests. The farm is situated within an Area of Outstanding Natural Beauty. The gently undulating farmland is crossed by footpaths, which lead down to the village and up to the downs. The village of Godshill is renowned for its pretty thatched cottages, 14th-century church and tea gardens. info@godshillparkfarm.uk.com   www.godshillparkfarm.uk.com/godshill_park_cottage.html

GODSHILL *(S-C)*

LAKE VIEW 245

Godshill Park Farm
Godshill PO38 3JF
Tel: 01983 840781

MAP 19

Cottage: sleeps 6
£220-£875 pw

Breakfast can be taken in the farmhouse by arrangement

Soil Association

Lake View is a recently refurbished wing of Godshill Park Farmhouse, providing spacious accommodation all on one level. French windows lead onto the south-facing patio, which looks out over the garden to the millpond and the woods and farmland beyond, stretching up to the Downs. Breakfast can be taken in the Great Hall of the farmhouse by arrangement if wished. Lake View is situated on our working organic farm, bordering Appuldurcombe estate in the heart of an Area of Outstanding Natural Beauty. Footpaths and bridleways cross the farm to the downs. The village of Godshill is renowned for its pretty thatched cottages, 14th-century church and tea gardens. Sandy beaches only a seven minute drive away.
info@godshillparkfarm.uk.com   www.godshillparkfarm.uk.com/self_catering.html

GODSHILL *(S-C)*

PHEASANT COTTAGE 246

Godshill Park Farm
Godshill PO38 3JF
Tel: 01983 840781

MAP 19

Cottage: sleeps 4-5
£180-£750 pw

Breakfast can be taken in the farmhouse by arrangement

Soil Association

A delightful detached cottage on a working organic farm bordering Appuldurcombe estate in the heart of an Area of Outstanding Natural Beauty. Breakfast can be taken in the Great Hall of Godshill Park farmhouse by arrangement if wished. The cottage looks out across the orchard to the nearby millpond, which has an abundance of waterfowl, and beyond to the downs. Godshill church can also be seen in the opposite direction. Our working organic farm has an Aberdeen Angus herd, rare breed sheep, arable fields, pasture, wooded hills and valleys. Footpaths and bridleways cross the farm. The picturesque village of Godshill is renowned for its pretty thatched cottages, 14th-century church and tea gardens.
info@godshillparkfarm.uk.com   www.godshillparkfarm.uk.com/self_catering.html

CRUNDALE (S-C)

RIPPLE FARM   247

Crundale
Canterbury CT4 7EB
Tel: 01227 730748   MAP 20

Farmhouse Accommodation: sleeps 5
£270-£475 pw

Organic vegetable box on Thursdays – small,
medium, large (order in advance)

Soil Association

An established horticultural farm specialising in organic produce, situated between the villages of Godmersham and Crundale. Spacious fully self-contained accommodation is provided in one half of the owner's Grade II listed 16th-century timber-framed farmhouse. Three rooms downstairs and two large timbered bedrooms, each with a gallery, overlook fields and across the valley to the North Downs. Guests are welcome to use the garden and may also use the owner's outdoor swimming pool by arrangement. A farmers' market is held in the nearby attractive village of Wye every alternate Saturday. Excellent walking and riding country. Several beaches are less than half an hour away.
ripplefarmhols@aol.com

OLD WIVES LEES (B&B)

POND COTTAGE   248

Selling Road
Old Wives Lees CT4 8BD
Tel: 01227 751828   MAP 20

Bed and Breakfast
£95 pn for two

90% organic and / or locally produced,
home-grown free-range eggs

A stylish, cool, quirky retreat in rural Kent. Exclusive and private. We offer our guests one luxurious spacious ground floor room. Step outside and wander around. There are many varieties of fruit tree, and a large natural pond with a rowing boat. Special emphasis is placed on organic and locally produced food. Home-grown free-range eggs and herbs fresh from our own garden. All other fresh produce will be from the Goods Shed in Canterbury – a permanent farmers' market. Even your welcome treats will be organic, including the goodies, teas and coffees in your room. We aim to be as environmentally friendly as possible in all other ways. An evening meal can be prepared for you (please request in advance).
jude@pondstays.com   www.pondstays.com

SUTTON *(B&B)*

ALE FARM   249

Vale Road
Sutton CT15 5DH
Tel: 01304 373374   MAP 20

Self-Contained B&B, £65 room pn
Caravan: sleeps 7, £250-£450 pw

All home-grown products are grown to an
organic standard

Bed and Breakfast in a charming self-contained annex with a spacious double bedroom, a bathroom, somewhere to make tea or coffee – and your own front door. Our 4-acre farm is home to Saddleback pigs grown for bacon and sausages and a large flock of hens and ducks for eggs. In our large greenhouse we have used organic seeds and organic compost to grow a wide range of vegetables, fruits, salads and herbs. Our bumper crop of tomatoes and cucumbers have benefited enormously from the worm composters. We make our own chutneys, jams, jellies and relishes from our produce. Ale Farm is set on the edge of the village of Sutton-by-Dover, ten minutes from the Port of Dover and twenty from the Channel Tunnel. rachel@alefarm.com   www.alefarm.co.uk

WINGHAM *(S-C)*

RETREAT AT WITHERDENS 250

Popsal Lane
Wingham CT3 1AT
Tel: 01227 720543   MAP 20

Cottage: sleeps 4
£35-£100 pppn

Delicious home-cooked food sourced locally
(around 90% organic)

The Retreat is situated in the grounds of 16th-century Witherdens Hall. Offering a relaxing break in tranquil surroundings, the cottage has two double bedrooms, bathroom, kitchen and sitting room for guests' exclusive use. It is beautifully furnished and fitted out, with Egyptian cotton sheets, jacuzzi bath, fluffy towelling robes and a magnet and crystal healing bed with Tempur mattress for a fabulous night's sleep. Organic food and beverages can be served to order using produce from the garden and the local organic farm shop, or guests can prepare food themselves. Treatments available in the privacy and comfort of The Retreat, from acupuncture and reiki to facials (Organic Pharmacy) and hairdressing. louisecox@fusemail.com   www.witherdenshall.co.uk

WINGHAM *(B&B)*

TWITHAM COURT 251

Staple Road
Wingham CT3 1LP
Tel: 01227 720265   MAP 20

Bed and Breakfast
£40-£55 pppn

Organic and locally produced breakfast (95% organic)

A traditional yet modern bed and breakfast. Nestled in the Kent countryside, Twitham Court Farm is a collection of buildings of architectural and historical importance, many are Grade II listed. The farmhouse dates from 1700s and was formerly part of the Goodnestone Park Estate. The house and grounds have recently been refurbished to provide modern accommodation. We are an environmentally-aware household with organic cotton bedding and towels, organic toiletries, organic teas and coffees in the rooms, and we provide an organic and locally sourced (where possible) breakfast. The rooms are a breath of fresh air. Beautifully decorated yet individual. Wonderful detail with a fantastic finish. Special but homely.
info@twitham.com   www.twitham.com

BASHALL EAVES *(S-C)*

COACH HOUSE 252

Clough Bottom Farm
Bashall Eaves BB7 3NA
Tel: 01254 826285   MAP 9

Cottage: sleeps 4
£405-£635 pw

Organic beef (subject to availability), pick your own organic vegetables in season

Organic Farmers & Growers

A Grade II listed coach house, lovingly-restored to retain its original features, unique charm and character. In a secluded setting with its own private lane running parallel to the stream, the approach is a welcoming sight with the orchard and vegetable garden just beyond. Pre-order one of our home-cooked ready-meals and have a wholesome meal ready to enjoy by the time you've unpacked. We can also supply a Lancashire breakfast hamper of organic and local produce, as well as home-produced organic beef and complimentary 'pick your own' organic vegetables (both subject to availability). The cottage is situated on an organic and conservation-minded hill farm in the idyllic and relaxing environment of the Forest of Bowland.
info@cloughbottom.co.uk   www.cloughbottom.co.uk/cottages

BASHALL EAVES *(S-C)*

SADDLE BARN 253

Clough Bottom Farm
Bashall Eaves BB7 3NA
Tel: 01254 826285   MAP 9

Cottage: sleeps 6
£490-£820 pw

Organic beef (subject to availability), pick
your own organic vegetables in season

Organic Farmers & Growers

A three bedroom property in an Area of Outstanding Natural Beauty in the heart of the beautiful Ribble Valley. Lovingly converted, it retains its natural country style charm. French doors lead to a private patio area overlooking fields and a stream. Pre-order one of our home-cooked ready-meals and have a wholesome meal ready to enjoy by the time you've unpacked. We can also supply a Lancashire breakfast hamper of organic and local produce, as well as home-produced organic beef and complimentary pick your own organic vegetables (both subject to availability). Situated on an organic farm in the idyllic and relaxing Forest of Bowland, the cottage is ideal for walking locally or for touring the Lakes and Dales.
info@cloughbottom.co.uk   www.cloughbottom.co.uk/cottages

BASHALL EAVES *(S-C)*

WOODCUTTER'S COTTAGE 254

Clough Bottom Farm
Bashall Eaves BB7 3NA
Tel: 01254 826285   MAP 9

Cottage: sleeps 4
£365-£595 pw

Organic beef (subject to availability), pick
your own organic vegetables in season

Organic Farmers & Growers

A lovingly-converted property in an Area of Outstanding Natural Beauty in the heart of the beautiful Ribble Valley. Dating back to the 16th-century, the cottage has been thoughtfully decorated to maintain its cosy and quaint feel. A private patio area overlooks fields and a stream. Pre-order one of our home-cooked ready-meals and have a wholesome meal ready to enjoy by the time you've unpacked. We can also supply a Lancashire breakfast hamper of organic and local produce, as well as home-produced organic beef and complimentary pick your own organic vegetables (both subject to availability). Situated on an organic farm in the idyllic and relaxing Forest of Bowland, the cottage is ideal for walking locally or for touring the Lakes and Dales.
info@cloughbottom.co.uk   www.cloughbottom.co.uk/cottages

BOLTON LE SANDS *(Camping)*

RED BANK FARM CAMPSITE 255

The Shore
Bolton Le Sands LA5 8JR
Tel: 01524 824981   MAP 9

Campsite (open Easter to October)
Adult £3.50 pn, Child £1.50, Hook-up £2.50

Our own organic produce is used in the café
and is also for sale

Soil Association

Red Bank Farm Campsite is a small family-run camping and motorhome site on a working organic farm in Bolton Le Sands. Situated on the shores of Morecambe Bay (a SSSI), it has stunning views of the Lakeland Hills. The on-site pets corner and beachside location make it ideal for young and old alike. After visiting pets corner you can ask to watch the cows being milked. In 2008 we opened our new café / tearoom, where we endeavour to source as much organic produce as possible. Our own meat (organic beef and organically reared salt marsh lamb) is used in the meals in the café and is also for sale for you to barbecue or take home. For those who enjoy walking, the Lancashire Coastal Way runs right through the farm.
archer_mark@lycos.co.uk   www.redbankfarm.co.uk

ROEBURNDALE WEST *(S-C)*

ROEBURNDALE BARN   256

Backsbottom Farm
Roeburndale West LA2 9LL
Tel: 015242 22214   MAP 9

Camping Barn: sleeps 16, £210 pw
£100 pwend, £40 pn

There is a small shop selling organic
preserves from the farm

Soil Association

The barn is situated in a secluded meadow in a beautiful steeply-wooded valley in North Lancashire, home to a small flock of Lleyn sheep, wild flowers and wildlife. Backsbottom Farm is really better described as a nature reserve. It has always been traditionally farmed in the past and now has Higher Level Organic Stewardship. Traditional apple varieties and organic fruit produce a small range of preserves. Wind turbines, solar energy and wood stoves provide power and heat. Other self-catering options are available in the study centre (10 bunks) and a yurt (sleeping 6), both just a short walk from the farm buildings. The study centre also promotes sustainable living by running courses, including Permaculture courses.
roeburndalecampingbarn@phonecoop.coop   www.middlewood.org.uk

WALCOTE *(B&B)*

HIGH HOUSE 257

Lutterworth Road
Walcote LE17 4JW
Tel: 01455 552413 MAP 15

Bed and Breakfast
Double, £70 pn

At least 60% organic food

Welcome to our Georgian home. We have two spacious double rooms available with private bath and shower room (robes provided). There is a lounge for guests' use and rooms have wireless internet access. For breakfast, we use organic produce wherever possible and all the bread is home-made. Special diets catered for, just ring us beforehand to discuss your requirements. The area is good for both cycling and walking and we can recommend several short circuits (including pub stops). Lovely organic shop (2 miles) in an old converted barn in the village of Cotesbach. Ryton Organic Gardens (23 miles). Please mention 'Organic Places to Stay' when booking for a 5% discount on the bed and breakfast price.
info@highhousebnb.co.uk   www.highhousebnb.co.uk

MARTIN *(B&B)*

CHAPLIN HOUSE 258

92 High Street
Martin LN4 3QT
Tel: 01526 378795 MAP 15

Bed and Breakfast, £32.50-£42.50 pppn
Special occasions meal (book in advance)

Most of our produce is locally sourced, free-range and organic

Chaplin House is situated in the heart of the Lincolnshire countryside. Our barn conversion has three *en suite* rooms together with a guests' lounge and a decked area for guests to enjoy. We have one guest room in the house. Enjoy tea with our home-made cake on arrival, relax in our peaceful garden, unwind with a book. We offer a range of options for breakfast. Most of our produce is locally sourced, free-range and organic. Sample honey from our own bee hives. Packed lunches on request. Winner, Tastes of Lincolnshire Accommodation Award. Winner, Lincolnshire Tourism's Accommodation of the Year Star Award. Gold Award, Guest Accommodation in the East Midlands Enjoy England Excellence Awards 2008.
info@chaplin-house.co.uk   www.chaplin-house.co.uk

NORTH SOMERCOTES *(B&B)* TITHE FARM   259

Church End
North Somercotes LN11 7PZ
Tel: 01507 358413   MAP 10

Farmhouse Bed and Breakfast, £27.50 pppn
Evening Meal (by arrangement)

Good quality food, mostly organic (around 80%) and local where possible

18th-century farmhouse set in 6 acres of naturally cultivated gardens and meadowland in a peaceful rural location near Louth and the Lincolnshire coast. We provide good quality food, mostly organic and local where possible, with home-made jam and freshly picked fruit in season. As well as accommodation in the house we also have a yurt, complete with a double futon and a woodstove (see separate listing). There's plenty of wildlife in the garden – rabbits, hedgehogs, water voles, shrews, voles, mice, frogs, toads and newts are resident – badgers, foxes, hares and squirrels visit. Tithe Farm is a great place to go bird-watching from. For several miles north and south of us the coast is a nature reserve.
biff@biffvernon.freeserve.co.uk   www.biffvernon.freeserve.co.uk

NORTH SOMERCOTES *(Camping)* TITHE FARM YURT   260

Church End
North Somercotes LN11 7PZ
Tel: 01507 358413   MAP 16

Yurt: sleeps 2-4, £27.50 pppn
Breakfast included in the price

Good quality food, mostly organic (around 80%) and local where possible

Our yurt is 16 feet in diameter and 9 feet high in the middle, made of about 150 willow rods and a lot of canvas. There's a transparent piece at the top to let the sunshine, or moonlight, in. The floor is solid timber and there's a woodstove, which gets the place warm in no time. Electricity is supplied but the candle lanterns are more fun. Surrounded by trees, flowers and vegetables, the yurt is set in our six-acre garden. Outside is the yurt's own lawn with picnic table. Round the back is an open air bathroom. Breakfast in the house is included in the price of your stay. For several miles north and south of us the coast is a nature reserve. We are close to the seal breeding colony at Donna Nook.
biff@biffvernon.freeserve.co.uk   www.biffvernon.freeserve.co.uk

OLD LEAKE *(S-C)*

ECO-LODGE 261

Rose Cottage
Station Road PE22 9RF
Tel: 01205 870062, 01205 871396   MAP 16

Eco Lodge: sleeps 4, £340 pw + £5 pp
Mon-Fri or Fri-Mon £170 + £5 pp

Local organic fruit and vegetables, organic
dairy produce

The eco-lodge is built from wood grown and harvested in Lincolnshire. The energy sources are wind and solar power and a large wood-burning range. It is set in 8 acres of naturally managed wood and meadowland with many native tree species. Organic produce is available to order. Situated in fenland six miles from the sea marshes, the lodge is also close to the Wolds. Beautiful walking and cycling country, interspersed with occasional country pubs. For more relaxation, Shiatsu massage and Japanese body-work workshops are available (see our website for more information). Visitors' comments: a wonderful break from the real world, freedom for children, magic moments, great hospitality, somewhere precious.
drgclarke@btinternet.com   www.internationalbusinessschool.net/ecolodge.htm

SKIDBROOKE *(B&B)*

CLODDYGATE FARM 262

Owes Lane
Skidbrooke LN11 7DE
Tel: 01507 358679   MAP 16

Bed and Breakfast, double £55 pn
A single supplement may be charged

Almost all organic, local where possible plus
fair trade or home-grown

Cloddygate Farm is a cosy and welcoming 19th-century farmhouse on the Lincolnshire coast, near the historic market town of Louth. Enjoy a comfortable guest room with far reaching rural views. We are passionate about good, seasonal, local food and prepare full English or vegetarian breakfasts using almost all organic ingredients. Special diets and delicious evening meals by arrangement. Close by the farm are coastal nature reserves with marsh orchids and samphire, full of wild birds and visited by Atlantic grey seals in winter. We have lots of room for storing bikes and safe off road parking. The quiet lanes and footpaths and miles of wild coastline are ideal for wildlife photography, walking, cycling, or just relaxing.
cloddygatefarm@tiscali.co.uk   myweb.tiscali.co.uk/cloddygatefarm

PRIMROSE HILL *(S-C)* FLAT A 263

192 Regent's Park Road
Primrose Hill NW1 8XP
Tel: 020 7722 7139 MAP 19

Double Room, £85-£95 per room pn
Flat: sleeps 4, £170-£190 pn

Generous organic breakfast (self-service) by
arrangement, £10 pp

Rent a room in this charming split-level two bedroom apartment in the heart of lovely Primrose Hill 'village'. Beds can be made up as a double or a twin and have either premier organic or club class mattresses. You will have the use of a fully equipped kitchen / living room. Alternatively you can rent both rooms as a self-contained flat. Bedrooms are *en suite* and serviced daily. On arrival guests receive a generous bowl of organic fresh fruit, organic snacks and fresh fair trade flowers where possible. Selection of organic teas, coffee and biscuits available from the kitchen at all times. Close to transport and walking distance to the West End. The ideal location for all that London has to offer. Prior booking essential.
info@primrosehill-london.co.uk   www.primrosehill-london.co.uk

PRIMROSE HILL *(S-C)* FLAT B 264

192 Regent's Park Road
Primrose Hill NW1 8XP
Tel: 020 7722 7139 MAP 19

Flat: sleeps 2-4
£130-£150 pn

Generous organic breakfast (self-service) by
arrangement, £10 pp

Flat B is a luxury one bedroom, self-contained, serviced apartment on the first floor of 192 Regent's Park Road. The apartment has been designed and refurbished to a very high standard, with the environment in mind. We have used eco-paints, insulated with Welsh wool, and used natural products where possible. We subscribe to Good Energy, the only UK supplier of 100% renewable electricity. We supply eco and organic soaps / shower shampoos, etc. A generous bowl of organic fruit, snacks, teas, coffee, herbal drinks and fresh flowers greet all guests on arrival. The flat is a stylish, modern oasis in the heart of the Primrose Hill village. Regent's Park Road is close to transport, making it the ideal London location.
info@primrosehill-london.co.uk   www.primrosehill-london.co.uk

BARNHAM BROOM *(B&B)*

THE FOXBURGH  265

PO Box 19
Barnham Broom NR9 4BZ
Tel: 01603 759791   MAP 16

Bed and Breakfast, £75-£95 pn
Natural Health and Wellness Centre

Breakfast is organic

Demeter

Country home within a secluded estate only eight miles south-west of Norwich. We offer an informal atmosphere for only a small number of guests, who are welcomed in comfortable *en suite* rooms in modern, country house style. In line with the holistic and biodynamic principles we practice and believe in, the water supply is fully energised with Grander Water Technology – one of the few properties in the country with this facility. In addition to offering bed and breakfast accommodation we are also an Holistic Therapies Centre, providing a wide range of holistic therapies. The four acres of our biodynamically managed garden provide many plants that are used in herbalism and flower remedies.
isabelle@foxburgh.co.uk   www.foxburgh.co.uk

BIRCHAM *(B&B)*

BAGTHORPE HALL 266

Bagthorpe
Nr Bircham PE31 6QY
Tel: 01485 578528   MAP 16

Bed and Breakfast
Double £75 pn, Single £45

Includes organic produce from the family farm

Soil Association

Bagthorpe Hall is situated in the countryside of North Norfolk, close to Sandringham and Burnham Market. One twin with own bathroom, one double with shower and one with *en suite*, plus a family room. We are devoted to organic farming and gardening. Breakfast includes organic produce from the family farm. Bagthorpe Hall is a large, elegant house offering a luxurious stay. Wonderful colours, good beds, and a fascinating and beautiful mural in the hall chronicling the family history. The house is surrounded by 50 acres of parkland, woodland and gardens, which are peaceful, quiet and full of birdlife. Many of the trees are over 150 years old. There is a lovely snowdrop walk in February. The coast is a fifteen minute drive.
enquiries@bagthorpehall.co.uk   www.bagthorpehall.co.uk

DEOPHAM *(S-C)*

STALLAND FARM   267

The Stalland
Deopham NR18 9ED
Tel: 01953 850873   MAP 16

Converted Stables: sleeps 2
£20 pppn

Naturally grown produce from our
smallholding

Simple but comfortable accommodation in a self-contained converted stables. It sleeps two in the sleeping loft and / or two on the futon sofa bed. Heating is by woodstove or electric. We run a 5-acre smallholding with bees, chickens and extensive vegetable gardens. Vegetables from the smallholding are available for guests to buy. Meals and bed and breakfast (vegetarian) in the house available by arrangement. Stalland Farm is in a very quiet rural situation. The surrounding area is good walking and cycling country (bikes available). For those who would like to travel here by train and bring their bikes with them, the nearest train station is four miles away at Wymondham. The historic city of Norwich is fifteen miles away.
stv_mhny@yahoo.co.uk

DRAYTON *(B&B)*

WEST LODGE   268

24 Fakenham Road
Drayton NR8 6PR
Tel: 01603 861191   MAP 16

Boutique Accommodation, £75-£125 room pn
Small Conference Centre

Exclusively vegetarian, all food organic and
fair trade where possible

West Lodge is a unique venue, an intimate and friendly large Victorian house with a light, airy, contemporary feel. It is 4-star rated with complimentary WiFi throughout. We are an exclusively vegetarian guest house and small conference centre, ideal for retreats, workshops and day / week courses. We use as much organic / local / fair trade produce as possible, and are happy to cater for most dietary requirements (providing they don't involve meat). Visit us as a guest for a single night's stay, or have exclusive occupancy of the house for reunions or get-togethers, where you create the atmosphere of your choice, or perhaps hire one of our rooms for workshops. Our gardens offer places to find solitude and peace.
info@vegetarian-bedandbreakfast-norwich.co.uk www.vegetarian-bedandbreakfast-norwich.co.uk

SWAFFHAM *(Hotel)*

STRATTONS HOTEL 269

4 Ash Close
Swaffham PE37 7NH
Tel: 01760 723845 MAP 16

Boutique Hotel, double B&B £150-£225 pn
Restaurant

Award-winning restaurant serves organic
and locally sourced produce

An art boutique hotel, hidden away in its own peaceful courtyard a minute's walk from the marketplace in Swaffham. Ten individual rooms. Environmentally sensitive restoration using environmental solutions, such as lambswool insulation and environmental paint systems. Award-winning restaurant, recently scooping the Considerate Hoteliers Food Award for sourcing locally, ethically and reducing air miles. Menus change daily sourcing organic local produce to create contemporary dishes. Strattons was the first hotel in the UK to win the prestigious Queen's Award for Outstanding Environmental Performance, and has since picked up a handful of awards for its environmental ethos, interiors and food.
enquiries@strattonshotel.com   www.strattonshotel.com

BARDON MILL *(S-C)*

FELBRIDGE COTTAGE 270

Gibbs Hill Farm
Bardon Mill NE47 7AP
Tel: 01434 344030 MAP 9

Cottage: sleeps 2-4
£200-£350 pw

Organic free-range eggs, organic tomatoes,
honey

Organic Farmers & Growers

Felbridge Cottage is a most attractive, surprisingly spacious two storey building on a traditional working hill farm dating back to before the 17th-century. The ground floor has a large living area incorporating the kitchen, dining area and a sitting area with a welcoming log burning stove set into the large stone-built fireplace. A stairway leads up to the bedroom and bathroom. The porchway faces west towards Felbrook. Natural spring water. Organic produce is available locally. There is access, via Gibbs Hill land, to a specially created boardwalk and bird-watching hide on the nearby Greenlee Lough nature reserve. Walk the best bits of the new Hadrian's Wall path from your own doorstep.
val@gibbshillfarm.co.uk   www.gibbshillfarm.co.uk/felbridge.htm

BARDON MILL *(S-C)*

FELBROOK COTTAGE   271

Gibbs Hill Farm
Bardon Mill NE47 7AP
Tel: 01434 344030   MAP 9

Cottage: sleeps 6
£250-£600 pw

Organic free-range eggs, organic tomatoes, honey

Organic Farmers & Growers

Converted from a stable on a traditional working hill farm. Felbrook has a spacious living room in which the original wooden beams have been left exposed complementing the huge stone fireplace and its wood-burning stove. Off this room is the large kitchen / dining area with original beams and stone fireplace. Organic produce is available locally. Natural spring water. A door to the rear from the sitting room leads to a patio with barbecue area and access to the farmland behind. Towards the northern boundary of Gibbs Hill Farm there is an ancient stone circle, thought to be an early Bronze Age burial site. This site is worth the walk, not only for its historical interest, but also for the views it offers.
val@gibbshillfarm.co.uk   www.gibbshillfarm.co.uk/felbrook.htm

BARDON MILL *(S-C)*

FELSTREAM   272

Gibbs Hill Farm
Bardon Mill NE47 7AP
Tel: 01434 344030   MAP 9

Cottage: sleeps 4
£330-£520 pw

Organic free-range eggs, organic tomatoes, honey

Organic Farmers & Growers

Newly refurbished to an extremely high standard, the cottage is furnished with locally made pine furniture. There's a spacious cosy living / dining area with a welcoming log-burning stove set into the large stone-built fireplace. French windows open onto a large patio with panoramic views southwards towards a lake, the Roman Wall and distant hills. At one end of this patio is a barbecue for relaxed summer evenings. Towards the northern boundary of the farm is an ancient stone circle. This site is worth the walk, not only for it's historical interest, but also for the views it offers. There is access from our land to a specially created boardwalk and bird watching hide on nearby Greenlee Lough nature reserve.
val@gibbshillfarm.co.uk   www.gibbshillfarm.co.uk/felstream.htm

BARDON MILL *(B&B)*

GIBBS HILL FARM B&B 273

Bardon Mill
Hexham NE47 7AP
Tel: 01434 344030 MAP 9

Farmhouse Bed and Breakfast, £30-£35 pppn
Packed lunches can be provided

Home or local produce, much of it
organically produced

Organic Farmers & Growers

Gibbs Hill is a traditional working organic hill farm dating back to before the 17th-century. The present owner's are the fourth generation to farm here. The farm carries fifty suckler cows and calves and over five hundred Swaledale cross ewes and lambs. There is also a small fold of Highland cattle. Integration into the Countryside Commission's Farm Stewardship Scheme and conversion under their DEFRA Organic Farming Scheme is indicative of the deep commitment that the family have to the countryside and environmental care. Within the farm's land there are two 50-acre areas of ancient peat bog, which have been designated SSSI and handed to the Northumberland National Park for their management.
val@gibbshillfarm.co.uk   www.gibbshillfarm.co.uk/bed-breakfast.htm

BARDON MILL *(S-C)*

GIBBS HILL HOSTEL 274

Gibbs Hill Farm
Bardon Mill NE47 7AP
Tel: 01434 344030 MAP 9

Hostel: sleeps up to 18
£12 pppn

Organic free-range eggs, organic tomatoes, honey

Organic Farmers & Growers

Converted from an old hay barn at Gibbs Hill Farm, the hostel accommodates up to eighteen people in three rooms. The three rooms each have six bunks. The hostel is centrally heated throughout, and to reduce energy consumption the barn is insulated with special panels. Low energy light bulbs are used throughout. To the rear of the hostel is a large decking area where guests may enjoy the evening sun, and also access the stables by the wooden staircase. Basic items of food may be purchased. Guests may order (in the evening for the next day) a continental breakfast (£4 pp) and packed lunches (£5 pp) from the farmhouse. Evening meals are available in the farmhouse (from £12.50 pp). Organic produce available locally.
val@gibbshillfarm.co.uk   www.gibbshillfarm.co.uk/bunkhouses.htm

BERWICK UPON TWEED (B&B)

GRANARY GUEST HOUSE 275

11 Bridge Street
Berwick upon Tweed TD15 1ES
Tel: 01289 304403   MAP 10

Bed and Breakfast, £45-£85 pppn
Packed Lunches (by arrangement)

We use locally sourced and produced
organic foods as much as possible

The Granary is an elegantly restored Georgian town house providing luxury 5-star bed and breakfast. Our aim is to make our guests as comfortable as we can and to provide the finest breakfast using locally sourced organic ingredients. All our meat, eggs and honey are from local farms. Fish is from Eyemouth merchants. Fruit, vegetables and all our baking ingredients are from our local Green Shop. Teas, coffees and breakfast juices are all organic. The toiletries in the *en suite* bathrooms are from Willow Organics. Bridge Street is in the oldest part of Berwick upon Tweed and retains many original Victorian shopfronts. Many restaurants and pubs are within easy reach and the River Tweed is just a stone's throw away.
pamwaddell@btinternet.com   www.granaryguesthouse.co.uk

EDLINGHAM (S-C)

GARDEN COTTAGE 276

Lumbylaw Farm
Edlingham NE66 2BW
Tel: 01665 574277   MAP 10

Cottage: sleeps 2
£205-£460 pw

Booklet with information on where to buy
local produce

Organic Farmers & Growers

Surround yourself with the peaceful, beautiful countryside of Lumbylaw. Our working organic farm specialises in pedigree Lleyn sheep and our prize-winning herd of South Devon cattle. Garden Cottage is centrally heated with one double bedroom and no steps. Set amidst the picturesque Cheviot and Simonside Hills it has its own garden and breathtaking views. You can walk in the grounds, which feature medieval Edlingham Castle and a five-arch Victorian viaduct over the valley. The cottage is adjacent to the hamlet of Edlingham and is the perfect location to explore the delights of Northumberland, both coastal and inland. Booklet for guests in the cottage, with information on where to buy local produce.
holidays@lumbylaw.co.uk   www.lumbylaw.co.uk

EDLINGHAM *(S-C)*

LUMBYLAW COTTAGE 277

Lumbylaw Farm
Edlingham NE66 2BW
Tel: 01665 574277   MAP 10

Cottage: sleeps 6
£308-£749 pw

Booklet with information on where to buy
local produce

Organic Farmers & Growers

Surround yourself with the peaceful, beautiful countryside of Lumbylaw. Our working organic farm specialises in pedigree Lleyn sheep and our prize-winning herd of South Devon cattle. Lumbylaw Cottage is centrally heated with three bedrooms, two bathrooms and no steps. Set amidst the picturesque Cheviot and Simonside Hills it has its own garden and breathtaking views. You can walk in the grounds, which feature medieval Edlingham Castle and a five-arch Victorian viaduct over the valley. The cottage is adjacent to the hamlet of Edlingham and is the perfect location to explore the delights of Northumberland, both coastal and inland. Booklet for guests with information on where to buy local produce.
holidays@lumbylaw.co.uk   www.lumbylaw.co.uk

HADRIAN'S WALL *(B&B)*

HOLMHEAD GUEST HOUSE 278

Hadrian's Wall
Greenhead CA8 7HY
Tel: 016977 47402   MAP 9

Bed and Breakfast, from £36-£40 pppn
Evening Meal, £28 pppn

40%-80% organic over the year (lamb, beef, pork, venison organic and local)

Holmhead Guest House (four stars) stands on the World Heritage Site of Hadrian's Wall and was built with stones taken from it. Set at the top of a valley beneath the ruins of a castle and beside a river, it is surrounded by fields and woodland. Guests dine at the large oak table in the lovely stone arched beamed dining room. Food is always freshly-prepared, and organically grown vegetables and organically reared local meat are served wherever possible. We specialise in organically grown and produced wine, with an award winners list from around the world. Our other speciality is Hadrian's Wall. You can read about it from our extensive library or watch videos, and you can take a guided or a self-guided tour.
holidays@holmhead.com   www.bandbhadrianswall.com

LONGHORSLEY (B&B)

THISTLEYHAUGH 279

Longhorsley
Morpeth NE65 8RG
Tel: 01665 570629   MAP 10

B&B, double £37.50 pppn, single £50-£70
Evening Meal, 3 course £20

Organically reared meat and seasonal local produce

Organic Farmers & Growers

A picturesque farmhouse on the banks of the River Coquet in the heart of rural Northumberland. We offer five *en suite* rooms, and guests have exclusive use of the farmhouse dining room and lounge. As well as a hearty Northumbrian breakfast, we also cook traditional roast dinners, home-made soups and puddings. The food is locally produced and seasonal. The meats we serve are organically reared, and the fish fresh wild North Sea salmon. We are a licensed premises. Set in 720 acres of organic farmland, Thistleyhaugh retains much of the charm and many of the historic features found in a traditional Georgian farmhouse. The working farm, with cattle and sheep, has been run by the same family for over a hundred years. thistleyhaugh@hotmail.com   www.thistleyhaugh.co.uk

SHIPLEY HILL (S-C)

FARM COTTAGE 280

Farmhouse
Shipley Hill NE66 2LX
Tel: 01665 579266   MAP 10

Cottage: sleeps 5, £280-£450 pw
Short breaks available from £165

Organic holiday boxes can be ordered locally and delivered to the cottage

Soil Association

Shipley Hill is a mixed organic farm of 450 acres situated in the heart of the beautiful Northumberland countryside. The cottage is set in an elevated position on a quiet lane leading to the farm. Visitors are very welcome to stroll around the farm. There are many fantastic walking destinations in the surrounding area, as well as miles of unspoiled sandy coastline to explore. It provides an excellent base for exploring Northumbria, with the coast, castles (Lindisfarne, Dunstanburgh, Bamburgh), miles of sandy beaches, the Cheviot hills and the Northumberland National Park, all well within a half hour drive. The town of Alnwick, with its magnificent castle and garden, is only five miles from the farm. www.cottageguide.co.uk/shipleyhill

WHITFIELD *(S-C)*

BURNLAW BUNKHOUSE 281

Whitfield
Hexham NE47 8HF
Tel: 01434 345359

MAP 9

Bunkhouse: sleeps 6
£10 pn (own linen), £13 pn (linen provided)

Organic produce available in season

Soil Association

Burnlaw is a 50-acre organic smallholding on the edge of the West Allen Valley, one of the most unspoiled and beautiful corners of Britain. Set in the North Pennines uplands, it enjoys steep wooded valleys and fast flowing limestone streams. The Tall Barn is part of a complex of traditional farm buildings. It has three bedrooms sleeping up to eight people in total, a reception room, a kitchen, a very large studio room, two showers, loos and a bath. It is centrally heated. We have suckler cows, horses, poultry, an orchard, a vegetable garden, a herb garden, woodland, nationally rated wild flower hay meadows. Guests are welcome to explore the farm, walk the labyrinth, meditate in the temple, use the disc golf course.
gvs38@hotmail.com   www.burnlaw.org.uk

WHITFIELD *(S-C)*

BURNLAW COTTAGE 282

Whitfield
Hexham NE47 8HF
Tel: 01434 345359

MAP 9

Cottage: sleeps 8
£300-£500 pw

Organic produce available in season

Soil Association

Burnlaw Cottage is on a 50-acre organic smallholding in an Area of Outstanding Natural Beauty. The converted 18th-century barn is part of a complex of stone farm buildings, which is home to five households – most of whom are members of the Baha'i Faith. On the edge of the West Allen Valley, it is one of the most unspoiled and beautiful corners of Britain. Part of the North Pennines, it has hilly uplands, steep wooded valleys, and fast flowing limestone streams. The farm has a small herd of suckler cows, horses, poultry, orchard, organic vegetable garden, and woodland. Guests are welcome to wander round the farm, use the games field, and also use the nationally recognised disc golf course.
gvs38@hotmail.com   www.burnlaw.org.uk

WHITFIELD (S-C)

THE TALL BARN   283

Burnlaw
Whitfield NE47 8HF
Tel: 01434 345359   MAP 9

Room: sleeps 6
£10 pn (own linen), £13 pn (linen provided)

Organic produce available in season

Soil Association

Burnlaw is on a 50-acre organic smallholding on the edge of the West Allen Valley, one of the most unspoiled and beautiful corners of Britain. Part of the North Pennines, it has hilly uplands, steep wooded valleys, fast flowing limestone streams. The Tall Barn is part of a complex of stone farm buildings. It has a large room with sleeping arrangements for six people, reception room, kitchen, very large studio room, two shower rooms, a bath and two loos, and is centrally heated. The farm has a small herd of suckler cows, horses, poultry, orchard, organic vegetable garden, woodland. Guests are welcome to explore the farm, walk the labyrinth, use the games field and the internationally recognised disc golf course.
gvs38@hotmail.com   www.burnlaw.org.uk

EAST BRIDGFORD (B&B)

BARN FARM COTTAGE   284

Kneeton Road
East Bridgford NG13 8PH
Tel: 01949 20196   MAP 15

Bed and Breakfast
£32 pppn

The delicious breakfast is almost always all organic

A warm welcome awaits you at this wonderful hideaway. It's a small biodynamic / organic holding in East Bridgford, overlooking fields and the Trent Valley. Ideal for walkers and fishermen, it is also well set up for children. Barn Farm Cottage has log fires, exposed beams, pretty gardens, a peaceful atmosphere, and good food. The delicious breakfast is almost always all organic, and includes home-made marmalade and jams. Many organic items are also available to buy from the village shop. East Bridgford is an attractive old village on the Trent Valley Way. For those who prefer a self-catering option, we have just completed a beautiful barn conversion which sleeps four to five persons. Early booking is essential.

BENSON *(B&B)*

FYFIELD MANOR 285

Brook Street
Benson OX10 6HA
Tel: 01491 835184   MAP 19

Bed and Breakfast
£35-£37.50 pppn (2 people sharing)
A range of organic produce is offered

Recently restored and refurbished, Fyfield Manor offers very comfortable accommodation in an interesting manor house with features which span seven centuries, many of which have been hidden for over 250 years. We pride ourselves on running an environmentally friendly bed and breakfast, using local produce, saving energy and the world's resources. A full English breakfast is served in the medieval dining room. A range of organic produce is offered, including naturally grown tomatoes and fruit in season from the garden. Guests have full use of the gardens and picnic areas. The gardens, with six acres of natural water gardens, are a haven for wildlife and totally organic. There is a surcharge for single occupancy.
chris_fyfield@hotmail.co.uk   www.fyfieldmanor.co.uk

SPARSHOLT DOWN *(B&B)*

DOWN BARN FARM 286

Sparsholt Down
Wantage OX12 9XD
Tel: 01367 820272   MAP 19

Farmhouse Bed and Breakfast, £30-£35 pppn
Evening Meal, from £15 (by arrangement)

Most of the food is from the organic farm and garden

Organic Farmers & Growers

Down Barn is a 100-acre grassland farm set in a hollow of the Ridgeway Downs. This organic cattle and pig enterprise is quietly situated and gives the impression of being completely isolated even though it is in fact close to Oxford and the Cotswolds. A full English cooked breakfast is included in the price of the rooms, and evening meals are available if required (with a little advance notice). Most of the food served is from the farm and garden, and is therefore all organic. Some of the special dining features offered are home cooking, home produce and vegetarian food. The countryside around the farm is ideal for walking, off-road cycling and riding. The whole area is renowned for its racehorse training stables.
pendomeffect@aol.com   www.nationaltrail.co.uk/Ridgeway/site.asp?PageId=50&SiteId=103&c=6

WALLINGFORD *(B&B)*

LITTLE GABLES 287

166 Crowmarsh Hill
Wallingford OX10 8BG
Tel: 01491 837834   MAP 19

Bed and Breakfast
Double from £65 pn, Single from £50

Fruits from our own garden are made into jams, chutneys, pickles, juices, etc

Little Gables is a 1930s detached house situated close to the medieval market town of Wallingford. English and continental breakfasts are served. Fruit juice, cereals (we make our own organic muesli), organic milk, yogurt, toast with preserves, plus a cooked breakfast. Organic bread. Fruits from our own garden are made into jams, chutneys, pickles, juices, etc. We also offer packed lunches and sandwich trays. Little Gables is close to the Ridgeway and Thames Path National Trails and the Oxfordshire Cycle Routes (we have a locked bike store). We are by the bus route to Oxford, Henley and Reading. Cholsey train station is a couple of miles from the house. We are members of the Green Tourism Business Scheme. mail@littlegables.co.uk   www.littlegables.co.uk

LEINTWARDINE *(B&B)*

LOWER BUCKTON 288

Buckton
Leintwardine SY7 0JU
Tel: 01547 540532   MAP 14

Private Restaurant with Rooms
B&B £90 room pn, Dinner £30-£35

Lots of organic food either home-produced or locally sought, bought and caught

Country house accommodation with award-winning breakfasts and delicious dinners. Situated off the beaten track in Mortimer Country on the north Herefordshire / south Shropshire borders, where England meets Wales. Our cooking is much praised for its ingredients and flair. We are members of Slow Food and believe in the importance of low food miles. Our productive vegetable garden, managed on organic principles, supplies the kitchen with year round fresh seasonal produce. We buy all other ingredients from small local growers, producers and suppliers, thus supporting the rural community and economy. Open all year for short breaks, private house parties, bring your own horse holidays, cookery courses, and food safaris. carolyn@lowerbuckton.co.uk   www.lowerbuckton.co.uk

NEWCASTLE ON CLUN *(S-C)*

BRYNMAWR FARM 289

Newcastle on Clun
Craven Arms SY7 8QU
Tel: 01588 640298   MAP 14

Caravan: sleeps 4-6, £200-£250 pw
Price pn on application

Organic vegetables subject to availability

Soil Association

The caravan is set on the Shropshire / Mid Wales border in the beautiful Clun Valley, an Area of Outstanding Natural Beauty. Brynmawr is a working organic farm situated within an environmentally sensitive area. The farm produces organic potatoes (including seed), carrots, swedes, organic beef and lamb. Enjoy the peace and quiet and the spectacular views, whether sitting in the caravan, walking on the hill top, or sitting in the self-contained garden having tea. The farm includes the Shropshire Wildlife Trust's Rhos Fiddle Nature Reserve, a beautiful expanse of upland moorland designated as a Site of Special Scientific Interest, where you will be able see Highland cattle and Hebridean sheep.
brynmawr@farmersweekly.net   www.clunvalleyorganics.co.uk

NEWCASTLE-ON-CLUN *(S-C)*

BUCKSHEAD ECO-COTTAGE 290

Brynmawr Farm
Newcastle-on-Clun SY7 8QU
Tel: 01588 640298   MAP 14

Cottage: sleeps 4, £200-£390 pw
Price pn on application

Pick your own organic vegetables from the garden (subject to availability)

Soil Association

The cottage is set within its own grounds on an organic hill farm in the Clun Valley. The kitchen floor and units are made using local wood, and the worktops from recycled coffee cups. The flagstones in the lounge are original and the high-efficiency Clearview wood-burning stove is made locally. The bedroom furniture, along with the floors, is made from local ash, alder and oak. The walls throughout the house have been traditionally lime plastered. The garden has a large patio and a raised seating area. Organic vegetables are grown in raised beds and these are freely available for use by the guests. There is ample opportunity to explore the local countryside and wildlife, either by foot or using the bicycles provided.
brynmawr@farmersweekly.net   www.buckshead-ecocottage.co.uk

OBLEY *(S-C)*

ECOCABIN 291

Obley
Bucknell SY7 0BZ
Tel: 01547 530183   MAP 14

Ecocabin: sleeps 4+cot, £420-£605 pw
£90-£105 pn (minimum 2 nights)

Organic foods can be delivered ready for
your arrival (£5 collection charge)

Ecocabin is constructed of home-grown timber, sheep's wool, reeds, lime and clay, and is heated by a wood pellet stove. It nestles peacefully in a secluded valley in the South Shropshire Hills and has stunning views. Fair trade tea, coffee and cocoa are provided and there is a small 'honesty' shop stocking many organic products. The Marches and Mid-Wales have a delicious variety of small scale food producers that sell at local outlets and farmers' markets. We provide a 'buy local' shopping service and a selection of foods of your choice can be delivered ready for your arrival (£5 collection charge). Organic cotton bed linen, towels and chemical-free toiletries provided for your stay. No short breaks in school holidays.
kate@ecocabin.co.uk   www.ecocabin.co.uk

RHYDYCROESAU *(Hotel)*

PEN-Y-DYFFRYN HOTEL 292

Rhydycroesau
Oswestry SY10 7JD
Tel: 01691 653700   MAP 14

Country House Hotel, B&B from £57 pppn
Restaurant (3 course dinner from £30 pp)

Food is healthy, locally sourced, and tends to
use organic produce

Perched almost a thousand feet up, this silver stone former Georgian rectory is situated in the Shropshire / Welsh hills, an area of unspoilt natural beauty. The restaurant (AA two rosette good food award), with its huge south-facing sash windows, is central to the Pen-y-Dyffryn experience. The relaxed and almost 'retreat like' feel of the hotel is complemented by the increasing use of local and organic produce in the kitchen, so that guests depart feeling thoroughly revitalised. Set in 5 acres of grounds the hotel offers superb accommodation including some bedrooms with private patios, others with spa baths. The gardens run down to the river marking the border, the banks of which are being managed as a nature reserve.
stay@peny.co.uk   www.peny.co.uk

WESTHOPE *(B&B)*

WARD FARM 293

Westhope
Craven Arms SY7 9JL
Tel: 01584 861601   MAP 14

Farmhouse Bed and Breakfast
£28-£38 pppn

Our own fresh eggs and our own sausage
and bacon for breakfast when available

Organic Farmers & Growers

Ward Farm is a certified organic working farm with a traditional herd of Hereford cattle, sheep, two Gloucester Old Spot pigs and two Berkshires. We also keep a variety of completely free-range poultry, providing fresh eggs for your farmhouse breakfast. Our spacious guest rooms (4-star Silver Award), including a ground floor twin room, have lovely views across fields and all the facilities you need to make your stay a comfortable one. The village of Westhope is in South Shropshire's Area of Outstanding Natural Beauty and is particularly picturesque. The area is ideal for walking or cycling. Ludlow and Church Stretton are fifteen minutes by car and Shrewsbury, Much Wenlock, Ironbridge and Bridgnorth are about thirty minutes. contact@wardfarm.co.uk   www.wardfarm.co.uk

WESTHOPE *(Camping)*

WARD FARM CAMPING   294

Westhope
Craven Arms SY7 9JL
Tel: 01584 861601   MAP 14

Camping and Caravanning Site (March-Oct)
£8 per pitch (£10-£12 with hook-up) pn

Organic Farmers & Growers

Ward Farm is a certified organic working farm with a traditional herd of Hereford cattle, sheep, two Gloucester Old Spot pigs and two Berkshires. We also keep completely free-range poultry. Our camping and caravanning Certified Location site has electric hook-ups, drinking water supply and chemical disposal point. We also have a shower room with wc and wash basin with hot and cold water. The site, which is for camping and caravanning club members only, is situated next to the farmhouse with views across the surrounding countryside. Westhope is in South Shropshire's Area of Outstanding Natural Beauty and is particularly picturesque. The area is very peaceful and is ideal for both walking and cycling. contact@wardfarm.co.uk   www.wardfarm.co.uk/Camping.htm

BATH *(B&B)*

MARLBOROUGH HOUSE 295

1 Marlborough Lane
Bath BA1 2NQ
Tel: 01225 318175 MAP 18

Vegetarian Bed and Breakfast
Double, £85-£125 pn

Organic food is a speciality of the house
(95%-100%)

Exquisitely furnished with antiques, Marlborough House is an enchanting small establishment in the heart of Georgian Bath. Served in either the elegant parlour or lovely dining room, breakfasts are cooked to order, using only the highest quality organic ingredients. Marlborough House specializes in organic foods which include a wide range of organic cereals, juices, yogurts, fresh fruits and jams, organic English cheeses, eggs and milk and a selection of excellent breads, and croissants, as well as fresh roasted continental coffees and various fair trade organic teas. Your friendly hosts will happily give you advice on your explorations of Bath, as well as the many fine walks in the gorgeous surroundings. mars@manque.dircon.co.uk   www.marlborough-house.net

BATHWICK *(B&B)*

NUMBER FOURTEEN 296

14 Raby Place
Bathwick Hill BA2 4EH
Tel: 01225 465120 MAP 18

Regency Town House Bed and Breakfast
Double £70 pn, Single £35 pn

About 80% organic produce

A delightful Georgian house situated on the lower slopes of Bathwick Hill, with superb views of the World Heritage City of Bath. The house is in a typical Georgian terrace, single fronted with a richly decorated interior. Bedrooms are tastefully done in an interesting mix of colours and styles. Healthy breakfasts, using organic products whenever possible, include eggs, bacon, yogurts, fruit salads and home-made jams, and are taken around a large mahogany table in the dining room. Visit Bath's hot springs and the Roman Baths, one of the best examples of a Roman bath complex in Europe. Number Fourteen is very close to the Bath Skyline Walk (created by the National Trust), and the Kennet and Avon Canal.

BURCOTT *(B&B)*

THE MILLER'S HOUSE   297

Burcott Mill
Burcott BA5 1NJ
Tel: 01749 673118   MAP 18

Guest House
Bed and Breakfast, £25-£35 pppn

Our wholemeal bread is made by a local baker using our own organic flour

Soil Association

The Miller's House, dating from around 1750, is a charming Grade II listed building adjoining Burcott Mill. There has been a mill on this site for over a thousand years, and few such watermills still operate commercially today. We specialise in the production of 100% organic wholemeal stoneground flour made from organic English wheat grain. Our breakfasts are highly praised by our guests. We offer a selection of locally made organic yogurts, marmalades and honey, West Country honey roast sausages and bacon to go with your free-range eggs, and of course our wholemeal bread, made by a local baker using our own organic flour. A private tour of the working mill with our miller is a feature of your stay here. theburts@burcottmill.com   www.burcottmill.com

COURSING BATCH *(B&B)*

SHAMBHALA RETREAT   298

Coursing Batch
Glastonbury BA6 8BH
Tel: 01458 831797   MAP 18

Vegetarian Retreat
Bed and Breakfast, £42-£56 pppn

Fresh organic ingredients (100% organic)

Everything you ever wanted. Shambhala Healing Retreat on the Tor in Glastonbury with magnificent views of the Vale of Avalon. This is a sacred site from ancient times, steeped in legend. The focus is a beautiful star of hundreds of clear crystal points that energy pulses through from deep in the earth. Enjoy our flock of peace doves, water gardens and meditation spaces, beautiful rooms and lots of love. Organic vegetarian food is lovingly prepared with fresh high quality ingredients. Our treatments for mind, body and spirit are renowned. We have been voted one of the top ten retreats in the UK by the Daily Mail, and we have a Gold Star Award from the Good Retreat Guide. Highly recommended. elisis@shambhalaheartcentre.com   www.shambhala.co.uk

GLASTONBURY *(B&B)*

TORDOWN B&B 299

5 Ashwell Lane
Glastonbury BA6 8BG
Tel: 01458 832287   MAP 18

Bed and Breakfast
£32-£45 pppn

Delicious organic, local and fair trade food served for your sumptuous breakfast

Comfortable, relaxing, peaceful family-run home on the southern slopes of Glastonbury Tor. Beautiful views over the Vale of Avalon from the garden, guest lounge and some of the bedrooms. We serve a sumptuous breakfast which includes fruit juices, fresh fruit, a large variety of cereals and teas as well as cooked vegetarian fare. We use as much organic, local and fair trade food as possible. Organic shampoos, etc. Glastonbury is a fabulous place to visit – historical, spiritual, and a great place to stay to visit many other places in the area. Come and find out for yourself at our environmentally aware home. Treat yourself to one of our treatments or a soothing hydrotherapy bath plus recommended treatments in town. torangel@aol.com   www.tordown.com

GOATHURST *(S-C)*

HUNTSTILE ORGANIC FARM 300

Goathurst
Bridgwater TA5 2DQ
Tel: 01278 662358   MAP 18

Self-Catering: sleeps 2+2/3
£250-£895 pw

We can provide all meals and organic farm produce is for sale

Soil Association

Huntstile offers three self-catering options: Apple Loft, Cider House, Seed Granary. On our farm we grow a wide variety of organic vegetables, soft fruit and herbs. With a little notice we can provide breakfasts, packed lunches and evening meals too. We cater for both meat and vegetarian. Delicious breakfasts £3.50 per person. Packed lunches £5-£7 per person, depending on your appetite. Evening meals around £10-£15 per person and we use as much of our own fresh organic produce as possible. All is available to buy from our farm gate sales area. For £6.50 you can order a mixed box of organic vegetables for your arrival and we can also provide you with a varied organic hamper for your stay.
lizziemyers@hotmail.com   www.huntstileorganicfarm.co.uk

GOATHURST (B&B)

HUNTSTILE FARM B&B 301

Goathurst
Bridgwater TA5 2DQ
Tel: 01278 662358   MAP 18

Bed and Breakfast, double from £60 pn
Evening Meal, from £10

Breakfast includes home-grown organic produce plus local organic sausages and bacon

Soil Association

A fascinating farmhouse, dating back to Henry VIII, with many original and beautiful features. Huntstile Organic Farm is set in the foothills of the Quantocks, with panoramic views across the county. We have six rooms for B&B guests (four double / family rooms and two twins). Evening meals are available from £10 per person. We are passionate about locally grown, well produced, quality food and we grow our own organic fruit, vegetables and herbs in our two and a half-acre kitchen garden. Our flock of organic chickens provides delicious eggs for breakfast. We also have a small herd of British White beef cattle. There are some lovely farm walks, and wonderful surrounding countryside.
lizziemyers@hotmail.com   www.huntstileorganicfarm.co.uk

GOATHURST (Camping)

HUNTSTILE ECOTENTS 302

Goathurst
Bridgwater TA5 2DQ
Tel: 01278 662358   MAP 18

EcoTents: sleep 5-12, £150-£550 pw
Camping £10 pn (2 man), Caravans £12 pn

Organic farm produce for sale in the farm shop

Soil Association

We have recently added the Sidelands into our wildlife project. This is a beautiful part of the valley, with far reaching views and a natural spring that feeds the wildlife lake. There are no vehicles, no electricity and no mains water. We have a water purification system for the spring water, composting loos, solar-powered showers fed from the spring (eco-friendly shampoo and soap only please). There is a recycling and composting area and a purpose built wood-burning community barbecue. The ecotents have a solid wooden base and are equipped with cooking facilities, table, benches, camp beds. All you have to do is bring your own sleeping bag and food. Very peaceful, very natural, very eco-friendly.
lizziemyers@hotmail.com   www.huntstileorganicfarm.co.uk

LUCKWELL BRIDGE *(B&B)*

CUTTHORNE 303

Luckwell Bridge
Wheddon Cross TA24 7EW
Tel: 01643 831255   MAP 18

Country House, B&B £38-£47 pppn
Dinner, £18-£24 pp

Approximately 50% organic produce over
the year

Hidden in a private valley, deep in the heart of the glorious Exmoor countryside, Cutthorne is a delightful country house with a rare tranquillity that is truly off the beaten track. At the centre of this 25-acre estate is the impressive Georgian farmhouse, which retains much of its original character and charm. We offer superb bed and breakfast accommodation in a choice of three *en suite* guest rooms or two adjoining cottages. We grow our own fruit, vegetables and salads naturally, and provide eggs from our own hens. All our meals are traditionally prepared and cooked in an Aga. Delicious home-baked puddings. Local organic produce used whenever possible. Fully licenced, with some organic wines.
durbin@cutthorne.co.uk   www.cutthorne.com

NETHER STOWEY *(B&B)*

THE OLD CIDER HOUSE 304

25 Castle Street
Nether Stowey TA5 1LN
Tel: 01278 732228   MAP 18

Guest House, £30-£40 pppn
Evening Meal, £14.50-£19.50

Somerset-sourced produce, organic where
available, home-grown in season

The Old Cider House was built in 1910 and produced local cider until the 1960s. Now a 4-star guest house with five *en suite* rooms, we are enthusiastic about producing good home cooking using seasonal and local ingredients. We grow as many of our own vegetables as possible in the summer, and keep naturally fed hens for fresh eggs. Meat comes from the local butcher, and we subscribe to a local organic box scheme. In 2006 we set up the Stowey Brewery, producing a small range of real ales for in-house consumption. We now offer 'Run a Brewery' residential workshop weekends. The thriving village of Nether Stowey, designated a Rural Centre, is situated at the foot of the largely unexplored Quantock Hills.
info@theoldciderhouse.co.uk   www.theoldciderhouse.co.uk

NEWTON SAINT LOE (B&B)

PENNSYLVANIA FARM B&B 305

Newton Saint Loe
Bath BA2 9JD
Tel: 01225 314912   MAP 18

Bed and Breakfast
Double, £60-£68 pn

Organic milk, organic eggs, organic yogurts, local bread, local sausages

Soil Association

Pennsylvania Farm is a working organic family farm set in 300 acres of unspoilt countryside close to the historic cities of Bath and Bristol. The farmhouse is a listed 17th-century building, warm and comfortable with a friendly atmosphere. It has three bedrooms, two with *en suite* facilities and one with its own bathroom. There's a cosy dining room and a pleasant sunny sitting room with a log fire. Whatever time of year you come there will be something to interest you and help you unwind, from fresh spring mornings in rural countryside to cold winter nights in front of a crackling log fire. Long lazy days in the peace and quiet, slow walks, visits to the beautiful towns of Cheddar and Wells for sightseeing and shopping. info@pennsylvaniafarm.co.uk   www.pennsylvaniafarm.co.uk/home.htm

NEWTON SAINT LOE (S-C)

PENNSYLVANIA FARM 306

Newton Saint Loe
Bath BA2 9JD
Tel: 01225 312451   MAP 18

Cottages: sleep 2-4, £250-£550 pw
Short Breaks, £50-£120 pn

It may be possible to purchase the farm's own organic beef, lamb and eggs

Soil Association

Pennsylvania Farm is a working organic family farm set in 300 acres of unspoilt countryside close to the historic cities of Bath and Bristol. Ivy and Stable cottages were converted from the farm's old stable buildings. They have been carefully modernised retaining exposed beams, flagstone flooring and exposed stonework to offer spacious comfortable accommodation furnished and equipped to a very high standard. Both have a patio garden with table and chairs where you can relax, have a barbecue and take in the lovely views of the Englishcombe valley. The Cheese House has gardens to the front and rear of the house with a barbecue and garden furniture to help make the most of those long summer evenings. info@pennsylvaniafarm.co.uk   www.pennsylvaniafarm.co.uk/selfcat.htm

OVER STOWEY *(B&B)*

PARSONAGE FARM 307

Over Stowey
Quantock Hills TA5 IHA
Tel: 01278 733237   MAP 18

Farmhouse B&B, double £55-£75 pn
Light Supper £10, Evening Meal £20-£25

We specialise in organic, home-grown food

A traditional 17th-century farmhouse and naturally run smallholding in a peaceful village in the Quantock Hills, an Area of Outstanding Natural Beauty. The farmhouse has three double bedrooms (two *en suite*), a cosy sitting room, log fires and quarry tiled floors. There is a walled kitchen garden with honeybees, hens, and an apple orchard with a flock of black Welsh sheep. A traditional or vegetarian English breakfast is served in front of an open fire in the dining room. Eggs from our hens, home-made breads and jams, and pancakes with maple syrup. We specialise in organic, home-grown food. Evening meals are served by candlelight. 5% discount if you arrive by bicycle, foot or public transport.
suki@parsonfarm.co.uk   www.parsonfarm.co.uk

SELWORTHY *(B&B)*

HINDON ORGANIC FARM 308

Nr Selworthy
Minehead TA24 8SH
Tel: 01643 705244   MAP 18

Farmhouse Bed and Breakfast
£35-£45 pppn

Our own organic / free-range meats, all organic and local produce breakfasts

Soil Association

Enjoy Exmoor National Park where red deer roam, on an award-winning 500-acre organic hill farm. 18th-century accommodation with 21st-century comforts and some style. Cotton linen, green toiletries, log fire. Aga-cooked breakfasts with our own home-made sausages and bacon, free-range eggs from our hens, fresh baked bread, fruit, honey on the comb, etc. Hindon is a working stock farm and country home, set in an idyllic secluded location 3 miles from Minehead. Ducks dabble in the garden stream. Wonderful walks from the door to the moor, the South West Coast Path, the sea, and Selworthy (a mile) for scrummy cream teas. Farm shop. Outdoor hot tub. Aromatherapy treatments. Self-catering cottage also available.
info@hindonfarm.co.uk   www.hindonfarm.co.uk

SELWORTHY (S-C)

HINDON FARM COTTAGE 309

Nr Selworthy
Minehead TA24 8SH
Tel: 01643 705244   MAP 18

Cottage: sleeps 1-6
£350-£950 pw

Our own organic and free-range meat,
home-made sausages, eggs, baked bread

Soil Association

Real farm. Real food. Relax. Stay in farm style for a perfect escape. Charming 18th-century traditional farm cottage with 21st-century comforts. Lovingly cared for. Set alone on an idyllic wooded hillside in its own enclosed garden with lovely views over the fields, hidden 100 yards from the farmhouse (for B&B) on our 500-acre award-winning organic stock farm within Exmoor National Park. Peacocks wander. Red deer roam. Complimentary welcome basket of organic / local produce. Log fire. Central heating. Crisp cotton linen. Eco toiletries. Wonderful walks from the door to coast, moorland and sea. On-site farm shop for our produce. National winners 'Organic Producers of the Year'. Food Heroes. Dogs welcome. Outdoor hot tub.
info@hindonfarm.co.uk   www.hindonfarm.co.uk

SHEPTON MONTAGUE (B&B)

LOWER FARM   310

Shepton Montague
Wincanton BA9 8JG
Tel: 01749 812253   MAP 18

Bed and Breakfast in the Barn, sleeps 6
£45 pppn (weekends minimum 2 nights)

Home-produced, organic, local (at least 80% organic)

A stylish self-contained barn attached to an 18th-century farmstead surrounded by organic farmland in deepest Somerset dairy country. Comfortable beds, crisp cotton sheets, downy duvets, toile de Jouy curtains, lime-washed walls, polished wood floors. The big window in the barn overlooks hens scratching in the orchard, an inspiring acre of compost-grown vegetables (we have been growing organic vegetables since 1983), abundant flower borders, and orchards. Breakfast consists of home-produced, local, and organic ingredients, and the bread is baked from organic wheat grown in the village. We can usually supply organic vegetables if you wish to cook for yourselves in the barn kitchen.
susie@lowerfarm.org.uk   www.lowerfarm.org.uk

THE QUANTOCKS *(B&B)*

WALKS AND FORKS 311

The Quantocks
Somerset
Tel: 01458 251060   MAP 18

Jacob's Barn: sleeps 10, from £210 pp for 3 nights. Includes all meals and guided walks

Local organic produce is used in all the meals

Walks and Forks offer long week-end breaks and tailor-made holidays for small groups of walkers on the Quantock Hills. Most of the food is sourced from local organic farms in Somerset. Fresh packed lunches are provided for the day walks, and evening meals and breakfasts celebrate seasonal organic food. Other local B&Bs are used for some of the walking holidays. These also specialise in organic seasonal food and can be seen on the website. The walks leader knows the area well and can introduce visitors to organic specialities of the area. There will be a chance to see some of the farms on the walking routes. Some of the weekends focus on the Coleridge Way, a 36 mile walk from Nether Stowey to Porlock.
info@walksandforks.co.uk www.walksandforks.co.uk

TRACEBRIDGE *(B&B)*

HESPERUS COTTAGE B&B 312

Tracebridge
Wellington TA21 0HG
Tel: 01823 672194   MAP 18

Bed and Breakfast, £35-£40 pppn

Packed Lunch, Dinner (by arrangement)
We offer an organic breakfast

Hesperus Cottage is set in an acre and a half of wooded area on the banks of the river Tone. We use local, natural, organic produce and eco-friendly products where possible. We believe in sourcing our produce locally so that it is fresher and to encourage small local businesses. To us eating well is conducive to a healthy life, which is why we offer an organic breakfast with cooked breakfast, cereals, spreads, fruit juices, fresh fruit, teas or coffee. For dinner, our fantastic local pub offers meals with fresh locally sourced produce. If what you're after is a few days of peace, quiet and relaxation you will not be disappointed. Set in a beautiful, tranquil valley our B&B is ideal for walks or as a sightseeing base.
info@hesperuscottage.com www.hesperuscottage.com

WAMBROOK (B&B)

WAMBROOK FARM 313

Wambrook
Chard TA20 3DF
Tel: 01460 62371 MAP 18

Farmhouse Bed and Breakfast
£29-£32.50 pppn

Generous farmhouse breakfast or
continental options

Soil Association

Wambrook Farm is in the beautiful countryside of the Blackdown Hills, two miles from Chard. We are a working mixed organic farm. We keep sheep that lamb in the spring, suckler beef cattle, rear heifers for dairy farms, and grow corn. The farmhouse and buildings are listed (built mid-1800), with a unique granary as a focal point in the yard. We offer a generous farmhouse breakfast or continental options, and use locally grown produce. We have a lovely garden to sit in or to play badminton. Guests are welcome to walk on the farm. Wambrook is a quiet rural village in an Area of Outstanding Natural Beauty. There is a pub in the village, which is a lovely mile walk in the summer, offering excellent food.
wambrookfarm@aol.com   www.wambrookfarm.co.uk

WICK (S-C)

PADDINGTON FARM TRUST 314

Maidencroft Farm
Wick BA6 8JN
Tel: 01458 832752 MAP 18

Farmhouse: sleeps 20, Mon-Fri £650 / Fri-Sun £325. Longhouse: sleeps 10, £15 pppn

Organic vegetables and eggs available to buy direct from farm

Soil Association

Low cost self-catering accommodation on a beautiful 43-acre organic educational farm. The farm is only a mile from the historic town of Glastonbury. Private bookings and groups of all kinds are welcome. The large farmhouse has its own private garden, picnic tables and barbecue. The longhouse, with three separate self-catering units (two units 2 beds, one unit 4-6 beds), is suitable for individuals, families or small groups. Panoramic views across the Somerset Levels to the Mendips. Glastonbury Tor is a twenty minute walk. Wildlife, walks, local attractions, tailored group activities on the farm as you wish (see our website for details of activities). Groups need to book activities on the farm in advance.
pft@onetel.net   www.paddingtonfarm.co.uk

WOOKEY *(S-C)*

MILL LODGE 315

Burcott Mill
Wookey BA5 1NJ
Tel: 01749 673118   MAP 18

Apartment: sleeps 2
£195-£350 pw (based on 2 people)

Our wholemeal bread is made by a local baker using our own organic flour

Soil Association

Discover this Victorian treasure. A unique holiday experience awaits you in the heart of a rare working watermill. Our twin bedroom apartment offers modern comforts in an historic setting with its private view onto the mill floor. A tour of the mill is a feature of your stay. There is a tearoom on-site (weekends Easter to September) serving bread, home-made cakes and cream teas made using our organic flour. Within our grounds are an adventure playground, picnic area, paddock, orchard, and a variety of small animals and wildfowl. You will also find a crafts workshop, a pottery and a post office here. Mill Lodge is in a rural setting opposite a country pub / restaurant. Ideal for Wells, Wookey Hole, Glastonbury, Cheddar. theburts@burcottmill.com   www.burcottmill.com

WOOLMINSTONE *(B&B)*

BARN COTTAGE 316

Lyminster Farm
Woolminstone TA18 8QP
Tel: 01460 75313   MAP 18

Bed and Breakfast, double £27.50-£30 pppn
Discount for over 3 nights, Supper £6.50

We endeavour to use locally sourced organic ingredients whenever possible

Barn Cottage is situated in a beautiful, tranquil corner of rural South Somerset, an Area of Outstanding Natural Beauty surrounded by organic farmland. We offer comfortable and spacious accommodation in king and twin *en suite* rooms. Both 'rooms with a view' are sunny and south-facing with stunning panoramic views of Pilsden Pen and Lewesdon Hill. Our aim is to offer guests plenty of the tastiest, freshest, best quality food by seeking out and using organic, local and home-grown ingredients. Breakfast includes rare breed eggs from a neighbour's farm gate, organic bread from Lyme Regis Town Mill, traditionally made Devon sausages, local organic rare breed bacon, and our own jams made with organic fruit. bandbbarncottage@aol.com   www.smoothhound.co.uk/hotels/barncottage

ALTON *(S-C)*

ROWAN HOUSE 317

Tythe Barn
Alton ST10 4AZ
Tel: 01889 591844   MAP 15

House: sleeps 7+, £600-£850 pw
Short Breaks, £400-£595

Complimentary organic breakfast basket, in-house catering

Four star self-catering accommodation on the edge of the historical and picturesque village of Alton in the Staffordshire Peak District. Organic and fair trade teas and coffees and a home made cake welcome you. Rowan House is sustainably run with a focus on supporting the local environment and economy. The pretty south-facing garden has been organically managed for 18 years. We are on the Staffordshire Way with miles of walks from the door and the Peak National Park ten minutes away. Chatsworth, the Potteries, Manifold Valley, Leek and the Roaches are all within easy reach. Routes, maps and organic picnics are available. Day and weekend courses from the basics of growing your own food to chemical-free cleaning. emily@simplystaffordshire.co.uk   www.simplystaffordshire.co.uk

KINGSLEY *(B&B)*

THE CHURCH FARM 318

Holt Lane
Kingsley ST10 2BA
Tel: 01538 754759   MAP 15

Farmhouse Bed and Breakfast
£25-£28 pppn

100% organic breakfast can be provided on request

Surrounded by beautiful countryside the farmhouse is situated in the quaint village of Kingsley, above the lovely Churnet Valley. The Grade II listed house features oak-beamed rooms and has beautiful period furnishings. It has a cottage garden with a large lawn. A full English breakfast is served using organic and local produce. On request, a 100% organic breakfast can be provided. The 50-hectare farm (dairy, poultry, beef) is a working farm with a tree-ringed farmyard and friendly farm animals. The farm is not far from the Churnet Valley steam railway station. It is close to the Staffordshire Way footpath, five and a half miles from Alton Towers, and an ideal base for exploring the Potteries and the Peak District. thechurchfarm@yahoo.co.uk

MARCHINGTON CLIFF *(Camping)*

FORESTSIDE FARM 319

Marchington Cliff
Uttoxeter ST14 8NA
Tel: 01283 820353 MAP 15

Camping and Caravan Site
Tents from £6 pn, Caravans from £10 pn

Fresh organic milk available from the farm

Soil Association

Forestside Farm is a 156-acre organic dairy farm overlooking the Dove Valley and Weaver Hills, set against the magnificent Needwood Forest. There are five hardstandings with electric hook-up for touring caravans and tent pitches in the adjacent paddock. Shower and toilet available. Also for campers' use are fridge, microwave and kettle, together with washing-up facilities. Rallies taken by arrangement. Fishing available on-site. Lots of lovely country walks and places to visit in the area. Sudbury Hall and Kedleston are two local National Trust properties. Tutbury Castle, Alton Towers and Uttoxeter Racecourse are also close by. There's a shop in the village and locally there are butchers, country pubs and restaurants.
forestside@uttoxeter.com   www.forestsidefarm.co.uk

BARSHAM *(B&B)*

2 THE OLD HALL 320

Barsham
Beccles NR34 8HB
Tel: 01502 714661 MAP 16

Bed and Breakfast, £20 pppn+£5 per car pn
Evening Meal, £7 pp

Around 98% organic, and 99% supermarket-free

We offer cycle-friendly accommodation in a 16th-century old hall on a 3-acre smallholding in the peaceful Waveney Valley. We grow much of our own food, and welcome informal visitors to share our lifestyle and the idyllic surroundings. Evening meals, using our own garden produce, can be provided. We are a non-smoking, vegetarian, child-friendly household. As our guests you share our home. We have a variety of rooms and can accommodate up to fifteen people. We also have a self-catering option sleeping up to eight in bunk beds. We are interested in food preservation (bottling, drying, juice, wine), spinning, dyeing, knitting, cycling, yoga, massage, green living. Camping £1 per person per night plus £5 per car per night.
graham@bikeways.org.uk   www.bikeways.org.uk

BECCLES *(B&B)*

PINETREES 321

Park Drive
Beccles NR34 7DQ
Tel: 01502 470796   MAP 16

B&B, double *en suite* from £55 pn
Single occupancy from £45 pn

We use organic, fair trade and local produce throughout

Enjoy the contemporary design and eco-friendly features at Pinetrees, set in six and a quarter acres of the peaceful Waveney Valley at Beccles. Pinetrees is a small family business. We offer a wide range of breakfasts including free-range eggs from our own hens, and packed lunches on request (£3.50). Although we don't have the Soil Association stamp of approval, all our foods are sourced organically, locally, and are free of harmful fertilisers and pesticides and anything which may damage the environment and wildlife. Beccles is on Route 1 of the National Cycle Network and there are four attractive regional radial routes of which we can supply details and maps. We offer £5 discount per room for cyclists and walkers.
info@pinetrees.net   www.pinetrees.net

BRAMFIELD *(B&B)*

BRIGHTS FARM  322

Bramfield
Halesworth IP19 9AG
Tel: 01986 784212   MAP 16

Bed and Breakfast
£35-£45 pppn

Breakfast includes organic produce from our farm

Soil Association

A classic three storey Grade II listed 15th-century farmhouse set at the heart of a working organic mixed farm. Breakfast is served in the garden room overlooking the farm pond. Organic and fresh locally produced ingredients are cooked for breakfast, including organic produce from the farm (eggs, bread, damson jam, raspberries, strawberries). This is a traditional Suffolk farm with three generations living on and involved with the farm. It has a Site of Special Scientific Interest, which is one of only 236 sites in England. From the farm you can access twelve miles of grass walks passing old meadows, ancient woods and ponds. One mile to The Queen's Head, where many ingredients are sourced from local organic farms.
mail@brightsfarm.co.uk   www.brightsfarm.co.uk

GUILDFORD *(Hotel)*

ASPERION   323

73 Farnham Road
Guildford GU2 7PF
Tel: 01483 579299   MAP 19

Small Hotel
Double £85-£120 pn, Single £50 pn

Our aim is to use organic, free-range, fair
trade and local produce wherever possible

Asperion offers contemporary accommodation within walking distance of historic Guildford town centre and the mainline train station. We aim to create a high quality guest experience that is ethical, sustainable and rewarding. Our fifteen stylish and comfortable *en suite* rooms and suites are luxuriously decorated, and feature cutting-edge technology. We are passionate about food and are committed to providing our guests with high quality, freshly cooked food. Our aim is to use organic, free-range, fair trade and local produce wherever possible. Relax and unwind with delicious food and drink in our organic bar (tapas menu). All Asperion's wines and spirits are organic, and we also offer an organic beer.
enquiries@asperion.co.uk   www.asperion.co.uk

○ ⇌

WORPLESDON *(Hotel)*

HILLSIDE HOTEL   324

Perry Hill
Worplesdon GU3 3RF
Tel: 01483 232051   MAP 19

Small Hotel
Double £75-£105 pn, Single £65 pn

Our aim is to use organic, free-range, fair
trade and local produce wherever possible

Soil Association

Situated on the beautiful rolling landscape of Surrey, the Hillside Hotel is adjacent to Whitmore Common. Set in award-winning gardens, the privately-owned and run hotel has fifteen *en suite* bedrooms. From the moment you are greeted at the door of the converted Georgian Post Office we aim to make you feel instantly at home and relaxed. Our large and comfortable sitting room overlooks the beautiful gardens and Koi-filled pond. All food is prepared on-site within our own kitchens. We take great pride in our personal attention to detail and have organic certification with the Soil Association for food served in the hotel. The village of Worplesdon is four miles from both Guildford and Woking.
info@thehillsidehotel.com   www.thehillsidehotel.com

○

BRIGHTON *(Hotel)*

FIVEHOTEL 325

5 New Steine
Brighton BN2 1PB
Tel: 01273 686547   MAP 20

Small Hotel, B&B £35-£70 pppn
Weekends minimum stay 2 nights

Freshly prepared organic breakfasts

This period townhouse offers beautiful panoramic sea views and overlooks a classic regency square. FiveHotel has ten rooms. The majority of rooms are *en suite* with views over the square and sea. Crisp white linen and luxurious duvets. Complimentary WiFi throughout. We serve a selection of fresh breakfasts to order, including a vegetarian option. Our organic breakfast is made from fresh produce sourced from local farms on the Sussex South Downs. Accredited with A Taste of Sussex breakfast award, FiveHotel is a stone's throw from the beach and the famous Brighton Palace Pier, and a short stroll from the city. With a backdrop of the Sussex Downs and traditional English countryside, it is a great base for exploring. info@fivehotel.com   www.fivehotel.com

BRIGHTON *(Hotel)*

PASKINS TOWN HOUSE 326

18/19 Charlotte Street
Brighton BN2 1AG
Tel: 01273 601203   MAP 20

Town House Hotel
Bed and Breakfast, £30-£67.50 pppn

Local organic, local farm, home-made

A 'green' hotel, environmentally friendly, and serving organic food. Paskins Town House, in the heart of one of Victorian England's most perfectly preserved conservation areas, is in a tranquil street lined with fine four-storey buildings (built around 1810), with intricate cast iron balconies and gracious bow fronts. Healthy cuisine. We pride ourselves that most of our fresh ingredients are organic, and many are grown on local Sussex farms, including the eggs, tomatoes and mushrooms. The beach is at the end of the road. Paskins is not far from the South Downs Way, imposing chalk cliffs, Beachy Head (with views across the sea), picturesque medieval villages, forests and bird sanctuaries. welcome@paskins.co.uk   www.paskins.co.uk

BRIGHTON (B&B)

THE BRIGHTON HOUSE 327

52 Regency Square
Brighton BN1 2FF
Tel: 01273 323282 MAP 20

Guest House
Bed and Breakfast, £40-£65 pppn

Big organic buffet-style breakfast (at least 80% organic)

The Brighton House is a recently refurbished historic Regency townhouse, centrally located by the West Pier. We are proud of our environmental and health concerns, and wish this to reflect in our fourteen-room guesthouse. The large buffet-style breakfast, suitable for both vegetarians and non, is almost entirely organic, with the exceptions being made known (if it is not organic, we say so). The environmental ethos extends to careful recycling, energy efficient heating systems, and electricity exclusively from renewable sources. Come and experience the clean *en suite* rooms and relax in our down duvet decked beds. Green Tourism Business Scheme Gold Award.
info@brighton-house.co.uk   www.brighton-house.co.uk

EAST DEAN (S-C)

BEACHY HEAD COTTAGES 328

Upper Street
East Dean BN20 0BS
Tel: 01323 423 878 MAP 20

Cottages: sleep 4/5/6 (or groups of up to 15)
£360-£1080 pw (short breaks available)

Tea room, pub, farmers' market and shop sell the farm's own produce

Organic Farming Scheme

Beachy Head Holiday Cottages look out over the stunning South Downs Area of Outstanding Natural Beauty, and are just twenty minutes from the sea through adjoining fields. The three cottages, situated in the heart of the old village of East Dean, are converted 18th-century farm buildings each with their own character and charm. Our organic farm produce is available every Wednesday morning at East Dean market and also from our local butcher in Willingdon. Our local pub, The Tiger Inn, sells our own Beachy Head Ale which is also available in bottles from the tea room. Walking and cycling opportunities are encouraged by the owner's of Beachy Head, who will be more than happy to point out the area's capacity for outdoor adventure.
jan@beachyhead.org.uk   beachyhead.org.uk

FONTWELL (B&B)

London Road
Fontwell BN18 0SG
Tel: 01243 544133   MAP 19

Bed and Breakfast|
£30-£40 pppn

Organic wholemeal and malted oat breads,
fruit, muesli, cheese, milk, orange juice

Enjoy an organic stay in an 18th-century Sussex flint cottage. An organic breakfast is served in the dining room overlooking the cottage gardens. Select from seasonal organic fruit, malted oat and wholemeal breads, organic cheeses, organic milk, organic orange juice with fair trade teas and coffee. The Cameron Room is a double bedroom with adjacent private bath and features an antique Spanish bedstead. The Fontwell Room is a single en suite with 1920s furniture. Both rooms offer Sky, wireless broadband and hospitality trays, with fair trade teas and coffees as well as the organic CocoaLoca Brownies. Park Cottage offers walking and cycling from the doorstep, and we have a walled garden with seating for guests. parkcottage1@btinternet.com   www.country-enterprise.co.uk/parkcottage

HEATHFIELD (Camping)

HIDDEN SPRING VINEYARD 330

Vines Cross Road
Horam TN21 0HG
Tel: 01435 812640   MAP 20

Caravan and Camping Site, 1st Mar-31st Oct
Adult £4.50, Child £2, Yurt (contact for prices)

Organic apples and pears, organic ciders,
vineyard honey

Soil Association

Hidden Spring combines a quiet rural caravan and camping site with the chance to stay on a working vineyard and organic orchards. There is a small touring caravan site, tented camping on the adjacent field and a yurt (available from 2009). Loos, showers, pot wash and Elsan point available. All sites have lovely views over the vines, orchards and the Sussex Weald. We offer on-site sales of our own wines, organic cider, organic apple juices as well as vineyard honey, free-range eggs and organic fruit in season. For day-to-day needs, the local village of Horam is within a short walk. With its proximity to the Cuckoo Trail there are many walks and cycle rides in the area, or simply come for a peaceful and relaxing stay. hiddenspring@btconnect.com   www.hiddenspring.co.uk

HEATHFIELD *(S-C)*

THE COACH HOUSE 331

Beech Hill Farm
Rushlake Green TN21 9QB
Tel: 01435 830203 MAP 20

Cottage: sleeps 2-3, £320-£420 pw
Short breaks available from £225

In season fruit, vegetables, naturally reared
rare breed lamb / mutton

20-acre smallholding, run organically, with two small lakes, formal gardens, traditional pasture. The artistically converted 18th-century coach house (separate entrance) is set within its own private garden with views over the unspoilt ancient High Weald, making it a wonderful place to relax and unwind. Public transport and food on your doorstep leaflets. WWOOF host, committed to sustainable ways of living wherever possible. SEEDA Sustainable Business Award for resource efficiency. BETRE Green Action Award for rain-harvesting scheme for vegetable, fruit and flower production. Fine textiles, locally spun yarn, fleece – all from our rare breed Black Wensleydale Longwools. Green Tourism Business Scheme Gold Award. julia@desch.go-plus.net   www.sussexcountryretreat.co.uk/farm-stay/the-coach-house.htm

HEATHFIELD *(S-C)*

THE STUDIO SANCTUARY 332

Beech Hill Farm
Rushlake Green TN21 9QB
Tel: 01435 830203 MAP 20

Studio: sleeps 2/3, £310-£360 pw
Short breaks available from £215

In season fruit, vegetables, naturally reared
rare breed lamb / mutton

20-acre smallholding, run organically, with two small lakes, formal gardens, traditional pasture. WWOOF host, committed to sustainable ways of living wherever possible. SEEDA Sustainable Business Award for resource efficiency. Green Tourism Business Scheme Gold Award. The studio offers dedicated space and seclusion for single / small groups, master classes / workshops, or as a personal retreat for rest and artistic inspiration. Woodburner now installed with BETRE Green Action Award 2008. We welcome walkers and cyclists as part of the East Sussex Paths to Prosperity Programme. Fine textiles, locally spun yarn and fleece available to purchase – all from our rare breed Black Wensleydale Longwools. julia@desch.go-plus.net   www.sussexcountryretreat.co.uk/farm-stay/the-studio-sanctuary.htm

ROBERTSBRIDGE *(B&B)*

SLIDES FARM B&B 333

Silverhill
Robertsbridge TN32 5PA
Tel: 01580 880106   MAP 20

Bed and Breakfast, £40 pppn
Dinner (by arrangement)

Local farm produce, with the emphasis on
organic and free-range

Slides Farm B&B (awarded 5 stars from Enjoy England) is set in 20'acres of fields and pasture in a secluded position above the historic village of Robertsbridge. It has magnificent views over the Sussex Weald, an Area of Outstanding Natural Beauty. Each of our *en suite* rooms are stylish and contemporary, with their own garden and terrace area. We pride ourselves in serving a delicious breakfast using the best of local farm produce, with the emphasis on organic (around 70%) and free-range wherever possible. Breakfast options include full English with local Salehurst bacon and sausages, local Wealden smoked haddock with organic poached egg, or Parmesan scrambled eggs with locally smoked salmon.
info@slidesfarm.com   www.slidesfarm.com

RYE *(B&B)*

HAYDEN'S 334

108 High Street
Rye TN31 7JE
Tel: 01797 224501   MAP 20

Bed and Breakfast, £30-£60 pppn
Lunch (daily), Evening Meal (Friday, Saturday)

Almost all our food is of organic and local
origin

Located in a beautiful 18th-century town house, Hayden's is a family run eco-friendly bed and breakfast in the centre of the ancient market town of Rye. Visitors have access to the rear terraces, which have panoramic views across Romney Marsh and out to the sea. Enjoy our home cooking, prepared using organic local produce, as you gaze at the views. We serve breakfast and lunch every day, and also open for evening dining on Fridays and Saturdays. As well as paying attention to natural wholesome food, we use green cleaning products in the kitchen, home laundry and rooms. We also think recycling is very important and participate in community trade waste recycling schemes for glass, plastic and cardboard.
haydens_in_rye@mac.com   www.haydensinrye.co.uk

STEYNING *(B&B)*

NASH MANOR  335

Horsham Road
Steyning BN44 3AA
Tel: 01903 814988 MAP 19

Bed and Breakfast, £37.50-£45 pppn
Workshops, from £80 pp for 2 days

75% of the food is organic over the year

Family-run bed and breakfast situated in the beautiful Sussex countryside. Totally refurbished, Nash Manor has six guest rooms (*en suite* or with private bathrooms). We use as much organic produce as possible when available. Set in eight acres of land overlooking Chanctonbury Ring, we grow our own vegetables and herbs and have our own chickens. We are very committed to protecting the environment in whatever way we can, and have achieved the Gold Award with the Green Tourism Business Scheme. In the grounds we have a stone circle and a labyrinth. At Nash Manor we hold weekend workshops on health-related or creative subjects. Close to the South Downs, this is a tranquil setting for walking and cycling. info@nashmanor.co.uk   www.nashmanor.co.uk

UCKFIELD *(Camping)*

WOWO CAMPSITE 336

Wapsbourne Manor Farm
Sheffield Park TN22 3QT
Tel: 01825 723414 MAP 20

Yurts: sleep 4-5, £84.60-£94.60 pn
Camping, adult £8, child £4 pn

Organic food (milk, eggs, cheese, bread) to order

Soil Association

Our 150-acre organic farm is situated at Sheffield Park. Wildlife is abundant – deer, badgers, woodpeckers, owls, etc. Bluebells, wild honeysuckle, blackberries and other wild food are plenty, so come and pick a feast. Have a yurt experience by a trickling stream with cosy woodstove, or choose from camp sites in our secluded tipi trail woodland sites (£10 extra per site) or nestle in by a stream. Signposted short or longer walks and cycle routes available from the site. Local attractions within walking distance include the Bluebell Railway and Sheffield Park NT garden. Organic bread, eggs, green top milk and award-winning cheeses to order. Musicians camp for free on a Friday night for entertainment of other guests. camping@wowo.co.uk

WINCHELSEA *(B&B)*

WICKHAM MANOR FARM 337

Wickham Rock Lane
Winchelsea TN36 4AG
Tel: 01797 226216   MAP 20

Farmhouse Bed and Breakfast
£40-£47.50 pppn (2 sharing)

Organic lamb, beef, pork

Soil Association

Wickham Manor is an historic property built in the 16th-century and now owned by the National Trust. It is our family home and the centre of our 750-acre organic farm, which surrounds the historic town of Winchelsea – the smallest town in England. The farm is home to many species of wildlife such as badgers, rabbits, foxes, swans and herons. Situated in the heart of the Sussex countryside the manor offers comfortable oak beamed bedrooms (refurbished to a high standard in 2007) with wonderful views, a beautiful breakfast / dining room where you will be served a traditional full English breakfast, and lovely gardens where you can sit and relax after a long day exploring the many local historic places of interest. info@wickhammanor.co.uk   www.wickhammanor.co.uk

○

BISHOPSTONE *(B&B)*

PREBENDAL FARM 338

Icknield Way
Bishopstone SN6 8PT
Tel: 01793 790485   MAP 19

Farmhouse Bed and Breakfast
£30-£40 pppn

Organic breakfasts are provided

Prebendal Farm, built in 1863, is only a mile from the Ridgeway – the most ancient road in Europe. The classic Victorian red brick farmhouse is enclosed within its own extensive walled gardens, which sweep away from the house in a succession of ancient terraces to the medieval fish pond. This working arable farm is situated in Bishopstone, a beautiful chalk downland village with an exquisite Norman church and a multitude of thatched cottages clustered around an old mill pond. Organic breakfasts are provided, using produce from the famous Eastbrook Farm next door. The Royal Oak pub (also run by Helen Browning of Eastbrook Farm) offers an extensive organic menu and is just five minutes walk from the house. prebendal@aol.com   www.prebendal.com

○ ⑤ ❺ ⅄ ♘ ⊞

BISHOPSTONE *(B&B)*

THE ROYAL OAK   339

Cues Lane
Bishopstone SN6 8PP
Tel: 01793 790481   MAP 19

Bed and Breakfast, double £60 pn
Bar snacks, full lunches, evening meals

The finest organic meat and good quality,
often home-grown, ingredients

The Royal Oak has been the heart of the village of Bishopstone since around 1650 and is now part of Helen Browning's organic food and farming business centred on Eastbrook Farm. Bed and Breakfast is in two rooms set away from the hubbub of the bar. Wake up to a glorious breakfast mostly provided by our own pigs and hens. Lunch and supper menus using the best meat and eggs from our own organic livestock, our own garden fruit, berries from our hedgerows, game from the farm, as seasons dictate. Open 11am-3pm and 6pm-11pm Monday to Friday. Saturdays and Sundays we open at noon and serve lunch till after 4pm. Simple supper menus Sunday and Monday evenings. Organic wines and champagnes. royaloak@helenbrowningorganics.co.uk www.helenbrowningorganics.co.uk/royal_oak_pub.phtml

EAST KNOYLE *(B&B)*

COOLS FARM   340

East Knoyle
Salisbury SP3 6DB
Tel: 01747 830720   MAP 18

Bed and Breakfast
£35-£45 pppn

Our own free-range eggs are included in
your farmhouse breakfast

Soil Association

Bed and breakfast in a historic 17th-century farmhouse on an organic farm within the Cranborne Chase Area of Outstanding Natural Beauty. The house is built in local stone and has beams, inglenooks and light sunny rooms. Part of coming away is having a good English breakfast and you'll have it here in true English farmhouse style. Eggs and beef from our suckler herd of Red Poll cattle are often for sale. Pythouse Organic Farmshop, situated in a beautiful 18th-century walled garden, is one mile. Longleat, Stonehenge, Salisbury, Bath nearby. Walk along the Wessex Ridgeway Path or visit Studland Beach and Nature Reserve (a haven for rare birds and other native wildlife), where glorious sandy beaches stretch for three miles. stay@coolsfarm.co.uk www.coolsfarm.co.uk

EAST KNOYLE *(S-C)*

THE OLD PIGGERY 341

Cools Farm
East Knoyle SP3 6DB
Tel: 01747 830720   MAP 18

Self-Catering: sleeps 2-3
£278-£466 pw

Full English breakfast in the farmhouse (£8 pp)

Soil Association

The Old Piggery is across the lawn from our 17th-century farmhouse, within the Cranborne Chase Area of Outstanding Natural Beauty. The self-contained accommodation has an *en suite* shower room and a fully equipped kitchen. The one large studio bedroom has a 5' double bed plus a single sofa bed. Centrally heated with a wood-burning stove providing a lovely focal point in colder periods. Own garden area. We have a herd of organic Red Poll cattle on the farm, our own chickens for delicious eggs and home-grown asparagus. Boxes of Red Poll beef, our eggs and asparagus are for sale. Well-behaved dogs welcome. Pythouse Organic Farmshop one mile. Longleat, Stonehenge, Salisbury, Bath nearby. Wessex Ridgeway path crosses our land.
stay@coolsfarm.co.uk   www.coolsfarm.co.uk

POULSHOT *(Camping)*

BELLE VUE FARM 342

Poulshot
Devizes SN10 1RZ
Tel: 01380 828351   MAP 19

Feather Down Tents: sleep 5+, £345-£679 pw
Short Breaks, £185-£395

As far as possible produce comes from the farm or from the fields around it

Soil Association

Belle Vue Farm is a 110-acre organic farm in Poulshot near the small market town of Devizes. Part of the Feather Down Farm group, our five tents are spacious and comfortable. The tents are beautifully sited between large hedges near a stream. In summer the stream offers a great opportunity for adventurous water play. Each Feather Down Farm has an 'honesty shop' in which fresh produce is sold. The food items are, where possible, from the farm and from the region and produced according to traditional methods. Fresh eggs can be gathered by guests every morning. During your stay we'll fire the wood-fired traditional oven so you can enjoy a home-made meal. Bikes can be hired to explore the local countryside.
edward.dyke@onetel.net   www.featherdown.co.uk/Farms/BelVue_Farm.htm

SHAW *(B&B)*

LOWER SHAW FARM 343

Old Shaw Lane
Shaw SN5 5PJ
Tel: 01793 771080 MAP 19

Activity Breaks / Courses, from £114 (inc meals). B&B, £20-£25 pppn

Full vegetarian board is provided (90% of the food we give our guests is organic)

Once a dairy farm deep in rural North Wiltshire, Lower Shaw Farm now has another life. It is a 3-acre organic oasis in an area of new development, with large organic vegetable, herb and flower gardens, poultry and Black Mountain sheep. There are wildlife areas with native shrubs and trees, ponds and play spaces. The outbuildings have been converted into dormitories, meeting rooms and workshops, and it is now a flourishing meeting place and residential centre, running courses, conferences and learning holidays. These include rural crafts, family activities, yoga, singing. The food is mostly home-grown or local and organic, and is all freshly-prepared. Not far away are the Ridgeway Path and Avebury stone circle.
enquiries@lowershawfarm.co.uk   www.lowershawfarm.co.uk

○

KNIGHTWICK *(B&B)*

THE TALBOT 344

Knightwick
Worcester WR6 5PH
Tel: 01886 821235 MAP 14

Coaching Inn, B&B £45-£50 pppn
Restaurant (lunch, dinner)

Strong emphasis on organic (40%-60%) and locally produced ingredients

In a peaceful setting on the River Teme, this traditional coaching inn has been welcoming enthusiasts of good food since the late 14th-century. There is a strong emphasis on organic and locally produced ingredients (with the exception of fish delivered from Cornwall and Wales), and traditional, seasonal and sometimes ancient recipes, all reworked with an imaginative flair and real emphasis on wholesome flavour. Home-made preserves, breads, black pudding and raised pies. Many of the vegetables, salads and herbs come from our own organic kitchen garden, and wild food is gathered from the fields and hedgerows. Home brewed ales are produced in our own brewery behind the inn.
info@the-talbot.co.uk   www.the-talbot.co.uk

○ ⑤ 🍷 👥 🐴 🚌

MATHON (B&B)

OLD COUNTRY HOUSE   345

Old Country Farm
Mathon WR13 5PS
Tel: 01886 880867   MAP 14

Farmhouse Bed and Breakfast
Double £60-£90 pn, Single £35-£55 pn

80% certified organic food on average

Stay in our 600 year old family home with its large and beautiful garden. Relax in the big farmhouse kitchen. The extensive farmhouse buffet breakfast encompasses organic and local food wherever possible. Enjoy the freedom of walking in the grassland, traditional orchards and ancient woodland of this 220-acre farm. The whole farm is managed for the benefit of wildlife and landscape, and to encourage the understanding of our relationship – physical, spiritual and creative – with the natural world. We have a Herefordshire Nature Trust Green Business Award and a Gold Wildlife Award. Visitors staying at Old Country House can view the historic and characteristic cider house and hopkilns building at their discretion.
ella@oldcountryhouse.co.uk   www.oldcountryhouse.co.uk

MATHON (S-C)

THE LIGHTHOUSE   346

Old Country Farm
Mathon WR13 5PS
Tel: 01886 880867   MAP 14

Green Oak House: sleeps 6-14, £650-£1450 (6 nights). Short Breaks, £500-£1050 (3 nights)

A welcome pack of organic and local food is provided

The Lighthouse is in a wonderful position in the orchards, overlooking the Malvern Hills. This is a newly built green oak building, with a large music / sitting room suitable for group use, a smaller study / twin bedroom, three double bedrooms with baths / showers, and further sleeping space for two people. Organic mattresses and bedlinen on the double beds. In the nearby studio / garage are facilities for washing clothes, cleaning palettes, etc. Two to four more beds available in the studio. Hang your work and host a final party at the 'Gallery in the Granary'. All the facilities of Old Country Farm are open to our guests. The Lighthouse is self-catering accommodation. Children should be over eight years old.
ella@oldcountryhouse.co.uk   www.oldcountryhouse.co.uk

RUSHWICK *(S-C)*

THE STEADING 347

Upper Wick Farm
Rushwick WR2 5SU
Tel: 01905 422243   MAP 14

Cottage: sleeps 2+2
£200-£275 pw (pppn by arrangement)

Home cooked meals can be provided made with our own seasonal organic produce

Soil Association

Upper Wick Farm is to the south-west of Worcester city, two miles from the magnificent Cathedral and Royal Worcester Porcelain works. We are a working organic farm of 300 acres rearing our own organic beef, lamb, chicken and eggs plus a large variety of vegetables, herbs and fruit that we sell at our own shop in the village. The Steading is all on the ground floor. It has a large double bedroom with room for a further bed / cot for children, family bathroom, fully equipped kitchen, large lounge (with sofa bed) / dining room with a beautiful aspect across the farm towards the Malvern Hills. The farm is bordered by the River Teme, a Site of Special Scientific Interest due to the wealth of wildlife it supports. roots@rushwick.com

DRIFFIELD *(S-C)*

WOLD VIEW 348

Foston on the Wolds
Driffield YO25 8BJ
Tel: 01262 488382   MAP 10

Apartment: sleeps 2
£226-£340 pw

Eggs and seasonal produce always available from the owner's organic nursery

Soil Association

A traditional first floor property, adjacent to the owner's house and small organic nursery business. Very comfortably furnished to provide excellent and cosy holiday accommodation, it overlooks the rear courtyard and vegetable garden. Complimentary fruit basket, milk and eggs. Small sun terrace with chairs (french window access from the lounge) and use of the owner's garden. The very pleasant outlook extends out over the surrounding countryside. The cottage is in a quiet and secluded position in the small village of Foston, deep in the Yorkshire Wolds. There are many lovely country walks in the immediate area, and plenty of local sights to visit. Visit the east coast of Yorkshire and the North Yorkshire Moors. www.theinternetfarmshop.com/foston-nurseries.htm

GUISBOROUGH *(Hotel)*

PINCHINTHORPE HALL   349

Pinchinthorpe
Guisborough TS14 8HG
Tel: 01287 630200   MAP 9

Country House Hotel, B&B from £65 pppn
Restaurant and Bistro

Menus include fresh seasonal produce from
our Georgian kitchen garden

Organic Food Federation

A 17th-century country house hotel situated in natural woodland within the North Yorkshire Moors National Park. Menus change daily, dependant on the choice of fresh seasonal produce available from our kitchen garden. Whenever possible all other produce is bought from local producers within a fifty mile radius, using organic as first choice and free trade if obtained from abroad. Our pedigree herd of Dexter cattle provides the chefs with beef that is second to none. The Manor Restaurant is grand but intimate, whereas the Brewhouse Bistro is less formal. The onsite brewery is certified by the Organic Food Federation, and the brewery tour includes a set meal. NB, the kitchen garden is not certified organic.
sales@nybrewery.co.uk   www.pinchinthorpehall.co.uk

HEBDEN BRIDGE *(B&B)*

MYRTLE GROVE   350

14 Old Lees Road
Hebden Bridge HX7 8HL
Tel: 01422 846078   MAP 9

Vegetarian Bed and Breakfast
Double £55-£65 pn, Single £35-£55 pn

Organic when possible; home-grown fruit,
home-made jams, home-baked bread

Beautifully furnished stone cottage overlooking the small town of Hebden Bridge. The self-contained *en suite* guest room has scenic views of the Calder Valley and across to Heptonstall. I cook vegetarian, and use organic produce wherever I can. I grow a wide selection of fruit (rhubarb, raspberries, gooseberries, damsons, blackcurrants, redcurrants), which is served with yogurt at breakfast time. What doesn't get eaten is bottled or made into jam and served throughout the year. I bake my own bread using organic products and buy local eggs and vegetables whenever possible. Plenty of footpath walks begin from the house. It's a pleasant walk down to the town with its thriving organic cafés and delicatessens.
myrtlegrove@btinternet.com   www.myrtlegrove.btinternet.co.uk

HOWDEN (S-C)

STRAW BALE CABIN 351

Barmby Grange
Eastrington DN14 7QN
Tel: 01430 410662 MAP 10

Straw Bale Cabin: sleeps 2 £245-£280 pw
Weekend and mid week breaks available

Complimentary larder basics, honesty shop,
vegetable box to order

Unique cottage built with locally grown straw bales and other natural materials. Powered with renewable energy. The cosy, well-equipped cabin stands in the corner of a wildflower meadow, overlooking a delightful pond. Curvy, clay plastered walls, oak beams and deep, oak windowsills give the cabin the feel of an old country cottage. Organic towels, bedding and cleaning materials are provided. Herbs growing on the doorstep. Miles of bramble-laden hedgerows in season. Local, organic and fair trade food available. Peaceful rural location. Explore this unspoilt corner of East Yorkshire. Free use of bicycles. Excellent train links for the complete environmentally friendly holiday. Station collection service.
carol@strawcottage.co.uk   www.strawcottage.co.uk

HUDDERSFIELD (B&B)

WEAVERS SHED 352

88 Knowl Road
Golcar HD7 4AN
Tel: 01484 654284 MAP 9

Bed and Breakfast, £50-£75 pppn
Restaurant (dinner from 7pm)

Dishes include naturally grown produce
from the kitchen garden

The Weavers Shed Restaurant with Rooms is a former cloth-finishing mill in the centre of the village of Golcar. Set in the heart of the Colne Valley it was converted to a restaurant over twenty five years ago and adjoins the former mill owner's residence, which now comprises five spacious luxury guest rooms. The restaurant offers a menu of suitably rustic dishes, in a setting of rough stone walls and flagstone floors. It is one of the few restaurants in the North to have its own kitchen garden. The restaurant grows fruit, vegetables and herbs as naturally as possible on over an acre of land, which is picked on an almost daily basis. Eggs are provided by the restaurant's own chickens and ducks.
info@weaversshed.co.uk   www.weaversshed.co.uk

PICKERING *(S-C)*

BEDFORD CORNER 353

Little Edstone Farm
Little Edstone YO62 6NY
Tel: 01751 431369 MAP 9

Self-Catering: sleeps 4+2
£400-£930 pw

Organic eggs and organic seasonal
vegetables always available to purchase

Soil Association

Little Edstone House and Farm is set in wonderful countryside on the edge of the North York Moors National Park. The beautiful cottages were created from a 300 year old stone barn, with many of the original features remaining, and are heated by renewable energy. Facilities include a heated indoor pool, tennis court, gym, sauna, table tennis, outdoor children's play area and a pets corner. You're welcome to explore the woodland, which although small is home to a variety of wildlife. Organic eggs and organic vegetables are available to buy direct from the owner's. Alternatively a box of home-grown organic vegetables can be picked to order and delivered to your cottage within minutes of picking, or you can pick your own.
pj.littleedstone@btinternet.com   www.littleedstone.co.uk

PICKERING *(S-C)*

FOXCOVER 354

Little Edstone Farm
Little Edstone YO62 6NY
Tel: 01751 431369 MAP 9

Self-Catering: sleeps 4+1
£380-£840 pw

Organic eggs and organic seasonal
vegetables always available to purchase

Soil Association

Little Edstone House and Farm is set in wonderful countryside on the edge of the North York Moors National Park. The beautiful cottages were created from a 300 year old stone barn, with many of the original features remaining, and are heated by renewable energy. Facilities include a heated indoor pool, tennis court, gym, sauna, table tennis, outdoor children's play area and a pets corner. You're welcome to explore the woodland, which although small is home to a variety of wildlife. Organic eggs and organic vegetables are available to buy direct from the owner's. Alternatively a box of home-grown organic vegetables can be picked to order and delivered to your cottage within minutes of picking, or you can pick your own.
pj.littleedstone@btinternet.com   www.littleedstone.co.uk

PICKERING (S-C)

SEPTEMBER LOFT 355

Little Edstone Farm
Little Edstone YO62 6NY
Tel: 01751 431369 MAP 9

Self-Catering: sleeps 2+1
£290-£610 pw

Organic eggs and organic seasonal
vegetables always available to purchase

Soil Association

Little Edstone House and Farm is set in wonderful countryside on the edge of the North York Moors National Park. The beautiful cottages were created from a 300 year old stone barn, with many of the original features remaining, and are heated by renewable energy. Facilities include a heated indoor pool, tennis court, gym, sauna, table tennis, outdoor children's play area and a pets corner. You're welcome to explore the woodland, which although small is home to a variety of wildlife. Organic eggs and organic vegetables are available to buy direct from the owner's. Alternatively a box of home-grown organic vegetables can be picked to order and delivered to your cottage within minutes of picking, or you can pick your own. pj.littleedstone@btinternet.com   www.littleedstone.co.uk

PICKERING (S-C)

STANDFIELD HALL 356

Standfield Hall Farm
Westgate Carr Road YO18 8LX
Tel: 01751 472249 MAP 10

Cottage: sleeps 4, £280-£766 pw
Free organic breakfast hamper

Soil Association

Dating back to the 1800s, this detached stone-built cottage is in an ideal location for exploring the North Yorkshire Moors and the Heritage coastline of East Yorkshire. The cottage is situated on our 67-acre working organic farm. A complimentary organic breakfast hamper (worth £20) and fresh flowers will be in the cottage at the beginning of your holiday. The four star accommodation has a fully fitted farmhouse kitchen and a lounge with a wood-burning stove on the ground floor, and king-size double and twin bedded rooms and a bathroom on the first floor. Outside there's a private patio and a large garden with barbecue and picnic table. The farm is down a quiet country lane, a mile from the small market town of Pickering. mike@theorganicfarmshop.com   www.theorganicfarmshop.com

PICKERING *(S-C)*

THE WHEELHOUSE 357

Little Edstone Farm
Little Edstone YO62 6NY
Tel: 01751 431369 MAP 9

Self-Catering: sleeps 8+2
£740-£1550 pw

Organic eggs and organic seasonal
vegetables always available to purchase

Soil Association

Little Edstone House and Farm is set in wonderful countryside on the edge of the North York Moors National Park. The beautiful cottages were created from a 300 year old stone barn, with many of the original features remaining, and are heated by renewable energy. Facilities include a heated indoor pool, tennis court, gym, sauna, table tennis, outdoor children's play area and a pets corner. You're welcome to explore the woodland, which although small is home to a variety of wildlife. Organic eggs and organic vegetables are available to buy direct from the owner's. Alternatively a box of home-grown organic vegetables can be picked to order and delivered to your cottage within minutes of picking, or you can pick your own. pj.littleedstone@btinternet.com   www.littleedstone.co.uk

PICKERING *(S-C)*

WESTEND 358

Little Edstone Farm
Little Edstone YO62 6NY
Tel: 01751 431369 MAP 9

Self-Catering: sleeps 4+1
£380-£840 pw

Organic eggs and organic seasonal
vegetables always available to purchase

Soil Association

Little Edstone House and Farm is set in wonderful countryside on the edge of the North York Moors National Park. The beautiful cottages were created from a 300 year old stone barn, with many of the original features remaining, and are heated by renewable energy. Facilities include a heated indoor pool, tennis court, gym, sauna, table tennis, outdoor children's play area and a pets corner. You're welcome to explore the woodland, which although small is home to a variety of wildlife. Organic eggs and organic vegetables are available to buy direct from the owner's. Alternatively a box of home-grown organic vegetables can be picked to order and delivered to your cottage within minutes of picking, or you can pick your own. pj.littleedstone@btinternet.com   www.littleedstone.co.uk

SALTBURN BY THE SEA (B&B)

THE ROSE GARDEN 359

20 Hilda Place
Saltburn by the Sea TS12 1BP
Tel: 01287 622947 MAP 9

Bed and Breakfast
Double £30 pppn, Single £40 pn

Carefully sourced high quality produce,
mainly organic / local / fair trade

The Rose Garden is a gracious Victorian terraced house situated within five minutes walk of the sea. This four star accommodation is also close to the shops and the train station. We have two excellently-furnished *en suite* double / twin bedrooms appointed to a high standard. They both have well stocked tea trays, with mineral water, a selection of teas, coffee, hot chocolate, herbal drinks, biscuits and organic chocolates. We believe that food should be produced in an environmentally friendly way using humane methods. We therefore use mainly organic / fair trade / locally produced products, and are more than happy to cater for those with various dietary requirements, such as vegetarians and vegans.
enquiries@therosegarden.co.uk   www.therosegarden.co.uk

SCARBOROUGH (S-C)

GRANARY COTTAGE 360

Spikers Hill Farm
West Ayton YO13 9LB
Tel: 01723 862537 MAP 10

Cottage: sleeps 4
£220-£400 pw

Local organic produce can be bought at the weekly farmers' market (two miles)

Soil Association

Granary Cottage is situated on a 570-acre farm, part of which is organic. It is on the west side of Spikers Hill farm steading, with views over farmland to Wykeham woods and the wolds. The cottage has two bedrooms – one double room with a double bed, and one twin with two single beds. Downstairs is open-plan, and heating is by oil-fired central heating. Local organic produce can be bought on Fridays at the weekly farmers' market in Wykeham, two miles away. A box of organic produce may be available to order from River Swale Organic Vegetables (please ask for details when booking). Set within the North Yorkshire National Park the farm cottage is six miles from the coast at Scarborough. Fishing can be arranged locally.
janet@spikershill.ndo.co.uk   www.spikershill.ndo.co.uk

SCARBOROUGH *(B&B)*

THE LODGE 361

98 Throxenby Lane
Scarborough YO12 5RE
Tel: 01723 363365 MAP 10

Bed and Breakfast, £35-£40 pppn
Evening Meal (by prior arrangement)

Almost 100% organic, sourced locally
wherever possible

The Lodge is a spacious, comfortable mid-Georgian detached property on the edge of the countryside yet within easy reach of the town centre and North and South Bays' beaches. Pleasant well-appointed rooms are complemented by hearty and wholesome breakfasts with home-made breads and preserves, using exclusively organic ingredients. Complimentary trays with organic tea, coffee and biscuits are provided in the bedrooms as well as a welcoming drink on arrival. On occasion, dinner is available by prior arrangement if, for example, a late arrival is envisaged. Healthy, delicious food and warm hospitality are the reasons behind The Lodge's growing reputation as we invite you to share our home with us. charles.betty@gmail.com   www.lodgeorganic.co.uk

SETTLE *(Hotel)*

THE TRADDOCK 362

Austwick
Settle LA2 8BY
Tel: 015242 51224 MAP 9

Small Hotel, B&B from £70 pppn
Fully certified organic restaurant

The award-winning restaurant uses organic, local and seasonal ingredients

Soil Association

Nestling in the unspoilt village of Austwick and flanked by the three peaks of Ingleborough, Penn-y-Ghent and Whernside with glorious views of the Forest of Bowland, this stylish, cosy and friendly hotel offers an authentic country house experience. There are stunning walks from the front door through Crummackdale, the Norber Erratics and the famous Limestone Pavements (as featured in Wainwright's Limestone Country), enabling you to enjoy the wonders of the surrounding countryside and work up a hearty appetite for the delicious organic food on offer at The Traddock's fully certified organic restaurant. The restaurant won Organic Restaurant of The Year for the Industry Awards 2006. AA Rosette. info@austwicktraddock.co.uk   www.thetraddock.co.uk

SKIPTON (B&B)

WEST WINDS 363

Buckden
Upper Wharfedale BD23 5JA
Tel: 01756 760883   MAP 9

Bed and Breakfast, £25-£27 pppn
Meals (lunch, high tea, early dinner)

Fresh organic fruit and vegetables supplied
by Farmaround, or grown in our garden

Homely, comfortable bed and breakfast within an old stone cottage in a beautiful and quiet Dales setting. Hearty Yorkshire food using local, in-season, organic and fair trade produce as much as possible. When you arrive, we provide a complimentary pot of tea and home-made cake in our tearooms. In your room you'll find flowers from our garden, a sample box of locally made Whitaker's chocolates and a help-yourself bowl of organic fruit. In the morning you can have a full cooked breakfast (English or vegetarian) or a continental option, served in our tearooms at a table set with bone china on a hand-embroidered cloth. We also offer Yorkshire high tea or early dinner, and if it's fine you can sit out in our attractive garden.
lynn@westwindsinyorkshire.co.uk   www.westwindsinyorkshire.co.uk

SKIPTON (B&B)

WHARFE VIEW FARM 364

Main Street
Burnsall BD23 6BP
Tel: 01756 720643   MAP 9

Bed and Breakfast
From £35 pppn

As many organic products as possible are
sourced locally for your breakfast

Soil Association

Wharfe View Farm House B&B is a family-run bed and breakfast accommodation situated in the beautiful village of Burnsall in the Yorkshire Dales. We offer two large spacious double and twin rooms and a private sitting / dining room with colour TV and open log fire. As many organic products as possible are sourced locally for our full English breakfast, and we offer organic cereals, fruit juice and fruit. The farm is a working organic farm with sheep and some cattle. Guided farm walk. Wharfe View Farm is an excellent base for many walks, including the first few days of the Dales Way walk (Ilkley to Windermere). Free off road parking is available to those staying with us who are doing the local three dale walk.
richard.hirst@ukgateway.net   www.burnsall.net

STAITHES *(S-C)*

RIDGE HALL COTTAGES   365

Ridge Lane
Staithes TS13 5DX
Tel: 01943 466988   MAP 10

Cottages: sleep 2-6, £290-£650 pw. Short
Breaks, £190-£295 (smaller cottages only)

Welcome basket of seasonal local produce
and home-produced preserves

These imaginatively-designed cottages have panoramic views of Borrowby Edge, Roxby, and eastward to the sea and Staithes Valley. We have an holistic approach to the environment and will be happy to share our enjoyment of our kitchen garden with guests. The kitchen garden is backed up by a sixty foot polytunnel providing exotic fruit and vegetables to complement the traditional orchard and plots. Ridge Hall gets its water from a spring at Twizzy Ghyll, and this is just filtered and purified. Rainwater is collected to water the gardens. A wind vane is soon to be situated in the kitchen garden. Future projects include planting a small vineyard, building a new greenhouse, a hen house for fresh eggs and a natural swimming lake. relax@ridgehallcottages.co.uk   www.ridgehallcottages.co.uk

YORK *(B&B)*

CORNMILL LODGE B&B   366

120 Haxby Road
York YO31 8JP
Tel: 01904 620566   MAP 9

Vegetarian Guest House
Bed and Breakfast, £30-£40 pppn

Vegetarian and vegan options, using organic
produce (around 90%) where possible

A deceptively large Edwardian terraced house, built on the site of an 18th-century mill in a popular residential area of this historic city. Comfortable accommodation in a friendly atmosphere. Start the day with a choice of vegetarian or vegan breakfasts. The delicious menu is prepared using organic produce wherever possible, with enough to satisfy the heartiest appetite. Cornmill Lodge is within fifteen minutes walk of York Minster and the city walls – in fact most of this beautiful city is accessible on foot. To the west lie the Yorkshire Dales, to the north the Yorkshire Moors. The rugged cliffs, bird sanctuaries and sandy beaches of Yorkshire's Heritage Coast are less than an hour's drive away. cornmillyork@aol.com   www.cornmillyork.co.uk

YORK *(B&B)*

YORK ALTERNATIVE B&B   367

82 Scarcroft Road
York YO24 1DD
Tel: 01904 625931   MAP 9

Bed and Breakfast
£30 pppn

Serving locally produced and organic foods
(choice of traditional or vegetarian menu)

A comfortable Bed and Breakfast with lots of character, only ten minutes walk from the railway station and the city centre. Everyone comments on the delicious breakfasts. Whenever possible produce will be organic, local, home-made and fair trade. I buy organic products from the local shops. All breads are home-made, and the preserves are home-made from fruit picked locally at Woodside Farm, Acaster Malbis or from our allotment. I also cater for special diets such as vegan, gluten-free, diabetics, etc. The secluded back garden attracts many varieties of birds and insects. York is very cycle friendly, with cycle lanes in many parts of the city. I welcome cyclists, and can house your bike in a lock-up garage overnight. direddeer@nahurac.freeserve.co.uk   www.yorkalternativebandb.co.uk

IRELAND

Clare Island Retreat Centre, County Mayo

INISHERE *(B&B)*

SOUTH ARAN HOUSE   368

Inishere
Aran Islands
Tel: 099 75073   MAP II

Guesthouse, B&B double €35-€45 pppn
Organic and Wild Café

We are aiming for around 90% organic

In Conversion

South Aran Centre provides a unique introduction to the beauty, peace and mystical nature of the Aran Islands. Our new guesthouse is situated in an exceptional location on the western side of the island, with absolutely amazing views of the Atlantic Ocean. The Organic and Wild Café at Fisherman's Cottage serves delicious and healthy organic food, complemented by daily fresh fish and abundance of the ocean. As Slow Food members we aim to do what we can to provide tasty local food that is unique to this island, so that our visitors can take with them memories deeply rooted in this special place in South Aran. The centre provides lifestyle and other courses, retreats, and seminars in a purpose built classroom.
foodwise@eircom.net   www.southaran.com

○ ⑤

INISHMORE *(B&B)*

THE MAN OF ARAN   369

Kilmurvey
Inishmore
Tel: 099 61301   MAP II

Bed and Breakfast, €40-€45 pppn
Restaurant (lunch, dinner)

Maura conjures up masterful meals utilizing the excellent produce from the garden

The cottages are cosy and well maintained, with an old world charm that has to be experienced to be appreciated. I am an avid organic gardener, and nearly half the acre of land the cottage is situated on is given over to this pursuit. Utilizing the excellent produce from the garden, my wife Maura conjures up masterful meals that she serves in the small restaurant located in the main building. The soups she creates are original, unique and exquisite, and I (while professing no artistic talent) fabricate amazing salads out of my garden, featuring a medley of greens as well as flowers, including squash flower and even pansies. Lunch from 6 Euros. Dinner (booking only) from 35 Euros. Packed lunches are also available.
manofaran@eircom.net   manofarancottage.com

○

ARDATTIN (S-C)

BALLIN TEMPLE 370

Ardattin
Carlow
Tel: 059 915 5037 MAP 12

Cottages: sleep 3+2, €600 pw
€150 pn, €400 for 3 nights

Organic produce from the farm and garden available to buy in season

Organic Trust

Ballin Temple is a rare nature sanctuary with ancient woods and three kilometres of river in a special area of conservation (Area of Outstanding Natural Beauty). It is ideal for a romantic rendezvous, a healthy break, an activity weekend, or touring the area. Accommodation is in cosy traditional cottages with views of the Blackstairs Mountains and refurbished with modern comforts. Enjoy walking or cycling in the woods and surrounding country lanes, learn to fly-fish, play archery or book a yoga lesson. Our organic produce, grown in a walled garden with a granite canal, is enjoyed by residents and guests. We've got vegetables, fruit and eggs from chickens and ducks. See our website for things to do and lots of photos. gardener@ballintemple.com   www.ballintemple.com

KILGREANEY (B&B)

LORUM OLD RECTORY 371

Kilgreaney
Bagenalstown
Tel: 059 977 5282 MAP 12

Bed and Breakfast, double €75-€80 pppn
Dinner, €45 (book by noon)

Home cooking incorporates mainly local and organically grown produce

A warm welcome is assured at Lorum Old Rectory, which nestles beneath the Blackstairs Mountains. Built in 1863 of cut granite, the rectory sits beneath Mount Leinster in the tranquil Barrow Valley. Photographs and family memorabilia combine to give that wonderful 'at home' feeling. We have built an international reputation for delicious and imaginative home cooking, incorporating mainly local and organically grown produce, and are members of Slow Food and Euro-Toques. There is fishing and walking alongside the Barrow River, or you can wander in the garden or play croquet. Celtic Cycling, based here at Lorum, organises self-guided 'go as you please' tours in South-East Ireland.
enquiry@lorum.com   www.lorum.com

ST MULLINS *(B&B)*

MULVARRA HOUSE 372

St Mullins
Graiguenamanagh
Tel: 051 424936 MAP 12

Bed and Breakfast, €40-€42 pppn
Dinner, €30 (book in advance)

Locally grown fresh organic herbs and
produce (50%-80% organic)

Mulvarra House is situated in the historic village of St Mullins in south County Carlow. The house emanates peacefulness and tranquillity as it overlooks the River Barrow Valley. All rooms are *en suite* with private balconies. Imaginative home baking and cooking is a speciality. Dinner is served at 7.30pm each evening. All the food is freshly-prepared to a very high standard, using home-grown and locally produced organic produce, herbs and free-range organic eggs. We also offer a wide selection of body treatments. Mulvarra House is set on 2 acres of mature gardens, which can be taken in along with local walks along the tow path to Graiguenamanagh. Short breaks, €155-€185 (2-3 nights B&B and two treatments). info@mulvarra.com www.mulvarra.com

MULLAGH *(S-C)*

THE MILL HOUSE 373

Lakeview Organic Farm and Gardens
Mullagh
Tel: 046 9242480 MAP 12

House: sleeps 4-6
€375-€850 pw

Organic eggs, vegetables, fruit (and flowers)
and fish from Mullagh Lake

Irish Organic Farmers and Growers

The Mill House is located 2km west of the picturesque village of Mullagh on a quiet lane beside Mullagh Lake. Formerly a sawmill and pumphouse for Lakeview Farm, it has been newly renovated to a high standard. The house is set amongst ancient beech trees and flower-filled meadows, all managed to certified organic standards. There is lots to see and do in the area – walk the lanes and nearby bog, climb Mullagh Hill, fish the lake, or explore the rich heritage of County Meath and Cavan. Surplus farm and garden produce will be available to purchase, and there may be a chance to see the now private and famous Lakeview Gardens. Farmers' markets and the best cheese supplier in Ireland are all nearby. daphne@levingeshackleton.com

ANNAGH *(B&B)*

BERRY LODGE 374

Annagh
Miltown Malbay
Tel: 065 708 7022   MAP 11

Bed and Breakfast, €45-€48 pppn
Restaurant (booking is recommended)

As far as possible we only use fresh, natural
and organically grown foods in season

A warm welcome awaits you at this charming Victorian family home, a renovated farmhouse close to the Atlantic offering superb accommodation, excellent food, and cookery tuition in the heart of picturesque County Clare. Berry Lodge dates back to 1775, and although modernised to 20th-century comforts it keeps the character, peaceful ambience and homeliness of an earlier age. The restaurant provides fresh natural foods, and all the ingredients used are sourced locally. As far as possible we only use fresh, natural and organically grown foods in season, flavoured with home-grown herbs and light vegetable stocks. Two-day cookery weekends and special cookery courses (see our website for more information).
info@berrylodge.com   www.berrylodge.com

FANORE *(B&B)*

ROCKYVIEW FARMHOUSE 375

Coast Road
Fanore
Tel: 065 707 6103, 065 707 6213   MAP 11

Farmhouse Bed and Breakfast, €32 pppn
sharing. Packed Lunch (by arrangement)

Organically grown home produce (tomatoes,
basil courgettes, lettuce, herbs, etc)

The farmhouse is situated in the seaside village of Fanore, with spectacular views of the Burren Hills, Galway Bay and the Aran Islands. We (Noel and Ita) are organic gardeners, and have been gardening organically for over thirty years. Breakfast is around 50% organic, and we provide freshly-baked bread and scones, local free-range eggs and organic soya milk. In season there are organic tomatoes, basil and courgettes from the tunnel. We have a vast knowledge of the Burren area, and are keen nature lovers and bird-watchers. The start of the Burren Way is two minutes from the house. The Burren is a limestone karst region, renowned for its geological features, archaeological remains, natural wonders and magnificent flora.
info@rockyviewfarmhouse.com   www.rockyviewfarmhouse.com

ADRIGOLE *(B&B)*

DROMAGOWLANE HOUSE 376

Adrigole
Beara Peninsula
Tel: 027 60330   MAP 11

Bed and Breakfast, double €66-€70 pn
Dinner, 3 course €25 (by arrangement)

Much of the produce comes from the organic garden and orchard surrounding the house

Irish Organic Farmers and Growers

Dromagowlane House is situated on the beautiful Beara Peninsula at the foot of the Sugar Loaf Mountains. The house dates back to the late 1700s and has been modernised and extended to the highest standards. It is set in its own grounds of about 20 acres, with an organic garden and orchard that supplies the house. A full choice breakfast menu is available every morning. Dinner is available by prior arrangement, and all food is sourced from our own organic garden and farm or nearby quality producers. A packed lunch is also available. Adrigole is a small village of exceptional beauty and wonderful tranquillity. The area enjoys a sub-tropical climate and crystal clear waters due to the influence of the Gulf Stream.
dromagowlanehouse@eircom.net   www.dromagowlanehouse.com

COOMLEIGH WEST *(B&B)*

HAGAL FARM   377

Coomleigh West
Bantry
Tel: 027 66179   MAP 11

Bed and Breakfast
Double, €35 pppn

Our vegetables are from our own organic garden or from the local organic market

Hagal Farm is situated in the beautiful natural landscape of West Cork. It nestles on the south slope of the Mealagh Valley with breathtaking views over Bantry Bay in the distance. We offer B&B in five rooms looking onto the gardens (some have a door opening directly into the garden) and we have a self-catering unit with its own garden. Delicious vegetarian food. Our large vegetable garden is fully organic. Our lifestyle and philosophy reflects respect for nature and our natural resources. The buildings and gardens have preserved natural features as much as possible. The five acres surrounding our farm are cultivated in an eco-friendly way, allowing native wild plants to flourish as well as introducing some new species.
hagalhealingfarm@eircom.net   hagalholistichealth.com

KEALKILL *(B&B)*

DOUCE MOUNTAIN FARM 378

Incharoe
Kealkill
Tel: 027 66263   MAP 11

Events (see website): Full Board €69 pppn
Occasional B&B or Self-Catering

Tasty and wholesome food using mainly our
own products (around 85% organic)

Organic Trust

Douce Mountain Farm is set on 49 acres of mountainside in the beautiful Shehy Mountains in West Cork. Our guesthouse is a traditional farmhouse with splendid views along the Owvane River valley and Bantry Bay. Groups, individuals, and families can take part in various activities – hillwalking, walking and meditation, family days (where the children are involved in farm-oriented activities while the parents explore this beautiful area), self-drive holidays (7 nights accommodation plus food €450 pp), and more. An essential part of your stay is the fresh and healthy food, to a large extent made with our own organic produce. Meditation in the style of Zazen is open to visitors. The farm hosts therapy, yoga and other groups.
mail@doucemountainfarm.com   www.doucemountainfarm.com

NOHOVAL *(B&B)*

GORT-NA-NAIN 379

Ballyherkin
Nohoval
Tel: 021 4770647   MAP 11

Vegetarian Guesthouse, double B&B €85-€95
pn. Evening Meal €30 pp (3-course set menu)

Sample the wonderful range of fresh
vegetables, grown on our organic smallholding

Facing the Atlantic on the south coast of County Cork, Gort-Na-Nain is the perfect location for those wanting a quiet rural break set within stunning coastal scenery. The guest rooms in our eco-friendly farmhouse look out towards the rolling agricultural landscape. All meals are based on seasonal vegetables grown onsite on our 9-acre organic smallholding, and prepared within minutes of picking. We keep our own hens for eggs, and all the food we serve is home-made, including breads, jams, pasta, ice cream and other desserts. We offer 3-course evening meals to our guests. Packed lunches are also available to enjoy while exploring the area, including unspoilt beaches, coastal walks and the nearby historic town of Kinsale.
lucy@gortnanain.com   www.gortnanain.com

SHANAGARRY *(S-C)*

BALLYMALOE COTTAGES 380

Ballymaloe Cookery School
Shanagarry
Tel: 021 464 6785 MAP 11

Cottages: sleep 6-12
€950-€1150 pw

Free-range eggs, pork, veg and fruit in season
are available from the farm

Organic Trust

The cottages are all converted from the 18th-century farm buildings beside Kinoith House, the regency home of Darina Allen. They overlook the orchards, gardens and courtyard at Kinoith, and guests are welcome to wander freely through the organic farm and gardens. Free-range eggs and pork, and vegetables and fruit in season are available from the farm. The cottages are available at Christmas, Easter, on a weekly basis during the summer, and occasional holiday weekends. Ballymaloe House, with its famous restaurant, is just two miles away (booking essential). Midleton farmers' market every Saturday. Kinoith is just outside the village of Shanagarry, and two miles from the little fishing village of Ballycotton. info@cookingisfun.ie cookingisfun.ie/pages/self_catering_cottages/

SHANAGARRY *(Hotel)*

BALLYMALOE HOUSE 381

Shanagarry
Midleton
Tel: 021 465 2531 MAP 11

Country House B&B, double from €220 pn
Restaurant (breakfast, lunch, dinner)

We base our menu on the food from our
own farms and our local area

Organic Trust

A large country house on a 400-acre farm, 30km east of Cork. The hotel is family run, on the family farm. We offer comfortable accommodation and an award-winning restaurant in pleasant rural surroundings. The Ballymaloe restaurant was started by Myrtle Allen as the Yeats Room, and has become world famous. At its heart is a culinary philosophy founded on enhancing the natural flavours of the best and freshest local ingredients. Ballymaloe has a two-acre walled vegetable and herb garden (not certified organic), where most of the restaurant's herbs and vegetables are grown, as well as some fruit. The organic farm and gardens surrounding the Ballymaloe Cookery School supplies pork and vegetables. res@ballymaloe.ie www.ballymaloe.ie

TRAGUMNA (S-C)

TRAG RETREAT 382

Gokane
Tragumna
Tel: 028 23283 MAP 11

Cottage: sleeps 6, €580-€1250 pw
Weekends €330 (off season)

Our own organic beef and lamb available to buy

Organic Trust

Beautiful self-catering dwelling house in an idyllic sea front location, set in over an acre of completely private garden in West Cork. The house is renovated to the highest of specifications while still retaining its original character. You have the exclusive use of a hot tub in private gardens with breathtaking views. The extensive timber decking is ideal for holiday barbecues. Garden furniture. Children's swings. We have a 60-hectare organic sheep and suckling beef farm adjacent to the house. We also have a traditional butchery which sells all home-produced fresh meat. The house is ideally located about a mile from the safe and secluded sandy beach of Tragumna. Two bicycles. Scenic walks. Local farmers' market.
tragretreat@gmail.com   www.tragretreat.com

UNION HALL (S-C)

SOUTH REEN FARM RETREAT 383

Union Hall
Skibbereen
Tel: 028 33258 MAP 11

Self-Catering: sleeps 8
€650-€1050 pw

Organic beef, chicken, vegetables and eggs available on request

Organic Trust

Self-catering accommodation on a 75-acre farm. The land is natural and organically tended. The retreat has been newly designed for the individual, group or families. The house has solar hot water, heating a wood-burning stove, washing machine, dishwasher etc. It has a spacious sitting room / kitchen, a sunroom, a conservatory good for group work, a large decking area and a private garden. Situated very close to a beach on a peninsula surrounded on three sides by the sea, its views look over to the sea and up hills and on to woodland, ponds and rivulets. Guests can wander freely, so you can walk through the land crossing ancient old paths, or climbing the peninsula. Organic food can be provided from the farm.
space@southreenfarm.com   www.southreenfarm.com

DOORIAN *(S-C)*

DONEGAL ORGANIC FARM 384

Doorian
Glenties
Tel: 074 955 1286 MAP 6

Apartments: sleep 4, €300-€500 pw.

100% organic (breakfast €5-€8 pp, meal €8-€20 pp)

Demeter

A biodynamic farm in the unspoilt pastoral landscape of Donegal on the north-west edge of the Blue Stack Mountains. It is set against a backdrop of beautiful mountain scenery in a Special Area of Conservation. We have three holiday apartments, each with two bedrooms. We cater for organic farm holidays, hillwalking holidays, eco holidays, seatrout and salmon fishing holidays. Organic vegetables, fruit and herbs are available all year round from our farmshop, as is home-baked bread. The tap water is our own spring water. The farm is 3km from the charming village of Glenties. Choice of walks. Close by is a rich variety of coastal scenery, with smooth white sandy beaches as well as stretches of rough, rocky coastline. tbecht@esatclear.ie   www.donegalorganic.ie

ATHENRY *(B&B)*

CAHEROYAN HOUSE 385

Athenry
Galway
Tel: 091 844858 MAP 5

Country House Bed and Breakfast
Self-Catering (contact for rates)

Our organic farm produces beef, lamb, fruit, etc

Organic Trust

Award-winning family-run country house offering bed and breakfast and self-catering. In a courtyard setting the cottages are only yards from the manor house and within five minutes walk of the town centre. The manor house itself has been tastefully refurbished to reflect its history and importance to the local heritage town of Athenry. The house is set amidst the fields of Athenry on 70 acres of organic farmlands and 30 acres of woodlands. Enjoy the peace and tranquillity of our nature walk or feed the animals with our special food. Around our eco-friendly farm you will see a windmill that pumps water around the farm, a restored lime kiln used to produce lime and whitewash in the olden days, a fish pond, lake and river. caheroynhouseandfarm@eircom.net   www.caheroyanhouseathenry.com

BALLYSEEDY *(S-C)*

GORTBRACK ORGANIC 386

Ballyseedy
Tralee
Tel: 066 7137042   MAP 11

Eco-Cabins
Contact for prices

Organic farm produce may be available

Organic Trust

The eco-cabins are situated on our 10-acre smallholding on the hills overlooking the Lee Valley. The three timber cabins run off solar panels and wood-burning stoves. They can be rented for a secluded getaway, or for attending courses at Gortbrack. The cabins are built in the heart of the farm, so you can wake up every morning in the beautiful peace and tranquillity of Gortbrack, take a wander on the bog or come and help out with the activities on the farm. The farm produces organic fruit, vegetables and herbs on a small scale, designs eco-gardens, propagates plants and trees, and plants native hedgerow and woodlands. Gortbrack is a unique area of native habitats and biodiversity, low impact living and natural beauty.
gortbrackorg@gmail.com   www.gortbrackorganicfarm.com/farmh_ecoc.htm

CASTLEMAINE *(B&B)*

THE PHOENIX 387

Shanahill East
Castlemaine
Tel: 066 976 6284   MAP 11

Bed and Breakfast, double *en suite* €40 pppn
Vegetarian Restaurant

Organic wines and the best of local and organic produce (at least 80% organic)

Uniquely-restored and decorated farmhouse with beautiful gardens, backed by the Slieve Mish Mountains. Over one acre of organic gardens, with a mountain stream, ponds, and exotic and natural flora provides a huge selection of culinary and medicinal herbs. Enjoy fresh home-grown organic salads and herbs, exotic Mediterranean style snacks, and romantic candle-lit dinners. We believe in using quality ingredients – organic wholefoods, local cheeses and produce – in our vegetarian restaurant's highly-praised cuisine. Residential courses include wholefood cookery and organic gardening. Guests are offered an opportunity to explore the natural garden, where most of the kitchen produce is picked fresh daily.
phoenixtyther@hotmail.com   www.thephoenixorganic.com

SNEEM (S-C)

KERRY ALTERNATIVE 388

Gortagowan
Sneem
Tel: 064 45 563   MAP 11

Cabin: sleeps 2-4, €20 pd
Courses, WWOOF Host

Complimentary seasonal home-grown produce

Kerry Alternative Technology provides an environment where you can learn about anything from battery maintenance to cheese-making, whilst touching on hydro power and pallet-building. We offer a variety of courses to suit all tastes. Located in the far west of Ireland, our hostel accommodation and home-grown organic food provides a great holiday too. The accommodation is basic but comfortable. The view is spectacular and the scenery fantastic. The gardens are run on strictly organic lines. They are divided into two main areas, one dedicated to herbs and perennials and the other to fruit and annuals. Polytunnels grow tomatoes, peppers, aubergines, courgettes, salad, melons, squash, early vegetables.
kerryat@eircom.net   www.kerryat.com

BALLITORE (S-C)

MOYLEABBEY ORGANIC 389

Ballitore
Athy
Tel: 059 8623800   MAP 12

Eco-Cabin: sleeps 2+2
Contact for prices

An organic fruit and vegetable box can be pre-ordered, or arranged on arrival

Irish Organic Farmers and Growers

We grow a wide range of organic fruit and vegetables on 13.5 acres in the townsland of Moyleabbey near to the historic Quaker village of Ballitore. We follow a macrobiotic way of life as well as a biodynamic approach to farming. Tourist accommodation is available for up to two adults and two children in a timber eco-cabin, with the option of experiencing the growing, harvesting and cooking of fresh organic fruit and vegetables. Our produce is available from our stall at the farm gate Fridays 12pm-8pm, Newbridge Farmers' Market (Georges Street) Saturdays 9am-2pm, Athy Farmers' Market on Sundays 10am-3pm. An organic fruit and veg box can be pre-ordered, or arranged on arrival.
organic@moyleabbey.ie   www.moyleabbey.ie

DUNAMAGGAN (S-C)

CROAN COTTAGES 390

Dunamaggan
Kilkenny
Tel: 087 236 8555, (0)56 7766 868   MAP 12

Cottages: sleep 4-6, from €325-€725 pw

Meals (ready to heat or ready to serve)

Wherever possible, local, fair trade, GM free and organic products are used

Croan Cottages are set in the grounds of Croan House, an 18th-century manor currently run as a small farm and adjoining almost 2000 acres of broadleaf woodland. Our walled garden and paddocks support a smallholding, with rare and friendly breeds of pigs, chickens, ducks, geese and goats providing fresh produce. We now produce most of the vegetables and fruit we need. Use is made of wild produce as well. We have recently begun offering our guests a range of meal options to enjoy in their cottages. The dishes include classics such as Irish stew, beef and Guinness pie and other popular favourites. For lunches and picnics we offer a range of quiches, frittata, pies, salads, sandwiches and sweet treats.
info@croancottages.com   www.croancottages.com

BALLICKMOYLER (S-C)

COOLANOWLE COTTAGES 391

Coolanowle House
Ballickmoyler
Tel: 059 862 5176   MAP 12

Cottages: sleep 4-6
€275-€460 pw

Organic produce available

Irish Organic Farmers and Growers

Two tastefully converted cottages, lovingly-restored from limestone stock barns. The cottages are surrounded by 3 acres of beechwood gardens, a lawn tennis court and 18th-century flax ponds. The farm at Coolanowle covers around 220 acres. It has been chosen as a demonstration organic farm, one of only seven in the country. Guests are most welcome to visit and view all aspects of the farm. Dairying is the main enterprise with fifty milking cows. Beef and lamb are also produced on the farm and sold locally to restaurants, butchers and, where possible, direct to the public. Fruit and vegetables, as well as our own organic beef and lamb, can be bought locally at Carlow Farmers' Market, which is held on Saturdays.
coolanowle@eircom.net   www.coolanowle.com

BALLICKMOYLER *(B&B)*

COOLANOWLE HOUSE   392

Ballickmoyler
Carlow
Tel: 059 862 5176   MAP 12

Bed and Breakfast, €40-€50 pn
Evening Meal, €30 (by arrangement)

We serve a wide variety of organic food produced here on the farm

Irish Organic Farmers and Growers

Experience the hospitality of a country farmhouse break at Coolanowle House on the Carlow / Laois border. We specialise in leisure and health farm breaks. The house is surrounded by three acres of beechwood gardens. The farm at Coolanowle covers around 250 acres. It has been chosen as an organic demonstration farm. Guests are most welcome to visit and view all aspects of the farm. Dairying is the main enterprise with fifty milking cows. Beef and lamb are also produced. Food lovers are in for a mouth-watering experience. From afternoon tea through to breakfast, home-made and organic are the order of the day. We serve our own organic beef and lamb for dinner, and fruit and vegetables which have been produced locally. coolanowle@eircom.net   www.coolanowle.com

MULLAGH *(S-C)*

ARD NAHOO ECO RETREAT   393

Mullagh
Dromahair
Tel: +353 71 9134939   MAP 6

Eco-cabins: sleep 4-7, €450-€750 pw
B&B, €100-€150 per cabin pn

Organic vegetarian catering available, green box available to order

Ard Nahoo is an eco retreat set in the hills of the North Leitrim glens. Our 6 acres of land are untouched by chemicals, and maintained in keeping with their natural form. Our unique eco-cabins are innovative structures, designed to provide an ethical stay in breathtaking surroundings. Items from an extensive menu can be ordered in advance and waiting for you in your eco-cabin on arrival, ready to be heated and enjoyed at your leisure. Local chef Maria offers delicious vegetarian dishes with Irish, European and Asian influences. Coming from one of Sydney's multi award-winning restaurants, Maria has over fifteen years experience in the cooking industry. All ingredients are sourced locally and are organic wherever possible. info@ardnahoo.com   www.ardnahoo.com

BALLYTOUGHEY *(B&B)*

CLARE ISLAND RETREAT   394

Ballytoughey
Clare Island
Tel: 098 25412   MAP 5

Vegetarian Retreat
€65 pd, full board (shared twin / double)

Most of the ingredients and fresh produce we use are organic (generally over 90%)

Eco-friendly retreat centre, located on a 240-acre farm on an island off the Mayo coast. It is a very peaceful location with stunning sea and mountain views. Clare Island offers wonderful hillwalking and interesting bird-watching. The accommodation is in a renovated cottage and its modern extension. This is an eco-friendly development with solar water-heating, wood-burning stoves and plenty of natural light. In the summer the centre offers residential yoga and meditation courses for all levels. Food is vegetarian and mostly organic, with local produce used whenever possible. Other courses include an introduction to vegetarian cooking and organic gardening. Organic vegetarian B&B or S/C is available off season. bookings@yogaretreats.ie   www.yogaretreats.ie

CAPPADUFF *(S-C)*

LOUGH MASK HOLIDAYS   396

Cappaduff
Tourmakeady
Tel: 094 954 4009   MAP 5

House, Cottages: sleep 5-6
€270-€600 pw

Vegetables grown organically can be purchased

Located on the unspoilt western edge of Europe, Ireland West offers a pollution-free environment with spectacular scenery the envy of Europe. The house and cottages are situated on our farm. Ard Aoibhinn Farm is in a peaceful location on the scenic western shore of Lough Mask. There are several restaurants and pubs in the village, with some of the best food and drink in the West of Ireland. If you have green fingers you could help out on the farm. Vegetables grown organically can be purchased by guests. We are members of a local organic grower's group and grow all our own vegetables (you could even take some home). The wild Atlantic Ocean, with its superb beaches, is twenty-five minutes drive from the farm. info@loughmaskholidays.com   www.loughmaskholidays.com

CASTLEHILL *(B&B)*

ENNISCOE HOUSE 397

Castlehill
Ballina
Tel: 096 31112   MAP 5

Country House, B&B double €192-€240 pn
Courtyard Apartments, €500-€850 pw

The organic garden supplies vegetables to the house

Organic Trust

A vibrant country estate situated in County Mayo, a region renowned for its wild unspoilt landscape, open peaceful spaces and friendly welcoming people. The house nestles in the tranquil surroundings of the countryside in the shadow of Mount Nephin. It has a restored Victorian walled garden, an organic walled vegetable garden and 19th-century pleasure grounds extending to the shores of Lough Conn. Also on the estate are the Courtyard Apartments, the Mayo North Family Heritage Centre and Cloonamoyne Fishery. Good food (organic / local produce where possible) and wine. The organic market garden supplies vegetables to the house. Evening Meal, €56. Courses in organic vegetable growing (contact for details). mail@enniscoe.com   www.enniscoe.com

ALTANELVICK *(B&B)*

LOUGH BRALLEE FARM 398

Altanelvick
Beltra
Tel: 07191 66037   MAP 6

Farmhouse Bed and Breakfast
€25 pppn (no single supplement)

Breakfast is made with organic ingredients

Organic Trust

The farmhouse is in a beautiful setting on a working farm on the Ox Mountains range. We offer bed and breakfast accommodation on our organic holding. All rooms are *en suite* and we can accommodate up to thirteen visitors. We provide an organically prepared breakfast. A log fire sitting room is available to guests. Lough Brallee Organic Farm is home to a flock of mountain ewes. The farm offers scenic walks, with a waterfall and a lake within easy reach. Unspoiled landscapes will greet you, with rich flora and fauna and panoramic views of Knocknarae and Ben Bulben. The Donegal mountains sitting on the edge of the Atlantic ocean are a sight to behold. Hill walking in the area. Self-catering €200 per week all year round. dymphnaohara@hotmail.com   www.organictrust.org

BALLINDERRY *(B&B)*

COOLANGATTA B&B 399

Brocka
Ballinderry
Tel: 067 22164 MAP 12

Bed and Breakfast
€35 pppn sharing, €45 single

Extensive breakfast menu using fresh
homegrown produce

Coolangatta Bed and Breakfast is a uniquely-built Scandinavian style guesthouse. It is located on a hill overlooking the River Shannon with a wonderful view of Lough Derg in the Tipperary Lakeside region. Our guest rooms are beautifully designed with wooden beams and floors and brick walls to give a natural, comfortable feel. Each room is *en suite* and has a stunning view of the surrounding countryside. Our guesthouse provides an extensive breakfast menu using fresh homegrown produce. The varied organic breakfast menu includes fruit juice, cereal, fresh fruit, yogurt, a full Irish breakfast of bacon, egg, sausage, tomato and mushroom, or scrambled egg and smoked salmon, and much more.
coolangatta@eircom.net   www.tipperaryguesthouse.com

CLOGHEEN *(S-C)*

ECOBOOLEY 400

Ronga
Clogheen
Tel: 052 65191 MAP 12

Eco Cottage: sleeps 4
€270-€350 pw

Organic produce is available from a farm shop across the fields

To stay in the Ronga EcoBooley is to stay in an old place in the lovely Galty Vee Valley landscape in the knowledge that you will leave the environment as you found it. The walls of the cottage are insulated with a hemp and lime mix, and local sheep's wool insulates the roof. The power supply comes from a water driven electric turbine. A wood-burning stove adds to the snug atmosphere. Looby Farm is part of the Rural Environmental Protection Scheme. Organic produce is available from a farm shop across the fields. You will also find local produce, such as cheese, apple juices, jams and chutneys in the area. There is direct foot access from the cottage to the Munster Way for endless hill and forest walking.
t.cunningham@tipperarysr.teagasc.ie   www.ecobooley.com

NEW INN *(S-C)*

GORTRUA ORGANIC FARM 401

Gortrua
New Inn
Tel: 062 72223   MAP 12

Cottage: sleeps 2
€150-€250 pw

Organic beef, bread, preserves, seasonal
vegetables

Irish Organic Farmers and Growers

Gortrua is a 100-acre organic farm on the banks of the Suir River deep in the heart of the Golden Vale of Tipperary. This old fashioned farm has been in the same family since 1800 and luckily escaped the destructive forces of so-called 'progressive farming'. The current generation have been farming organically for over twenty years. Aberdeen Angus cattle, as well as pony mares and their foals, keep the grasses mown and fresh. The stone cottage has been renovated and is ideal for a holiday in a peaceful and tranquil rural setting. This is a place where you can relax and enjoy a genuine working farm. Full of wild places the farm abounds in trees, grasses and wildflowers. There are many beautiful walks on the farm itself.
gortruaorganic@eircom.net   http://homepage.eircom.net/~gortruaorganic/index.html

TERRYGLASS *(S-C)*

THE LIMEKILN   402

Tir na Fiuise Farm
Terryglass
Tel: 067 22041   MAP 11

Cottage: sleeps 6
€400-€580 pw

Home baked bread, local organic vegetable
box by arrangement

Irish Organic Farmers and Growers

Tir na Fiuise cottages are situated on our organic farm in a peaceful setting in the heart of rural Tipperary. They are restored farm buildings, renovated in traditional style using natural materials and non-toxic finishes. Relax in the gardens of this country retreat, take a walk into the adjacent bog or stroll along the farm walk. The 160-acre family farm now has 5th generation Heenans living here. 70 acres is devoted to organic agriculture, sheep, cereals and cattle, while the rest of the farm has some recently established woodlands and grain crops. The land is farmed under the Rural Environment Protection Scheme, which encourages environmentally friendly practices. 2km from Terryglass village on the shore of Lough Derg.
info@countrycottages.ie   www.countrycottages.ie/our_lime.php

TERRYGLASS *(S-C)*

TIR NA FIUISE GRANARY 403

Tir na Fiuise Farm
Terryglass
Tel: 067 22041   MAP 11

Cottage: sleeps 2
€280-€400 pw

Home baked bread, local organic vegetable box by arrangement

Irish Organic Farmers and Growers

Tir na Fiuise cottages are situated on our organic farm in a peaceful setting in the heart of rural Tipperary. They are restored farm buildings, renovated in traditional style using natural materials and non-toxic finishes. Relax in the gardens of this country retreat, take a walk into the adjacent bog or stroll along the farm walk. The 160-acre family farm now has 5th generation Heenans living here. 70 acres is devoted to organic agriculture, sheep, cereals and cattle, while the rest of the farm has some recently established woodlands and grain crops. The land is farmed under the Rural Environment Protection Scheme, which encourages environmentally friendly practices. 2km from Terryglass village on the shore of Lough Derg. info@countrycottages.ie   www.countrycottages.ie/our_granary.php

TERRYGLASS *(S-C)*

TIR NA FIUISE STABLES 404

Tir na Fiuise Farm
Terryglass
Tel: 067 22041   MAP 11

Cottage: sleeps 4
€350-€530 pw

Home-baked bread, local organic vegetable box by arrangement

Irish Organic Farmers and Growers

Tir na Fiuise cottages are situated on our organic farm in a peaceful setting in the heart of rural Tipperary. They are restored farm buildings, renovated in traditional style using natural materials and non-toxic finishes. Relax in the gardens of this country retreat, take a walk into the adjacent bog or stroll along the farm walk. The 160-acre family farm now has 5th generation Heenans living here. 70 acres is devoted to organic agriculture, sheep, cereals and cattle, while the rest of the farm has some recently established woodlands and grain crops. The land is farmed under the Rural Environment Protection Scheme, which encourages environmentally friendly practices. 2km from Terryglass village on the shore of Lough Derg. info@countrycottages.ie   www.countrycottages.ie/our_stables.php

LADESTOWN *(B&B)*

LAKESHORE B&B   405

Ladestown
Mullingar
Tel: 044 9340618   MAP 6

Farmhouse Bed and Breakfast
Double, €80-€90 pn

Organic breakfast on request

Irish Organic Farmers and Growers

Lakeshore B&B is situated in beautiful unspoilt Irish countryside on the shores of Lough Ennell. My husband has farmed here for almost forty years and since 2000 we have farmed organically. We are fully certified as an organic farm by Irish Organic Farmers and Growers. We have a dairy herd, beef cattle, sheep and ponies. Guest accommodation is in four *en suite* rooms. A good hearty country breakfast is guaranteed or you can choose the continental breakfast with organic yogurt and cheese from our own farm. As artisan-scale producers, we produce a range of fresh cow's milk cheeses, probiotic yogurts and yogurt drinks. Ideally situated to suit the fisherman, Lakeshore B&B is within reasonable driving distance of the main Midland fishing lakes. lakeshorebb1@eircom.net   www.lakeshorebnb.com

GREAT ISLAND *(B&B)*

KILMOKEA MANOR   406

Great Island
Campile
Tel: 051 388109   MAP 12

Bed and Breakfast, double €75-€150 pn
Dinner, 2-3 course €48-€54

Meals prepared with organic and home-grown produce (up to 80%-90% organic)

An 18th-century Georgian stone rectory nestled on the shores of the River Barrow. The guest rooms have been lavishly decorated, and all have wonderful views over the formal walled garden. Seven acres of heritage gardens are tended for without using any chemicals. It is labour intensive but the results are inspiring and beautiful. We have developed a new acre of potager, which produces fresh produce for guests to enjoy in the house for dinner in our main dining room, and lunch in the Pink Teacup Café in the conservatory. The potager produces vegetables and herbs, and also edible flowers. Visitors can purchase home-made fare, jam, marmalade and bread. Self-catering options available (€750-€1250 pw). kilmokea@eircom.net   www.kilmokea.com

BALLYCULLEN (B&B)

BALLYCULLEN LODGE   407

Birch Hill
Ballycullen
Tel: +353 404 40000   MAP 12

Bed and Breakfast, double €69 pp sharing
Dinners are available by prior arrangement

All food is freshly-prepared from local,
home-grown, wild and organic produce

Set in 5 acres on the fringe of the Wicklow Uplands National Park, Ballycullen Lodge is a lovingly-restored and extended 1850s traditional Irish stone cottage. Features include a wealth of local stone, wood and stained glass. A nutritious, delicious, and if you wish, healthy breakfast is included in the room price. All food is freshly-prepared from local, home-grown, wild and organic produce. A 4 or 5 course dinner is available by prior arrangement. Menus are varied and interesting, reflecting the best of Irish cooking. Wellness packages include yoga classes, wellness weekends, rejuvenating holidays, forest walks and delicious organic meals in this 'wonderful relaxing retreat in the countryside with magnificent vistas'.
info@ballycullenlodge.com   www.ballycullenlodge.com

MACREDDIN (Hotel)

BROOKLODGE & WELLS SPA 408

Macreddin
Aughrim
Tel: 0402 36444   MAP 12

BIO-Hotel
See website for prices

Our certified organic restaurant serves only
wild and organic foods

Organic Trust

The BrookLodge is a stunning luxury hotel in a remote Wicklow Valley. It is home to Ireland's only certified organic restaurant, The Strawberry Tree, which serves only wild and organic foods sourced from local artisan food suppliers. Savour great food in sublime settings. Macreddin Village is known as 'the food village' and has a variety of venues offering free-range, organic and wild food options. The hotel has its own wine cellar and microbrewery, and we serve our very own organic lager and stout in the lively surroundings of Actons Country Pub. The innovative cuisine is matched by the dramatic surroundings. A wealth of outdoor activities are available to enjoy the flora and fauna of this beautiful area of Wicklow.
brooklodge@macreddin.ie   www.brooklodge.com

NORTHERN IRELAND

Omagh Hostel, County Tyrone

CASTLEWELLAN *(S-C)*

BURRENWOOD FARM 409

38 Burrenbridge Road
Castlewellan BT31 9HT
Tel: 028 4377 0241   MAP 7

Apartments: both sleep 4
£350 pw

Complimentary organic farm produce

Soil Association

Burrenwood Farm is located at the northern foot of the Mourne Mountains, midway between Tollymore and Castlewellan forest parks. Enjoy the freshest of food on your doorstep. Burrenwood is an organic vegetable farm growing all sorts of food on 12 acres for weekly delivery to a hundred households, and for free to our guests. Situated between the Irish Sea and two scenic lakes, the Burren River flows by these five fields next to a 60-acre woodland. There is plenty of space to roam and all manner of outdoor pursuits in the area. In keeping with the theme of room to breathe, both apartments boast huge conservatories with spiral staircases, offering ever changing wonderful views of mountain and sea. burrenwood@btinternet.com   www.burrenwood.com

NEWRY *(S-C)*

PLUMTREE COTTAGE 410

25 Lurganconary Road
Kilkeel BT34 4LL
Tel: 028 3025 4595   MAP 7

Cottage: sleeps 4+2
£600-£650 pw

Fresh organic fruit and vegetables available for guests to buy in season

Soil Association

Plumtree Cottage is set in idyllic landscaped gardens on a 100-acre organic farm at the foot of the majestic Mourne Mountains and within walking distance to the Blue Flag Cranfield beach. This charming cottage has the perfect blend of luxury and comfort, with underfloor heating powered by geo thermal heating systems. During your stay on the farm fishing is available on the White Water River, there is complimentary use of bicycles and outdoor wear, a children's playground on-site, and guests can explore one of the many nature trails. Hiking, horse riding, sailing, golf in the area. Fresh organic fruit and vegetables available to buy from the farm depending on season. Organic produce can be bought locally. info@lurganconaryfarms.com   www.lurganconaryfarms.com

NEWRY *(S-C)*

SAND COTTAGE 411

27 Lurganconary Road
Kilkeel BT34 4LL
Tel: 028 3025 4595   MAP 7

Cottage: sleeps 4+2
£600-£650 pw

Fresh organic fruit and vegetables available for guests to buy in season

Soil Association

Set in idyllic landscaped gardens on a 100-acre organic farm at the foot of the majestic Mourne Mountains and within walking distance to the Blue Flag Cranfield beach. This charming cottage has the perfect blend of luxury and comfort, with underfloor heating powered by geo thermal heating systems. During your stay fishing is available on the White Water River, there is complimentary use of bicycles and outdoor wear, a children's playground on-site, and guests can explore one of the many nature trails. Hiking, horse riding, sailing, golf in the area. Fresh organic fruit and vegetables available for guests to purchase from the farm, depending on the season. Organic produce can also be bought locally.
info@lurganconaryfarms.com   www.lurganconaryfarms.com

NEWTOWNARDS *(B&B)*

ANNA'S HOUSE 412

35 Lisbarnet Road
Comber BT23 6AW
Tel: 028 9754 1566   MAP 7

Bed and Breakfast, £40-£50 pp sharing
£60 for single occupancy

The food is guaranteed to be 75%-80% organic at any one time

This serene and secret place fourteen miles from the centre of Belfast is situated in the middle of Northern Ireland. The house stands within its own 20 acres of farmland with a two-acre organic garden and panoramic views over a wildfowl lake and meadows down to the Mountains of Mourne on the horizon. All breads are home-baked and the food is guaranteed to be 75%-80% organic at any one time. Ours is the only establishment in Northern Ireland to subscribe to the Soil Association's Catering Code of Practise. The field in front of the house supplies geo-thermal underfloor heating and solar panels provide hot water. Wildlife-friendly copses and shrubberies are in the process of being planted in meadow margins.
anna@annashouse.com   www.annashouse.com

LISNARICK *(S-C)*

ORCHARD ACRE FARM 413

Moynaghan North Road
Lisnarick BT94 1LQ
Tel: 028 686 21066   MAP 6

Standard tipi package, 2 nights £260, 6n £660
Deluxe full board, 2 nights £400, 6n £990

We serve gorgeous grub grown without the
use of chemicals

Experience real camping with space and comfort. Our 18ft hand-painted tipi sleeps four adults, tucked into a quiet corner of the farm beside the coolness of the river, a world away from traffic noise and modern mayhem. Internal and external rain protection, warmth from a real fire. Our standard package includes a free organic and local food hamper. Home cooked evening meals can be delivered to your tipi at extra cost. Packed lunches to go. The deluxe full board package includes a free breakfast food hamper, sumptuous packed lunches and home-cooked evening suppers. Free copy of local map. Optional extras at reasonable rates (bikes, canoe, laundry). Weekend retreat, midweek special, four day getaway, etc from £260.

info@orchardacrefarm.com   www.orchardacrefarm.com

LIMAVADY *(S-C)*

THE OFFICE 414

Mullan's Organic Farm
84 Ringsend Road, Limavady BT49 0QJ
Tel: 028 777 64940   MAP 7

Self-Catering House: sleeps 9
£350-£380 pw

Fresh organic produce is available (beef, lamb, poultry, eggs)

Irish Organic Farmers and Growers

Elevated on a mountain outside Limavady, there is a panoramic outlook across the valley from Dungiven to Donegal. The Office is located beside the main farmhouse in the middle of a working organic farm. It is a practical family-friendly house with exceptional views. Guests can enjoy walks (and jobs if they wish) around the farm. The overall aim of the farm is to sell good quality, locally produced organic food to local people. Our farm butcher's provides organic produce for local farmers' markets, so Aberdeen Angus Beef, local spring lamb, free-range chicken and eggs are available if required. Organic vegetable boxes can also be delivered. The farm is ideally located for touring the north west coastal attractions.

info@mullansorganicfarm.com   www.mullansorganicfarm.com

OMAGH HOSTEL 415

Glenhordial Farm
9a Waterworks Road BT79 7JS
Tel: 028 8224 1973 MAP 6

Dorm / Private Rooms, £12.50-£15 pppn
£20 tent up to 5 people pn, single £10 pn

Fruit and vegetables grown using organic
principles available in season

Imagine driving down a long country lane with flowery banks and ancient hedges to a place that feels like home. This remote, peaceful, small family farm nestles at the edge of the Sperrin mountains and offers simple self-catering accommodation with both dormitory and private rooms. Here you can breathe fresh air, wander green valleys, participate in community activities, plant a tree and offset your carbon. Our green ethos is a threaded through the farm – recently awarded the EU Ecolabel. We grow our own vegetables and fruit according to organic / permaculture principles. Feel free to explore the vegetable and fruit gardens. Introduction to organic gardening workshops for groups. Closed 1st November-1st March. marella@omaghhostel.co.uk   www.omaghhostel.co.uk

SCOTLAND

Bluebell Croft, Argyll

CUSHNIE *(S-C)*

WARK FARM HAYLOFT   416

Cushnie
Alford AB33 8LL
Tel: 01975 581149   MAP 2

Apartment: sleeps 2
£200-£300 pw

Organic traditional breed meats and charcuterie grown and processed on the farm

Soil Association

This recently-renovated accommodation has been created from the traditional farm steading in the centre of a family-run working organic farm with many nature conservation features. It has been sensitively converted to a high standard using local and sustainable features (local beech flooring and stairs, heating from a biomass boiler, etc). A variety of organic produce is always available to purchase from the farm, including Belted Galloway beef, Oxford, Sandy and Black pork, Hebridean lamb and Aylesbury duck as well as our charcuterie range including bacon, hams, sausages, pork pies and other cured and smoked items. There are several farmers markets and farm shops in the area also selling organic and local produce. dugie@warkfarm.co.uk   www.warkfarm.co.uk

BARGUILLEAN *(S-C)*

SITHEAN   417

Barguillean
Taynuilt PA35 1HY
Tel: 01866 822110   MAP 3

House: sleeps 8
£420-£800 pw

Our own organic produce may be available for guests to buy (eggs, meat, vegetables)

Soil Association

Sithean is a stunning new house on a working organic hill farm overlooking Glen Lonan. It is secluded and peaceful, yet only two miles away from Taynuilt on the shores of Loch Etive. We buy local produce from the nearby farmshop for the guests and our meals. We produce our own organic beef and lamb and in the future would like to make that available to our guests, as well as organic vegetables from the garden. If there are surplus eggs from our chickens we pass them on to guests. The water supply to the house is natural spring water. We have achieved the Gold Award in the Green Tourism Business Scheme. The location is ideal for walking and cycling for the whole family, and there's an amazing range of wildlife. info@sitheanselfcatering.co.uk   www.sitheanselfcatering.co.uk

CAMPBELTOWN *(S-C)*

BALLIMENEACH COTTAGE 418

Kildalloig Estate
Campbeltown PA28 6RE
Tel: 07979 855930   MAP 3

Cottage: sleeps 8
£470-£995 pw

Organic beef and lamb to order

Soil Association

The cottage is set within its own large garden, very close to the sea on the beautiful Mull of Kintyre on the west coast of Scotland. In a secluded position with outstanding sea views, this lovely house is ideal for families. Situated on the Kildalloig Estate, providing acres of unspoilt and remote rolling countryside with stretches of secluded beaches and stunning sea views, including the fascinating Island of Davaar with its cave painting and wild goats. Kildalloig is an organic farm producing organic beef and lamb. Organic breeding stock includes Aberdeen Angus heifers, pedigree registered Blueface Leicester, Blackface and North Ronaldsay rams or ewe lambs. Natural spring water supply.
marycturner@btinternet.com www.kintyrecottages.com/ballimeneach-cottage.html

CAMPBELTOWN *(S-C)*

FISHERMAN'S COTTAGE 419

Kildalloig Estate
Campbeltown PA28 6RE
Tel: 07979 855930   MAP 3

Cottage: sleeps 2
£350-£650 pw

Organic beef and lamb to order

Soil Association

Fisherman's Cottage is set on a secluded beach. This cosy single-storey accommodation enjoys a very romantic and peaceful setting with spectacular views over the Kilbrannan Sound to Arran and the Island of Davaar. Situated on the Kildalloig Estate, providing acres of unspoilt and remote rolling countryside with stretches of secluded beaches and stunning sea views, including the fascinating Island of Davaar with its cave painting and wild goats. Kildalloig is an organic farm producing beef and lamb. Organic breeding stock includes Aberdeen Angus heifers, pedigree registered Blueface Leicester, Blackface and North Ronaldsay rams or ewe lambs. Natural spring water supply.
marycturner@btinternet.com www.kintyrecottages.com/fishermans-cottage.html

CAMPBELTOWN *(S-C)* ISLAND COTTAGES 420

Kildalloig Estate
Campbeltown PA28 6RE
Tel: 07979 855930 MAP 3

Cottages: sleep 2-4
£220-£430 pw

Organic beef and lamb to order

Soil Association

In a superb, secluded location by the sea on the 160-acre private island of Davaar, this unique pair of cottages enjoy stunning views. Otter (sleeps 2) and Island (sleeps 4) are an adjoining pair of cosy and spacious lighthouse keepers' cottages. Natural spring water supply. The cottages share a walled enclosure with the neighbouring caretaker. Set at the northern tip of Davaar Island, they are connected to the mainland by a causeway, revealed by the sea for six hours at low tide. On arrival and departure, and for arranged shopping trips, visitors will be ferried by Landrover across the causeway (leaving their cars at the quayside). Kildalloig is an organic farm producing beef and lamb.
marycturner@btinternet.com www.kintyrecottages.com/island-cottages.html

CAMPBELTOWN *(S-C)* STABLE COTTAGE 421

Kildalloig Estate
Campbeltown PA28 6RE
Tel: 07979 855930 MAP 3

Cottage: sleeps 4
£360-£700 pw

Organic beef and lamb to order

Soil Association

Stable Cottage lies within a quarter mile of a secluded beach (reached via a steep track) near the southern tip of the romantic Mull of Kintyre. There are marvellous walks through woodland on the estate, on the coast (where seals, otters, and a variety of birds can be seen), and in the hills, where golden eagles soar. This spacious ground floor cottage, near to a working farm, stands in its own secure garden with fine sea views towards Ailsa Craig. Kildalloig is an organic farm producing beef and lamb. Organic breeding stock includes Aberdeen Angus heifers, pedigree registered Blueface Leicester, Blackface and North Ronaldsay rams or ewe lambs. Natural spring water supply.
marycturner@btinternet.com www.kintyrecottages.com/stable-cottage.html

CAMPBELTOWN (S-C)

THE LOOKOUT 422

Kildalloig Estate
Campbeltown PA28 6RE
Tel: 07979 855930   MAP 3

Cottage: sleeps 2
£300-£550 pw

Organic beef and lamb to order

Soil Association

The Lookout is a former wartime lookout post situated 100 yards away from the lighthouse enclosure. This cottage has an extra sitting room and sun terrace, formed from the original lookout, with superb long distance views from windows all around. The Lookout has its own area of lawn. Set at the northern tip of Davaar Island, the cottage is connected to the mainland by a causeway revealed by the sea for six hours at low tide (a 15 minute walk). On arrival and departure, and for arranged shopping trips, visitors will be ferried by Landrover across the causeway (leaving their cars at the quayside). Kildalloig is an organic farm producing beef and lamb. Natural spring water supply.
marycturner@btinternet.com   www.kintyrecottages.com/the-lookout.html

CLACHAN (Hotel)

BALINAKILL HOTEL 423

Clachan
Tarbert PA29 6XL
Tel: 01880 740206   MAP 3

Small Hotel, B&B £40-£50 pppn
Dinner, 3 course £28.95

About 70% of all the food we offer is organic

Balinakill is a relaxed and friendly country house set among glorious coastal scenery in an area abundant in wildlife, flowers, birds and outdoor activities. Most of the food in our AA Rosetted restaurant is sourced locally – venison from the hills behind the hotel, local free-range eggs, superb seafood from the waters around Kintyre, and organic beef and lamb from the Borders. Our dry goods come from Greencity workers co-op and are all fair trade, GM free and organic. We do not use chemicals for cleaning, and our grounds are pesticide free. Hot stone massage, reflexology and other therapies are available. Green Tourism Silver Leaf. Hotel Reservation Service Hotels of the Year 2006 (Green Award). AA Rosette.
info@balinakill.com   www.balinakill.com

KILCHRENAN (B&B)

ROINEABHAL HOUSE 424

Kilchrenan
Taynuilt PA35 1HD
Tel: 01866 833207 MAP 3

Bed and Breakfast, £45-£65 pppn
Dinner, £40 including wine

100% organic meals are available for a small surcharge

Roineabhal is situated in the very picturesque village of Kilchrenan. Enjoy the friendly family atmosphere. You can relax in front of the log fire, meander round the grounds or walk in the open countryside, or just sit outside in the sun-traps and listen to the tumbling burn. Savour fine cuisine – local Scottish game and seafood are on the menu daily. Fresh bread, muffins and shortbread are just a few baked items offered on a regular basis. 100% organic meals available at a slight extra cost. Vegetarian food can be prepared. Nearby, lonely Glen Nant is a hidden treasure teeming with wildlife, and a great place for gentle or strenuous walks. Loch Awe provides rambles, fishing, and some of the finest scenery in Scotland.
maria@roineabhal.com   www.roineabhal.com

OTTER FERRY (S-C)

SHEPHERD'S COTTAGE 425

Otter Ferry
Tighnabruaich PA21 2DH
Tel: 01700 821284 MAP 3

Cottage: sleeps 4
£200-£450 pw

Seasonal organic produce available to buy

Scottish Organic Producers Association

Situated high up on an organic hill farm, this small stone-built cottage has breathtaking views overlooking Loch Fyne. Facing south-west, the detached cottage has been created from an old shepherd's cottage near the farmhouse. Seasonal organic farm produce is usually available to buy. The friendly neighbours consist of blackface sheep, collie dogs, Jersey cows, bay mares and speckly hens, all of which combine to complement the surrounding wildlife. For a bit of activity there is a tennis court on the farm, pony rides for children, hiking, hill walking and sheep gathering. The beautiful Cowal Peninsula offers wonderful scenery, a variety of water sports, fishing and golf. Swimming and boating at Loch Fyne.
a.barge@otterferry.com

STRONTIAN *(S-C)*

HONEYSUCKLE HOUSE 426

Bluebell Croft
15 Anaheilt PH36 4JA
Tel: 01967 402226   MAP 3

House: sleeps 8+, £550-£1650 pw
Supper, 1-5 course £6-£40

All our produce is grown on the croft
following organic principles

A single house with six *en suite* bedrooms sleeping 12-16 (£1600-£2200 pw), or two houses separated by the conservatory sleeping 8+ (Honeysuckle) and 2-4+ (Rose). 5-star, gold green award, wheelchair-friendly and giant hot tub. A generous hamper can be ordered for your arrival which can contain home-made bread, eggs, preserves, home smoked goodies such as bacon, cheese and salmon, beef and chicken and seasonal vegetables, fruit, salads from the polytunnel / garden. We also offer a range of cooked meals, such as a casserole in the Aga waiting for you on arrival, supper during the week, or a full dinner (up to five courses) from the 'Rural Chef of the Year'. We will pick guests up from the train station at no extra cost.
billandsukie@bluebellcroft.co.uk   www.bluebellcroft.co.uk

STRONTIAN *(S-C)*

ROSE COTTAGE 427

Bluebell Croft
15 Anaheilt PH36 4JA
Tel: 01967 402226   MAP 3

Cottage: sleeps 2-4+, £500-£850 pw
Supper, 1-5 course £6-£40

All our produce is grown on the croft
following organic principles

Rose Cottage has two *en suite* rooms. The house is rated five star, with simple luxury throughout. A generous hamper can be ordered for your arrival, with more produce available during the week. The hamper could include home-made bread, eggs, preserves and home smoked goodies such as bacon from our own pigs, cheese and fish, and depending on the season we hope to include fresh vegetables, fruit and salads from the polytunnel / garden. We will also be offering a range of cooked meals, such as a casserole in the oven waiting for you on arrival, supper during the week, or a full dinner (up to five courses) from the 'Rural Chef of the Year'. We will pick guests up from the train station at no extra cost.
billandsukie@bluebellcroft.co.uk   www.bluebellcroft.co.uk

BARASSIE *(B&B)*

ARRAN GARDENS B&B   428

36 Arran Gardens
Troon KA10 6TE
Tel: 01292 679532   MAP 3

Shelldun Suite, B&B £35-£45 pppn
Evening Meal, £20-£30 (by arrangement)

Organic and free-range breakfasts and
evening meals, local and seasonal as available

A bright and spacious detached bungalow, within sight of Barassie beach with its views over the Firth of Clyde to the Isle of Arran. The Shelldun Suite is a unique, private, self-contained accommodation comprising one single bedroom, two twin bedrooms, a bathroom, and a lounge with french doors onto a patio within our walled garden. Breakfasts and evening meals are served in the conservatory, which overlooks the secluded garden. Imaginative breakfasts using organic / free-range and locally sourced produce as much as possible. Gluten-free meals with notice. Home-made preserves, home-grown fruits and tomatoes are seasonally available. Ideally located for many golf courses and exploring Western Scotland. shelldunsuite@wightcablenorth.net   www.shelldunsuite.co.uk

PINWHERRY *(B&B)*

DRUMSKEOCH FARM B&B   429

Drumskeoch Farm
Pinwherry KA26 0QB
Tel: 01465 841172   MAP 8

Vegetarian Bed and Breakfast, £25-£35 pppn
Evening Meal (by prior arrangement)

All food is organic and where possible
locally produced

A warm welcome and a comfortable relaxing stay awaits you in this unique organic vegetarian / vegan bed and breakfast. The traditionally and naturally renovated rural farmhouse has beautiful views of the surrounding hills, sunrises, sunsets, and the unspoilt night sky. The food is all organic, vegetarian / vegan and home-cooked. The farmhouse also has its own water source. Packed lunches and evening meals are available, and special dietary requirements are catered for. The bedding, towels, toiletries, and the paint on the walls are all organic. Our light bulbs are low energy. The loo is low flush. We run courses in rural sustainable crafts – willow structures, treebogs, drystone dyking, herbal medicine. drumskeoch@wildmail.com   www.drumskeoch.co.uk

DOLLARBEG *(B&B)*

KENNELS COTTAGE 430

Dollarbeg
Dollar FK14 7PA
Tel: 01259 742476 MAP 3

Bed and Breakfast
£30-£35 pppn

All the food we use is either local or organic

Set in one-acre of garden, Kennels Cottage 4-star bed and breakfast is a fresh, stylish former gamekeeper's cottage. White walls, soft white sofas, the odd splash of gold, and light airy *en suite* bedrooms all go to create a calm, peaceful atmosphere. Guests have use of their own sitting room and reading area. Breakfast is sourced locally using organic and free-range products wherever possible. We have our own hens so our eggs are very fresh, and we also grow some of our own produce. We use environmentally friendly cleaning products as much as we can and recycle as much as possible. We also offer classic car hire and classic car hire packages. The cottage is an ideal base to tour Scotland.
tanya.worsfold@btinternet.com   www.guesthousescotland.co.uk

FREUCHIE *(B&B)*

OCHIL VILLA B&B 431

High Street
Freuchie, by Cupar KY15 7EZ
Tel: 01337 858031 MAP 3

Bed and Breakfast, £60 per room pn
Price based on single or double occupancy

Organic dairy produce and home-baked
organic bread

For our breakfasts we use locally sourced quality ingredients, organic where possible, with enough variety to satisfy vegetarians and carnivores alike. Wild boar sausages from Perthshire, raspberries, strawberries and redcurrants grown nearby, our own home-made breads and oatcakes made using organic flours, and Scottish cheeses and honeys. The ingredients we use are not exclusively organic but are chosen on the basis of quality and low food miles as well as production methods. Pillars of Hercules organic farm shop, less than two miles away, supplies most of our yogurts and cheeses. They also have an organic café. If you have particular food needs or wants, email us in advance and we'll see what we can do.
bandb@ochilvilla.co.uk   www.ochilvilla.co.uk

ST ANDREWS *(B&B)*

DRUMTILLY HOUSE 432

2 Drumcarrow Road
St Andrews KY16 8SE
Tel: 01334 470954   MAP 3

Bed and Breakfast
£42 pppn

Full Scottish organic breakfast, home-made jam or marmalade, local honey

Small family-run bed and breakfast with newly-converted accommodation, situated in a quiet residential area of St Andrews. We serve a full Scottish organic breakfast. Organic cereal followed by a cooked breakfast of organic sausages, bacon, eggs, tomatoes, home-made potato scones, toast, preserves, organic juice, tea or coffee, milk and sugar. Enjoy a good night's sleep in organic bedding. We have two twin *en suite* bedrooms with organic tea and coffee making facilities as well as organic and 100% chemical-free complementary toiletries. Drumtilly House is two minutes walk from the Botanic Gardens. Ten minutes walk takes you into town, and it's fifteen minutes to the beach or, for golfers, the first tee of the Old Course. Drumtillyhouse@aol.com   www.drumtillyhouse.co.uk

AULDEARN *(Hotel)*

BOATH HOUSE HOTEL 433

Auldearn
Nairn IV12 5TE
Tel: 01667 454896   MAP 2

Regency House, B&B £110 pppn
Evening Meal, £65 pp (6 course set menu)

Home-grown, local (organic 60%-90%)

Beautiful Georgian mansion (4 rosettes, 3 red stars) set in 20 acres of lawns, woodland and streams. Eight rooms individually decorated to a very high standard. The grounds were set out around 1730, prior to the building of the present house. Lake with brown trout. A wildflower meadow and woodland walks have now been established. The kitchen gardens provide most of the vegetables and herbs for the award-winning restaurant. Organic meats, cheeses and vegetables are sourced locally through several suppliers. Supporters of the Slow Food movement. The Spa specialises in Ayurvedic treatments, using only organic petrochemical-free ingredients sourced from pure plant and flower extracts. wendy@boath-house.com   www.boath-house.com

BUNCHREW *(Hotel)*

BUNCHREW HOUSE HOTEL 434

Bunchrew
Inverness IV3 8TA
Tel: 01463 234917   MAP 2

Country House, B&B £75-£130 pppn
Restaurant

Organic produce (35%-45%), natural and
wild produce, local produce

A 17th-century Scottish mansion only yards from the sea. It is set amidst 20 acres of beautiful landscaped gardens and woodland where no pesticides are used, and where areas are left deliberately wild to provide a natural habitat for wildlife. Award-winning food, fresh, local or organic, is served in the wood-panelled dining room overlooking the sea. The chef uses naturally reared meat and fish, which wherever possible is locally and organically produced. Try the organic muesli from Brin Herbs near Farr, and the smoked duck or organic smoked salmon from the Summer Isles. Bunchrew House grows its own organic potatoes, herbs and cooking apples, and uses locally produced organic vegetables.
welcome@bunchrewhousehotel.com   www.bunchrewhousehotel.com

GLENURQUHART *(B&B)*

SHENVAL B&B   435

Glenurquhart
Drumnadrochit IV63 6TW
Tel: 01456 476363   MAP 1

Bed and Breakfast, £25 pppn
Dinner, £22-£27 (by prior arrangement)

Mostly organic, Scottish and international
cuisine with a French touch

On the gateway to Glen Affric National Nature Reserve, Shenval nestles in a secluded and peaceful hamlet ten minutes' drive from Loch Ness. You'll find a heartfelt friendly welcome in our comfortable B&B. Always freshly-prepared on the premises, our fare is mostly organic, and includes seasonal fruit and vegetables from our own garden. Packed lunches are available. Optional evening meal (2-3 courses) inclusive of non-alcoholic drinks and after dinner herbal tea, tea or coffee and biscuits. Hill and forest walks, cycling, bird-watching and fishing are readily available from our very doorstep. We'll be delighted to share our many years experience of hill walking in the Highlands and our extensive knowledge of the area.
info@shenval-welcome.co.uk   www.shenval-welcome.co.uk

LAGGAN (B&B)

THE RUMBLIE 436

Gergask Avenue
Laggan PH20 1AH
Tel: 01528 544766 MAP 2

Bed and Breakfast, £35 pppn
Evening Meal, £20-£25 (by arrangement)

Breakfast is around 70% organic, evening meals 80% to 90% organic

The Rumblie experience is about quality organic food and service in a relaxed Highland home. Our focus is on local produce, and on many occasions this would be Rumblie-grown by organic methods and organic seed stock. We use organic products extensively, and follow an ethical approach with many fair trade goods. All this and other measures led to our Green Tourism Business Scheme Gold Award. We offer a home-cooked evening meal on a set menu based on seasonal produce and served in our new sunroom. This will be 80% to 90% organic depending upon what is available at the time. We can provide a pick up service in our hybrid car for those guests who are planning to travel here by train or bus.
mail@rumblie.com   www.rumblie.com

ONICH (B&B)

CUILDORAG HOUSE 437

Onich
Fort William PH33 6SD
Tel: 01855 821529 MAP 3

Vegetarian / Vegan B&B, £25-£30 pppn
Evening Meal, £17.50 (by arrangement)

Breakfast up to 50% organic, evening meal 80%-100% organic

Cuildorag House is a vegetarian and vegan bed and breakfast, situated ten miles south of Fort William in the village of Onich. The house has mountain and loch views to the south and west. A warm welcome and delicious home-cooked meals are our speciality. Our house is set within 1.5 acres of mature garden where we grow, without chemicals, a variety of fruit and vegetables which we use in the preparation of our evening meals (3 courses with coffee). The garden is also home to our free-range hens, who provide the eggs for your large and delicious breakfast, and is visited by deer, red squirrels, badgers and pine martens. Walk the 150 metres to the shore of the loch. You may spot otters and basking sharks.
enquiries@cuildoraghouse.com   www.cuildoraghouse.com

SPEAN BRIDGE *(Hotel)*

OLD PINES HOTEL 438

Spean Bridge
Fort William PH34 4EG
Tel: 01397 712324   MAP 3

Small Hotel, B&B £45-£55 pppn
Evening meal £15-£30 pp

50%-70% organic ingredients

Old Pines is a small yet high quality hotel with a relaxed atmosphere. Set among mature Scots Pines in 30 acres of grounds north of the village of Spean Bridge, three hundred yards below the famous Commando Memorial. We consciously source organic ingredients for our home-made bread, pasta, ice cream, cakes and preserves. We have our own vegetable garden growing organic potatoes, carrots, leeks, salads, fruits and herbs. Only fresh local seafood, beef, venison and lamb are used to create the sumptuous contemporary Scottish dishes. Take a stroll down the quiet country lanes for amazing views of Ben Nevis, Loch Lochy and the Great Glen, and work up an appetite for dinner.
enquiries@oldpines.co.uk   www.oldpines.co.uk

TORLUNDY *(S-C)*

GREAT GLEN CHALETS 439

Torlundy Farm
Torlundy PH33 6SW
Tel: 01397 703015   MAP 3

Chalets: sleep 4
£330-£560 pw

Delicious organic lamb available from our deep freeze at the farm

Scottish Organic Producers Association

Eight Finnish chalets on an organic farm, individually sited with superb views of three of the highest mountains in the British Isles These two-bedroom chalets are pine-panelled throughout, and fitted with three full length double-glazed windows in the living room to make you feel part of the great outdoors. A variety of birds will feed from your balcony, and roe deer are frequently seen in the early morning amongst the trees. Torlundy Farm breeds Highland ponies, Highland cattle and Cheviot sheep. You are welcome to walk along any of the attractive tracks which lead down to the River Lochy, or up on to the hill which has wonderful views down Loch Linnhe. Fort William is three miles down the road.
info@fortwilliam-chalets.co.uk   www.fortwilliam-chalets.co.uk

TORLUNDY *(S-C)*

LONE PINE LODGE 440

Torlundy Farm
Torlundy PH33 6SW
Tel: 01397 703015 MAP 3

Lodge: sleeps 7
£550-£950 pw

Delicious organic lamb available from our deep freeze at the farm

Scottish Organic Producers Association

Superb log house from Carolina USA. Lone Pine Lodge is in an attractive rural location on an organic farm, with superb views of the spectacular north face of Ben Nevis and down Loch Linnhe. The one and a half storey timber house has an open-plan living room with a cathedral ceiling and large windows, and doors which open onto the balcony. Experience the peace and tranquillity from this elevated site, overlooking fields and forest to the mountains. The early morning and late evening views are often amazing. Enjoy a farm walk up into the hills behind, or take a couple of hours out and discover the fun of fly fishing – there's a trout loch just twenty yards from your balcony. Fort William is four miles away.
info@fortwilliam-chalets.co.uk   www.fortwilliam-chalets.co.uk/lonepine.htm

IONA *(Hotel)*

ARGYLL HOTEL 441

Iona
Isle of Iona PA76 6SJ
Tel: 01681 700334

Room only rate £44-£170 per room pn. Full breakfast, lunch, dinner menus all a la carte

The best of local produce and vegetables from our certified organic kitchen garden

Soil Association

Built in 1868 as the village inn, the hotel overlooks the Sound of Iona to the pink and blue hills of Mull. We have a strong environmental ethos, and this encompasses the entire range of activities surrounding the hotel's day to day management. For the past forty years the hotel has had its own organic garden, producing fresh produce for the kitchen. Eggs are local and free-range. We also promote Scottish organic meat. Baking and dry goods are sourced from Greencity Wholefoods (fair trade and organically produced goods). We achieved a Gold Award for sustainability from the Green Tourism Business Scheme in 2001, and full organic certification from the Soil Association in 2004. Booking a table is essential for dinner.
reception@argyllhoteliona.co.uk   www.argyllhoteliona.co.uk

IONA *(Hotel)*

ST COLUMBA HOTEL 442

Iona
Isle of Iona PA76 6SL
Tel: 01681 700304 MAP 3

Small Hotel, Dinner B&B £40-£74 pppn
Restaurant (breakfast, lunch, dinner)

All meals and baking are home-cooked using organic ingredients where possible

Soil Association

Situated next to Iona Abbey the hotel is owned by a partnership of ten individuals, nine of whom live and work on Iona. We aim to continue the tradition of hospitality that this hotel has offered for more than 100 years. Our sun lounges, dining room and many of our rooms enjoy spectacular views over the sound of Iona towards the mountains of Mull. All our food and baking is prepared from scratch on the premises. Our kitchen garden is run on organic principles and we achieved full organic certification in August 2008. The garden supplies much of the vegetables and most of the salads used in the kitchen. All other food is sourced as locally as possible and we use fair trade products where available. Free broadband internet.
info@stcolumba-hotel.co.uk   www.stcolumba-hotel.co.uk

LAGANDORAIN *(S-C)*

IONA HOSTEL 443

Lagandorain
Isle of Iona PA76 6SW
Tel: 01681 700781 MAP 3

Hostel, Adult £18.50 pn
Child £12.50 pn

We sell our own traditionally reared Hebridean mutton and duck eggs

Iona Hostel is situated on our working croft at the north end of the Isle of Iona in the Inner Hebrides. It is simply and beautifully furnished, has five bedrooms (sleeping two to six in bunkbeds), and has a wonderful kitchen / sitting room with woodburning stove. The views are spectacular. Iona Hostel holds a Green Tourism Gold Award and is graded as 4-star by the Tourist Board. Lagandorain croft has been worked for countless generations. The fields are now grazed by our flock of black Hebridean sheep from which we produce beautiful blankets and, in season, mutton. The only fertiliser used on the hay parks is seaweed from the beach. We are members of Linking Environment and Farming and the Slow Food movement.
info@ionahostel.co.uk   www.ionahostel.co.uk

LAGANDORAIN *(S-C)*

LAGANDORAIN COTTAGE 444

Lagandorain
Isle of Iona PA76 6SW
Tel: 01681 700642   MAP 3

Cottage: sleeps 4-6
£450 pw plus metered electricity used

We sell our own traditionally reared
Hebridean mutton and duck eggs

This newly refurbished and homely cottage is situated on our working croft at the north end of the Isle of Iona. It is the only house on Iona where at night you can see no other house lights – only the stars. The views (in the daytime) out past Staffa to Skye are fabulous. The croftlands of Lagandorain have been worked traditionally for countless generations and are a botanical gem. A very special and beautiful place, reaching from the beach below the cottage to the highest point on the island. The fields are now grazed by our flock of black Hebridean sheep from which we produce beautiful blankets and, in season, mutton. Such richness needs only time and space and care – the way it's been done for generations. john@lagandorain.f9.co.uk   www.lagandorain.com

CALGARY *(S-C)*

HAUNN COTTAGES 445

Calgary
Isle of Mull PA75 6QX
Tel: 01688 400249   MAP 3

Cottages: sleep 2-5
£225-£510 pw

Organic vegetables are sometimes for sale

Scottish Organic Producers Association

The Haunn cottages are remote, situated on our organic farm at the end of a two mile farm track. The sense of peace and quiet is strong. Surrounded by herb-rich grassy fields and with the dramatic Treshnish coastline five minutes walk away, the three crofters cottages (with thick rounded corner stone walls) provide a unique, simple yet comfortable place to stay. The fourth cottage, extensively renovated using sheep's wool insulation, solar-heated water, reclaimed maple floors and environmentally friendly paints, sits on its own with wonderful views from an open-plan kitchen / living room. Sheep tracks lead to hidden settlements in secluded glens and along wide open grassy raised beaches. enquiries@treshnish.co.uk   www.treshnish.co.uk/haunn.html

CALGARY (S-C)

TRESHNISH COTTAGES · 446

Calgary
Isle of Mull PA75 6QX
Tel: 0845 458 1971   MAP 3

Cottages: sleep 2-6
£225-£560 pw

Organic vegetables are sometimes for sale

Scottish Organic Producers Association

Situated on a dramatic headland with wonderful views and abundant wildlife, Treshnish is a working organic farm with Angus cattle and Blackface sheep. The Treshnish cottages (awarded a Gold Award by the Green Tourism Business Scheme) are located around the stone farm buildings and provide a peaceful base from which to explore this magical area. The cottages are all individually decorated with a mixture of modern and antique furnishings. Flora and fauna on the headland is rich and varied – we use a complex grazing regime to nurture and protect this biodiversity. On the farm itself there is plenty to explore, and within a few miles of here there are several secluded sandy beaches.
enquiries@treshnish.co.uk   www.treshnish.co.uk/treshnish.html

FIONNPHORT (S-C)

ISLE OF ERRAID   447

Fionnphort
Isle of Mull PA66 6BN
Tel: 01681 700384   MAP 3

Shared Cottages
Contributions between £120 and £260 pw

The fruit and vegetable garden is managed organically

The beautiful and tiny island of Erraid stands at the southern most tip of Mull, only a short way from the island of Iona. Comprising sandy beaches, lush peat bogs and stark craggy granite outcrops, the island, which has been in the care of the Findhorn Foundation for over twenty years, offers sanctuary to a small community as they enjoy a simple, but richly rewarding life. Being here allows them to connect with nature and the elements in a very immediate way, be it growing fruit and vegetables, caring for the animals, confronting the tides and weather or simply enjoying the rugged landscape of the island itself. The heart of the community is the organic garden, and much of the work here is outdoors.
leben.mk@gmx.net   www.erraid.com

FIONNPHORT *(B&B)*

STAFFA HOUSE   448

Fionnphort
Isle of Mull PA66 6BL
Tel: 01681 700677   MAP 3

Bed and Breakfast, £34-£42 pppn
Evening Meal (by arrangement)

Organic / locally sourced ingredients used
for meals where possible

Staffa House is situated in the village of Fionnphort on the Hebridean island of Mull. Inside the house, away from the hustle and bustle at the jetty, you will find a peaceful atmosphere. Meals are served in the lovely conservatory with views west to the Sound of Iona (great for sunsets) and east to Ben More. We believe that food plays a central role in offering genuine welcome and hospitality. Ali is a qualified chef with twenty years experience. Her professional skills and passion for organic / local, ethically sourced food ensures that nourishing meals are made with love and care, attractively presented and delicious to eat. A place to relax, unwind and feel close to the elemental rocks and seas on your doorstep.
enquiries@staffahouse.co.uk   www.staffahouse.co.uk

LOCHDON *(B&B)*

HIGH OATFIELD   449

Lochdon
Isle of Mull PA64 6AP
Tel: 01680 812323   MAP 3

Bed and Breakfast
£30 pppn

Organic continental breakfast (cereal, juice, yogurts, home-made bread, preserves)

Our aim is to offer you a relaxing holiday in a tranquil location, with an organic approach to your bed and breakfast stay. We have two double *en suite* guest rooms. An organic continental breakfast is served in your room. Teas and coffees on the room trays are organically sourced. We only use environmentally friendly products in the B&B. Bedding, towels and complimentary guest toiletries are all organic. Our house is situated next to our organic vegetable business, which supplies fresh salads and vegetables to local businesses. We also supply free-range organic eggs from our flock of chickens. The Gaelic name for our area is Ardchoirk, which translates as High Oatfield. Wildlife abounds just outside your window.
oatfieldorganics@btinternet.com   www.oatfieldorganics.co.uk

CULNACNOC *(B&B)*

THE GLENVIEW 450

Culnacnoc
By Staffin IV51 9JH
Tel: 01470 562248   MAP 1

Bed and Breakfast £32-£45 pppn
Evening Meals (2 or 3 course £22.50-£27.50)

We our passionate about sourcing organic free-range local produce

We are a friendly and creative team with a passion for food and hospitality. Situated on the beautiful Trotternish Peninsula we have five spacious guest rooms, a small restaurant (AA rosette) and a guest lounge with log fire. Breakfast is an important event, with organic and free-range options as well as seasonal fruit and home-baked organic bread. Our restaurant has a daily changing evening menu with the emphasis on organic and quality produce. Using local suppliers is of utmost importance to us, not only to minimise the environmental impact of the transportation of the food but also because we believe Scottish produce is among the best in the world and are privileged to have such an abundant larder on our doorstep. enquiries@glenviewskye.co.uk   www.glenviewskye.co.uk

LYNDALE *(S-C)*

LAUNDRY COTTAGE 451

Lyndale House
Lyndale IV51 9PX
Tel: 01470 582329   MAP 1

Cottage: sleeps 2
£400-£700 pw

Surplus organic produce may be available

Soil Association

Laundry Cottage offers an intimate and romantic holiday retreat, having been lovingly and sympathetically restored from an original estate building. Renovated with flair and imagination, the single storey cottage provides unique accommodation, combining modern comforts with traditional ambiance. Surplus fresh produce from Lyndale's one and a half-acre certified organic walled garden may be available to buy. Lyndale's organic produce can also be bought from the farmers' market in Portree on Thursdays. The cottage enjoys lovely views over woodland teeming with wildlife and flowers. There is easy walking access right from the door, and the cottage is within a very short walk of the sea. linda@lyndale.net   www.lyndale.net/the-laundry.php

LYNDALE (S-C)

LYNDALE GATE LODGE   452

Lyndale House
Lyndale IV51 9PX
Tel: 01470 582329   MAP 1

Gate Lodge: sleeps 4
£550-£900 pw

Surplus organic produce may be available

Soil Association

This delightful Grade B listed 'ink pot' style gate lodge stands in the grounds of Lyndale Estate, nestling in the woods at the top of the private drive. Renovated to a high standard, it offers cosy, comfortable, self-catering accommodation of great character. Surplus fresh produce from Lyndale's certified organic one and a half-acre walled garden may be available to buy. Lyndale's organic produce can be bought from the farmers' market in Portree on Thursdays. Guests enjoy the freedom of the Lyndale estate grounds and the nearby shorefront. It's just a short stroll down the wooded driveway to the sea, with panoramic views to the Outer Hebrides. The seashore teems with birds and other wildlife.
linda@lyndale.net   www.lyndale.net/gate-lodge.php

LYNDALE (S-C)

STABLE COTTAGE, PORTREE   453

Lyndale House
Lyndale IV51 9PX
Tel: 01470 582329   MAP 1

Cottage: sleeps 2
£400-£700 pw

Surplus organic produce may be available

Soil Association

Stable Cottage offers an intimate and romantic holiday retreat, having been lovingly and sympathetically restored from an original estate building. Renovated with flair and imagination, the single storey cottage provides unique accommodation, combining modern comforts with traditional ambiance. Surplus fresh produce from Lyndale's one and a half-acre certified organic walled garden may be available to buy. Lyndale's organic produce can also be bought from the farmers' market in Portree on Thursdays. Stable Cottage enjoys lovely views over woodland teeming with wildlife and flowers. There is easy walking access right from the door, and the cottage is within a short walk of the sea.
linda@lyndale.net   www.lyndale.net/lyndale-cottages.php

SKEABOST BRIDGE *(S-C)*

CROFT ORGANICS OF SKYE 454

5 Tote
Skeabost Bridge IV51 9PQ
Tel: 01470 532251　　　　　　　　MAP 1

Cottage: sleeps 2-4/5, £275-£350 pw
Camping, £2 adult, £1 child, tent £2-£4 pn

We grow much of our own salad and
vegetables and this is available to guests

In Conversion

An 18-acre family-run working croft situated approximately six miles north of Portree. We offer simple, clean, comfortable accommodation in our self-catering cottage and the chance to camp on our small adjacent camping field. We have our own 5kw wind turbine which supplies the croft's electricity. Campers travelling on foot or by bike are especially welcome and we offer special rates if you arrive without a car. We have a trampoline, cycles and Canadian canoes, which you are welcome to make use of while you are here. Families are very welcome. There is fishing locally. The croft is ideally placed for exploring the north of the island. Skye is a wonderful place to see wildlife and the area abounds with colourful history. wrightrutland@phonecoop.coop　www.croftorganicsofskye.co.uk

BALMACLELLAN *(S-C)*

WEST HOLMHEAD 455

Craig Farm
Balmaclellan DG7 3QS
Tel: 01644 420636　　　　　　　　MAP 8

Cottage: sleeps 5, £300-£500 pw
Short Breaks (out of season)

Surplus organic beef, lamb, apples, plums,
courgettes

Biodynamic Agricultural Association

West Holmhead is an old stone cottage on the edge of our organic (biodynamic) farm in deepest Galloway. The cottage has beamed ceilings and a big birchwood garden, and looks out through trees onto green fields and hills. Sometimes we can provide fresh organic eggs, apples, or meat – please ask. You'll find an excellent organic farm shop within thirty minutes drive (Beeswing). We have a mixture of sheep and cattle (White Galloways), orchid meadows, bluebell woods, splashy burns, heather moor, and abundant wildlife. From the front door you can walk or cycle (there's a pair of traditional bikes for your use) along the quiet 'hidden road' to Balmaclellan, through dark forests and over the green hills. mas@craigfarm.co.uk　www.craigfarm.co.uk

KIRKPATRICK DURHAM (B&B)

CRAIGADAM 456

Kirkpatrick Durham
Castle Douglas DG7 3HU
Tel: 01556 650233   MAP 8

Country House, B&B £44 pppn
Dinner, £24 pp

Organic lamb, organic vegetables, wild game

Scottish Organic Producers Association

A tastefully converted 18th-century farm steading within a working farm in Dumfries and Gallaway. Craigadam has been a past winner of the Taste of Scotland awards for its quality home cooking. Meals, including a hearty Galloway breakfast, are sumptuous and are enjoyed in our oak-panelled dining room around our magnificent oak table. We use organic lamb and organic vegetables. Sample our game cooking – the venison is wild,.as are the pheasants and partridges. Honesty bar and wine list. The estate is committed to organic farming and is run with conservation and sustainability in mind. The 25,000 acres of farmland, lochs, moorland and woodland are rich in wildlife, ideal for hiking, rambling and bird-watching.
inquiry@craigadam.com   www.craigadam.com

KIRKPATRICK DURHAM (S-C)

CRAIGADAM COTTAGE 457

Kirkpatrick Durham
Castle Douglas DG7 3HU
Tel: 01556 650233   MAP 8

Cottage: sleeps 4-6
£500-£550 pw

Organic lamb, organic vegetables, wild game

Scottish Organic Producers Association

Craigadam Estate covers 25,000 acres of farmland, lochs and moorland. It is committed to organic farming and is run with conservation and sustainability in mind. The self-catering cottage has three twin bedrooms individually decorated to a theme – African, Florentine, and Scottish. The cottage has a comfortable sitting / dining room with French windows and a lovely view of the orchard. The orchard is particularly suitable for sitting out, for barbecues and for children. Visitors can choose to come to the house for a meal or to make use of other facilities, or cater for themselves (the luxury fitted kitchen has all modern appliances) in one of the most pleasant homes from home in Dumfries and Galloway.
inquiry@craigadam.com   www.craigadam.com/accommodation/index.htm

MOSSDALE *(B&B)*

KEEPERS LODGE 458

Slogarie
By Mossdale DG7 2NL
Tel: 01644 450317 MAP 8

Bed and Breakfast
£62.50-£89.50 per room

Traditional wood-fired cooking using only
certified organic ingredients

Located within the peaceful 400-acre Slogarie Estate, we offer bed and breakfast in Keepers Lodge or Alice Cottage. The cottage can also be rented on a self-catering basis (£435-£535 pw). Eco-friendly products and Ecos paints are used throughout both properties. Bed linen, towels and bathrobes are made from the finest organic cotton. Toiletries are made on the Isle of Arran from local natural ingredients. We have been committed to an organic lifestyle for many years. Organic home baking and seasonal fruit and vegetables available daily. Galloway (the area west of Dumfries along the coast to Stranraer and north as far as Ayr) is one of the undiscovered jewels of Europe with stunning scenery and diverse outdoor pursuits. inskipsorganics@tiscali.co.uk   www.keeperslodge.co.uk

EDINBURGH *(B&B)*

McCRAE'S B&B 459

44 East Claremont Street
Edinburgh EH7 4JR
Tel: 0131 556 2610 MAP 3

Bed and Breakfast
£35-£50 pppn

Extensive organic breakfast menu, sourced
as locally as possible

A family-run guest house, located in Edinburgh's historic New Town close to the city centre. As a family we've been supporting the organic movement for many years, and now our Bed and Breakfast is too. Our extensive breakfast menu is 100% organic, apart from wild smoked salmon. We source our produce as locally as possible so you'll be getting a taste of the best Scotland has to offer. We offer our guests high quality accommodation that quite literally doesn't cost the earth and will help reduce your carbon footprint while enjoying our wonderful city. At McCrae's you'll enjoy the personal touch that a family-run establishment has to offer and we'll be on hand with lots of advice to help you make the most of your visit. info@mccraes.co.uk   www.mccraes.co.uk

EDINBURGH *(B&B)*

TANTALLON B&B 460

17 Tantallon Place
Edinburgh EH9 1NZ
Tel: 0131 667 1708 MAP 3

Bed and Breakfast
£26-£30 pppn

Breakfast is between 70%-90% organic

Tantallon Place is situated in the Grange, a quiet conservation area with tree lined streets and Victorian houses, close to the centre of Edinburgh. Breakfast is between 70%-90% organic. We offer a cooked breakfast with organic free-range eggs from East Lothian, organic wholemeal bread, grilled organic sausages and bacon, grilled tomatoes, mushrooms, freshly squeezed orange juice, home-made jams and marmalade, plus a wide range of teas and coffee. If you prefer, there's a lighter option with freshly made fruit salads, fresh grapefruit and melon, natural yogurt, local honey, organic porridge oats or muesli, scrambled or poached eggs, vegetarian sausages, and poached undyed smoked haddock.
mcw@ecosse.net   www.tantallonbandb.co.uk

○

EDINBURGH *(B&B)*

GLENORA GUEST HOUSE 461

14 Rosebery Crescent
Edinburgh EH12 5JY
Tel: 01313 371186 MAP 3

Bed and Breakfast
£35-£67 pppn

100% organic authentic Scottish breakfast from local producers and suppliers

The Glenora Guest House is a beautiful Victorian townhouse in the centre of Edinburgh. After a full refurbishment we have been awarded 4-stars by the Scottish Tourist Board. We serve a continental buffet and full cooked breakfast, all of which is entirely organic, in our large bright dining room on the ground floor. We also offer complimentary tea and coffee making facilities in the bedrooms, again all of which is both organic and fair trade. The guest house is located in Edinburgh's West End, where quiet streets with terraces of fine Victorian townhouses and private gardens exist close to the city centre. The nearby railway station at Haymarket makes excursions to other parts of Scotland very convenient.
enquiries@glenorahotel.co.uk   www.glenorahotel.co.uk

○ ⑤ ♣ ⇌ 🚆

FINDHORN (B&B)

SUNFLOWER B&B 462

404 The Field of Dreams
The Park IV36 3TA
Tel: 01309 692080 MAP 2

Bed and Breakfast
Double, £55 pn

Products certified organic and sourced
locally where possible (around 90% organic)

The B&B is situated in the middle of The Park as part of the world renowned Findhorn Community and Eco Village. All its attractions are within walking distance. A totally organic breakfast is served in the dining room, consisting of fresh fruit, yogurt, fruit juices, cereals, porridge, eggs and wholemeal bread. You also have the choice of a range of teas or coffees. Tea and coffee facilities are available at any time. All the products we are sourced locally wherever possible (bread is from Findhorn Bakery) and are certified organic. From the front door it's just a short stroll to Findhorn Bay and it's a fifteen minute walk to the beautiful sandy beach that extends for seven miles from Findhorn Village to Burghead.
info@sunflower-findhorn.co.uk   www.sunflower-findhorn.co.uk

FORRES (S-C)

MARCASSIE FARM 463

Rafford
Forres IV36 2RH
Tel: 01309 671700 MAP 2

Self-Catering: sleeps 2-4
£250-£430 per unit pw

Eggs, mayonnaise, wheatgrass, vegetables and herbs available in season

Soil Association

We run a certified organic smallholding growing vegetables, herbs and fruit. Accommodation is in the self-contained west wing of our farmhouse and comprises one bedroom, a bathroom and a large airy open-plan living-dining area. We have a small flock of laying hens, possibly to be joined by some sheep. Eggs, mayonnaise, wheatgrass (order in advance), fresh vegetables and herbs in season available for purchase on-site. Locally sourced organic fruit and vegetable box available to order on request, also meat and cheese. We run a sawmill and bespoke joinery manufacturing facility on-site, specialising in Scottish timber and timber products. Close to the coastal village of Findhorn, beaches, rivers, rolling hills and mountains.
marcassie@marcassie.fsnet.co.uk

NAIRN (S-C)

HIDDENGLEN HOLIDAYS   464

Laikenbuie
Grantown Road IV12 5QN
Tel: 01667 454630   MAP 2

Lodges, Chalet, Caravan
£120-£620 pw

Organic lamb (frozen), eggs, excess
vegetables

Soil Association

Watch red squirrels and woodpeckers on the balcony, plus roe deer among the abundant wildlife on a tranquil croft with a beautiful outlook over a trout loch amid birch woods. Guests are welcome to collect eggs, feed pet lambs (if present), tour the croft. Large warm lodges (85 square metres) provide comfortable accommodation, plus a chalet or residential caravan, all kept very clean and well equipped. There is also a camping area. It is safe for children, with trampoline, bikes and a boat. Laikenbuie is an excellent holiday centre with low rainfall, plentiful sunshine, and few midges. Near Loch Ness, sandy beaches, Moray Firth dolphins, Cairngorm Mountains, Speyside distilleries, golf, walking, pony trekking, fishing. info@hiddenglen.co.uk   www.hiddenglen.co.uk

EVIE (B&B)

WOODWICK HOUSE   465

Evie
Orkney KW17 2PQ
Tel: 01856 751330   MAP 2

Country House, B&B £34-£55 pppn
Evening Meal, 3 course £26 pp

Award-winning cuisine includes organic or
naturally grown produce where possible

Warm and welcoming historic country house overlooking the island of Gairsay and beyond. An extraordinary, peaceful location set in unique and beautiful surroundings on this sheltered part of Orkney. Only twenty minutes from Stromness and Kirkwall, and within easy reach of the main historic sites, bird reserves and sandy beaches. With its twelve acres of bluebell woodland, a burn cascading down to the sea and its own bay, this is an ideal location for bird-watching, seal watching or simply relaxing. A member of 'Eat Scotland' and 'Taste of Orkney' for our farmhouse style cuisine, which makes use of the excellent prime local produce and seafoods, using organic / naturally grown produce wherever possible. mail@woodwickhouse.co.uk   www.woodwickhouse.co.uk

HOLM *(S-C)*

NEW HOLLAND BOTHY 466

New Holland Organic Farm
Holm KW17 2SA
Tel: 01856 781345   MAP 2

Bothy: sleeps 2
£120-£250 pw

Home reared organic meat (beef, pork, lamb)

Scottish Organic Producers Association

Comfortable self-catering accommodation for two people in a converted farm bothy. It is surrounded by beautiful countryside on the main island of Orkney. New Holland is a working organic farm with cattle, sheep and hens. We can supply our own organic meat (beef, pork, lamb), sausages, and sometimes our own potatoes. We are passionate about our way of farming here, and love to discuss our methods and aims with our visitors, who are free to walk around our 900 acres of pastures and heather. There are scenic walks along breathtaking cliffs or beautiful deserted beaches. Orkney is also a well known bird-watchers' paradise, with many native and migrating species to be seen.
info@holidayorganic.co.uk   www.holidayorganic.co.uk

ROUSAY *(S-C)*

ROUSAY HOSTEL 467

Trumland Organic Farm
Rousay KW17 2PU
Tel: 01856 821252   MAP 2

Hostel, £10-£12 pppn
Camping, £5 pppn

Organic produce may be available to buy

Soil Association

A working organic farm within easy walking distance from the pier. Modern, purpose built and well equipped, the hostel has two dormitories and one single room, showers, kitchen and laundry facilities. The camp site is adjacent to the hostel. Campers have use of the hostel facilities. Organic produce may be available to buy from the farm. We are also WWOOF hosts. Visitors can walk to a shop, restaurant and pub. Bike hire is available at the hostel. A walker and birdwatcher's paradise (we are close to an RSPB reserve), the island has many footpaths of outstanding scenic and environmental beauty. Rousay's small friendly community creates a unique welcome for the visitor to this beautiful Orkney island.
trumland@btopenworld.com   www.hostel-scotland.co.uk/hostels/index.asp?ID=84

SOUTH RONALDSAY (S-C)

WHEEMS BOTHY 468

Wheems
Eastside KW17 2TJ
Tel: 01856 831556 MAP 2

Bothy: sleeps 8, £40 pn (min 2 nights), £190 pw
Camping, from £4 pn

Organic salads, vegetables, eggs available

Soil Association

20-acre organic farm on a south-facing slope, looking down onto a large sandy bay and cliffs. We specialise in a broad range of vegetable products for local market, sold at our farm and via a box scheme and farmers' market in Kirkwall. Small scale field crops and a large polytunnel provide salads, herbs, tomatoes, peppers etc, and our own chicken eggs. Accommodation is above a converted barn for individual / family / group use, booked as a single unit. One double and two single beds on pine platforms and two sets of timber bunks. Bathroom area with hot showers. Heating, cooking, bed linen included. Small camping field in front of our 200 year old farmhouse with spectacular views. Cliff walking, bathing, birds, seals. wheemsbothy@gmail.com

ST MARGARET'S HOPE (B&B)

ORCADIAN WILDLIFE 469

Gerraquoy Organic Farm
St Margaret's Hope KW17 2TH
Tel: 01856 831240 MAP 2

Orkney Island Tours, £800-£900 pw all inclusive / Short Breaks, £300-£450 pp

We do our best to provide organic food, utilising our own organic produce

Scottish Organic Producers Association

Orcadian Wildlife runs tailor-made birdwatching, wildlife and culture tours from April to October for up to a maximum of four guests. We specialise in a blend of wildlife tours (featuring our seabirds and birds of prey) and Orkney's 5000 year old Neolithic monuments. The base for your holiday will be our traditional family farmhouse and organic smallholding, embellished with a small herd of the placid and beautiful Shetland cattle, one of the rarest breeds in the UK. We produce our own organic beef and eggs, and have access to locally reared pork and lamb, so the farmhouse food that we serve is fresh and tasty. The price for six nights is £900 and includes accommodation, meals, and guiding services. enquiries@orcadianwildlife.co.uk   www.orcadianwildlife.co.uk

ST MARGARET'S HOPE (S-C)

THE PEEDIE HOUSE 470

Gerraquoy Organic Farm
St Margaret's Hope KW17 2TH
Tel: 01856 831240 MAP 2

Cottage: sleeps 2
£300-£325 pw

Our own organic beef and free-range eggs
for sale

Scottish Organic Producers Association

Visit Scotland 4-stars. The Peedie House is designed and constructed to enable full disabled access, and to the highest green tourism standards with solar-powered water heating, full roof and wall insulation, under-floor heating. The cottage has a double bedroom, bathroom with shower, first class kitchen facilities, large conservatory overlooking the island of Copinsay. Organic beef is for sale, produced on the farm from our small herd of native Shetland cattle, as well as free-range eggs produced by our own chickens. As part of our Orcadian Wildlife and Gerraquoy Farm businesses we offer to share our knowledge of Orkney's wildlife and 5000 year old neolithic sites, with day or half-day tours at preferential rates.
enquiries@orcadianwildlife.co.uk   www.orcadianwildlife.co.uk/Self-catering.htm

BALQUHIDDER (Hotel)

MONACHYLE MHOR HOTEL 471

Balquhidder
Lochearnhead FK19 8PQ
Tel: 01877 384622 MAP 3

Lochside Hotel, B&B from £47.50 pppn
Restaurant (lunch, dinner)

Fresh bread, eggs, meat and vegetables from
our farm, fish from the west coast

A small family-run farmhouse hotel in the heart of the Trossachs. Peacefully set in 2000 acres, it enjoys magnificent views across two crystal clear lochs. The menu in the award-winning restaurant changes daily. Most of our produce comes from within a thirty mile radius. Fish is delivered from the west coast, selected for optimum freshness and quality. Our garden supplies as many herbs as we can manage, plus all the basics from strawberries and salads to high summer favourites like broad beans and carrots, then on to cabbages and kale as the season progresses. We are great believers in preserving the best of our produce, from home-made jams and pickles to cured beef and bacon.
monachyle@mhor.net   www.mhor.net

BLAIR ATHOLL *(S-C)*

GLEN BRUAR LODGE 472

Atholl Estates
Blair Atholl PH18 5TH
Tel: 01796 481355 MAP 3

Lodge: sleeps 18
£1340-£1825 pw

Atholl Glens Organic Meat (beef and lamb)

Scottish Organic Producers Association

Set in a dramatic glen, nine miles along a private track from the public road at the village of Calvine, Glen Bruar is the ideal remote retreat for up to eighteen people. Many miles of pony and foot tracks start from the front door. Free from the trappings of everyday life (no TV or mobile signal), guests can watch wildlife such as red deer and golden eagles, pat the lodge's farm animals and enjoy organic produce. The lodge is part of Atholl Estates, most of which is under organic status. The estates' farms are part of the Atholl Glens Organic Meat co-operative, producing top quality organic beef and lamb, which can be pre-ordered (delivered frozen), as can organic fruit and vegetable boxes from a local company.
enquiries@atholl-estates.co.uk www.athollestateslodges.co.uk/lodges/glenbruar.asp

BLAIR ATHOLL *(S-C)*

OLD BLAIR LODGE 473

Atholl Estates
Blair Atholl PH18 5TH
Tel: 01796 481355 MAP 3

Lodge: sleeps 10-12
£1340-£2680 pw

Atholl Glens Organic Meat (beef and lamb)

Scottish Organic Producers Association

Originally an inn, Old Blair is located minutes walk from historic Blair Castle (part of Atholl Estates) and is surrounded by the castle's organic home farm. Tours of the farm run regularly throughout the year (admission charge). The estates' farms are part of the Atholl Glens Organic Meat co-operative, producing top quality organic beef and lamb, which can be pre-ordered (delivered frozen). Organic fruit and vegetable boxes are available from a local company. Perth (35 miles away) has a large farmers' market on the first Saturday of the month. Old Blair is only a short walk from the village of Blair Atholl. The house is ideally located for hill walking and mountaineering. Pony trekking can be provided on the estate.
enquiries@atholl-estates.co.uk www.athollestateslodges.co.uk/lodges/oldblair.asp

DOUNE *(B&B)*

MACKEANSTON HOUSE   474

Doune
Stirling FK16 6AX
Tel: 01786 850213   MAP 3

Country House, B&B £45-£48 pppn
Dinner, 4 course £28

Includes fresh vegetables, fruit and herbs
from the garden

We offer a warm welcome and a touch of luxury at Mackeanston in the heart of Scotland. Wake to the sound of the skylark, drink in the pure air of the highlands, enjoy the panorama of lochs and mountains which make up the beautiful Trossachs area. Breakfast and dinner are served in the dining room or in the conservatory overlooking the beautiful old walled garden. Delicious home-made Aga-baked breads. Home-made jams and marmalade. Cooking is largely organic using the Aga. We use local organic ingredients wherever possible, including herbs, fruit and vegetables from our own garden. Menus regularly include local fish, game and beef from hill and river. Organic venison, and fish, used where possible. WiFi available.
fiona@mackeanstonhouse.co.uk   www.stirling-flexible-lettings.co.uk

DOUNE *(S-C)*

THE GLED COTTAGE   475

Doune
Stirling FK16 6AX
Tel: 01786 850213   MAP 3

Cottage: sleeps 4-5, £395-£595
Visitors are welcome to book dinner

Includes fresh vegetables, fruit and herbs
from the garden

This charming and comfortable cottage stands in its own garden, facing south in the midst of farmland with distant views to the Gargunnock Hills. Nearby, across the fields, is an old tower built to mark the centre of Scotland. Visitors are welcome to book dinner at Mackeanston House (two minutes drive away or five minutes walk), where Fiona cooks delicious food with local produce and naturally grown fresh vegetables, fruit and herbs from her garden. Meals are served in the dining room or in the conservatory overlooking the beautiful walled garden. Menus regularly include local fish, game and beef from hill and river, and delicious home-made Aga-baked breads. Organic venison, and fish, used wherever possible. WiFi provided.
fiona@mackeanstonhouse.co.uk   www.stirling-flexible-lettings.co.uk

DULL *(S-C)*

CRUCK COTTAGE 476

Drumdewan
Dull PH15 2JQ
Tel: 01887 820071   MAP 3

Cottage: sleeps 2, from £425 pw
Short breaks are available

Buy organic produce from our farm shop, or
eat in our farm shop café

The ultimate in luxury for the discerning couple, whether on honeymoon, a romantic break, or just a 'get away from it all' experience. No expense has been spared in the decoration of the cottage, the fittings, or the wonderfully landscaped garden. This idyllic five star experience will leave you refreshed, invigorated and rejuvenated. Situated in the small village of Drumdewan the cottage is only two minutes walk from our farm shop. Here you can choose from an array of organic produce from Highland Perthshire and beyond (discount available for guests). You can even have a box of produce ready for your arrival, or you could choose to eat in the farm shop café where the majority of the food is organic.

info@aberfeldycountrycottages.co.uk   www.aberfeldycountrycottages.co.uk

GLENFARG *(S-C)*

BRACKEN LOG CABIN 477

Duncrievie Farm
Glenfarg PH2 9PD
Tel: 01502 502588   MAP 3

Log Cabin S4468: sleeps 2
Usually available for short breaks

Organic restaurant, organic farm shops, organic café all within 15 minutes drive

Scottish Organic Producers Association

New luxury log cabin offering every comfort, with a king-size four-poster bed, double spa bath, and sauna. The log cabin is centrally situated on an organic farm, with stunning panoramic views over the village. We have been awarded the Green Tourism Business Scheme Gold Award for excellence in environmental practice. The cabin has a thermostatically controlled ground source heating system. We have our own fresh water supply. We provide information on the local farmers' market, organic produce providers and farm shops. Jamesfield Organic Centre (organic restaurant, shop, butchery, bakery) and Pillars of Hercules (organic café, farm shop) are within fifteen minutes drive of Duncrievie Farm.

mail@hoseasons.co.uk   www.hoseasons.co.uk

GLENFARG *(S-C)*

FINGASK LOG CABIN 478

Duncrievie Farm
Glenfarg PH2 9PD
Tel: 01502 502588 MAP 3

Log Cabin S4394: sleeps 2
Usually available for short breaks

Organic restaurant, organic farm shops,
organic café all within 15 minutes drive

Scottish Organic Producers Association

A luxury one bedroom log cabin built from Finnish logs. The log cabin is centrally situated on an organic farm, with stunning panoramic views over the village. We have been awarded the Green Tourism Business Scheme Gold Award for excellence in environmental practice. The cabin has a thermostatically controlled ground source heating system, a wind turbine supplies electricity, and we have our own fresh water supply. Lots of local information is provided, including info on the local farmers' market, organic produce providers and farm shops. Jamesfield Organic Centre (organic restaurant, shop, butchery, bakery) and Pillars of Hercules (organic café, farm shop) are both within fifteen minutes drive.
mail@hoseasons.co.uk   www.hoseasons.co.uk

GLENFARG *(S-C)*

HILTON LOG CABIN 479

Duncrievie Farm
Glenfarg PH2 9PD
Tel: 01502 502588 MAP 3

Log Cabin S4345: sleeps 2+1
Usually available for short breaks

Organic restaurant, organic farm shops,
organic café all within 15 minutes drive

Scottish Organic Producers Association

One bedroom log cabin with wooden floors throughout. The log cabin is centrally situated on an organic farm, with stunning panoramic views over the village. We have been awarded the Green Tourism Business Scheme Gold Award for excellence in environmental practice. The cabin has a thermostatically controlled ground source heating system, a wind turbine supplies electricity, and we have our own fresh water supply. Lots of local information is provided, including info on the local farmers' market, organic produce providers and farm shops. Jamesfield Organic Centre (organic restaurant, shop, butchery, bakery) and Pillars of Hercules (organic café, farm shop) are both within fifteen minutes drive.
mail@hoseasons.co.uk   www.hoseasons.co.uk

INVERGOWRIE (S-C)

REDMYRE FARMHOUSE   480

Invergowrie
Dundee DD2 5LH   MAP 3

Farmhouse: sleeps 8
£675-£999 pw

You will find details of local organic suppliers in the farmhouse

Scottish Organic Producers Association

Nestling in the heart of a 320-acre organic arable and livestock farm, with panoramic views of the countryside, this spacious modern farmhouse is perfect for an idyllic country holiday. The house sits beside a wood where red squirrels scurry through the trees. It is five minutes walk to a pond, which ducks and swans call home, with a summerhouse. The woods are full of wildlife and over sixty different species of birds have been seen. The house has a large enclosed garden offering uninterrupted views of the Sidlaw hills over the organic grazing land, where sheep and cattle graze, and a barbecue area with seating ideal for the long Scottish evenings. There is ample walking and cycling on the farm and in the local area. alison.kaye@culfargie-estates.co.uk

KILLIN (B&B)

INVERTAY HOUSE   481

Killin
Stirling FK21 8TN
Tel: 01567 820492   MAP 3

Guest House
Dinner, B&B from £57 pppn

45%-65% organic over the year

Situated on the outskirts of the picturesque village of Killin, at the western end of Loch Tay. This former manse, the oldest part dating from 1744, stands in extensive walled gardens looking out across the River Lochay with spectacular views of the Tarmachan Mountains, Beinn Ghlas and Ben Lawers, and the wonderful Breadalbane countryside. The dinner menu changes daily and all meals are prepared using only fresh produce, including an abundance of naturally grown seasonal fruit, herbs and vegetables from our own garden, home-made jams and preserves, and honey from our beehives. All other produce used is carefully sourced and supplied directly to us from the highest quality producers in Scotland. invertay@btinternet.com www.invertayhouse.co.uk

LOGIEALMOND (B&B)

GREENACRES 482

Chapelhill
Logiealmond PHI 3TQ
Tel: 01738 880302   MAP 3

Bed and Breakfast
£25-£32.50 pppn

Minimum 70% organic, at times it may be as
much as 85%-90%

Set in lovely rural countryside with far reaching views of the surrounding hills, only a few
miles from Perth. Naturally home-grown or locally sourced food for breakfast. The house is
secluded, quiet, comfortable, and elegantly furnished. It is surrounded by a sheltered half-acre
garden, which is a sanctuary for birds, and includes an organic fruit and vegetable garden, hens
providing free-range eggs, decorative fantail pigeons and a wildlife pond. Greenacres is a plant
collector's paradise. It has held the Gold Award from the Green Tourism Business Scheme
for excellence in environmental practice for the past three years, and was also runner up in
the Big Tree Country Awards 2007 for business development.
enquiry@bedandbreakfast-perthshire.co.uk   www.bedandbreakfast-perthshire.co.uk

TULLIEMET (S-C)

CONVALLOCH LODGE   483

Atholl Estates
Tulliemet PHI8 5TH
Tel: 01796 481355   MAP 3

Lodge: sleeps 10-12
£980-£2000 pw

Atholl Glens Organic Meat (beef and lamb)

Scottish Organic Producers Association

Situated in an attractive and secluded highland location, with elevated views over lower
Strathtay, Convalloch is surrounded by organic farmland. As part of Atholl Estates, guests
receive tickets to nearby Blair Castle, where tours of the organic home farm run throughout
the year (at an additional cost). The estates' farms are part of the Atholl Glens Organic Meat
co-operative, producing top quality organic beef and lamb, which can be pre-ordered
(delivered frozen). Alternatively, Atholl Glens sell fresh meat at the Perth Farmers' Market
(20 miles away) on the first Saturday of the month. Organic fruit and vegetable boxes are
also available to order from a local company. River and hill loch fishing available nearby.
enquiries@atholl-estates.co.uk   www.athollestateslodges.co.uk/lodges/convalloch.asp

BAYFIELD *(B&B)*

WEMYSS HOUSE B&B 484

Bayfield
By Tain IV19 1QW
Tel: 01862 851212   MAP 2

B&B, double or twin *en suite* from £80 per room. Evening Meal, £30 (by arrangement)

Organic / local / home produce available

Set in a peaceful rural landscape near Tain in the Highlands of Scotland, Wemyss House has three comfortably furnished *en suite* rooms (two doubles and a twin) and stunning views over the Cromarty Firth to the mountains beyond. Enjoy a full traditional Scottish breakfast. Organic produce is important at Wemyss House. We (Christine and Stuart) grow most of our own vegetables in the two-acre garden, where the roaming free-range chickens provide the eggs for your breakfast. Together with home-made organic bread, home-made preserves and other locally sourced organic and traditional fare, you can be assured of a good wholesome start to your day. Four course evening meals plus coffee by arrangement. stay@wemysshouse.com   www.wemysshouse.com

BLACK ISLE *(B&B)*

SOLUS OR 485

Findon Hill
Culbokie IV7 8JH
Tel: 01349 877828   MAP 2

Bed and Breakfast
From £30 pppn

A healthy natural breakfast is provided, all our produce is organic

The Harmonology Centre evolved from an organic therapeutic centre to incorporate a Visit Scotland 4-star Bed and Breakfast. Set in 3 acres with panoramic views of mountains, sea, forest and pastures. Our emphasis is on 'natural'. This includes organic food, structured purified water throughout, and an EMG stress-free environment. We pick our own cherries, plums, herbs. Forest walks provide us with chanterelles, bilberries. We are beautifully located. Visit castles, gardens. View dolphins, seals, black swans, red kites, buzzards. Experience Pictish Trails, hill walks, stunning beaches. Return, relax on the patio, or treat yourself to a massage or sauna and steam shower – naturally chemical-free.
info@harmonology.eu   www.harmonology.eu/holidays.htm

POOLEWE *(S-C)*

COILLE BHEAG 486

14 Midtown of Inverasdale
Poolewe IV22 2LW
Tel: 01445 781783 MAP 1

Crofter's Cottage: sleeps 6, £245-£470 pw
Eco-Lodge: sleeps 4, £245-£550 pw

Our own produce (mixed salads, herbs, vegetables), free-range eggs

Two properties available for rental. A fully renovated crofter's cottage furnished in traditional style with a solid fuel fire, and a modern open-plan luxury eco-lodge with energy-efficient heating. Our 6-acre family croft has its own meadowland and wood, access to the shores of Loch Ewe, and amazing views of the wild rugged mountains. Home-grown vegetables and fruits are available in season. Ready prepared salads and herbs with fresh ingredients from the croft. Fresh, new laid free-range eggs. Wester Ross is one of the most beautiful parts of the Scottish Highlands. We are near to stunning coastal beaches, the Torridon Mountains, and world famous Inverewe Garden. Pets welcome in the cottage, but not in the lodge.
alasdairwright@btinternet.com www.coillebheag.com

POOLEWE *(Hotel)*

POOLEWE HOTEL 487

Poolewe
Achnasheen IV22 2JX
Tel: 01445 781241 MAP 1

Retreat, £67 pppn
3 day winter and spring offers

Minimum 65% organic, produced locally

The setting of Poolewe Hotel is magnificent: it looks both down the loch to the open sea and across to the world famous gardens at Inverewe. Many people have discovered the wonderful value of hill walking combined with rest and relaxation. In this beautiful setting we offer a holiday that combines the benefits of gentle exercise, great food and like-minded company. Your holiday cost is all-inclusive of accommodation and local food. Our aim is to offer at least 85% organic food (presently 65%) which will be determined by the growth and development of our local producers. Most of our vegetables and fruits are grown on local crofts, which enhances the fabulous meals we offer in our restaurant and family-friendly bistro.
info@poolewehotel.co.uk www.poolewehotel.co.uk

SCORAIG (S-C)

TOM'S BOTHY 488

Achmore
Scoraig IV23 2RE
Tel: 01854 633354   MAP 3

Bothy: sleeps 5
£15 per adult pn

Fresh vegetables, fruit, herbs, eggs, home-baked bread

The bothy is furnished with a fully equipped kitchen and is very comfortable, with a large wood-burning stove that also heats the water. There is a bath in the bothy and a basic outside loo. Our house is five minutes walk away behind the trees and our three-acre organic garden, where we grow and harvest the best quality organic vegetables, fruit and herbs. Depending on the season, fresh vegetables, fruit, herbs, eggs and home-baked bread (all organic) are available for you to purchase. Sometimes there may be the opportunity to catch fish, or lobsters and crabs in creels. Tom's Bothy is situated on the south side of Loch Broom. There are many local hill and coastal walks on the peninsula offering breathtaking views.
annanogood@freeuk.com

ULLAPOOL (Camping)

LECKMELM FARM 489

Leckmelm Estate
Loch Broom IV23 2RL
Tel: 01854 612471   MAP 1

Camping
£5 pppn

Meat and vegetables according to seasonal availability

Biodynamic Agricultural Association

Basic camping facilities in a walled garden with an onsite tipi. Situated on Leckmelm Farm the tipi sleeps two, or alternatively it can be used as a living room in addition to tents. The tipi has a groundsheet inside with rugs. It's in a very sheltered spot close to the loch, where you can swim in warm weather and fish. Long drop compost loo and tap nearby. We aim to manage the land in a way that benefits the environment and peripheral ecosystems as well as providing jobs and homes for local people. We are involved in the Rural Stewardship scheme and have been using traditional cropping techniques, tree planting in shelterbelts and grazing the pastures using traditional breeds of animal.
info@leckmelmholidays.co.uk   www.leckmelmholidays.co.uk/Tipi-Camping-g.asp

ULLAPOOL *(S-C)*

LECKMELM COTTAGES 490

Leckmelm Estate
Loch Broom IV23 2RL
Tel: 01854 612471 MAP 1

Cottages: sleep 2-6, £190-£600 pw
Green Weekends

Meat and vegetables according to seasonal availability

Biodynamic Agricultural Association

Eleven cottages in a rural situation, some by the loch, with the farm at the heart of Leckmelm Estate. STB Green Tourism Business Scheme Gold standard. Leckmelm Farm produces vegetables from the walled garden using biodynamic methods and markets via a box scheme and farm gate sales. We keep Highland Cattle predominantly for conservation grazing of species-rich grassland and production of store calves. The family of pigs produce many sets of piglets each year, which are either sold locally or kept for home-produced meat. Meat is reared organically but not certified due to the expense. There are plenty of good walks in the stunning landscape of Wester Ross from your doorstep.
organicholidays@leckmelmholidays.co.uk   www.leckmelmholidays.co.uk

EDNAM *(S-C)*

PLUM BRAES BARN 491

Cliftonhill
Ednam TD5 7QE
Tel: 01573 225028 MAP 3

Cottages: sleep 2-10 (4 bathrooms)
£260-£550 pw

We grow a small area of vegetables and fresh eggs are available

Scottish Organic Producers Association

Situated in a quiet corner of the Scottish Borders, with panoramic views over beautiful countryside, the cottages are only three miles from the attractive market town of Kelso. Cliftonhill is an organic farm growing wheat, barley and oats, and grass for sheep. We grow a small area of vegetables including asparagus, lettuce, tomatoes, herbs and potatoes for our holidaymakers. Fresh eggs are also available. Walks are breathtaking straight from your door. The river Eden is a small tributary of the Tweed, which meanders through Cliftonhill. There is nothing to disturb you but perhaps a grey heron or a kingfisher darting up the river in a blaze of colour. Trout and grayling can be caught, and there are plenty minnows.
maggie@kelsocottages.co.uk   www.kelsocottages.co.uk

LADYRIG *(B&B)*

JERPOINT 492

Ladyrig
Kelso TD5 8JP
Tel: 01573 450311   MAP 3

Bed and Breakfast, £135 pn per suite
Evening Meal £28, Picnic Hampers £10

Organic or locally sourced, home-reared
bacon, sausages and eggs

A luxury suite of rooms with stunning views from the private roof terrace overlooking open countryside towards Floors Castle. This romantic hideaway, with its own private entrance, is just a couple of miles from Kelso in the beautiful Scottish Borders. Food means a lot to us. We are members of the Slow Food movement which promotes the enjoyment and protection of locally produced food products and regional cooking, and we embrace this fully. We keep pigs and chickens and use organic ingredients or locally sourced produce at all times. We can provide a picnic hamper or a delicious three course evening meal if required.
karenandvalkelly@btinternet.com   www.jerpoint.co.uk

◯

LANGSHAW *(B&B)*

OVER LANGSHAW FARM 493

Langshaw
Galashiels TD1 2PE
Tel: 01896 860244   MAP 3

Farmhouse Bed and Breakfast
£30-£35 pppn

Breakfast cereals, yogurt, fruits, eggs, home-made breads, jams, marmalade, etc

Scottish Organic Producers Association

A welcoming family farm with wonderful views in the beautiful Scottish Borders. A family room is available with a private bathroom and there is a ground floor double with *en suite* shower room. Over Langshaw has been run organically for nine years, producing delicious organic milk from eighty beautiful British Friesian and Danish Red milkers. The four hundred pretty Lleyn ewes have their lambs in the spring and enjoy the grassy pastures on this hillside farm. More recently organic egg-producing poultry have been established – they have access to open areas with trees and lots of space for scratching (eggs like they used to taste). Home-produced ice cream and sorbets are made on the farm and find a ready market locally.
overlangshaw@btconnect.com

LANGSHAW *(S-C)*

THE HEN HOOSE 494

Over Langshaw Farm
Langshaw TD1 2PE
Tel: 01896 860244   MAP 3

Cottage: sleeps 4, £300-£475 pw
Short breaks available, prices vary

Organic milk, eggs, garden fresh vegetables,
ice-cream

Scottish Organic Producers Association

Stone cottage on a 500-acre working organic farm in the beautiful Scottish Borders. The south-facing sun room and traditional materials give the cottage much charm. Natural materials include cotton sheets, oak and recycled pitch pine floors, organic paint. 'Start you off' food hampers with organic and local produce. Eggs and, in season, garden fresh vegetables available to buy, plus Over Langshaw farmhouse ice-cream. An 'all seasons' place, in spring you'll see the sweet young lambs; In summer wildflowers and butterflies fill the clover meadows. Autumn colours and hazy days will bring out the photographer in you. Winter can be as cold and wild as it likes, you'll be snug and warm in your 'hoose'.
overlangshaw@btconnect.com

WALLS *(Hotel)*

BURRASTOW HOUSE 495

Walls
Shetland ZE2 9PD
Tel: 01595 809307   MAP 2

Country House Hotel
Dinner B&B, £70-£80 pppn

70%-90% organic (salads and vegetables fresh from our own garden)

18th-century house on a promontory facing the island of Vaila, on the remote and peaceful west coast of Shetland. Burrastow welcomes you with peat fires, a cosy library, and all the marvellous food you could want after a day's exploring. Delicious cuisine using fresh Shetland produce – lamb which is almost 100% organic and natural, locally raised beef and pork, a wide variety of freshly caught fish. Salads and vegetables come from the garden. Fine fresh ingredients, simply cooked with uncomplicated sauces that enhance or complement the natural favours. Organic wines. Otters and seals may be seen from the windows and wild orchids flourish in the grounds. The hotel is open from April to October.
burr.hs@zetnet.co.uk   www.users.zetnet.co.uk/burrastow-house

BY LAIRG *(B&B)*

RUDDYGLOW PARK 496

Loch Assynt
By Lairg IV27 4HB
Tel: 01571 822216 MAP 1

Country House, B&B £40-£100 pppn
Supper £25, Dinner £45

We aim to be as organic as possible (average at least 90% organic)

Small, exclusive, boutique bed and breakfast (5-star) located in the beautiful North West Highlands of Scotland. Luxurious accommodation combining antique furniture, original paintings and individually designed rooms. A much loved four-acre garden, full of well established trees and shrubs, surrounds the house giving a feel of incredible space, peace and tranquillity. As breakfast is the most important meal of the day we pride ourselves on ours. Lots of fresh organic fruits and fruit juices, delicious smoothies, home-made venison sausages, local free-range eggs, organic breads, and delicious jams and honeys. Dinners are designed to be both relaxing and delicious, just what's required after a long day out.
info@ruddyglowpark.com   www.ruddyglowpark.com

SGARASTA BHEAG *(Hotel)*

SCARISTA HOUSE 497

Sgarasta Bheag
Isle of Harris HS3 3HX
Tel: 01859 550238 MAP 1

Small Hotel, B&B £175-£199 room pn
Dinner, 3 course £39.50

Organic, local, home-grown, home-made

The views from Scarista House, a Georgian former manse, are stunning-heather-covered mountains, the ocean, and a three mile long shell sand beach. It is one of the most beautiful and remote places to stay in Britain. We offer traditional comfort in well-furnished guest rooms and two self-catering 'cottages'. We aim for natural, skilled cooking of the ingredients most immediately available, especially the island's wild seafood, lamb, beef and game. We carefully source organic, local or home-grown vegetables and herbs wherever possible. We bake our own bread and cakes, and make our own jam, marmalade, ice cream and yogurt. Three-course-dinner, £39.50 per person. Wines from £10 a bottle.
timandpatricia@scaristahouse.com   www.scaristahouse.com

GARLIESTON *(S-C)*

PAVILION COTTAGE 498

Garlieston House
Garlieston DG8 8HF
Tel: 01988 600600 MAP 8

Cottage: sleeps 5+3
£495-£1075 pw

Eggs from free-range naturally reared hens,
vegetables and salad in season

A delightfully secluded cottage within the beautiful walled garden of the Galloway House estate. Beams, woodburner, Rayburn, large enclosed private lawn, heated open air pool in summer. Our smallholding (free-range ducks, hens, guineafowl, naturally reared rare breed sheep, Dexter cows) borders an organic dairy farm, woodland and the sandy beach of Rigg Bay. Guests can order eggs, rare breed meat and garden produce such as artichokes, potatoes, salad. Lobster is available locally, and other seafood can be delivered to your door. Catch your own mackerel and sea bass. Local shops sell local produce including organic ice cream and preserves. Home baking is served from our tea-tent in the summer.

info@escapetogalloway.co.uk   www.escapetogalloway.co.uk

WALES

Seaview Cottage, Isle of Anglesey

BRECHFA *(S-C)*

LLYSTYN FARM 499

Brechfa
Carmarthen SA32 7RB
Tel: 01267 202463 MAP 13

Barn Conversion: sleeps 6
£250-£460 pw

Organic produce can be delivered by
arrangement

Soil Association

Situated on a 200-acre organic beef and sheep farm with beautiful views across the valley. The barn conversion provides excellent spacious family accommodation with pine furnishings, exposed beams, stone walls and a woodstove. A large games room includes table tennis and six foot snooker table. Free fuel and electric. Bed linen provided, no towels. You are welcome to explore the farm which is half a mile off the road up an unmade track. It includes 14 acres of broadleaf woodland, ancient flower meadows and varied bird life in an area known as Brechfa Forest. Free guided farm walks. Within fifty minutes of Llystyn Farm are Wales National Botanic Garden, castles, a goldmine, wonderful coastline, beaches. cliffcarnell@hotmail.com

CWMDU *(S-C)*

TY CERRIG 500

Cwmcochied
Cwmdu SA19 7EE
Tel: 01558 685815 MAP 13

Cottage: sleeps 2
£218-£452 pw

Welcome pack includes our own eggs,
(organic poultry, sausages, etc can be ordered)

Soil Association

Ty Cerrig is the old threshing barn. Renovated with five star specification by local craftsmen, it features oak and slate floors, underfloor heating, handmade fitted kitchens, original art and crafts. The cottage has a terrace with wonderful views to the Brecon Beacons, and also a private garden planted with herbs and cottage flowers. Cwmcochied is a 64-acre working farm. Our family have been organic farmers for over twenty years. Visitors are very welcome to walk around the farm and to enjoy the bluebell wood, lake and the spectacular views. There are wonderful walks from the farm to the village of Talley with its ruined abbey, lakes and community forest. We are members of the Quiet Garden Trust. info@mountainviewcottages.co.uk www.mountainviewcottages.co.uk/TyCerrig.html

CWMDU *(S-C)*

TY'R WENNOL 501

Cwmcochied
Cwmdu SA19 7EE
Tel: 01558 685815 MAP 13

Apartment: sleeps 2
£193-£399 pw

Welcome pack includes our own eggs,
(organic poultry, sausages, etc can be ordered)

Soil Association

Ty'r Wennol is the upper floor of the old stable block. Built into the hillside with its own entrance, there are no stairs to negotiate. It has its own private garden in the old orchard. Renovated with five star specification by local craftsmen, the apartment features oak and slate floors, underfloor heating, handmade fitted kitchens, original art and crafts. Cwmcochied is a 64-acre working farm. Our family have been organic farmers for over twenty years. Visitors are welcome to walk around the farm and enjoy the bluebell wood, lake and spectacular views. There are wonderful walks from the farm to the village of Talley with its ruined abbey, lakes and community forest. We are members of the Quiet Garden Trust.
info@mountainviewcottages.co.uk   www.mountainviewcottages.co.uk/TyrWennol.html

CWMDU *(S-C)*

Y STABL 502

Cwmcochied
Cwmdu SA19 7EE
Tel: 01558 685815 MAP 13

Apartment: sleeps 2
£193-£399 pw

Welcome pack includes our own eggs,
(organic poultry, sausages, etc can be ordered)

Soil Association

Y Stabl is the lower floor of the old stable block. Built into the hillside with its own entrance, there are no stairs to negotiate. Patio doors open from the living area onto a private paved garden planted with herbs and cottage flowers. Renovated with five star specification by local craftsmen, the apartment features oak and slate floors, underfloor heating, handmade fitted kitchens, original art and crafts. Cwmcochied is a 64-acre working farm. Our family have been organic farmers for over twenty years. Visitors are welcome to walk around the farm and enjoy the bluebell wood, lake and spectacular views. There are wonderful walks from the farm to the village of Talley. We are members of the Quiet Garden Trust.
info@mountainviewcottages.co.uk   www.mountainviewcottages.co.uk/YStabl.html

LLANBOIDY (B&B)

MAESGWYN ISAF   503

Llanboidy
Whitland SA34 0ET
Tel: 01994 448758   MAP 13

Farmhouse Bed and Breakfast
£26 pppn

Continental buffet breakfast (about 80% organic and local)

Small, clean, quiet bed and breakfast in beautiful Carmarthenshire, on the border with Pembrokeshire. Everything provided is home-made or locally sourced, organic or fairly-traded. Experience an ecological stay, where sustainability is offered without compromising your comfort and well-being. Awarded the Green Dragon Environmental Standard Level 2. We run the smallholding using permaculture principles, and have made it into a haven for wildlife and trees. Enjoy the atmosphere, beauty and wildlife on land managed with love and respect. Talk with us about our fruit and vegetable gardens. Visit our stone circle, extended woodlands, shelter woods, and meadows. Enjoy the stars, birds, flowers and wonderful views. carters@gn.apc.org   www.maesgwynisaf.co.uk

LLANDEILO (B&B)

FRONLAS   504

7 Thomas Street
Llandeilo SA19 6LB
Tel: 01558 824733   MAP 13

Boutique Bed and Breakfast. Double £35-£50 pppn, including full organic breakfast

Full organic and locally sourced breakfast, from mid and west Wales where possible

Located in the colourful market town of Llandeilo in West Wales, Fronlas is an impressive Edwardian townhouse offering stylish, contemporary 5-star bed and breakfast accommodation. Combining the designer looks of a boutique hotel with the personal touches you'd expect from a luxury B&B, all our individually styled boutique rooms offer views of the Towy and Brecon Beacons, designer wallpaper, flat-screen TVs, DVD players and luxury organic mattresses. All the ingredients in our breakfast are organic. We make every effort to source only the best and freshest ingredients, from mid and west Wales where possible. With eco-electricity and solar panels, Fronlas is also eco-friendly.
post@fronlas.com   www.fronlas.com

LLANDYSUL *(S-C)*

PEN PYNFARCH 505

Llandysul
Carmarthen SA44 4RU
Tel: 01559 384948 MAP 13

Cottage: sleeps 4-6
£300-£420 pw

Box of wholefoods and local organic
produce on request for self-catering guests

A self-contained cottage, part of the range of stone farm buildings, in a peaceful woodland valley. Simple décor using traditional and reclaimed materials and antique furniture. Woodburner with supply of logs from site. Green electricity. An organic / local food box can be ordered from a local company. An additional bunkroom (sleeps 5) and dining room are also available – please enquire. Pen Pynfarch is a smallholding working towards sustainability. We also host a seasonal programme of arts and environment workshops with vegetarian catering (bed, full board, use of studio, £60 pppn). Meals are cooked with wholefoods and fresh organic vegetables and fruit, using local produce plus our own eggs, honey and garden produce. enquiries@penpynfarch.co.uk   www.penpynfarch.co.uk

LLANSADWRN *(B&B)*

GLANMARLAIS FARM 506

Llansadwrn
Llanwrda SA19 8HU
Tel: 01550 777425 MAP 14

Farmhouse Bed and Breakfast, £25-£30 pppn
Evening Meal, 4 course £15 (by arrangement)

Organic produce served (also available to buy)

Soil Association

Glanmarlais is a 200 year old working organic farm, beautifully situated in the Towy Valley. We produce organic lamb, bacon and pork (and will shortly produce beef), all from rare or endangered breeds. Comfortable accommodation, with ample room for indoor relaxation should the weather invite you to sit by the open log-burning fire. Organic foods are available – most meat and vegetables served are home-grown or locally produced organic. The farm is surrounded by secluded woodland and hill pastures, with our own meandering stream. Farm walks connect with the local footpath network. Children are welcome, and they can help feed and handle farm animals such as chickens, geese, ducks, sheep and pigs. john@glanmarlaisfarm.co.uk   www.glanmarlaisfarm.co.uk

LLANSTEFFAN *(S-C)*

HEARTSPRING RETREAT 507

Hill House
Llansteffan SA33 5JG
Tel: 01267 241999 MAP 13

Apartments: sleep 2-6, from £195 for 3 nights
5 Day Retreats, all inclusive from £380

Organic vegan meals available and organic
vegetable boxes to order

Heartspring is a small retreat centre specialising in relaxing and nurturing holidays in a stunning coastal setting. We are easy to reach and have a neutral spiritual focus. We use toxic-free paints and natural furnishings. We have our own spring water. We offer three self-catering vegetarian apartments, and can provide organic meals and fruit and vegetables from our gardens. Organic vegetable boxes are available through Organics To Go at Werndolau Farm. We also offer tailor-made retreat programmes, which include organic meals and a choice of many complementary therapies. Heartspring Retreat Centre offers an inspiring, tranquil environment to help those looking to find their own healing and peace.
info@heartspring.co.uk   www.heartspring.co.uk

MARROS *(B&B)*

CLYNGWYN FARM B&B 508

Marros
Pendine SA33 4PW
Tel: 01994 453214 MAP 13

Farmhouse Bed and Breakfast
From £22 pppn

Breakfast includes organic produce when available

Soil Association

B&B on a working organic farm at the heart of Carmarthen Bay. Breakfast includes organic produce when available. Clyngwyn Farm is set in 100 acres of farmland. Surrounded by woodland and streams the farm is in a peaceful, idyllic location with an abundance of wildlife and fauna. An ideal setting for the family as we have many animals, such as sheep, cows, horses, ducks, geese and dogs. We have recently erected thirty nest boxes over the farm. Riding, clay shooting, beautiful beaches and coastal walks are all within walking distance. Amroth, less than a mile away, is a small coastal village set within breathtaking countryside and outstanding coastline. Colby Woodland Garden (National Trust) nearby.
clyngwyn@tiscali.co.uk

MARROS *(S-C)*

CLYNGWYN FARM 509

Clyngwyn Farm
Marros SA33 4PW
Tel: 01994 453214　　　　　　　　MAP 13

Cottages: sleep 2-6, £250-£475 pw
Breakfast, 4 course £4.50

Seasonal organic farm produce may be available

Soil Association

Four cottages on a working organic farm (three adapted for wheelchair use) at the heart of Carmarthen Bay. Clyngwyn is set in 100 acres of organic farmland. Seasonal organic farm produce may be available. Surrounded by woodland and streams the farm is in a peaceful, idyllic location with an abundance of wildlife and fauna. Amroth, a small coastal village set within beautiful countryside, is less than a mile away. We are one mile from a blue flag beach. The Pembrokeshire Coast Path, which takes you along one of the most outstanding stretches of coastline in Britain, starts at Marros. A Welsh farmhouse breakfast is available in the farmhouse for people staying in the cottages (by arrangement).
clyngwyn@tiscali.co.uk

PENTRE-CWRT *(S-C)*

PENYRALLT FACH 510

Penyrallt Home Farm
Pentre-Cwrt SA44 5DW
Tel: 01559 370341　　　　　　　　MAP 13

Cottage: sleeps 4, £250-£400 pw (Sat-Sat)
Short Breaks, £30 pppn (1 Nov-30 Apr)

Our farm shop sells meat, milk, eggs and basic groceries

Soil Association

Converted from an old piggery this comfortable cottage with wood-burning stove and exposed beams is all on one floor. Fully equipped kitchen / dining / sitting room. Two bedrooms, simply and attractively furnished. All bed linen and towels supplied. All fuel and electricity included in the price. The cottage is situated on an organic dairy and sheep farm in the beautiful Teifi Valley. Penyrallt Home Farm is a member of the Soil Association Organic Farm Network and is open for farm walks and tours by groups or individuals. The farm shop sells home-reared organic meat and basic groceries. Freshly home-baked cakes, scones and bread, made with organic and fair trade ingredients, can be ordered in advance or during your stay.
djwj@penyrallt.freeserve.co.uk　　www.penyrallt.co.uk

PONTYBEREM *(B&B)*

BRYNGWENYN FARM B&B 511

Pontyberem
Llanelli SA15 5NG
Tel: 01269 843990   MAP 13

Farmhouse B&B, double from £55 pn.
Evening Meal £18, Packed Lunch (on request)

Local produce and home-grown vegetables

Soil Association

Comfortable *en suite* accommodation in a 17th-century farmhouse, located in peaceful countryside with panoramic views across the Gwendraeth Valley. Enjoy a superb breakfast cooked for you on the Aga, which includes eggs laid by our free-range hens and home-made preserves. Evening meals can be provided by arrangement and are prepared using local produce and home-grown vegetables. Bryngwenyn is an organic farm with a flock of eighty Suffolk / Lleyn cross ewes and some Welsh Black suckler cows. Sandy the Golden Guernsey and Cleo the angora goat share the orchard with rabbits, chickens, ducks, geese, ponies. Our farm shop sells a good selection of organic and local produce. Fishing available on-site.
elizabeth.hedges@btinternet.com   www.bryngwenynfarm.co.uk

PONTYBEREM *(S-C)*

BRYNGWENYN FARM 512

Pontyberem
Llanelli SA15 5NG
Tel: 01269 843990   MAP 13

Cottages: sleep 5, £320-£525 pw
Short Breaks, from £150 (min 2 nights)

Our farm shop has a good selection of
organic and local produce

Soil Association

The three self-catering cottages, which have two or three bedrooms, are comfortably furnished. They are situated just across the yard from the farmhouse in peaceful countryside, with panoramic views across the Gwendraeth Valley. Evening meals can be provided for self-catering guests, either in the farmhouse or brought to your cottage. Our farm shop sells a good selection of organic and local produce. Bryngwenyn is an organic farm with a flock of eighty Suffolk / Lleyn ewes and Welsh Black suckler cows. Sandy the Golden Guernsey and Cleo the angora goat share the orchard with rabbits, chickens, ducks, geese and ponies. Children are very welcome and can join in the farm activities. Fishing is available on-site.
elizabeth.hedges@btinternet.com   www.bryngwenynfarm.co.uk/Cottages.htm

CAPEL DEWI *(S-C)*

THE LONGBARN 513

Penrhiw Farm
Capel Dewi SA44 4PG
Tel: 01559 363200　　　　　　　MAP 13

Bunkhouse: sleeps 34
Adult £10 pn (£8 pn under 18)

Organic meat, local organic vegetables, dairy produce

Soil Association

Our traditional long stone barn provides comfortable bunkhouse accommodation in beautiful West Wales. The 18th-century fully converted barn is situated in the yard of a working organic farm involved in crop and livestock production. The yard is in a lovely position, with a spectacular view across the Teifi Valley. Our own organic meat (beef, lamb and burgers) is available for visitors to buy. Organic vegetable boxes can be ordered by prior arrangement and we can have organic milk, cheese, butter and yogurt delivered from Calon Wen. There is walking locally on footpaths, or on our own farm trail. Both the stunning Ceredigion coast and the wild Cambrian Mountains are within easy reach of Penrhiw Farm. cowcher@thelongbarn.co.uk　www.thelongbarn.co.uk

COED Y BRYN *(S-C)*

COWSHED COTTAGE 514

Penbeili Mawr Farm
Coed Y Bryn SA44 5NA
Tel: 01239 851059　　　　　　　MAP 13

Cottage: sleeps 2+cot, £230-£425 pw
Short Breaks (prices on application)

Organic food hampers to order, honey from our own bees available

Quality Welsh Food Certification Ltd

Cowshed Cottage is a spacious detached cottage with comfortable accommodation all on ground level (refurbished 2007). Logs provided for the woodburner and full oil central heating. Private walled courtyard. Penbeili Mawr is a secluded 87-acre organic sheep and beef farm, nestling in tranquil countryside, yet within twenty minutes of the stunning Ceredigion Heritage Coast. The farm encompasses 30 acres of broadleaf woodland, providing beautiful walks and the opportunity to sight owls, woodpeckers, badgers and the majestic Red Kite. Coastal footpaths offer the opportunity to see dolphins and seals. Golf courses and riding stables are within easy reach. Fishing and canoeing are available on the River Teifi. penbeilicottages@hotmail.co.uk　www.penbeilicottages.co.uk

COED Y BRYN (S-C)

DAIRY COTTAGE 515

Penbeili Mawr Farm
Coed Y Bryn SA44 5NA
Tel: 01239 851059 MAP 13

Cottage: sleeps 6+cot or Z bed, £270-£645 pw
Short Breaks (prices on application)

Organic food hampers to order, honey from
our own bees available

Quality Welsh Food Certification Ltd

Dairy Cottage offers spacious comfortable accommodation on two levels (one bathroom with shower and one shower room). Refurbished 2008. Full oil central heating. Ample parking. Large enclosed child-safe garden with gas barbecue, overlooking woodland and rolling hills. Penbeili Mawr is a secluded 87-acre organic sheep and beef farm nestling in tranquil countryside, yet within twenty minutes of the stunning Ceredigion Heritage Coast. The farm encompasses 30 acres of broadleaf woodland, providing beautiful walks and the opportunity to sight owls, woodpeckers, badgers and red kites. Coastal footpaths offer the opportunity to see dolphins and seals. Golf, riding, fishing, canoeing available locally.
penbeilicottages@hotmail.co.uk   www.penbeilicottages.co.uk

COED Y BRYN (S-C)

STABLE COTTAGE 516

Penbeili Mawr Farm
Coed Y Bryn SA44 5NA
Tel: 01239 851059 MAP 13

Cottage: sleeps 4+cot, £250-£545 pw
Short Breaks (prices on application)

Organic food hampers to order, honey from
our own bees available

Quality Welsh Food Certification Ltd

Stable Cottage offers ground level spacious comfortable accommodation (one bathroom and one en suite shower room). Ample parking. Full oil central heating. Refurbished in 2008. Large enclosed child-safe garden with gas barbecue, overlooking woodland and rolling hills. Penbeili Mawr is a secluded 87-acre organic sheep and beef farm nestling in tranquil countryside, yet within twenty minutes of the stunning Ceredigion Heritage Coast. The farm encompasses 30 acres of broadleaf woodland, providing beautiful walks and the opportunity to sight owls, woodpeckers, badgers and red kites. Coastal footpaths offer the opportunity to see dolphins and seals. Golf, riding, fishing, canoeing available locally.
penbeilicottages@hotmail.co.uk   www.penbeilicottages.co.uk

CROESLAN *(B&B)*

NANTGWYNFAEN ORGANIC 517

Nantgwynfaen
Croeslan SA44 4SR
Tel: 01239 851914   MAP 13

Bed and Breakfast, £37 pppn
Evening Meal, £15 (2 course)

Meals include our own organic produce
(meat, vegetables, eggs, apple juice)

Soil Association

Nantgwynfaen is a working farm of 62 acres in beautiful West Wales, near beaches, castles and cliff top walks. We produce free-range organic eggs (which we sell in the farm shop and serve in our B&B) and grow our own vegetables. Meat is sourced from local organic farmers, whom we know well, and whose stock is kept to the highest welfare standards. We make and sell our own organic speciality sausages and bacon and make bread and jam using only organic ingredients. We have three *en suite* bedrooms, and a living room with log burner for guests to enjoy. Families and their wellies are most welcome to explore the farm. Our bespoke wooden furniture can be seen in the farmhouse and in production in the workshop. amanda@organicfarmwales.co.uk   www.organicfarmwales.co.uk

DIHEWYD *(S-C)*

TREBERFEDD FARMHOUSE 518

Treberfedd Farm
Dihewyd SA48 7NW
Tel: 01570 470672   MAP 13

Farmhouse: sleeps 7
Short breaks start from £89

Seasonal rare breed organic beef and lamb
from our farm

Soil Association

A country retreat with all the comforts of a modern home, with spacious accommodation for up to seven people. The house occupies an idyllic position, with panoramic views over rolling green hills to the front and organic fields at the back. The poet Dylan Thomas once described the Aeron Valley as 'the most precious place in the world'. Come and find out what makes it so special. The beautiful Cardigan Bay coast is fifteen minutes away, with great sandy beaches to discover. You can spend time exploring the Treberfedd nature trail and then enjoy a hearty meal around the farmhouse table. Organic beef and lamb from our farm is seasonally available to guests as well as organic vegetables from local growers. jack@treberfedd.co.uk   www.treberfedd.co.uk/white_house.php

DIHEWYD *(S-C)*

TREBERFEDD GRANARY   519

Treberfedd Farm
Dihewyd SA48 7NW
Tel: 01570 470672   MAP 13

Barn Conversion: sleeps 5
Short breaks start from £89

Seasonal rare breed organic beef and lamb
from our farm

Soil Association

Created from one of the farm's lovely traditional buildings this cottage provides beautiful contemporary accommodation whilst retaining much of the character of its origins. It has a large open-plan living space with lime washed walls and original stone features. An attractive summer room gives fantastic views of the woodland and surrounding valley. This cottage is an ideal holiday getaway. The beautiful Cardigan Bay coast is just fifteen minutes away and there is a nature trail to explore around our organic farm. Organic beef and lamb is available from Treberfedd, and fresh seafood is seasonally available at the nearby harbour towns of Aberaeron and New Quay. Short breaks start from just £89.
jack@treberfedd.co.uk   www.treberfedd.co.uk/granary_cottage.php

DIHEWYD *(S-C)*

THE OLD CART HOUSE   520

Treberfedd Farm
Dihewyd SA48 7NW
Tel: 01570 470672   MAP 13

Converted Barn: sleeps 9
Short breaks start from £89

Seasonal rare breed organic beef and lamb
from our farm

Soil Association

This award-winning barn conversion can sleep up to nine people. It provides the ideal country escape for families and groups. The accommodation was created from a traditional stone farm range. Many original features remain, with the beautifully crafted stone work of this Welsh building visible both inside and out. The main entrance to the house is through the archway which was originally made for the farm's horse-drawn cart. A large window in the kitchen / diner affords fantastic views of the valley and hills beyond. Our way marked nature trail around the organic farm and woodland is great fun. Organic beef and lamb from the home farm is seasonally available to guests. Short breaks from just £89.
jack@treberfedd.co.uk   www.treberfedd.co.uk/cart_house.php

DIHEWYD (S-C)

THATCHED COTTAGE 521

Treberfedd Farm
Dihewyd SA48 7NW
Tel: 01570 470672 MAP 13

Cottage: sleeps 6
Short breaks start from £89

Seasonal rare breed organic beef and lamb from our farm

Soil Association

The original thatched farmhouse at Treberfedd is surrounded by some of the finest scenery in Ceredigion. It sits in 67 acres of organic meadow and woodland that is yours to explore. The poet Dylan Thomas described this landscape as 'the most precious place in the world' – come and find out what makes it so special. Built in the late 1600s (and with original wall paintings to prove it), the house was modernised in 1802, and restored in 2002. It is furnished with beautiful Welsh country furniture. With its wood-burning stove and under-floor heating this Georgian farmhouse is the perfect place for a relaxing country break. Rare breed organic beef and lamb from our farm is seasonally available to guests.
jack@treberfedd.co.uk www.treberfedd.co.uk/thatched_cottage.php

PENUWCH (Camping)

THE YURT FARM 522

Crynfryn
Penuwch SY25 6RE
Tel: 01974 821594 MAP 13

Yurts: sleep 4-8
From £75 pn

Farm shop sells a wide range of veg, eggs, herbs and seasonal lamb and beef

Soil Association

Come and stay in simple luxury in one of four yurts in a beautiful rich hay meadow hidden between the Cambrian mountains and Cardigan Bay. Our farm will be yours to explore while you stay. It is the perfect spot for bird watching, fishing, cycling and walking. The farm has been organic for four generations, and is home to a beautiful herd of Hereford cattle, a carnival of colourful chickens and a large flock of sheep. We also grow a field of delicious vegetables, which we sell in our farm shop. Our site is as environmentally sensitive as we can make it – even your mattress is organic, and your showers are warmed by the sun. Children can enjoy the play area while you watch the red kites soar overhead.
info@theyurtfarm.co.uk www.theyurtfarm.co.uk

RHYDLEWIS *(B&B)*

BRONIWAN 523

Rhydlewis
Llandysul SA44 5PF
Tel: 01239 851261   MAP 13

Farmhouse Bed and Breakfast, £32 pppn
Evening Meal, £20 (by arrangement)

Our own Aberdeen Angus beef, eggs, soft
fruit, vegetables

Soil Association

A small farm (45 acres) with organic beef suckler cows in the far west of Wales. The grey stone house, with ancient ivy growing round the porch, was built in 1867. Its pine-panelled windows look towards the Preseli Hills. Delicious home-cooked meals with vegetarian options. We use our own organic produce, including eggs, beef, fruit and vegetables. Soups, cakes and marmalade are all home-made. Visitors may walk anywhere around the farm. There are sketch maps with rambles down to the stream or up to the high fields. Part of a Welsh conservation scheme, the front meadow is being devoted to new planting (crab apple, rowan, black thorn). The long, sandy Cardiganshire coast is ten minutes drive.
broniwan@btinternet.com   www.broniwan.com

UPPER ABERARTH *(S-C)*

TY-RHOS COTTAGE 524

Ty-rhos Organic Farm
Upper Aberarth SA46 0LA
Tel: 01545 571430   MAP 13

Cottage: sleeps 2-4
£160-£185 pw

Seasonal organic salad and vegetables gratis

Soil Association

Ty-rhos is set in 31 acres of organic farmland, 2 acres of which is used for protected horticulture, with the remainder being natural grassland and habitat for wildlife conservation. We produce salads and seasonal vegetables for the wholesale market and several local outlets. The cottage (double bedroom, lounge with kitchen area, shower room) is adjacent to the farmhouse. Seasonal organic salad and vegetables are available gratis. An abundance of birds, butterflies and wild flowers can be seen on the farm. Ty-rhos has all the feeling of remoteness, being set well back from a country lane, yet is only two miles from the Georgian harbour town of Aberaeron and the Ceredigion Heritage Coastline.
john@johnwalsh7.orangehome.co.uk

ABERCARN *(B&B)*

AWEN VEGETARIAN B&B 525

1 Penrhiwgwair Cottage
Twyn Road NP11 5AS
Tel: 01495 244615   MAP 18

Bed and Breakfast, £35-£40 pppn
Packed Lunch £8, Meal £12-£25

All food is locally sourced and organic
wherever possible

A peaceful and cosy retreat from the modern world. Awen Vegetarian B&B, a converted 16th-century Welsh longhouse, nestles high on a mountainside in the heart of the Welsh valleys. Accommodation for up to six people consists of one bedroom with a double four-poster bed and a single bed, and a second bedroom with a double bed and a single bed. Packed lunches and evening meals are available on request. Delicious organic veggie breakfasts – vegetarian sausages, eggs, beans, tomatoes, mushrooms, toast, marmalade, jams, cereals, fresh fruit salad, yogurt and freshly baked bread. Organic soaps, shampoos and cleaning products are used in the house. Healing available on a donations basis.
info@awenbandb.com   www.awenbandb.com

BRONABER *(B&B)*

CAE GWYN FARM RESERVE 526

Bronaber
Nr Trawsfynydd LL41 4YE
Tel: 01766 540245   MAP 14

B&B, £27 pppn (farmhouse continental
breakfast). Room only, £21 pppn

Our average organic food percentage is 90%

Cae Gwyn is a naturally run sheep farm in the valley of the Rhinog mountain range in the Snowdonia National Park. Our stone-built B&B hay barn conversion is part of the range of farm buildings which are over 200 years old. Our farmhouse continental breakfast, using organic, fairly-traded and local food as much as possible, is a healthier alternative to a cooked breakfast. Drinking water is sourced from our own mountain spring. Guests are invited to walk freely around our 190-acre farm and nature reserve, designated a SSSI for its rare fauna, flora and aquatic life, and enjoy the splendid mountain views. Self-catering options are available (camping fields £7.50 pppn, caravan £13 pppn, camping barn £10-£12 pppn).
enquiries@caegwynfarm.co.uk   www.caegwynfarm.co.uk

FRONGOCH *(B&B)*

CYSGOD Y GARN  527

Frongoch
Bala LL23 7NT
Tel: 01678 521457 MAP 14

Farmhouse Bed and Breakfast, £26-£34 pppn
Evening Meal (by arrangement)

Organic and local produce

Soil Association

Our small country farmhouse bed and breakfast is surrounded by beautiful organic farmland and spectacular views in the heart of Snowdonia (close to Bala Lake). Our family have been farming this land for two generations, and we are currently rearing sheep and the famous Welsh Black cattle. We are very proud of our farmhouse cuisine, and we are members of Blas ar Cymru (A Taste of Wales). Organic produce is used where possible for your tasty breakfast and evening meals. The three course evening meal (by prior arrangement) is from a set menu, cooked in the traditional way using fresh local produce. Our guests are most welcome to visit the farm during their stay, and farm tours are available on request.
carys@snowdoniafrongoch.co.uk   www.snowdoniafrongoch.co.uk

GYFFIN *(S-C)*

BRYN DOWSI  528

Gyffin
Conwy LL32 8YF
Tel: 01492 592182 MAP 14

Cottages: sleep 2-6
Short Breaks (1 Oct-23 Mar)

Organic Welsh lamb and beef available direct from us

Organic Farmers & Growers

Bryn Dowsi is a 200-acre organic beef and sheep farm a mile from Conwy in North Wales. There are four hundred Welsh mountain sheep and twenty beef cattle on the farm, where for the last ten years conservation has been a high priority. Organic Welsh Black and Charolais cross beef and Welsh Mountain lamb raised on our farm is available direct from us (please contact us for more information on our meat). Traditional farm buildings have been converted into quality self-catering cottage accommodation. The cottages are ideally placed for exploring the whole of North Wales, including the lakes and mountains of Snowdonia, historic castles and gardens, and beaches from Llandudno to Anglesey and beyond.
berylanddafydd@bryndowsicottages.co.uk   www.bryndowsicottages.co.uk

LLANGYBI *(S-C)*

GWYNDY 529

Mur Crusto
Llangybi LL53 6LX
Tel: 01766 819109   MAP 13

Cottage: sleeps 4+cot
£185-£565 pw

Organic fruit and vegetables available
according to season

Soil Association

Small organic farm set between the lovely scenery and unspoilt beaches of the Lleyn Peninsula and Snowdonia National Park. We have lovingly converted our milking parlour into a beautifully furnished eco-cottage (Gwyndy) with underfloor heating and insulation, making it cosy and warm even in winter. Enjoy magnificent sea and mountain views from the conservatory. Stroll round our 13 acres of land, with ducks, sheep, and cows in summer, lake and nature reserve. We mainly grow vegetables and are Rick Stein Food Heroes. Organic vegetables are available to buy all year, organic fruit according to season. There are wonderful walks locally and a cycle route passes the end of our drive.
info@llangybi-organics.co.uk   www.llangybi-organics.co.uk

LLANNOR *(S-C)*

GWYNFRYN ORGANIC FARM 530

Llannor
Pwllheli LL53 5UF
Tel: 01758 612536   MAP 13

Cottages: sleep 2-8
£240-£1070 pw

Freshly cooked meals, made with local
produce

Soil Association

This 100-acre working organic dairy farm is a peaceful haven for nature lovers. Derelict farm buildings have been sympathetically transformed into quality houses in this idyllic rural setting. Indoor swimming pool, sauna, jacuzzi, gym, tennis court, soft play area in the games room. Home-made takeaway meals are available, made with local produce. Glasfryn Farm Shop (five miles) sells some organic and local produce. Guests are welcome to help feed the animals, help bring in the cows for milking, or study the varied vegetation in the colourful meadows. The old market town of Pwllheli, gateway to the beautiful Lleyn Peninsula, is just over a mile away. The farm is within easy reach of numerous coastal activities.
gwynfrynfarm@btconnect.com   www.gwynfrynfarm.co.uk

LLITHFAEN *(S-C)*

ORGANIG PARC 531

Carnguwch
Llithfaen LL53 6NH
Tel: 01758 750000 MAP 13

Luxury Cottages: sleep 4-7
£335-£997 pw

Complimentary organic produce on arrival

Soil Association

Organig Parc offers a unique blend of eco-friendly design and 5-star luxury on a 300-acre working organic farm in the heart of the Llyn Peninsula. The five self-catering cottages have been designed and constructed using eco-friendly techniques, yet are fully equipped with modern conveniences. Situated in an Area of Outstanding Natural Beauty with some of the finest views in Cymru / Wales, Organig Parc is a short journey away from award-winning beaches and the mountains of Eryri / Snowdonia. Organig Parc has its own organic trout fishing lake. Running water is supplied by our own spring. We also supply organic linen and organic cleaning products. Complimentary organic produce on arrival.
info@organigparc.com   www.organigparc.com

LLITHFAEN *(S-C)*

TREDDAFYDD FARM 532

Llithfaen
Pwllheli LL53 6NL
Tel: 01758 750418 MAP 13

Caravan: sleeps 4-6, £195-£295 pw
Welcome grocery pack (on request)

Eggs, fresh vegetables and soft fruit available when in season

In Conversion

The caravan has stunning views across fields to the sea. Outside there's a private patio with seating and a barbecue. Our 7.5-acre organic smallholding is in a beautiful rural setting on the Lleyn Peninsula on the edge of Snowdonia. We have a flock of free-range hens, and produce soft fruit and vegetables. Farm gate sales of surplus seasonal fruit and veg (blueberries, strawberries, red / blackcurrants, potatoes, carrots, parsnips, swedes, sprouts, turnips, peas, runner beans, courgettes, cabbage, purple sprouting broccoli, beetroot, spinach, artichokes, etc). Children can help feed the hens and collect an egg each for breakfast. The Lleyn Coastal Path runs along the rear of the property. Short breaks £40 per night.
sharmear@aol.com   www.treddafyddfarmholidays.co.uk

PENMACHNO *(S-C)*

TY NEWYDD UCHAF 533

Ty Newydd Uchaf
Penmachno LL24 0AJ
Tel: 01690 760350   MAP 14

Farmhouse: sleeps 4-5, £500-£750 pw
Short Breaks, £100 pn

Organic eggs always available, meat and
poultry in season

Soil Association

An off-road, detached traditional stone Welsh farmhouse with attached barns. The farmhouse dates from the early 18th-century and is surrounded by organic farmland. Recently restored using lime, it has an Aga cooker, underfloor heating, a working Victorian kitchen range and a wood-burning stove. All rooms have extensive views of the surrounding countryside. Sheep, llamas and geese graze in the fields adjacent to the farmhouse. Organic eggs are always available, meat and poultry in season. Dogs and ponies are welcome. Ty Newydd is situated a mile from the village of Penmachno within the Snowdonia National Park. Betws-y-Coed and the popular Swallow Falls waterfall are set in a beautiful valley nearby.
clairebarnardburrows@yahoo.co.uk   www.tnorganics.co.uk

TALSARNAU *(Hotel)*

MAES-Y-NEUADD 534

Talsarnau
Harlech LL47 6YA
Tel: 01766 780200   MAP 14

Country House Hotel, B&B from £48.50 pppn
Restaurant (breakfast, lunch, dinner)

Annually over 8 tonnes of produce are
supplied to our kitchens from our gardens

Maes-y-Neuadd nestles on a hillside in the heart of the Snowdonia National Park, with magnificent views of the mountains and coast. The highlight of our 85 acres of grounds are the walled kitchen gardens which produce most of the herbs, hard and soft fruit, vegetables and flowers gathered daily for use in our highly-acclaimed 2 rosette restaurant. Only the finest, freshest, locally sourced ingredients are used in the imaginative dishes – Welsh lamb and beef, fish from Cardigan Bay and the Menai Strait, a wide selection of Welsh Farmhouse cheeses, accompanied by freshly squeezed juices, Welsh wines, spirits, liqueurs. Home-grown produce and home-made preserves for sale. Member of the National Gardens Scheme.
maes@neuadd.com   www.neuadd.com

TALSARNAU *(Hotel)*

TREMEIFION HOTEL 535

Soar Road
Talsarnau LL47 6UH
Tel: 01766 770491 MAP 13

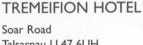

Vegetarian Country Hotel
Dinner Bed and Breakfast, £70-£80 pppn

Much of the produce is from our own
organic garden

Situated deep within the Snowdonia National Park, with beautiful, unspoilt scenery all around. Excellent walks, historic interest, miles of safe sandy beaches are all on the doorstep. Exclusively vegetarian / vegan, we take pride in serving home-cooked, high-quality food which is both healthy and imaginative. We use organic ingredients whenever possible, including produce from our own organic fruit, vegetable and herb gardens. We offer a full cooked, American, or Continental breakfast, and a 3 course evening meal. A wide range of organic wines and juices are available. Wander in our three acres of garden. Enjoy superb views over the estuary to Portmeirion. Relax with a drink in the garden room and watch the sunset. enquire@tremeifionvegetarianhotel.co.uk www.tremeifionvegetarianhotel.co.uk

Y FFOR *(Camping)*

RHOSFAWR PARK CAMPSITE 536

Rhosfawr
Y Ffor LL53 6YA
Tel: 01766 810545 MAP 13

Touring Caravan and Camping Park
From £10 pd

Organic vegetables may be available in season

Soil Association

Rhosfawr Park is an award-winning, secluded family-run site situated in the heart of the Llyn Peninsula. It offers a peaceful environment, panoramic views and space to enjoy. This quiet, sheltered, level site makes an ideal base either for exploring or simply taking it easy. Abersoch, Nefyn, Pwllheli, Criccieth, Porthmadog, Caernarfon and the Snowdonia National Park are all within easy access. You're never far from unspoilt beaches, fantastic scenery, magnificent mountains, historic castles. Also available to let are two holiday cottages sleeping 5 and 8 (£350-£750 per week), and a static caravan sleeping 6 (£200-£350 per week). A small selection of organic vegetables are grown in season.
Info@northwalesholidayhomes.co.uk www.northwalesholidayhomes.co.uk

YSTUMGWERN *(S-C)*

YSTUMGWERN HALL FARM 537

Ystumgwern
Dyffryn Ardudwy LL44 2DD
Tel: 01341 247249 MAP 13

Self-Catering: sleep 1-8
£240-£1080 pw

Information given about where to buy
organic food locally

Quality Welsh Food Certification Ltd

Luxury self-catering on a 16th-century traditional Welsh farm set between sea and mountains on the west coast of the Snowdonia National Park. The guest accommodation is in traditional stone farm buildings and farmhouses about a mile's walk from sandy beaches or rambling mountains. The properties have been awarded the highest grade of five stars by the Wales Tourist Board. We are a 1000-acre working organic beef and sheep farm. There are numerous footpaths and ample opportunities to explore the open countryside with its breathtaking views. Snowdonia is a contrast of rugged mountains and wooded valleys, rushing streams and peaceful lakes, glorious beaches and boat-dotted harbours.
ynys@ystumgwern.co.uk   www.ystumgwern.co.uk

TYN-Y-GONGL *(S-C)*

SEAVIEW COTTAGE 538

Plas Llanfair
Tyn-y-Gongl LL74 8NU
Tel: 01248 852316 MAP 13

Cottage: sleeps 4-5, £450-£725 pw
Meal for your arrival on request

Seasonal organic fresh fruit, vegetables, jams, chutneys

Soil Association

An upstairs sitting room with a simple truss timbered roof and log-burning stove takes advantage of extensive sea, countryside and mountain views. Ledged oak doors, Welsh green oak staircase, slate tiled finish to the ground floor, solid oak flooring upstairs. Guests are provided with a complimentary seasonal basket of our own organic produce on arrival. We are a 3 hectare organic producer of a range of fruit and vegetables, specialising in soft fruits. We process the finest quality organic jams, preserves and chutneys from our own produce. Organic home-grown produce is available to buy. On request, visitors may order a meal for their arrival. The cottage is half a mile from the coastal path, the village and the beach.
plasllanfaircottages@fsmail.net   www.plasllanfaircottages.co.uk

TYN-Y-GONGL *(S-C)*

SWALLOW COTTAGE 539

Plas Llanfair
Tyn-y-Gongl LL74 8NU
Tel: 01248 852316 MAP 13

Cottage: sleeps 4, £400-£650 pw
Meal for your arrival on request

Seasonal organic fresh fruit, vegetables, jams, chutneys

Soil Association

Swallow Cottage is in a private and secluded setting with beautiful countryside views from the patios and garden. The sitting room, with an open king post and truss timbered roof, features a log burning stove. Guests are provided with a complimentary seasonal basket of our own organic produce. On request, visitors may also order a meal for their arrival. Organic home-grown produce is available to buy. We are a 3 hectare organic producer of a range of fruit and vegetables, specialising in soft fruits. We process the finest quality organic jams, preserves and chutneys from our own produce. The land has a diverse range of species and habitats. Plas Llanfair is half a mile from the coastal path, the village and the beach. mikeparker@fsmail.net www.plasllanfaircottages.co.uk

GROSMONT *(B&B)*

PART-Y-SEAL 540

Grosmont
Abergavenny NP7 8LE
Tel: 01981 240814 MAP 14

Country House B&B, double £75 pn
Tearoom (morning coffee, lunch, afternoon tea)

Breakfasts organic home-grown and home-made produce whenever possible

Part-Y-Seal is a peaceful and relaxing haven set in the beautiful Monnow Valley. Our rooms are *en suite* with a choice of king-size, four-poster or twin beds, and all have magnificent views. Within our four acres of mature gardens is a large organic kitchen garden with greenhouses, where we try to produce crops for eating all year. Our free-range chickens give us delicious eggs and our latest addition, bees, have provided us with natural honey. All food is home-made from breads to preserves. Guests are welcome to take their breakfast outside in summer, where you'll see the vast amount of birds and wildlife around, or by log fires in winter. A truly relaxing break, which starts with complimentary cream teas on arrival. fred@ong55.freeserve.co.uk www.partyseal.co.uk

LLANVIHANGEL LEWERN *(B&B)*

UPPER RED HOUSE FARM   541

Llanvihangel Ystern Llewern
Monmouth NP25 5HL
Tel: 01600 780501   MAP 14

Bed and Vegetarian Breakfast
£35-£50 pppn

Organic vegetarian food includes home-made
marmalade and jams from our orchard fruit

Soil Association

Our 17th-century Grade II* listed farmhouse has two double guest bedrooms and one single, with two shared bathrooms. We offer a generous organic vegetarian breakfast, which includes home-made produce. The farmhouse stands in wonderful country at the end of a small lane close to the Offa's Dyke Path. It is surrounded by its own and neighbours' organic farmland, ponds and orchards. Fully organic spring cereals are grown, and permanent pastures grazed by cattle and sheep. We specialise in conservation, so the farm is ideal for walking and wildlife watching. Organic vegetarian packed lunches are available by arrangement. Close to all the beauties of the Welsh borders. Advance booking is essential.
upperredhouse@mac.com   www.upperredhouse.co.uk

TINTERN *(S-C)*

THE NURTONS APARTMENT 542

Tintern
Chepstow NP16 7NX
Tel: 01291 689253   MAP 18

Apartment: sleeps 4, £350 pw
Short Breaks, (min 3 nights stay) £220

Seasonal home-grown produce may be
available

The Nurtons is an intriguing old house with a fascinating history, set in a secluded and peaceful spot in the glorious Wye Valley. The apartment is situated on the second floor of the house and has stunning views of the gardens and the valley. Used on a bed and breakfast basis for group participants, it is available for self-catering at other times. Newly refurbished, the apartment has a large bedroom with a king-size bed and two single beds, a large sitting room, a simply equipped kitchen area (vegetarian cooking preferred), and a bathroom. The gardens and woodlands are for your enjoyment and relaxation. We have been organic for over forty years with continuing commitment to the ethos of the Soil Association.
info@thenurtons.co.uk   www.thenurtons.co.uk

TINTERN *(B&B)*

THE NURTONS B&B   543

Tintern
Chepstow NP16 7NX
Tel: 01291 689253   MAP 18

Bed and Breakfast, from £30 pppn
Evening Platter (by arrangement)

We've been growing fruit and vegetables
organically here for over forty years

The Nurtons is an intriguing old house with comfortable B&B suites of strikingly different characters, set in a secluded and peaceful spot in the glorious Wye Valley. The 30 acres of gardens and woodlands are for your relaxation and enjoyment – quiet reflection, views, abundant wildlife, picnics, walks, a play lawn for children. We have been organic for over forty years with continuing commitment to the ethos of the Soil Association. We have our own spring water and honey from our bees. Continental buffet breakfasts (including freshly-prepared fruit juices, seasonal fruits, nuts, yogurt, home-made mueslis, breads, Welsh cakes, spreads and more) provide a healthy, delicious alternative to the traditional cooked breakfast. info@thenurtons.co.uk   www.thenurtons.co.uk

ABERCASTLE *(Camping)*

TRELLYN WOODLAND   544

Abercastle
Haverfordwest SA62 5HJ
Tel: 01348 837762   MAP 13

Campsite, from £170 pw
Yurts and Tipis, £ 510-£700 pw

On-site home-grown vegetables, fresh local
landed fish, lobster, crab, mackerel

A very small campsite with two yurts, two tipis and five pitches, set in 16 acres of a conservation project just yards from the sea in the Pembrokeshire National Park. We take a maximum of forty guests or so on our holding. We provide wood and adjustable barbecue / grills, and encourage visitors to cook as much as possible on the open fire. Chill out around your very own campfire – this is what we are all about. Look up at the stars and watch the bats come out to play. The yurts and tipis provide a luxury camping experience that won't be spoilt by the weather. An organic ethos smallholding with meadows, ponds and woods to explore, aimed primarily at those looking for a low impact family holiday. camping@trellyn.co.uk   www.trellyn.co.uk

DRUIDSTON (B&B)

LOWER DRUIDSTON B&B   545

Druidston
Haverfordwest SA62 3NE
Tel: 01437 781318   MAP 13

Farmhouse Bed and Breakfast
£29-£35 pppn

Home produce, local produce, organic produce

Lower Druidston Farm (WTB 4-star) is situated at the end of a no-through road, 600 yards from the coastal path. On our 5-acre smallholding we grow a wide range of naturally produced vegetables and, in particular, soft fruit. Our own produce is served, in season, as part of your breakfast or packed lunch. Home-made preserves are a feature of both breakfasts and the welcoming afternoon teas. Other local produce, such as free-range eggs and organic meat, are obtained from farms within a mile of Lower Druidston. Druidston beach, a beautiful natural sandy beach with high cliffs, caves and rock pools, is just twenty minutes walk away. Two other natural sandy beaches are within three miles, both ideal for families. druidston@madasafish.com

DRUIDSTON (S-C)

LOWER DRUIDSTON FARM 546

Druidston
Haverfordwest SA62 3NE
Tel: 01437 781318   MAP 13

Caravan: sleeps 4
£185-£310 pw

Chemical-free fruit and vegetables grown on the farm are available to buy

Lower Druidston Farm is a 5-acre smallholding, growing chemical-free fruit and vegetables. Situated at the end of a no through road it is 600 yards from the 180-mile coastal path. Magnificent views of St Brides Bay can be enjoyed from the adjacent fields. The 28-foot caravan is situated in its own secluded area with private access. There is only one caravan on the farm and guests have access to two nearby fields. Chemical-free fruit and vegetables grown on the farm are available for you to buy. Druidston beach, a beautiful natural sandy beach with high cliffs, caves and rock pools, is just twenty minutes walk away. There are also two other natural sandy beaches within three miles of the caravan, both ideal for families. druidston@madasafish.com

DWRBACH (S-C)

THE HAYLOFT & THE BARN 547

Ffynnonston
Dwrbach SA65 9QT
Tel: 01348 873004   MAP 13

Hayloft: sleeps 2, £200-£400 pw
Barn: sleeps 6, £250-£600 pw

A variety of fresh organic produce is
available in season

Soil Association

This stone-built 18th-century hayloft is to be found down a little lane, set within an organic smallholding about a mile from Fishguard. The character of the building has been retained through stone walls, pine cladding and antique quarry tiles. Windows are small with glimpses of garden, lane and distant hills. One door opens onto a secluded garden, the other onto the old farmyard. There is also a stone barn, which sleeps six. A variety of fresh organic produce is available in season. The area is quiet and peaceful and there are many good walks. The Pembrokeshire Coast National Park, the Gwaun Valley, the Preseli Hills, and beautiful secluded beaches are all within easy reach. Short breaks by agreement.
annhicks@waitrose.com   www.ffynnonston.co.uk

DYFFRYN ISAF (S-C)

DOVE COTTAGE   548

Dyffryn Isaf
Llandissilio SA66 7QD
Tel: 01437 563657   MAP 13

Cottage: sleeps 4, £160-£340 pw
Short Breaks (October-April)

Honey, eggs, some home-produced
vegetables

Soil Association

Come and enjoy a relaxing holiday on our small organic farm. The holiday cottage has two bedrooms. We are located in a quiet valley, central for the beautiful Pembrokeshire coast and the Preseli Hills. You can also spend your time walking over our fields meeting our sheep, goats and chickens, learn about organic farming, or you can relax in the small private garden behind the cottage. Take a seat next to our pond and observe the wildlife, or enjoy a local walk through the quiet rural landscape around us. We also use and sell the wool from our Shetland sheep, so be inspired for your next craft project. Fresh farm produce for sale – normally we have home-produced vegetables, eggs and honey available.
bettinab@dsl.pipex.com   www.pembrokeshire-organic-holidays.co.uk

LAWRENNY *(B&B)*

KNOWLES FARM 549

Lawrenny
Kilgetty SA68 0PX
Tel: 01834 891221   MAP 13

Farmhouse Bed and Breakfast, £35-£37 pppn
Evening Meal £12, 4 course organic £22

80% organic breakfast, organic meals on request

Soil Association

A lovely farmhouse amidst an organic arable and dairy farm (the milk from our cows goes into Rachel's Yogurt). A romantic estuary snakes its way around the boundary. Bring your own wine and you can dine here on delicious organic meals in the evenings. The natural beauty of the farm, with its ancient hanging woods, teeming bird and wild animal life, makes for a holiday in itself. There are walks through the woods and along the shore, boating on the river, picnics on the front lawn – and then there's the coast. Only nine miles away, you will find beaches, cliffs and coves. Castles, gardens, galleries, theme parks, fishing and riding – all these are only minutes away. Come and share our special corner of Pembrokeshire. ginilp@lawrenny.org.uk   www.lawrenny.org.uk

LAWRENNY *(B&B)*

TEDION FARM B&B  550

Lawrenny
Kilgetty SA68 0QB
Tel: 01834 891253   MAP 13

Bed and Breakfast
Contact for prices

The farmhouse breakfast is made with organic and local produce

Soil Association

Tedion farmhouse has large gardens and overlooks our 300-acre working organic dairy farm. The farm is set in deepest rural South Pembrokeshire, where life remains uncomplicated. It is within easy reach of a wealth of glorious beaches in all directions and close to the Pembrokeshire Coast National Park, famous for its stunning scenery, globally important birdlife and proliferation of wild flowers. Known as the Landsker region, it is sparsely populated and life moves at a pace that your grandparents probably reminisce about. Quiet country lanes mean you can walk and cycle where you like. The nearby Cleddau estuary is rich with wildlife. The pretty town of Narberth, with its 'real' shops and great deli, is not far away. tedionfarm@btconnect.com

LAWRENNY (S-C)

TEDION FARM COTTAGE 551

Lawrenny
Kilgetty SA68 0QB
Tel: 01834 891253   MAP 13

Cottage: sleeps 6
£300-£800 pw

There's an ample supply of fresh organic
vegetables for sale at the local pub

Soil Association

With its many rooms, Tedion Cottage is an Aladdin's Cave. Outside, there is garden on three sides so you can follow the sun as it tracks from front to back. A patio and barbecue provide a private alfresco dining area, and there's an enclosed garden complete with playhouse. Guests are welcome to wander through our woods and fields as well as neighbouring Little Pen Coed Farm. Organic farming methods ensure wild flowers and wildlife thrive in this stunning part of Pembrokeshire. Tedion is very much a working farm with 300 acres of organic fields providing pasture for our dairy herd. Their coming and going marks the start and end of each day – part of the gentle rhythm of the countryside. Beaches, walking, horseriding nearby.
tedionfarm@btconnect.com   www.vallenfarmcottages.co.uk/cottages/tedion.htm

LLANFALLTEG (S-C)

GWARMACWYDD FARM 552

Gwarmacwydd Farm
Llanfallteg SA34 0XH
Tel: 01437 563260   MAP 13

Cottages: sleep 2-6
£240-£570 pw

Local organic produce can be ordered

Organic Farmers & Growers

A country estate of over 450 acres set in the Vale of the River Taf. Our working organic farm uses a sustainable system of farming which respects the welfare needs of the land, environment, animals and people. Wildlife abounds. Enjoy the beauty of the South West Wales countryside. Amble for one and a half miles along the river banks, or pause to fish for salmon or trout. Walk the old Whitland to Cardigan railway, a fantastic nature trail. Picnic amidst wooded glades. Explore the many paths that lead among grassy meadows. Walk through 50 acres of ancient oak and ash woodlands. Sandy beaches with rock pools and old county towns only twenty minutes drive. Book online via our website.
ghg2008@gwarmacwydd.co.uk   www.gwarmacwydd.co.uk

LLANGOLMAN *(S-C)*

FFYNNON SAMSON 553

Llangolman
Clynderwen SA66 7QL
Tel: 01437 532542　　　　　MAP 13

Farmhouse: sleeps 4-5, £250-£565 pw
Home cooked organic meals (Fri, Sat, Sun)

Complimentary organic box of food,
vegetables and eggs

Soil Association

A working organic farm nestled beneath the enchanting Preseli hills. Located on the crest of a hill, the farm affords breathtaking views. On the border of the National Park we link to a large network of footpaths and bridleways and the Bluestone cycle trails. You are welcome to roam on the farm which comprises of pastureland, mixed woodland, and a marshland hosting rare butterflies and orchids near the river border. An area is given over to an organic market garden, and seasonally produced vegetables, fruit and eggs are available for guests to order. Home-cooked organic three course meals are on offer on Friday, Saturday and Sunday evenings. We do our utmost to use locally produced ingredients.
admin@organic-holiday.co.uk　www.organic-holiday.co.uk

LLANTEG *(S-C)*

ROSE PARK ORGANIC FARM 554

Llanteg
Narberth SA67 8QJ
Tel: 01834 831111　　　　　MAP 13

Cottage: sleeps 4, £470 pw
Camping, Caravan £10-£12 pn

Our own organic lamb is sold at the farm
shop in season

Soil Association

Rose Park is a 50-acre organic farm set in the heart of the beautiful Pembrokeshire countryside. Wake up to breathtaking views of Caldey Island and the beautiful Colby Lodge estate on our recently landscaped three and a half-acre touring caravan and camping site. We have twenty eight hard standing pitches for tourers / motor homes, and a separate area for twenty tents. The newly-built cottage has a patio with a picnic table. We have a newly restored bridleway and footpath running through the farm that leads on to the coastal path. Staying at Rose Park Organic Farm is an ideal retreat from the hustle and bustle of the towns, but within easy reach of Amroth, Saundersfoot, Pendine Sands and Tenby.

LUDCHURCH (S-C)

BLACKMOOR FARM 555

Ludchurch
Narberth SA67 8JH
Tel: 01834 831242   MAP 13

Cottages: sleep 2-6, £292-£540 pw
Short breaks (min 3 nights), £58-£80 pn

Organic and local produce at Wisebuys farm shop (3 miles)

Soil Association

Blackmoor Farm, surrounded by our own 36 acres of pastureland, offers a relaxed holiday atmosphere where children can play in safety. The three cottages are set in an attractive sunny courtyard, architect-designed and purpose-built with country-style furniture and equipment. The caravans are set in a lawned area with a concrete path to each one and excellent parking facilities. The site is pleasantly sheltered by mature trees and there is every opportunity for a relaxed holiday away from the bustle of everyday life. The farm is within two miles of Amroth on the coast, with its large sandy beach backed by cliffs. The National Park footpath starts here, stretching for 168 miles around the stunning Pembrokeshire coast. ltecornth@aol.com   www.blackmoorfarm.co.uk

NEWPORT (Camping)

TYCANOL FARM CAMPING 556

Newport
SA42 0ST
Tel: 01239 820264   MAP 13

Camping Barn: sleeps 4, £15 pppn
Caravan: sleeps 4 £30 p2pn, Camping £8 pppn

Organic food available locally

Soil Association

Tycanol is an organic farm close to the beautiful Pembrokeshire coast. The farm offers simple old-fashioned accommodation for four in a small camping barn with a fantastic view. For larger groups there is a campsite for tents and caravans, which overlooks the whole of Newport Bay. There are no meals provided on this two star site but the camping barn has self-catering facilities. Organic produce can be bought from the wholefood shop in Newport, which is fifteen minutes walk away, and also from Fishguard farmers' market (held fortnightly). There is a nature trail on the farm, which contains badger setts. The campsite is situated on the coastal walking path, and we are just two minutes from our own beach. www.caravancampingsites.co.uk/pembrokeshire/tycanolfarm.htm

ROCH (B&B)

CUFFERN MANOR 557

Roch
Haverfordwest SA62 6HB
Tel: 01437 710071 MAP 13

Country House Bed and Breakfast,
£30-£35 pppn

Vegetarian Evening Meal (by arrangement)

Meals are at least 90% organic (we aim for 100% organic)

A Georgian manor house and a walled kitchen garden in 3 acres of woods. Three double *en suites*, two twin, two singles (each with wash hand basin), three standard double rooms. A substantial packed lunch can be provided. Vegetarian or vegan evening meals available when required. All our own soft fruit and vegetables, from our one-acre walled garden, are grown without chemicals. We aim for 100% organic / naturally grown but sometimes buy fair trade fruit, which may not be organic. Pembrokeshire Produce Award for 'best use of local food'. Cuffern Manor is three miles from the coastal path and the two mile sandy beach at Newgale. Ideal for family occasions, courses, conferences (we can take groups of up to twenty). enquiries@cuffernmanor.co.uk   www.cuffernmanor.co.uk

ST DAVID'S (Hotel)

TYF ECO HOTEL 558

Caerfai Road
St David's SA62 6QS
Tel: 01437 721678 MAP 13

B&B £30-£40, HB £45-£55,
FB £50-£60 pppn

Almost all the food and drink we serve in the restaurant is organic

Quality Welsh Food Certification Ltd

TYF Eco Hotel is an 18th-century converted windmill with green credentials. The hotel recently became the first organic certified hotel in Wales, through the Welsh Organic Scheme. The kitchen works with the rhythms of the seasons, and the core of our organic restaurant's repertoire is focused on high quality Welsh produce that's bursting with flavour. An excellent range of organic wine, beer and cider is available to complement your meal. The hotel is only a few minutes walk away from the beach, the Pembrokeshire Coast Path, and the centre of the historic city of St David's. This small city, surrounded by awe-inspiring landscapes and seascapes, is aiming to become Britain's first carbon-neutral city. stay@tyf.com   www.tyf.com/?c=acc-felin

ST DAVIDS *(S-C)*

CAERFAI BAY COTTAGES   559

Caerfai Organic Farm
St Davids SA62 6QT
Tel: 01437 720548   MAP 13

Cottages: sleep 1-6
£240-£895 pw

Organic farm shop (open May-August)

Soil Association

Caerfai Organic Farm, a 140-acre coastal farm, is just half a mile from the unique city of St David's. The farm's organic enterprises include milk ('green top' licensed), cheeses, potatoes, beef and cereals. We use our own organic unpasteurised milk to produce three types of cheese on the farm – Cheddar, Caerfilly, and Caerfilly with leek and garlic. In high season (May-August) we operate a small organic shop. Set within the Pembrokeshire Coast National Park, the cottages once formed part of the old farmstead at Caerfai Farm. Each of the four cottages has its own grounds, away from the present farm buildings. It's a 350 yard walk to beautiful Caerfai Bay, a sandy bathing cove with many colourful and fascinating rock pools. chrismevans69@hotmail.com   www.caerfai.co.uk

ST DAVID'S *(Camping)*

TREGINNIS UCHAF   560

Treginnis Uchaf
St David's SA62 6RS
Tel: 01437 720234   MAP 13

CL Caravan Site, from £6 pn
Open all year (phone to check availability)

Organic produce in St Davids (one and a half miles)

Soil Association

Spectacular views of the countryside can be seen from your caravan on the spacious level ground grass site. Sheep graze in the nearby fields, in March / April with their newborn lambs. Ducks, cormorants, and the occasional heron visit the man-made pond across the fields. Foxes and badgers can also be seen in the valley from the caravan site. The most spectacular sunsets can be enjoyed. Walking access to the Pembrokeshire Coastal Path is within five minutes to Porthllisky Bay with its fascinating rock pools and clear waters for bathing. Cold water drinking tap. Chemical disposal point with cold water tap. Batteries can be charged. Treginnis Uchaf is only one and a half miles from St Davids. davies@treginnis.co.uk   www.treginnis.co.uk/caravan/index.html

ST DAVID'S *(S-C)*

TY MORTIMER — 561

Treginnis Uchaf
St David's SA62 6RS
Tel: 01437 720234 — MAP 13

Cottage: sleeps 5, £300-£670 pw
Short Breaks, from £160

Organic produce in St Davids (one and a half miles)

Soil Association

With outstanding views, Treginnis is situated in one of the most picturesque peninsula areas of the Pembrokeshire National Park. Ty Mortimer is set in a farmyard complex of traditional stone buildings. The quiet beach of Porthllisky, with its beautiful rock pools, is five hundred yards away. Easy accessibility to explore the magnificent coastal path. Many varied walks nearby – some coastal and spectacular, particularly with the sunsets – others more serene and gentle, capturing the essence of wild flowers and bird-watching. Porpoises and seals are a delight to see. Treginnis is a National Trust working organic farm with a breeding flock of 800 ewes. During spring and early summer lambs gambol in the fields.
davies@treginnis.co.uk   www.treginnis.co.uk

⑤

ABERHOSAN *(S-C)*

HENDRERON COTTAGE — 562

Penyglog
Aberhosan SY20 8SG
Tel: 01654 702033 — MAP 14

Cottage: sleeps 6
£220-£500 pw

Local organic food is readily available in Machynlleth (4 miles)

Quality Welsh Food Certification Ltd

The tastefully renovated 18th-century miner's cottage is part of an organic beef and sheep farm with glorious views of the surrounding unspoilt Mid-Wales countryside. There are three bedrooms sleeping six people with bedlinen and towels provided. The kitchen diner is all electric. There is a large family lounge with the original beams, inglenook and original bread oven retained. Outside is an enclosed garden with a barbecue and garden furniture. Visitors are more than welcome to take walks on the farm to see the abundant wildlife and wide variety of birds, especially the red kite. Local organic food is readily available in the small market town of Machynlleth (4 miles). The Centre for Alternative Technology is 8 miles.
d.b.evans@btinternet.com

BOUGHROOD (B&B)

UPPER MIDDLE ROAD FARM 563

Boughrood
Brecon LD3 0BX
Tel: 01874 754407   MAP 14

Farm Bed and Breakfast, from £25 pppn
Evening Meal, £12-£15 (by arrangement)

Produce is from our own farm and garden
or locally sourced

Our 5-acre working smallholding is set at 550 feet above the Wye Valley in the quiet and beautiful landscape of Mid Wales. The house is over 150 years old. We keep a small flock of sheep, which provide meat for the house and fleece to spin and dye. Free-range hens provide the eggs. Most of our food is produced without artificial fertilisers or chemicals. Breakfast includes freshly home-baked bread using Doves Farm organic flour, home-made yogurt, jams and marmalade. Fruit from the garden is available in season. All meals are freshly cooked with a Welsh flavour. Produce is mainly from our own farm and garden, otherwise locally sourced. We have achieved level two of the Green Dragon environmental award.
info@uppermiddleroad.co.uk   www.uppermiddleroad.co.uk

CARNO (S-C)

THE HIDEAWAY   564

Gorfanc
Carno SY17 5JP
Tel: 01686 420423   MAP 14

Barn Loft: sleeps 2+2, £244-£262 pw
Short Breaks, £89-£97 for 2 nights

Naturally grown home produce in season

From the balcony entrance to The Hideaway you will see only hills, woods and sky. Trannon Moor is on the edge of the Cambrian Mountains where, surrounded by meadows, hedgerows and wild open upland, you can walk for miles with only sheep paths to follow or potter along a tree-lined stream valley. Gorfanc is a traditional stone upland dwelling set in a peaceful, wild and productive garden. Naturally grown produce from the garden may be available to buy, along with honey from our bees, home-made organic wholemeal bread, and jams and pickles. Eggs come from Muriel's free-range hens at the bottom of the hill. Tents are also welcome (£4 pppn) in secluded locations, with camp fires and lovely views.
wildwood@deeppool.fsnet.co.uk

CEMMAES *(B&B)*

GWALIA FARM B&B 565

Cemmaes
Machynlleth SY20 9PZ
Tel: 01650 511377 MAP 14

Vegetarian Bed and Breakfast, £25 pppn
Evening Meal (by arrangement)

Wholefood, home-made, organic meals

Gwalia Farm is a peaceful, traditional smallholding with goats, hens and sheep in the remote hills of Mid Wales. The large organic garden provides an abundance of vegetables and soft fruit for home-cooked, wholefood vegetarian meals, together with our own milk, free-range eggs and home-made jams. A conservation area has a tranquil lake with native trees and amazing pond life, and here you will also find a diving board and canoes. There are beautiful views of the mountains at the southern edge of Snowdonia National Park. Enjoy a log fire, spring water, good walking, bird-watching, dragonflies, stargazing – and silence. The Centre for Alternative Technology is about seven miles from the farm.
www.gwaliafarm.co.uk

CRAI *(S-C)*

BRYNIAU PELL 566

Aberhyddnant Organic Farm
Crai LD3 8YS
Tel: 01874 636797

Cottage: sleeps 4+2 cots, from £288 pw
Short Breaks, from £72 pn

A wide selection of organic produce is available to order in advance

Quality Welsh Food Certification Ltd

Tranquil organic hill farm nestling in the breathtaking scenery of the Brecon Beacons National Park. The cottage has been converted to a high standard from an existing farm building, providing comfortable accommodation with a cottage feel. Fresh spring water flows from the taps. Our 220-acre farm produces organic beef, pork and lamb (which you can buy along with our organic eggs and vegetables) whilst caring for the environment and abundant wildlife. The fields, sheltered by hedgerows and woodland, are managed under a whole farm environmental scheme. There are thousands of acres of hillside adjoining the farm waiting to be explored. Our farm shop and tearoom in nearby Trecastle is open from Wednesday to Sunday.
info@abercottages.com www.abercottages.com

CRAI *(S-C)*

NYTH Y WENNOL 567

Aberhyddnant Organic Farm
Crai LD3 8YS
Tel: 01874 636797 MAP 14

Cottage: sleeps 6+2 cots from £300 pw
Short Breaks, from £75 pn

Organic food and produce available to visitors

Quality Welsh Food Certification Ltd

Tranquil organic hill farm nestling in the breathtaking scenery of the Brecon Beacons National Park. The cottage has been converted to a high standard from an existing farm building, providing comfortable accommodation with a cottage feel. Fresh spring water flows from the taps. Our 220-acre farm produces organic beef, pork and lamb (which you can buy along with our organic eggs and vegetables) whilst caring for the environment and abundant wildlife. The fields, sheltered by hedgerows and woodland, are managed under a whole farm environmental scheme. There are thousands of acres of hillside adjoining the farm waiting to be explored. Our farm shop and tearoom in nearby Trecastle is open from Wednesday to Sunday.
info@abercottages.com   www.abercottages.com

CRIGGION *(B&B)*

LANE FARM 568

Criggion
Shrewsbury SY5 9BG
Tel: 01743 884288 MAP 14

Farmhouse Bed and Breakfast
£25-£27 pppn

Full Welsh breakfast using local produce

Organic Farmers & Growers

A warm welcome awaits you at our traditional family-run working organic farm, set beneath the Breidden Hills in the picturesque Severn Valley. At Lane Farm a large farmhouse breakfast is assured using local produce and, when possible, our own eggs. Relax and enjoy the house farm and gardens. You are welcome to walk around our tranquil 400 acres, but remember this is a working farm with moving machinery and animals and children must always be supervised. Private free fishing is available on the River Severn (please bring your own rods). For those feeling energetic, a walk to the top of the Breiddens to Rodney's Pillar will afford spectacular views of the Severn Valley on a clear day.
lane.farm@ukgateway.net   www.lanefarmbedandbreakfast.co.uk

DINAS MAWDDWY *(S-C)*

GLANLLYNMAWR 569

Nant-y-Nodyn
Dinas Mawddwy SY20 9AG
Tel: 01650 531330   MAP 14

Farmhouse: sleeps 6
£250-£580 pw

Organic and local produce at the Quarry
Shop and Café in Machynlleth

Soil Association

This 17th-century farmhouse nestles in the valley above the River Dovey. The interior of the house retains its traditional character with a wealth of original beams and is tastefully furnished. Mawddwy is an unspoilt, quiet valley in the superb scenery of the southern Snowdonia National Park. Nant-y-Nodyn's four self-catering cottages, a quarter of a mile apart, are situated in this valley about two miles from the wool village of Dinas Mawddwy and near the highest pass in Wales, which leads to Lake Vyrnwy and Bala Lake. The cottages are part of a sheep and beef organic farm, which has been positively managed with conservation in mind, and guests are welcome to explore and enjoy the wildlife.
elwyn@nantynodyn.fsnet.co.uk   www.nantynodyn.co.uk/cottage_detail.php?ID=1

DINAS MAWDDWY *(S-C)*

LLANERCH 570

Nant-y-Nodyn
Dinas Mawddwy SY20 9AG
Tel: 01650 531330   MAP 14

Farmhouse: sleeps 6
£250-£580 pw

Organic and local produce at the Quarry
Shop and Café in Machynlleth

Soil Association

This 16th-century Grade II listed farmhouse is surrounded by lovely, peaceful mountain scenery near the River Dovey. Beautifully restored with original oak beams and an inglenook fireplace. Mawddwy is an unspoilt, quiet valley in the superb scenery of the southern Snowdonia National Park. Nant-y-Nodyn's four self-catering cottages, a quarter of a mile apart, are situated in this valley about two miles from the wool village of Dinas Mawddwy and near the highest pass in Wales, which leads to Lake Vyrnwy and Bala Lake. The cottages are part of a sheep and beef organic farm, which has been positively managed with conservation in mind, and guests are welcome to explore and enjoy the wildlife.
elwyn@nantynodyn.fsnet.co.uk   www.nantynodyn.co.uk/cottage_detail.php?ID=3

DINAS MAWDDWY (S-C)

TY'N Y FFORDD   571

Nant-y-Nodyn
Dinas Mawddwy SY20 9AG
Tel: 01650 531330   MAP 14

Cottage: sleeps 6
£395-£750 pw

Organic and local produce at the Quarry
Shop and Café in Machynlleth

Soil Association

This is an enchanting Grade II listed beamed whitewashed cottage. The accommodation is on the ground floor. French doors open onto a patio from where you can enjoy glorious views. Mawddwy is an unspoilt, quiet valley in the superb scenery of the southern Snowdonia National Park. Nant-y-Nodyn's four self-catering cottages, a quarter of a mile apart, are situated in this valley about two miles from the wool village of Dinas Mawddwy and near the highest pass in Wales, which leads to Lake Vyrnwy and Bala Lake. The cottages are part of a sheep and beef organic farm, which has been positively managed with conservation in mind, and guests are welcome to explore and enjoy the wildlife.

elwyn@nantynodyn.fsnet.co.uk   www.nantynodyn.co.uk/cottage_detail.php?ID=2

DINAS MAWDDWY (S-C)

YR EFAIL   572

Nant-y-Nodyn
Dinas Mawddwy SY20 9AG
Tel: 01650 531330   MAP 14

Cottage: sleeps 2
£260-£477 pw

Organic and local produce at the Quarry
Shop and Café in Machynlleth

Soil Association

This is a beautifully renovated stone smithy, refurbished to a luxuriously high standard. All the accommodation is on the ground floor. Enclosed garden with barbecue and garden furniture. Mawddwy is an unspoilt, quiet valley in the superb scenery of the southern Snowdonia National Park. Nant-y-Nodyn's four self-catering cottages, a quarter of a mile apart, are situated in this valley about two miles from the wool village of Dinas Mawddwy and near the highest pass in Wales, which leads to Lake Vyrnwy and Bala Lake. The cottages are part of a sheep and beef organic farm, which has been positively managed with conservation in mind, and guests are welcome to explore and enjoy the wildlife.

elwyn@nantynodyn.fsnet.co.uk   www.nantynodyn.co.uk/cottage_detail.php?ID=4

DOLFOR *(B&B)*

OLD VICARAGE DOLFOR   573

Dolfor
Newtown SY16 4BN
Tel: 01686 629051   MAP 14

Guest House, B&B £47.50-£65 pppn
Restaurant (lunch, dinner)

Organic local produce with home-grown
vegetables and free-range eggs

This Victorian vicarage offers 5-star comforts in the beautiful Montgomeryshire countryside. There are hills, fields and views that stretch for miles. Luxury *en suite* bedrooms have everything you need. The dining room is perfect for a leisurely organic breakfast, benefiting from the morning sun with a view over the front garden and the hills beyond. There are log fires, a cosy sitting room and candlelit dinners. Wines are organic, and Tim's menus use the best of local organic produce. Meat from Welsh Farm Organics, smoked salmon from The Organic Smokehouse, and flour from Bacheldre Watermill for the home-made bread. There is a kitchen garden, polytunnel and free-range hens, all of which contribute to the experience. tim@theoldvicaragedolfor.co.uk   www.theoldvicaragedolfor.co.uk

DYFI VALLEY *(Camping)*

ECO RETREATS   574

Dyfi Valley
SY20 8PG
Tel: 01654 781375   MAP 14

Tipis: sleep 2
£305-£359 per tipi for two nights

All food products we provide are certified
organic and fair trade

Organic Farmers & Growers

The Eco Retreats site is in a remote and stunningly beautiful location. Close to the river, our new yurt is furnished with a double bed, organic sheepskins and simple but beautiful furniture. Where possible our furnishings are from local, recycled or fair trade sources. All food products we provide are certified organic and fair trade. In the heart of beautiful mountains, live for two or more nights in this traditional yurt, experiencing the tranquillity of the natural world while still being surrounded by all the necessary modern creature comforts. Forest and mountain walks, open fires, holistic therapy, a visit to the Centre for Alternative Technology and magnificent views combine to give you an elemental experience. chananb@ecoretreats.co.uk   www.ecoretreats.co.uk

DYFI VALLEY *(S-C)*

ECO RETREATS YURT 575

Dyfi Valley
SY20 8PG
Tel: 01654 781375 · MAP 14

Yurt: sleeps 2
From £315 for two nights

All food products we provide are certified
organic and fair trade

Organic Farmers & Growers

The Eco Retreats site is in a remote and stunningly beautiful location. Close to the river, our new yurt is furnished with a comfy double bed, organic sheepskins and simple but beautiful furniture. Furnishings are from local, recycled or fair trade sources where possible. All food products we provide are certified organic and fair trade. In the heart of beautiful mountains, spend two or more nights in this traditional yurt, experiencing the tranquillity of the natural world while still being surrounded by all the necessary modern creature comforts. Forest and mountain walks, open fires, holistic therapy, a visit to the Centre for Alternative Technology and magnificent views combine to give you an elemental experience.
chananb@ecoretreats.co.uk   www.ecoretreats.co.uk/page5.htm

ELAN VALLEY *(S-C)*

THE CLYN 576

Elan Valley
Rhayader LD6 5HP
Tel: 01597 810120 MAP 14

Granary: sleeps 4, £245-£419 pw / £49-£62 pn
Cottage: sleeps 7, £257-£648 pw / £51-£93 pn

Seasonal home produce (naturally grown
vegetables, soft fruit, meat, honey, eggs)

The two cottages are on a remote smallholding with naturally reared sheep, poultry, bees, and sometimes pigs, as well as extensive vegetable, fruit and flower gardens. The focus is on 'green living' – our electricity comes from renewable sources (wind and water turbines), and we have solar water heating panels. A range of home produce is available in season. Pure spring water on tap. The Clyn is in a superb setting, high on the edge of open moorland, and ideally situated for walking, mountain biking, fishing, bird-watching. National Trust / Elan Valley Trust moorland, RSPB reserves, the Elan Valley reservoirs are all literally on the doorstep. Children welcome. Dogs on leads welcome. Short breaks available.
theclyn@tiscali.co.uk   www.clyncottages.co.uk

ERWOOD *(B&B)*

TRERICKET MILL   577

Erwood
Builth Wells LD2 3TQ
Tel: 01982 560312   MAP 14

Vegetarian Guest House, B&B £29-£36.50
pppn. Supper £8, Evening Meal £14-£18

Wholesome meals using organic and local
produce where possible

Grade II listed water corn mill overlooking the River Wye offering a range of informal accommodation – bed and breakfast in the guest house, a cosy traditional bunkhouse, and a campsite set in the old cider orchard. Trericket Mill has a unique historic atmosphere, complete with original milling machinery, log fires, books, games, a riverside garden within a designated Site of Special Scientific Interest. All the catering is vegetarian, from breakfast (£7.50) to simple suppers or evening meals, using local, organic, free-range and fair trade produce wherever possible. Eggs are from our own free-range ducks and hens during the laying season. Natural chemical-free water is provided by our private source.
mail@trericket.co.uk   www.trericket.co.uk

FELINDRE *(B&B)*

PRIMROSE EARTH RETREATS 578

Felindre
Hay-on-Wye LD3 0ST
Tel: 01497 847636   MAP 14

B&B on self-serve basis from £130 pppw
Full board from £270 pppw

Mainly organic food from the farm or
sourced locally where possible

Soil Association

Variety of holistic courses encouraging respect for the earth. Courses on sound healing and sustainable living; encouraging a connection with nature and the earth for grounding; understanding of growing healthy food in harmony with the environment and creatively turning into nutritious and flavoursome meals. Quiet retreats for de-stressing from busy lives. Full board includes light or packed lunches and 2-course evening meals. Situated at the foot of the Black Mountains. A peaceful setting amidst beautiful gardens on a well established organic fruit and vegetable smallholding using permaculture principles. Simple but lovely retreat space in the peace garden. Alternatively one double, one twin, one single room available.
jan.benham@ukonline.co.uk   www.organic-sacred-earth.co.uk

FELINDRE *(B&B)*

PRIMROSE ORGANIC 579

Felindre
Hay-on-Wye LD3 0ST
Tel: 01497 847636   MAP 14

Bed and Breakfast
From £22 pppn

Mainly organic and sourced locally where possible

Soil Association

Our B&B (one double, one twin, one single, two bathrooms) is traditional and simple but comfortable. We have a well established organic fruit and vegetable smallholding at the foot of the Black Mountains near Hay-on-Wye. Managed using organic and sustainable permaculture principles, it's a wonderful example of productivity in harmony with nature. The productive area includes half an acre of forest garden with a hundred varieties of fruit and nut trees. The holding is a Soil Association demonstration farm. We focus on creating healthy and wholesome food, using organic where possible, some straight from our abundant garden. We have been awarded Level 2 of the Green Dragon environmental standard.
jan.benham@ukonline.co.uk   www.organic-sacred-earth.co.uk

LLANGENNY *(S-C)*

OAKVIEW 580

Graig Barn Farm
Llangenny Lane NP8 1HB
Tel: 01873 810275   MAP 14

Apartments: sleep 2-6, £350-£500 pw
Short Breaks, £70-£100 pn (min 2 nights)

Provisions can be ordered from Graig Farm Organics on-line shop

Quality Welsh Food Certification Ltd

Superbly-located barn conversion to two self-contained 4-star apartments with magnificent views over the Usk Valley. The top floor apartment caters for six, the ground floor accommodates four (both can be let as one unit for a maximum of ten). Significant reductions made for just two people staying. Drying room to facilitate walkers and cyclists. Outside there's a summerhouse with a barbecue area. To the rear of the property is a 10-acre bluebell wood. Graig Barn, our small family-run organic farm, is situated in the Brecon Beacons National Park. It's in a peaceful location on the slopes of the Black Mountains, near the quaint little town of Crickhowell. Our latest venture is an organic apple juice business.
johng.morris@virgin.net   www.oakview-cottages.co.uk

LLANHAMLACH *(B&B)*

PETERSTONE COURT 581

Llanhamlach
Brecon LD3 7YB
Tel: 01874 665387   MAP 14

Restaurant with Rooms
B&B, double £100-£220 pn

Food from our family farm, all locally
sourced and organic where possible

Peterstone Court Country House and Spa is situated in the heart of the Brecon Beacons National Park. The Georgian house is avant-garde and distinctive in style, and the bedrooms are all large, light spaces. Food is of huge importance to us – most of the meat and poultry on our menu is reared on our family farm (Glaisfer Uchaf) just down the road, so we know exactly what our animals have been fed throughout their life. We hope this will help lessen our carbon impact on the environment. Our food is always seasonal, sustainable and simple, using fresh, organic where possible, home reared ingredients. Our spa also uses only natural, organic products, a philosophy which has filtered down from the main house.
info@peterstone-court.com   www.peterstone-court.com

LLANWRTHWL *(B&B)*

PENLANOLE 582

Llanwrthwl
Llandrindod Wells LD1 6NN
Tel: 01597 810266   MAP 14

Bed and Breakfast
£25 pppn

Organic breakfast with bacon, sausages and
eggs sourced from our own farm

Organic Farmers & Growers

Penlanole nestles in forty acres of breathtaking Wye Valley land. Our 40-acre organic farm is home to cows, sheep, and saddleback pigs ranging over ancient woodland, orchards and peat bog through to a kitchen garden, duck pond and hay meadow. Choose from a double room with an *en suite* bathroom, or two double rooms with use of a shared bathroom, all with fabulous views of the surrounding countryside. Attic bedrooms are also available for children, or adults, who fancy something more adventurous. An organic breakfast, with bacon, sausages and eggs sourced from our own farm, can be served in the bright elegance of the dining room or in the warm informality of the family kitchen.
info@penlanole-organics.co.uk   www.penlanole-organics.co.uk

LLANWRTHWL *(S-C)*

PENLANOLE COTTAGE 583

Llanwrthwl
Llandrindod Wells LD1 6NN
Tel: 01597 810266   MAP 14

Cottage: sleeps 5
Contact for prices

You can buy fresh organic produce from the farm

Organic Farmers & Growers

Nestling in 40 acres of breathtaking Wye Valley land, Penlanole is a special place. The cottage has three bedrooms and has recently been modernised. Our 40-acre organic farm is home to cows, sheep, and saddleback pigs ranging over ancient woodland, orchards and peat bog through to a kitchen garden, duck pond and hay meadow. We rear our own stock to supply organic beef, mutton, lamb and pork to local butcher's, hotels, farmers markets and consumers, and our Christmas turkeys are a famous favourite. In October / November the annual apple harvesting and pressing party yields delicious fresh apple juice, which we also sell as a speciality. As a private nature reserve, we host informative farm walks.
info@penlanole-organics.co.uk   www.penlanole-organics.co.uk

LLANWRTHWL *(Camping)*

PENLANOLE STABLE 584

Llanwrthwl
Llandrindod Wells LD1 6NN
Tel: 01597 810266   MAP 14

Stable: sleeps 4, £50 pn
Camping

Buy fresh organic produce from the farm

Organic Farmers & Growers

A family of four or a group of friends can take over the converted stable block, which has a youth hostel-style shared sleeping platform, loo and basin, and basic cooking facilities. For the more outdoorsy types, camping pitches are available in the apple orchard and well-drained field close to the main house. In October / November the annual apple harvesting and pressing party yields delicious fresh organic apple juice, which we sell as a speciality. We welcome and encourage volunteers of all ages to join in with farm tasks and seasonal activities such as haymaking, lambing and apple pressing. Exhausted farm hands can then collapse under the stunning star-spangled Penlanole night sky.
info@penlanole-organics.co.uk   www.penlanole-organics.co.uk

LLANWRTYD WELLS *(B&B)*

LASSWADE HOUSE 585

Station Road
Llanwrtyd Wells LD5 4RW
Tel: 01591 610515   MAP 14

Restaurant with Rooms,
B&B from £37.50 pppn

Restaurant (3 course dinner £28)

Choose from a selection of fresh, local,
mostly organic food

4-star period country house with magnificent views, set in the heart of Wales between the Cambrian Mountains and the Brecon Beacons. We offer friendly hospitality and high quality food and drink (the restaurant has two AA Rosettes). All our produce is sourced fresh, local and mostly organic, with a daily changing menu. We use single estate tea, coffee and fair trade products. We were the first eco-friendly and organic hotel and restaurant in Wales. Good Food Guide listed 2004-2008. Other accolades include the Green Dragon Environmental Award and the Considerate Hoteliers Sustain Food Challenge Award. We are the pioneers of food transportation by railway. Discount available for those travelling here by train.
info@lasswadehotel.co.uk   www.lasswadehotel.co.uk

PENPONT *(S-C)*

PENPONT SELF-CATERING 586

Penpont
Brecon LD3 8EU
Tel: 01874 636202   MAP 14

Courtyard Wing: sleeps 13-17, £1450-£1850
pw. 2n £850, 3n £950, Camping £10 pp

Fresh fruit and veg, salad bags and local eggs
for sale in our organic farm shop

Soil Association

Penpont is one of the finest houses situated within the heart of the Brecon Beacons National Park. This privately owned Grade I listed house has been home to the same family since it was first built in about 1666. It lies in the middle of a 2000-acre working rural estate. Guest accommodation is in the courtyard wing. Around the house lie extensive grounds, sweeping lawns, the old Victorian rose and walled gardens, riverside and woodland walks, and an all weather tennis court. We have an organic farm shop in the back courtyard which sells produce from the Penpont Estate. The walled gardens are certified organic by the Soil Association. On sale are fresh fruit and vegetables, salad bags and local eggs.
penpont@btconnect.com   www.penpont.com

TALGARTH *(Camping)*

SMALL FARMS CAMPSITE 587

Lower Porthamel
Talgarth LD3 0DL
Tel: 01874 712125   MAP 14

Camping: Adult £6, Child £2.50
Small children free of charge

Farm shop and café on-site

Organic Farmers & Growers

Camp in the orchard at Lower Porthamel organic farm in the beautiful Wye Valley. Facilities include a loo block with hot showers, and a wash room. We have a small children's play area. Walk our Nature Trail through fields, down the old railway line and along the River Llynfi. The shop sells our own beef, lamb, pork, poultry. Fresh seasonal vegetables are available straight from the farm, and we have chosen the very best organic Welsh cheeses. Enjoy organic fair trade coffee and tea, lemonade, and home-made cakes and tarts at our café. We can make up a delicious plate for you from our deli range, with garden salad leaves and healthy locally baked breads. Dogs very welcome with well-trained owner's.
joeldurrell@yahoo.com   www.smallfarms.co.uk

LLANGENNITH *(S-C)*

HARDINGSDOWN B/HOUSE 588

Lower Hardingsdown Farm
Llangennith SA3 1HT
Tel: 01792 386222   MAP 17

Bunkhouse: sleeps 14, £15 pppn shared
£180 pn sole occupancy

Organic fruit and vegetables can be delivered

Soil Association

Hardingsdown Bunkhouse at Lower Hardingsdown Farm is a renovated stone barn situated on an organic working farm on the Gower Peninsula. The bunkhouse provides comfortable self-catering accommodation for families or groups, sleeping up to fourteen people. Fully equipped kitchen, three shower / toilet rooms, living room with comfy sofas, chairs and two single sofa beds, four bedrooms. Fully centrally heated throughout with underfloor heating downstairs. Patio area and lawned garden. Separate drying room and lock up for storage. Ample parking. Shops and pubs nearby. Access to all that the Gower Peninsula has to offer within easy reach. Level 2 Green Dragon Environmental Award Scheme achieved.
bunkhousegower@tiscali.co.uk   www.bunkhousegower.co.uk

ACCOMMODATION INDEX

FEEDBACK FORM

We would welcome your feedback on the contents or organisation of this third edition of **Organic Places to Stay**. If you have any comments, or would like to suggest places for inclusion in the next edition, please email them to us at sales@greenbooks.co.uk, or write them below and post this form to Green Books, Foxhole, Dartington, Totnes, Devon TQ9 6EB.

....

....

....

....

....

....

....

....

....

....

Your name and address, or email (for our identification purposes only – these details will not be disclosed to any other party):

....

....

....

....

❑ Please tick here if you would like to receive information about future editions of **Organic Places to Stay** or related books that we publish.

Thank you for your help.